LITERACY FOR ALL

Literacy for All
ISSUES IN TEACHING AND LEARNING

Edited by

JEAN OSBORN
FRAN LEHR

Introduction by Richard C. Anderson

THE GUILFORD PRESS
New York   London

©1998 The Guilford Press
A Division of Guilford Publications, Inc.
72 Spring Street, New York, NY 10012
http://www.guilford.com

Printed in the United States of America

This book is printed on acid-free paper.

Last digit is print number: 9 8 7 6 5 4

Library of Congress Cataloging-in-Publication Data

Literacy for all: issues in teaching and learning / edited by Jean
   Osborn and Fran Lehr.
      p.   cm.
   Includes bibliographical references and index.
   ISBN 1-57230-348-4. — ISBN 1-57230-349-2 (pbk.)
   1. Language arts (Early childhood) 2. Reading (Early childhood)
3. Literacy. 4. Language arts (Early childhood)—Ability testing.
I. Osborn, Jean. II. Lehr, Fran.
LB1139.5.L35L58 1998
372.6—DC21   98-6175
                                                                CIP

Contributors

Marilyn Jager Adams, PhD, Harvard University Graduate School of Education, Cambridge, MA

Peter Afflerbach, PhD, Department of Curriculum and Instruction, National Reading Research Center, University of Maryland, College Park, College Park, MD

Richard C. Anderson, PhD, Center for the Study of Reading, University of Illinois at Urbana–Champaign, Champaign, IL

Isabel L. Beck, PhD, Learning, Research, and Development Center, University of Pittsburgh, Pittsburgh, PA

Clark Chinn, PhD, Graduate School of Education, Rutgers University, New Brunswick, NJ

Sarah Warshauer Freedman, PhD, School of Education, University of California, Berkeley, Berkeley, CA

Vivian L. Gadsden, PhD, Graduate School of Education, University of Pennsylvania, Philadelphia, PA

Janet S. Gaffney, PhD, Department of Special Education, University of Illinois at Urbana–Champaign, Champaign, IL

Jane Hansen, PhD, Department of Education, University of New Hampshire, Durham, NH

James V. Hoffman, PhD, Department of Curriculum and Instruction, College of Education, The University of Texas at Austin, Austin, TX

Edward J. Kameenui, PhD, College of Education, University of Oregon, Eugene, OR

Fran Lehr, MA, Center for the Study of Reading, University of Illinois at Urbana–Champaign, Champaign, IL

Kim Nguyen, MA, Research Assistant, University of Illinois at Urbana–Champaign, Champaign, IL

Jean Osborn, MEd, Center for the Study of Reading, University of Illinois at Urbana–Champaign, Champaign, IL

P. David Pearson, PhD, Department of Education, Michigan State University, East Lansing, MI

Michael Pressley, PhD, Department of Psychology, University of Notre Dame, Notre Dame, IN

Victoria Purcell-Gates, PhD, Graduate School of Education, Harvard University, Cambridge, MA

Taffy E. Raphael, PhD, Department of Reading and Language Arts, Oakland University, Rochester, MI

Virginia Richardson, PhD, School of Education, University of Michigan, Ann Arbor, MI

Nancy L. Roser, EdD, Department of Curriculum and Instruction, College of Education, The University of Texas at Austin, Austin, TX

William Rutherford, EdD, Department of Curriculum and Instruction, College of Education, The University of Texas at Austin, Austin, TX

Martha Waggoner, PhD, Teacher, Danville, IL

Jo Worthy, PhD, Department of Curriculum and Instruction, College of Education, The University of Texas at Austin, Austin, TX

Acknowledgments

The warm and homelike atmosphere of the Wingspread Conference Center, generously made available for our use by the Johnson Foundation, encouraged conference participants to discuss issues that arose from the presentations. Discussions took place at breakfast, lunch, and dinner, and often into the evening. We thank Charles W. Bray, President of the Johnson Foundation, for making the facilities of the center available and for making us feel so welcome. Although the hospitality of the entire Wingspread Center staff was remarkable, Susan J. Poulsen, Program Officer of the Johnson Foundation, was always particularly gracious and attentive. We give special thanks to her for the smooth operation of each day of the conference.

Additional support for the conference was provided by the Ball Foundation, Carus Corporation, and the McDougal Foundation. We are grateful for each of these contributions.

The conference plans originated in discussions among Richard C. Anderson of the Center for the Study of Reading, P. David Pearson of Michigan State University, and M. Blouke Carus of Carus Corporation. The focus of these discussions was the possibility of developing a framework that could be used by educators to make reasoned decisions about reading and writing instruction. We are glad they had these discussions and hope that this book promotes equally fruitful discussions among those who read it.

JEAN OSBORN and FRAN LEHR
Center for the Study of Reading
University of Illinois at Urbana–Champaign

Preface

The Wingspread conference provided its participants with a forum for a lively, and, as Richard Anderson notes in his introduction, sometimes intense exchange of ideas. Our hope is that this book will capture and convey to its readers the vibrancy of the conference.

That the conference prompted heated discussions is not surprising. People hold strong views about reading, its instruction, its assessment, and about how best to help students—all students—become literate. The chapters in this book reflect many deeply held views on issues related to literacy teaching and learning.

The chapters are grouped into five parts: "Learning to Read," "Purposes for Reading and Talking about Books," "Writing and Learning to Write," "Standards and Assessment," and "Teaching and Teacher Education."

The five chapters in Part 1 focus on a number of issues crucial to young children, their families, their communities, and for their teachers and administrators who must plan instruction that will result in literacy for all children. Isabel Beck begins this part of the book by recounting how her experiences as a teacher, parent, and researcher led her to conclude that for children to become successful readers, they must first gain control of the print-to-speech mapping system. In Chapter 2, Vivian Gadsden discusses the home and community contexts that affect whether and how children become engaged and sustain their engagement in literacy learning and how they themselves construct images of their possibilities as learners. In Chapter 3, Victoria Purcell-Gates cautions those who are concerned with young children's literacy development to approach instructional and curricular decisions with the assumption that *all* children are learners and to work from the beginning to even the playing field. In Chapter 4, Marilyn Jager Adams examines the three-cueing system of reading. Adams traces the origins of a popular schematic that is used frequently to depict key aspects of beginning reading instruction. She argues that the schematic is often misinterpreted to imply that teachers should minimize attention to graphophonemic relationships. Adams recommends an interpretation of the system that more closely matches research-based knowledge about how children learn to read. After reviewing options for teaching low-achieving students, Janet Gaffney, in Chapter 5, poses four questions designed to stimulate discussions among educators as they plan how to implement the most effective conventional instruction, interventions, and long-term remedial and special education services.

Part 2, "Purposes for Reading and Talking about Books," contains three chapters that address a range of literacy issues. In Chapter 6, Michael Pressley urges members of the profession to get beyond the whole language–decoding skills debate in beginning reading and to devote attention to the crucial area of comprehension. Pressley reviews the research on comprehension instruction, concluding that comprehension can be improved by explicitly teaching students to use a repertoire of comprehension strategies. The remaining two chapters of Part 2 look at ways that teachers and students can work together to ensure that students learn how to use reading and the knowledge gained from reading in a variety of useful and productive contexts. In Chapter 7, Taffy Raphael stresses the value of talk in the classroom—talk that is balanced among the students and teacher participants, across the content being discussed, and across grouping arrangements. Raphael provides a detailed look at one classroom program, the Book Club, as a means of laying out a curricular framework that captures the content of classroom talk about literacy and for illustrating the contexts and opportunities for teaching this curriculum through classroom discourse. In Chapter 8, Richard Anderson and his colleagues also focus on classroom talk—specifically the talk that takes place in classrooms during story reading. The researchers compare *recitation,* the conventional approach to story discussion, with *collaborative reasoning,* a new approach to story discussion designed to be more intellectually stimulating.

An essential partner of reading, writing is the subject of the two chapters in Part 3. In Chapter 9, Sarah Warshauer Freedman describes a project that looked at learning to write in schools in the United States and in England. She relates in detail the literacy growth of one classroom of low-tracked ninth-grade students in the United States that occurred over the school year as the students exchanged writing with a similar group of English students. In Chapter 10, Jane Hansen describes similar growth in the writing of very young children as they strive to communicate with real audiences and for real purposes.

Over the past decade, the setting of standards for the attainment of reading and writing achievement and the development of assessment procedures to measure that achievement have become central themes of the national education agenda. The three chapters in Part 4 address issues related to the setting of standards and to the assessment of literacy achievement. In Chapter 11, Peter Afflerbach argues for the centrality of effective, well-designed assessment in helping young children become literate. He concludes that effective assessment results from systemic and inclusive development efforts that focus on the validity, reliability, and utility of assessment information. In Chapter 12, David Pearson examines the role of standards and assessments in shaping the teaching and learning of reading. Following an analysis of the conceptual and technical issues surrounding assessment, Pearson offers suggestions for research studies that focus on assessments of early literacy. James Hoffman and his colleagues focus, in Chapter 13, on performance assessment, basing their discussion on personal experiences gained while working with a group of teachers to develop a better way of assessing the literacy growth of their first-grade children. The researchers connect their experiences to a broader understanding of performance assessment and its potential for teacher education.

In Part 5, "Teaching and Teacher Education," two topics pivotal to the successful literacy achievement of all students are addressed: staff development and the development of criteria that will formulate an agreed-upon knowledge base for the profession. Virginia Richardson begins Chapter 14 with a brief description of two forms of staff development: a traditional, training approach and a new inquiry-based approach called Practical Argument Staff Development. Posing the question: Why don't school districts implement staff development in a way that takes advantage of the relatively clear-cut, research-based findings about effective staff development? Richardson then addresses the question of whether the new form of staff development actually meets the needs of students. In Chapter 15, the final chapter of the book, Edward Kameenui explores the challenges inherent in the phrase "literacy for all." He notes the need for literacy professionals to reach agreement on the knowledge base that determines how best to teach all children and to insist upon a proactive accountability system.

Contents

Introduction: Reflections on Literacy Education

RICHARD C. ANDERSON

University of Illinois at Urbana–Champaign

Once again the pendulum in the field of literacy education is moving. This time it is swinging away from an emphasis on whole language and toward an emphasis on instruction grounded in skills. Among the reasons are the recent decline in NAEP reading scores in California, a state in which many teachers fervently embraced whole language; a growing discontent among the general public with the state of reading instruction in America, and federal and state mandates aimed at improving students' reading perform-ance and test scores. As is usually the case in times of change, the pendulum swing is accompanied by increased conflict and confusion: conflict between the champions of whole language and those of skills-based instruction; confusion among teachers, school administrators, and the general public about what should be taught and how best to teach it.

In early 1996, the Center for the Study of Reading, with support from the Carus Corporation, the Ball Foundation, the Johnson Foundation, and the McDougal Foundation, began organizing a conference with the intent not simply of reviewing what research has to say about reading and language instruction in a broad way but of addressing the transition that is taking place. The goal was to show that there is an intermediate position on the pendulum's arc between pure whole language and pure basic skills that makes good sense and is not just an unhappy compromise between the two extremes. We sought, in other words, not a negotiated settlement but a creative synthesis of the best ideas in reading and language instruction, whatever their source.

In this introduction, I describe the conference as we envisioned it, the conference as it actually unfolded, and my personal reflections on two of the major themes at the conference—the issue of how children best learn to read, and the issue of the best mode for educational reform.

THE WINGSPREAD CONFERENCE

The conference was convened in October 1996 at the Wingspread Conference Center near Racine, Wisconsin. The invited participants were literacy researchers, educators, education writers for the popular media, and representatives of state agencies involved in educational policy making. Participants were chosen who represented a range of positions on issues in learning to read and write.

Those among the conference participants who made presentations were asked to prepare thoughtful, balanced, research-based papers that discussed major issues in literacy education. They were to focus their presentations on the following questions:

- What are the essential components of reading and writing instruction in American schools?
- What is the agreed-upon common knowledge base for the teaching and learning of reading and writing?
- How do we prepare teachers and manage schools so that all students achieve acceptable standards of performance in reading and writing?
- What are the strategies to use to change educational policy and to communicate with teachers, administrators, and the general public?

The hope was that the conference would lead reasonable people to seek an end to the seemingly endless conflict between whole language and skills advocates. The further hope was that the conference would help to end the confusion over the ways and means of teaching reading and writing and, thus, to lay the foundation for a national agenda that educators, schools, and states might use to make reasoned decisions about instruction.

Presentations at the conference were thoughtful. Discussion was spirited. Inevitably, perhaps, considering the range and strength of the commitments of the participants, tempers sometimes flared. During a presentation on site-based management and teacher-based performance assessment, a participant known for his advocacy of state-mandated educational reform was heard to mutter "bull shit," provoking an angry retort from the speaker. Another speaker, whose presentation was excellent, could not be persuaded to submit a chapter for this volume, because he believed the conference was dominated by "phonics firsters."

At the initiative of Bill Honing, a former chief state school officer in California, an informal, self-nominated subgroup of participants drafted what they hoped would be a consensus statement that all, or most, of the conferees would endorse. The chair of the conference ruled that the statement would not come to a vote of the participants, because reaching a consensus statement had not been in the call for the conference and, therefore, pressure to endorse it would be unfair to participants who had reservations or alternate viewpoints. For the record, the subgroup's draft entitled "A Principled Statement about Beginning Reading" is incorporated as an appendix to this book. The statement should be read with the understanding that it does not necessarily represent the final thinking of even the subgroup that wrote it and, to reiterate, it is not a consensus statement of the conference.

So the conference proved to be a microcosm of the entire field, revealing a fair amount of conflict and some confusion. That the conference was unable to fulfill the hopes that we had for it prompts this warning: A field divided into warring camps is not a profession.

An agreed-upon body of knowledge is typical of and I will go further and say, essential to a true profession. Although an enormous amount of writing and research has focused on various aspects of reading, it is sad to have to acknowledge that this work has not coalesced into an agreed-upon body of knowledge about the content or form of reading instruction, particularly beginning reading instruction.

THE CONTINUING DEBATE ABOUT LEARNING TO READ

Within the field of literacy education, there have been developments on all manner of important topics over the past 30 years, but at the intersection of literacy education with the broader public arena of educational policy, the Great Debate (Chall, 1967) continues to be almost entirely about: whether phonics is essential for all children; whether phonics is being taught; if not, why not; and, if phonics for all is the best policy, what can be done to guarantee that phonics is taught?

The litany of the phonics advocate is that children should receive explicit, systematic, intensive, phonics instruction. Each of the italicized terms raises a point of contention. I will take the opportunity afforded to a conference chair to outline what I regard as the sensible positions on these points. Then I address a couple of questions framed within the whole-language perspective. I have to take the space to define my terms to

avoid the Punch and Judy impasse: "You don't teach phonics." "Yes, I do!"
"No you don't!!" "Yes, I do!!!"

Is Knowledge of Letter–Sound Patterns
Essential for Reading Development?

By a letter–sound pattern I mean individual letters, onset-rimes, prefixes,
suffixes, roots—along with their associated speech sounds. The answer to
this question is an unqualified yes. Evidence of several kinds converges on
this conclusion. For instance, the speed and accuracy with which students
can name pronounceable pseudowords such as *bave* and *zim* will neatly
separate the good, average, and poor readers as determined by teacher
judgment of overall reading level or scores on a standardized reading
comprehension test. Lists of pseudowords can not be pronounced on the
basis of meaning, syntax, or helpful illustrations. The only possible basis
is knowledge of letter–sound patterns. During normal reading, of course,
readers of all ages draw on semantic, syntactic, and contextual information,
but anyone who thinks that a child can achieve a high level of reading
proficiency relying on other "cueing systems" (cf. Adams, Chapter 4)
without mastering the letter–sound patterns of the language is simply
uninformed.

Does Phonics Instruction Promote Reading Development?

The answer to this question is also yes, although the evidence that
supports it is not as strong or as consistent as that bearing on the first
question. The best evidence comes from studies that compare the reading
achievement of children from classrooms receiving phonics instruction
with the reading achievement of comparable children from classrooms
receiving little or no phonics instruction (for reviews, see Chall, 1967,
1983; Adams, 1990). On average, the research indicates that phonics
instruction proves helpful.

Should Phonics Instruction Be Explicit?

In "explicit" or direct phonics instruction, the teacher attempts to get across
letter–sound patterns by telling, explaining, modeling, and leading students
in group and individual exercises. All of the evidence mentioned above was
evidence about explicit phonics instruction. Thus, this is the proven way,
but perhaps not the only way. The success of the Reading Recovery
program suggests that indirect instructional methods may also be effective.
Reader Recovery tutors seldom tell, explain, or model. Rather, for instance,
if a child who is writing the sentence "We got a new rug for the TV room"
pauses at *rug*, the tutor might have the child say *rug* slowly and clearly and
then ask, "What sound do you hear at the beginning?" The reason for

asking, where possible, instead of telling is to encourage children to be actively involved in searching for patterns.

Must Phonics Instruction Be Systematic?

By systematic I mean that there is a predetermined set of letter–sound patterns to be taught and a predetermined sequence for teaching them. Published phonics programs are always systematic, in this sense, but this may be an incidental rather than a critical feature. I do not know of convincing evidence that bears directly on the question. The assumption behind the belief that phonics instruction should be systematic is that children must be provided with a rather complete map of letter–sound patterns. An alternate assumption is that the point of phonics instruction is to get across the lesson that there is a logical relationship, albeit a complicated and only semiregular one, between letters and sounds; if this is the point, then letter–sound patterns are taught just as illustrations to enable children to understand how to complete the map for themselves, and maybe phonics teaching does not have to be systematic. More research is needed to resolve this issue.

Must Phonics Instruction Be Intensive?

In the context of this discussion, *intensive* means spending a lot of time and making good use of this time so as to provide plenty of opportunities for children to learn. There is evidence that more phonics is better (see Rosenshine & Stevens, 1984). I think it likely that a major shortcoming of many whole-language classrooms is the failure to provide children with enough opportunities to learn letter–sound patterns.

Could Embedded Instruction of Phonics Be Effective?

By "embedded" phonics instruction I mean seizing "teachable moments" afforded during language arts activities to advance children's under-standing of letter–sound patterns. Stahl and his colleagues report that studies comparing whole language with conventional instruction in the early grades show little difference in average reading achievement but a much greater range of achievement among whole-language classrooms (Stahl, McKenna, & Pagnucco, 1994; Stahl & Miller, 1989). This implies that some whole-language teachers are ineffective, whereas others are effective beyond the ordinary. My conjecture is that the effective whole-language teachers are employing techniques of embedded phonics instruc-tion frequently and well. Discovering whether this indeed is so, and identifying what the specific techniques are, are worthwhile goals for future research.

What Sorts of Books Are Best
for Promoting Early Reading Development?

In Chapter 1, Beck presents an attractive argument for books made decodable, in the sense of containing a high proportion of words with regular letter–sound patterns, because, she maintains, such books will enable easier and more certain acquisition of letter–sound knowledge.

Others argue that books for young children should be made *predictable* by using common (but not necessarily regular) vocabulary, familiar events from everyday life, plots with a repeating theme, and illustrations that picture the things and actions described in the story. The rationale for predictable books is to provide children with a scaffold that, among other benefits, supports them to work out letter–sound patterns. The counterargument is that predictable books promote the illusion of "reading" and are a crutch that may even interfere with learning letter–sound patterns because the child has alternate routes to pronunciation. The best available evidence shows that predictable books are more often a scaffold than a crutch (Phillips, Norris, & Mason, 1996).

Still others maintain that only authentic literature should be used in reading and language arts instruction. The rationale is that authentic literature is more deeply meaningful and engaging than contrived texts written for school. Among the selections for young children that could be called authentic, few, if any, are decodable, whereas many, but not all, are predictable. I think there is good reason to doubt that any but the highest performing first graders can make much headway in reading when they are supposed to learn from unpredictable texts. The known provides the framework for tackling the unknown; when too little is known, there is no framework. I am led to wonder whether whole-language teachers who are effective beyond the ordinary employ predictable texts to promote reading development, reserving rich, interesting, but less predictable and therefore more difficult texts for oral language development. (I get this idea from Beck, who in Chapter 1 develops it with respect to decodable text and authentic literature.)

Surely the answer to the question of which kinds of books are most helpful in learning to read depends on exactly how the books are used. But little systematic is known about which kinds of books work best with which kinds of children under which kinds of instructional regimen. With little actual knowledge available, perhaps it is inevitable that some will try to settle the issues in flaming matches on the Internet.

COMPETING CONCEPTIONS OF REFORM
IN LITERACY EDUCATION

At least four papers at the conference (see Chapters 11–14 by Afflerbach, Pearson, Hoffman and colleagues, and Richardson) were premised on the assumption that worthwhile and lasting reforms in literacy education originate in the initiatives of local schools and individual teachers, a view sharply opposed by many conferees who envision reform through holding schools and teachers accountable for achieving state mandates. To some extent, positions on how reform ought to take place are pragmatic and tactical. If you believe that teachers are eager to put your favorite idea into practice, you will be inclined to endorse local initiative. If you think teachers are resistant, you may favor state mandates. Thus phonics advocates tend to believe in state mandates, because many teachers appear to resist phonics (or is it the brand of phonics? or the fact that phonics is mandated?), whereas phonics seems like common sense to governors and state legislators.

Views about reform are conditioned by beliefs about the nature of teachers and teaching. In one conception, teachers at their best are artists who create lessons in response to circumstances. In another view, teachers are conceived of as technicians whose job is to efficiently implement a curriculum developed by others. My position is that a professional teacher is both an artist and a technician. This is an uncomfortable position because many of the entailments of the two positions—teacher as artist, teacher as technician—are contradictory. I have learned from my student Maria da Venza Tillmanns that it is often better to live with some discomfort than to resolve dilemmas by discarding one position in favor of another. She has educated me about Buber's idea of "holding the tension" between opposing positions (Tillmanns, 1998). When one remains open to both positions, turning from one to the other, thinking can be invigorated and decision making informed.

Ultimately, views of educational reform hinge on core beliefs about the purposes of education. One conception is that the main business of education is the transmission of a codified body of knowledge and skill. A contrasting conception seeks to reach enlightenment goals: people committed to a humane and civil society; people who possess the habits of mind for independent, reflective, and critical thinking; people who can take delight in life and in literature. Again, we must hold the tension; education will be impoverished if either conception is suppressed.

As I attempt to hold the tension among competing conceptions of reform in literacy education, I am led to the following reflection. Certainly, as a nation we are not doing as good a job as we might in assuring basic literacy for all. We must take every reasonable step to do better. However, a state mandate for phonics, enforced with performance standards on a competency test, is strong medicine. I am persuaded by Richardson's argument (Chapter 14) that, if you do not treat teachers as reflective people, you can hardly expect them to treat students as reflective beings. School environments that sustain civility, reflectiveness, and zest are fragile and not seen everywhere. These environments are threatened by state-mandated treatment of subjects on penalty of examination failure, in my judgment.

It is up to advocates of state mandates and competency exams to show otherwise. In the meantime, I oppose them.

REFERENCES

Adams, M. J. (1990). *Beginning to read: Thinking and learning about print.* Cambridge, MA: MIT Press.

Chall, J. S. (1967). *Learning to read: The great debate.* New York: McGraw-Hill.

Chall, J. S. (1983). *Learning to read: The great debate* (rev. ed.). New York: McGraw-Hill.

da Venza Tillmanns, M. (1998). *Philosophical counseling and teaching: Holding the tension in a dualistic world.* Unpublished dissertation, University of Illinois, Urbana–Champaign, Urbana–Champaign, IL.

Phillips, L. M., Norris, S. P., & Mason, J. M. (1996). Longitudinal effects of early literacy concepts on reading achievement: A kindergarten intervention and five-year follow-up. *Journal of Literacy Research, 28,* 173–195.

Rosenshine, B., & Stevens, R. (1984). Classroom instruction in reading. In P. D. Pearson, R. Barr, M. L. Kamil, & P. Mosenthal (Eds.), *Handbook of research in reading* (pp. 745–798). New York: Longman.

Stahl, S. A., McKenna, M. C., & Pagnucco, J. (1994). The effects of whole language instruction: An update and a reappraisal. *Educational Psychology, 29,* 175–186.

Stahl, S. A., & Miller, P. D. (1989). Whole language and language experience approaches for beginning reading: A quantitative research synthesis. *Review of Educational Research, 59,* 87–116.

PART ONE

LEARNING TO READ

CHAPTER ONE

Understanding Beginning Reading: A Journey through Teaching and Research

ISABEL L. BECK
University of Pittsburgh

PROLOGUE

My journey through reading education began about 40 years ago, initially, as a first-grade teacher and then as a teacher of third-, fourth-, and fifth-grade students. I finished my public school teaching experience as a kindergarten teacher. In addition, two other practical experiences were enormously important to the development of my understanding of reading. One was teaching sergeants who did not know how to read at an Army camp in Arkansas. The other was watching and interacting with my own two children in the course of their reading development.

My journey through reading research began soon after my youngest child was born. While waiting for acceptance to law school, I started working as a part-time research assistant at the Learning Research and Development Center at the University of Pittsburgh. It was there that I happened upon some psychological research and theory on reading that addressed some curiosities that had emerged from my experience with first-graders as well as the sergeants in Arkansas. What first got my attention was that some of the people who were writing articles on reading (psychologists) had never taught anyone to read, yet they were able to describe phenomena that I had observed in the course of teaching reading. That made me really curious. In the course of reading some of the psychological literature on reading, I became fascinated with some potential explanations for real-world phenomena I had witnessed in students' attempts to learn to read—so fascinated, that I decided against law school and pursued a PhD in reading education.

Although my longest and most sustained research has involved comprehension and learning from text, I have never given up my study of and interest in beginning reading. Thus, the purpose of this chapter is to relate my teaching experiences to research in beginning reading. To do so, I am going to speak to you in two voices: a personal voice that describes several of my teaching experiences; and an analytical voice about those experiences, which I attempt to connect with reading research.

TRAVELS IN FIRST GRADE

My first-grade teaching experiences were in southern California and on the East Coast in an urban school district. Forty-some children in each of those classes tells you how long ago it was. Both classrooms were similarly arranged: The focus in each room was the "reading circle," about 10 little chairs in a semicircle in front of a pocket chart; a library corner with pillows, illustrated color words and days of the week along the borders, class-developed experience charts on a large stand, individually dictated and illustrated little books, and many other such enduring first-grade paraphernalia and props.

In both classrooms the children and I had built a "post office" where the children delivered letters to each other. The post office, which I had read about in a description of the University of Chicago's lab school, consisted of cubbyhole mail slots made out of cut-down shoe boxes. Near the post office was my desk. On one side of my desk was an ever-changing collection of such classics as *Make Way for Ducklings* and *Ping on the Yangtze River*, which I read to the children. On the other side of my desk sat the "Dick and Jane" teacher's manuals—dog-eared, clipped, bookmarked.

Let me tell you a little about those "Dick and Jane" teacher's manuals. When I started my student teaching in a first-grade classroom, I knew a lot about children's literature and about reading to children. I knew something about the development of young children and had learned from instructors who exemplified an attitude of kindness and respect for children. As for reading and writing, I knew about developing experience charts, labeling children's drawings, and taking dictation. But, from my critic teacher, during student teaching, I learned the most "useful" thing of all: I learned how to follow the "Dick and Jane" teacher's manuals.

So when I entered my very own first-grade classroom, with the sobering responsibility of teaching 43 children to read on my shoulders, I felt enormous relief in finding the "Dick and Jane" manuals in the cupboard. Those manuals were not only a source of great comfort throughout the year, they were a source of great wisdom; I did virtually everything they suggested. We finished the readiness book, went on to the first preprimer, and virtually all the children were learning to read. That is, they could read the words in the first preprimer. The second preprimer, however, did not go quite as well as the first; it seemed that several children were forgetting words they used to know and misreading new words as old words. So I used flashcards, both in isolation and context, and devised game-like ways to make the cards more interesting.

At about this time in the instructional sequence, activities directed to beginning sounds appeared in my manual. The manual suggested putting a letter *B* on a piece of chart paper and having the children bring in pictures of things that begin with *B*. Over the weeks, we developed *C* charts, *M* charts, *S* charts, and the like. The students enjoyed bringing in the pictures, and I did what the manual told me to do: I would ask the children what was the same about the names of the pictures, and we would get to the point that they told me that all the picture names began with *B*.

As we reached the last pages of the third preprimer, however, it was quite clear that more than a few children were forgetting words they had once known. How was that possible? How could they know a word and then not know it? And it did not get better with the primer; in fact, it got worse. More children misread words they once knew, and they were not remembering new words. After that year in California, I moved to the East and taught first grade again, with about 40 children in a large urban environment. And similar things happened.

At the end of those 2 years, there was good news, not-so-good news, and bad news. The good news was that about 50 of the 80 children were developing into good readers. The not-so-good news was that about half of the remaining 30 were kind of shaky. They could read target materials correctly, but they did not seem to have much confidence. The bad news was that of the remaining 15, most were in trouble. With some, the difficulties started earlier in the process; with others, it appeared later. Some seemed to forget words right from the start—after 15 or 20 words had accumulated; others did not forget words until well into the second and third preprimers, when perhaps 70 or 80 words had accumulated.

Analysis of Travels in First Grade

Why did some of those children misread words they once knew, and why did they guess old words for new words?[1] Somewhere along the line, probably soon after I had discovered reading research and became more analytical, I became consciously aware that in the "Dick and Jane" materials, the misreading index grew as the word corpus got larger. Why was this occurring when the whole-word basals of that time provided extensive exposure to the words introduced including repetition of words across stories, within books, and across books?

I offer two related reasons, both of which concern the key role of learning letter–sound correspondences early in the acquisition of reading. First, the period in which I used the "Dick and Jane" materials was the heyday of the whole-word/look–say orientation in which the approach for teaching words was memorization of the whole word unit. The pedagogical strategies involved presenting new words in sentences, in isolation, matching them to pictures, cutting up sentence strips and reading the words, putting the words back into sentences, and the like. It was my experience that early on—when the word corpus was small—those kinds of repetition of whole words seemed to work for most children.

At this point, let me assert that because those kinds of procedures work when the word corpus is small, many children pay little, if any, attention to all the constituent parts of words. Moreover, looking at all the parts of words (i.e., all the letters from beginning to end of words) is not particularly natural. Observations of young children's first unguided attempts to use print show that they often find a distinctive feature as a cue to identify a word (Gough & Hillinger, 1980). Distinctive features might include a picture or a page location (e.g., *owl* is the last short string of letters on the page with a picture of birds); a mental image (e.g., *yellow* is a long string of letters with two straight lines in the middle); or initial letters, which are frequently used as recall cues (e.g., *birthday* starts with *b*).

Such word recognition involves "rote associations between unanalyzed spoken words and one or more salient and often arbitrary graphic feature of the printed word or its context" (Share, 1995, p. 159). Spelling-to-speech connections at subword units play little, if any role. Thus the whole-word/look–say method for teaching word recognition resembles the teaching of Chinese, a logographic-like writing system in which one symbol represents an entire word. But it takes a very long time to learn to read Chinese, and it is not expected that students learn more than a few hundred items per year (Mason, Anderson, Omura, Uchida, & Imai, 1989; Perfetti & Zhang, 1996).

I believe that in the "Dick and Jane" materials, as the number of words grew too large, those children who had not induced spelling–sound relationships simply could not keep up because the arbitrary graphic features they may have been using as recall cues lost their saliency. In this regard, Share (1995) emphasizes a point noted by others (see Ehri, 1992; Perfetti, 1992) that "it is questionable whether providing the identity of a printed word at the whole-word level is likely to draw a child's attention to the detailed orthographic structure which ultimately forms the basis for proficient word recognition" (p. 153).

The second and intimately related issue to what I think caused some of my students to experience serious difficulty by the end of first grade concerns the vocabulary used in the early "Dick and Jane" materials. Specifically, the words included in the early text materials of the whole-word basals were selected on the basis of frequency in the language and the likelihood that young children would know those words from their aural repertoires. For example, those materials could have included in close proximity *coat, boy, hot, look, no,* and *slow.* Although all these words contain the letter *o,* the spelling-to-sound pattern is unique in each. When frequency is the major criterion for selecting words, it will result in the inclusion of many complex spelling patterns as well as irregular words. Including many words in early texts that represent complex spelling–sound patterns makes it difficult to induce the systematicity of the spelling–sound mapping system. Thus in terms of the kinds of words that children encounter in early texts, Juel and Roper-Schneider (1985) have noted that "the types of words which appear in beginning reading texts may well exert a more powerful influence in shaping children's word identification strategies than the method of reading instruction" (p. 151).

Conclusions and Misunderstandings from Travels in First Grade

Although I had some misgivings about how those 15 poor readers would fare, my general conclusion was optimistic. That is, if they did not get discouraged, they would be all right. It would just take them longer.

My optimistic conclusion was likely wrong for many children and perhaps dangerous for some. Research now offers persuasive evidence that children who get off to a slow start rarely become strong readers (Stanovich, 1986). There are many reasons that this is the case. Early learning of the code leads to wider reading habits both in and out of school (Juel, 1988). Wide reading provides opportunities to grow in vocabulary, concepts, and knowledge of how text is written. Children who do not learn to decode do not have this avenue for growth. This phenomenon of the "rich get richer" (i.e., the children who learn to decode early continue to make improvement in their reading) and the "poor get poorer" (i.e., children who do not learn to decode early become increasingly distanced in reading ability from the "rich"), has been termed the *Matthew Effect* (Stanovich, 1986). A particularly chilling finding about the results of a weak start comes from Juel's (1988) longitudinal study of 54 children from first through fourth grade that showed a .88 probability that a child at the bottom quartile on the Iowa Reading Comprehension subtest at the end of first grade would still be a poor reader at the end of fourth grade. A similar finding was identified earlier by Clay (1979).

TRAVELS IN THE ARMY

For personal reasons, after I finished my second year of first-grade teaching, I relocated to Fort Smith, Arkansas. There were no available jobs there in the public schools, but through a serendipitous circumstance, I got a job at Camp Chaffee Army base teaching noncommissioned officers (NCOs), mostly sergeants, to read. Some of the NCOs could read, albeit haltingly, and the Army had simplified *Reader's Digest* kinds of things for them to read. However, others virtually could not read at all. What to do with them?

Not to worry! The Army had figured it all out, it had developed a basal, directly modeled on the "Dick and Jane" materials. On the first page of this reader, there was a picture of a young man in a farm scene. His name was Pete.[2] Following this was a two-page spread in which Pete's mother was shown in her apron, canning something, and his father was shown on a tractor, waving to a neighbor. On the following page, there was a recruiting sergeant. And the story—well, in contrast to Dick and Jane who visit the country, Pete joins the Army to serve his country. And instead of sentences such as "Dick and Jane ride in the car. They are riding to grandfather's," the Army basal read, "Pete rides the bus. He is riding to the Army camp."

I knew exactly how to teach that kind of basal with its whole-word/look–say approach, and I threw myself into doing it well. I introduced new words in context sentences; we practiced reading the sentences; we reviewed the words on flash cards; we read the story silently, then orally, and so on. And it didn't work. Not even a little. The men forgot words, virtually immediately. So in frustration I began to break the rules that I had learned about teaching beginning reading. I found myself saying things such as "Look, it says *bus. bbuuss.* Sergeant Hiram, point to the letters in *bbuuss*, and say the sounds slowly." It seemed that with that kind of showing and practicing, I could see a crack here and there in the men's memory for words.

What was I doing? Well, I was teaching phonics, and I was making it up as I went along. Phonics had been mentioned in the one reading methods class I had taken, but it had seemed to me to have a negative connotation. And, the *phonetic* [sic] analysis in the "Dick and Jane" manuals I had been using in my first grades did not get much beyond initial, and, maybe, final consonant sounds. It was easy to see that it was often the sequence of letters after the initial one that caused my sergeants the most trouble in reading. When they got to a word that they did not recognize, some of the men would start it correctly, but after the initial sound they'd switch to a word that made sense in the context, even when it did not begin with the initial sound of the target word (not unlike some of my 15 first-graders). With the sergeants, however, I started to insist that they stay with the correct beginning sound and try to figure out the word. (I had not done that with my first-graders, as I had learned in college and from the manuals, to tell them the words they could not read, so as not to interrupt meaning.) Moreover, perhaps I saw what the sergeants were doing because, in contrast to 40-some children, many of whom did not do what I just described about my sergeants, I worked with small classes, often on a one-to-one basis.

So I began to insist that the sergeants try to figure out a word after they had produced an initial correct sound. At first chaos broke out: *bus* might become *bat*; *truck* might become *take*, and the like. They did not like that because they knew it did not make sense. They would have much preferred to call *truck*, *vehicle*. But I would not let them, because doing so would not advance them on the road to independent reading. What I did do was require that they deal with the sounds of every letter from the beginning to the end of words. (In retrospect, although my idea was right, my procedures were primitive.) Be that as it may, what I was doing began to work a little, and some of the virtually nonreading sergeants began to pick their way through *Private Pete in Basic Training* texts, menus, and movie marquees. And the men and I were very happy.

Enormously important to the development of my understanding of how to teach these men was that when I asked, they would tell me what I did that helped. Most often the things that helped had something to do with showing them the system by which print and speech connect—although those were not their words—or for that matter, at the time, mine.

My conclusion after several years with these men was that the reason they needed such explicit instruction was that when they first went to school, they had not been *ready* to learn to read, and *that*, at least in part, was because they had likely come from backgrounds with very limited exposure to print.

Before providing an analysis of my conclusion about the men in Arkansas, I turn to what I learned about beginning reading from my two children, Mark and Elizabeth.

TRAVELS IN MY HOME

Our home was print-rich, language-rich, and child-centered. Let me give you a glimpse of each of my children as he or she engaged in an aspect of literacy. I'll start with Mark who, at age 5, moved around some magnetic letters on the refrigerator and formed the sequence *t i i p*. Mark asked me to try to figure out what the letters said but warned me that although it was a real word, it was not spelled right. I read *type*, then *tip*. "No, no," Mark said to each of these attempts. And with lots of giggling, he told me that there was a clue in the word *portion*, which was in a recipe on the refrigerator. When that clue did not help me, Mark told me that the word was *ship*. I didn't get it and asked him how *portion* should have helped me figure out that *t i i p* was ship. With that, Mark pointed to the *ti* in *portion* and said, "See."

Now let me tell you about Elizabeth. She adored books, she begged to be read to, and her father and I were enormously responsive. Elizabeth did not engage with the magnetic letters on the refrigerator; instead, for magnetic posting she drew pictures of stories that she had heard, and she dictated notes to the characters in the stories. Elizabeth was not interested in letters or for that matter in words; she was interested in stories and ideas and feelings.

Let me compare what happened to Mark and Elizabeth in school. Both went to the same kind of first grade, one with the whole-word approach to reading. Mark flourished as a reader. But Mark would have flourished in any context. Without having been directly taught, Mark's figuring out of the print-to-speech system was quite extraordinary. Elizabeth did not flourish. And, the print-rich environment in which she grew up did not help her observe the patterns in written language.

Elizabeth's teacher told me not to worry. Elizabeth was so creative and smart, she would catch on. And I believed what her teacher said. But Elizabeth knew she was not doing well, and eventually she showed her unhappiness. At this point I set about to teach her to read. And what did I teach her? I taught her what I had taught my sergeants—I taught her the letter–sound mappings directly and systematically. But I did it less primatively.

By the time I started to work with Elizabeth, a variety of "code-emphasis" programs had come on the market. I discovered these programs through Jeanne Chall's (1967) book.[3] Whereas today I think that the code-emphasis programs of the 1960s were too narrow, the a priori sequence of letter-sounds and the related textual material that included words that exemplified the letter-sounds taught were enormously helpful to me in teaching Elizabeth.

Anyway, Elizabeth learned what she was taught, but she had to be taught everything. Somehow, despite growing up in a print-rich environment with sympathetic and encouraging parents, Elizabeth did not figure out many of the intricacies required to apply the alphabetic principle.

As an aside, for those of you who have your own Elizabeth, I can report that today she is an excellent and avid reader. As Elizabeth grew up, she articulated her learning-to-read experiences, and there was a period in her life when she would tell me often that she knew she had been lucky to have had me as a "teacher." And she was. But those 15 first graders were not lucky to have me as a teacher.

Analysis of Travels in My Home

My own children's stories point to two important issues. First, the Elizabeth story renders suspect, at least partly, my conclusion that the reason my sergeants needed to have the code presented systematically was that they had not come from print-rich backgrounds. Leaving the acquisition of reading aside for a moment, the face validity of the advantages of a literacy-rich home in which parents often read to and talk with their children about what they read cannot, be denied. Among the advantages are learning about the wonders that can be encountered between the cover of books, including both knowledge about the world and the universality of human feelings. So who would not wish that all children could have the thousands of hours of literacy experiences that Elizabeth had? But all that experience did not make early reading acquisition easy for Elizabeth. Is she rare? Apparently not. In a recent review of research, Scarborough and Dobrich (1994) found a median correlation of .28 between parents reading to children and their subsequent reading achievement. The .28 correlation accounted for less than 8% of the variance in reading achievement.

In consideration of the Scarborough and Dobrich data, as well as some other data, Gough (1996) makes the point "that while it may be true that children who are immersed in literacy in their home will tend to read better than those who aren't, there are numerous children who are read to but have difficulty learning to read, and many children who are not read to but readily learn to read. Clearly, a literate environment does not guarantee literacy" (p. 4).

Conclusions from Travels in My Home

The second issue my own children's story points to is that of individual differences. It seems clear that individual differences are what account for the enormous dissimilarity in Mark's and Elizabeth's early competence with words and subword units. In this regard, Share and Stanovich (1995) have described the problems of Elizabeth and her counterparts (e.g., some of my first-graders and sergeants) as follows:

> Successful reading acquisition seems to require the development of an analytic processing stance towards words that is probably not the "natural" processing set adopted by most children, and some children have extreme difficulty in adopting an analytic processing set. The latter group will, as a result, have considerable difficulty building up knowledge of subword spelling–sound correspondences—and such knowledge appears to be a necessary prerequisite of fluent reading. (p. 153)

Relatedly, it should be noted that theories about and research on individual differences point to phonological factors, especially difficulties in converting spellings to sounds, as the primary area that differentiates skilled from less-skilled young readers (Stanovich, 1988). Phonological difficulties can be overcome by phonemic training and by direct letter–sound instruction (see, e.g., Blachman, 1994).

We do not know how many children there are like Elizabeth, that is, children who have difficulty learning to read. Estimates once were perhaps 20% of all children, but there are indications that that number has grown toward, perhaps, 40% (Adams, 1996). And, although there are higher incidences of poor children who have difficulty learning to read, Elizabeth is by no means unique.

PATHS TO RESEARCH

When I discussed my sergeants, I said, "Some of the NCOs could read a little, albeit haltingly, and the Army had simplified *Reader's Digest* kinds of things for them to read." Also recall that I described some of my first-graders, not the ones in trouble, but another group as "shaky." They read correctly, but they did not seem to have confidence. I later observed this even more clearly, when I taught third grade. I would tell such children, "You're right, you're doing fine, have more confidence." It didn't help; they just weren't as confident as the good readers.

Then, at a colloquium given by Charles Perfetti in the early 1970s, I became acquainted with issues of *automaticity* of lower-level processes, and I had a revelation. What I had mistaken as lack of confidence in my students and the sergeants was more likely lack of automaticity. Such understanding produces an instructional implication different from the one I had developed.

Research over the last several decades has made it abundantly clear that comprehension (which, of course, is the purpose of reading) is not a single process; rather, it is a complex process that is made up of many interrelated component subprocesses (Just & Carpenter, 1987; Perfetti, 1985). These subprocesses include recognizing words and associating them with concepts stored in memory; developing meaningful ideas from strings of words (phrases, clauses, sentences); drawing inferences—relating what is already known to what is being read; and more. For a reader to comprehend a text, all these mental operations must take place, many of them concurrently. But it is well established that human information processing is limited (Kiss & Savage, 1977); that is, people simply cannot pay attention to too many things at once. Thus, when a complex process comprises a number of subprocesses, some of the lower-level processes must be developed so that they can be carried out without direct attention, or what is known as "automaticity."

The negative impact of engaging in a complex process in which a lower-level subprocess has not been developed to automaticity is easily recognized in the psychomotor domain. For example, compare a competent basketball player with a novice basketball player as each dribbles the ball during a game. The competent player dribbles efficiently, giving no conscious attention to dribbling. That player can direct attention to the higher level components of the game, such as avoiding a steal, getting into position to pass, or maneuvering to a place where the ball can be dunked. Now think of a novice player who knows how to dribble the ball but who needs to pay a certain amount of conscious attention to dribbling to do it well. If that player devotes too much attention to dribbling the ball in a game, he or she may not perform the higher-level components such as passing and shooting. However, if the novice diverts too much attention to the higher-level components, his or her dribbling ability might break down, and the player might lose the ball.

I consider word recognition somewhat analogous to dribbling a basketball. Although one might argue the appropriateness of the analogy, the dependency of comprehension on efficient levels of word recognition processes is not arguable. Adams (Adams & Bruck, 1995) summarizes the point as:

> Scientific research converges on the point that the association of spellings with sounds is a fundamental step in the early stages of literacy instruction. . . . There are literally hundreds of articles to support [this] conclusion. Over and over, children's knowledge of the correspondences between spellings and sounds is found to predict the speed and accuracy with which they can read single words, while the speed and accuracy with which they can read single words is found to predict their ability to comprehend written text. (p. 15)

THE PHONICS PATH

What one needs for competence does not necessarily dictate how one reaches that competence. In the case of reading, there is ample evidence that those approaches to beginning reading that fall in the code-emphasis/linguistic/phonics domain produce advantages in word recognition with no disadvantages in comprehension (Adams, 1990).

In considering the term "phonics" it is important to underscore that it is an umbrella term for a variety of ways of "showing" (be it explicit or implicit) young learners how the print-to-speech system works. As is the case with most umbrella terms, there are both better and less good instantiations. In the section that follows, I examine what I view as the two most important features of phonics instruction: the text materials and the instructional strategies.

Text Materials

I believe that *it is efficient for most children and essential for some children that the early textual material they read be developed using vocabulary that maximizes the regularity of the print-to-speech mapping system of English.*

This speaks to "controlled vocabulary," which many may consider to be more of a dirty term than phonics (see Foorman, 1995), to the extent that whole language advocates do not eschew bringing attention to sub-word units as they are encountered in familiar stories (see Freppon & Headings, 1996; Strickland & Cullinan, 1990). But artificial texts are anathema (Bergeron, 1990). To discuss some of the issues involved in vocabulary control, I now consider three ways the field has developed for providing text materials for beginning reading.[4]

The High-Frequency Vocabulary Way

One way to develop materials for beginning readers is to write selections using words that appear with high frequency in the language and that are likely to be in young children's spoken vocabularies. In each new selection the children encounter, some previously introduced words are repeated and several new words are added. As a result, there is a lot of repetition of an accumulating word list across stories within books and across books. This approach is the one used in the "Dick and Jane" series. The following example is a current version of this approach. It presents the first 39 words of the last story from the second preprimer of a 1991 basal reading program that was published by a major publisher. The page shows a girl reading a picture book:

> Pam likes to read at night.
> "I like the big bird in this book," she says.
> "I wish this bird could come out and play."
> She sees the clock.
> "It is time to put my book down," she says.

After this opening, the bird steps out of the picture book, and in the remaining pages Pam rides the bird to the zoo, they see some things, day breaks, they come back, and the bird steps back into the book.

In this short example, the words *book, could, come, out, clock, to,* and *down* represent multiple graphemes for the same phoneme, and multiple phonemes for the same grapheme. Given that so many complex spelling sequences are presented early and in close proximity, it is difficult to "see" how the system works. Now, one might say that this is the problem with English; English letter–sound relationships, especially vowels, are influenced by the letters around them, so there really is not much systematicity to English. Well . . . yes there is.[5] But that systematicity will not be seen easily by beginning readers if we present texts that throw a lot of complexities at them too early on.

The whole-word/look–say approach to word recognition goes hand and glove with the kind of vocabulary in the Pam story. The reason the whole word approach is necessary for such vocabulary is as follows: Given that so many complex spelling sequences and irregularities are represented early, how do we *teach* children about how the system works? Human beings can tolerate and understand complications in and exceptions to a system—*if* they understand that there *is* a system. In the case of reading, as I have said, if the early words children encounter include too many words in which the spelling-to-speech patterns exaggerate the complexities and exceptions, it very difficult for the child to figure out the systematic relationship between written and spoken language.

The Letter–Sound Relationship Way

The second way to develop texts for beginning readers is to use words that highlight the regularity of the print-to-speech system. In the early 1960s, Fries (1962), who revived the notions that Bloomfield (1942) had discussed several decades earlier, argued that the whole word approach as exemplified in the basal readers of the period made learning to read unnecessarily difficult. The linguists urged that instructional materials be arranged to expose beginning readers to words that maximize the regularities of print-to-sound mapping rather than to those that exacerbate the complexities.

Thus regularity from simple to more complex patterns is the major criterion used by the linguistic/phonics approaches to text development. The text developer establishes an a priori sequence of specific letter–sound correspondences and spelling sequences that are arranged to move from simple to more complex patterns (e.g., CVC, CCVC, CVCe, CVVC, etc.) then creates texts using words that exemplify the sequence. The most extreme version of this approach produces the "Sam can see a tan pan" variety of text.

The following text is the opening 39 words from a story in book 7 of a series of 18 little books for first-graders that was published in 1995 by a publisher that has always controlled vocabulary on the basis of letter–sound correspondences.

Wendell wanted a pet.
He got his net and went to the pond.
Frogs swam in the pond.
One frog was on a pad.

>Wendell grabbed his net.
>He stepped on a log
>to get next to the frog.

As the story continues, the frog gets away, Wendell slips on a log, ends up in the pond with frogs on his body, and thus the punch line to the story is "Wendell was wet, but he got lots of pets."

With the kind of vocabulary used in this story, the strategies for word recognition involve telling students directly or having them induce from the regular patterns the sounds for letters and spelling sequences.

After the introduction of the whole-word/look–say approach in the 1930s, the linguistic/phonic approaches never had the sales of the major mainstream basals. From the 1960s to the 1980s, however, there were six or so complete but narrow linguistic/phonic programs available. For the most part, these programs have disappeared since the literature-based/whole-language movement began to dominate commercial basal reading programs.

The Tell-a-Good-Story Way

The third way to provide textual materials for beginning readers is not to create texts but to use delightful existing children's literature. This literature-based orientation eschews vocabulary control. Generally this means that from the beginning the stories children read in their basal anthologies come from published trade books. Basal program publishers put the stories into grade levels, using such criteria as age-appropriate content and a face-validity sense of difficulty.

The following text presents the opening 49 words from a trade book by Mem Fox entitled *Hattie and the Fox,* which was reproduced in its entirety in the second of five first-grade books that make up a 1993 basal literature anthology. Virtually all the selections in this program—both narrative and expository—are previously published children's literature.

>Hattie was a big black hen.
>One morning she looked up and said,
>"Goodness gracious me!
>I can see a nose in the bushes!"
>"Good grief!" said the goose.
>"Well, well!" said the pig.
>"Who cares?" said the sheep.
>"So what?" said the horse.
>"What next?" said the cow.

As the story continues, Hattie sees more and more parts of the mysterious creature in the bushes, and, as she announces what she sees, the animals provide their standard responses. When Hattie sees enough parts to identify a fox, all of the animals scatter, and there is a cute ending in which the cow changes his repetitive "What next?" to a loud "Moo" and frightens the fox away.

The major strategies for presenting new words and developing word recognition in literature-based early reading materials involve reading and rereading a story. Often this process begins by having children follow along as the teacher reads, then moves to choral reading, and then, perhaps, to partner reading. Use of the context to figure out a word is recommended. In terms of context, because beginning readers cannot read many words, an important criterion for choosing which stories to include in the early months is predictability. After reading, the teacher may employ various whole word approaches (e.g., sentence strips) and what Adams (1990) has referred to as "light and late" phonics. For example, the teacher may bring attention to several words in the selection read that begin with the same initial sounds or identify a phonogram that appears in several words.

Which Texts for What?

Looking across the three types of texts in terms of story interest and natural and delightful language, I assert that the Hattie story wins hands down. When considering the difference among the three stories in terms of quality on delightfulness/natural language dimensions, many might ask who in his or her right mind would deny children the Hattie story in favor of the others. Well . . . although I won't deny children experiences with the Hattie type of literature, I will deny them that type of literature as the vehicle for learning to read in the early months in favor of the Wendell type. Additionally, I would obliterate altogether the "Pam rides" orientation.

I would like to make a point about controlled vocabulary: I find controlling vocabulary on the basis of high-frequency words—the Dick and Jane and Pam variety—supremely wrong-headed because it makes learning the system so much more difficult than it need be and produces bland, boring texts. So I cast my lot with controlling vocabulary on the basis of exemplifying spelling–sound sequences—the Wendell type of material— because to do so makes learning the system easier for children, even though the texts produced are less than wonderful. Second, in the Wendell story, per se, the kind of extreme regularity of the orthodox "The man sat on a tan can" linguistic text has been reduced, and I suspect it could probably be reduced more without harming the value of such texts.[6]

Why then reject the Hattie type of story as the major vehicle for beginning reading? Because the words an author uses to tell a good story independently can never correspond to a preestablished sequence of letter–sounds and spelling patterns. The purposes of a good story and the purpose of stories that include many words that exemplify letter–sound relationships are two entirely different things.

Instructional Strategies

The second feature about phonics instruction that I think most important is that *the instructional strategies include requiring learners to decode phonologically from the beginning to the end of words.*[7] This assertion that instructional strategies require the learner to attend to all the letters in a word comes from both my observations as a teacher and from the nature of reading in an alphabetic orthography. In terms of the former, the negative results I saw from the "light and late" phonics of the "Dick and Jane" materials and from my sergeants' inability to move through a word has been reinforced by numerous recent tape recordings that my master's students have made of young students reading, both in context and in lists, in which they do *partial* decoding and fail. In this regard, Share and Stanovich (1995) make the point that "By its very nature, *partial* decoding must fail in identifying words presented in *isolation* owing to the complete or near-complete processing of letter information required by an alphabetic orthography" (p. 22). In fact, the specific representation of all the letters of a word is a hallmark of competent reading (Perfetti, 1992).

As I have already noted several times, although the whole-word/look–say basals gave some attention to initial sounds and eventually to final sounds, they were extremely limited in bringing attention to letter–sound correspondences in *all* positions from beginning to end. So when the corpus of whole words the children were memorizing grew to include such words as *likes, leads, loses, lets,* the strategies of first letter, final letter, and context were not reliable. Each of these words can make sense in a local context, but if the wrong one is identified, it can greatly misrepresent meaning. The strategy that is most reliable is looking at all the letters.

THE ROLE OF LITERATURE IN EARLY LITERACY

Now I have to face the music of denying children the kind of delightful material represented by the Hattie example in favor of the less-than-wonderful plots and sometimes phonologically obvious linguistic/phonic materials. My rationale is as follows:

First, under no circumstances would I deny children delightful literature—what I deny is using the delightful literature as the vehicle for beginning reading instruction. The problem with using the excellent available stories is that the kind of control that can make the systematicity of written English apparent does not occur in these wonderful stories.

I do not underestimate the role of literature as a resource for dealing with the universals that make us human and in the "discourse of a civil society." Thus I believe children should engage with good literature. But children who do not know how to read need to engage with good literature by listening to, talking about, thinking through, and creatively dramatizing it. As the vehicle for teaching children to read, however, given the lack of vocabulary control, this wonderful genre complicates the early learning-to-read task. For some children, this complication is disastrous. The extra-strong contexts and predictability of the stories most frequently used at the early levels do not require looking at all the parts of some words. And although one can be a successful reader without looking at all the parts of words when the word corpus is small, when the corpus becomes large enough, one will not be successful by not looking at all the parts of words.

The second point, in terms of my rationale for denying the use of marvelous literature as the vehicle for early reading instruction, is that by not making it easier to figure out the orthographic/phonological system, too many children are denied the kind of instruction that will enable them to read literature on their own. In this regard, let me note that the kind of control and systematicity that I ask for does not need to last long—perhaps 6 months, a year, and certainly not with excessive rigidity. Moreover, I think a very strong case can be made that good literature actually can become the basis of reading instruction sooner, *if* we do not depend on it at the beginning.

That a plethora of supplementary little books that are supposed to exemplify letter–sounds have been and are being developed by publishers offers ample evidence that the lack of vocabulary control in literature-based material is an issue. However, there are two problems with these new little books. First, in the books that I have seen, there is not enough control. Second, even if there were enough control, the books provide no real connections to the authentic literature that children read in their literature anthologies. So why not use the literature for reading to children and develop books for children to read themselves in which the lawful ways that spelling-to-speech works are made apparent?

Now it may be the case that the supplementary and add-on materials that are being developed will help. But the print-to-speech mapping system is the core of what children need to learn early; it is not an add-on. Putting that at the core of beginning reading instruction in interesting and intelligent ways requires that publishers and teachers really understand what needs to be learned.

FINAL COMMENT

The gist of my story is this: From the multiple lenses of having taught first-graders and army sergeants to read; from watching my own two children; from being familiar with large bodies of research about the psychology of word recognition and the role of lower-level processes in comprehension; from engaging in my own lines of related research; from working with teachers training to become reading specialists; and from visits to current primary-grade classrooms, the most significant understanding that I have about beginning reading is that it is crucial for children to gain control of the print-to-speech mapping system early. And, this will not happen for a substantial number of children if we do not do it systematically. Doing it systematically, however, does not need to diminish the development of a language-rich environment.

NOTES

1. In terms of guessing old words for new words, in a study of Scottish primary school children who were taught by the whole-word method and no phonics, Seymour and Elder (1986) report that their word recognition errors were drawn from the words they had been taught. This points to the children's nongenerative word skills. They did not attempt to figure out the phonological details of words; rather, when they could not recognize a word, they simply called on another word, from the set of words they had encountered in their reading instruction.

2. In another chapter in which I described the scene, I called the young man Jim but indicated that I was not sure that this was his correct name. Tom Sticht, who did research on reading with Army recruits, and who well may be the only other person now in the reading field who remembers the Army materials, informed me that the young man's name was Pete and that the materials carried the title *Private Pete*.

3. It is questionable whether, in the late 1960s, I would have discovered that code-emphasis programs (in contrast to phonics workbooks) existed had I not read Chall's books. One reason, perhaps, is that after my 2 years of teaching first grade and my time with the sergeants, I had taught intermediate grades, and thus beginning reading programs were not of direct interest to me. Be that as it may, code-emphasis programs never had the marketing and distribution of the mainstream whole-word basals, and I can report that I never saw any code-emphasis programs in the schools in which I taught.

4. The examples I provide for each of the three ways of creating texts for beginning readers come from programs that are currently in use in this country. Moreover, if children are moving along in the materials as the developers of the three programs anticipate—give or take classroom differences—on average, first-grade children will read the stories sometime in October. As such, the texts can be considered as typical—in terms of being representative of the three ways that early texts are developed—of what first graders are reading in their classrooms the second month of first grade.

5. Moats (1995), who has studied the relationship between speech and print, makes the point that "The spelling patterns of English are predictable and logical if one takes into account several major layers of language represented in the orthography" (p. 19). In this regard, it is notable that the massive predictability of English pronunciations can be seen in the success of connectionists models, which can pronounce 90% of a corpus of words after training on some subset (Plaut, McClelland, Seidenberg, & Patterson, 1996).

6. Let me suggest that it is unfortunate that, to the best of my knowledge, the Wendell story comes from the only new complete program on the market that represents the linguistic/phonic approach. It is unfortunate because I believe if there

were competition, the field would craft the orientation better and better. I do not mean this as a negative judgment of the program that produced Wendell. Rather, the point is that if the orientation were widespread enough, other instantiations might bring more creativity to the general notions.

7. Although research evidence is not clear about "optimal" units, especially whether the grapheme–phoneme or onset-rime units should be emphasized early or later or always (Haskell, Foorman, & Swank, 1992; Iversen & Tunmer, 1993; Treiman, 1992). As far as I know, all researchers who have studied word recognition and extrapolated their results to early reading instruction have called for instruction that brings attention to subword spelling-sound units, be they single or multiletter units. It is my position that single-letters need to be reached sooner than later but that onset-rime units may be a good starting place for a short while because they may provide a natural phonological unit (Treiman, 1992). Thus, the sequence that appears sensible is one that starts with onset-rime units, goes to grapheme–phonemes, and then provides practice in larger chunks. Would that the field were in the position to study this kind of detail empirically in acquisition studies.

REFERENCES

Adams, M. J. (1990). *Beginning to read: Thinking and learning about print.* Cambridge, MA: MIT Press.

Adams, M. J. (1996). *Adventures in mind-tuning: From thinking skills to enlightened phonics.* Sylvia Scribner address delivered at the meeting of the American Educational Research Association, New York.

Adams, M. J., & Bruck, M. (1995). Resolving "The Great Debate." *American Educator, 19*(2), 7–20.

Bergeron, B. (1990). What does the term whole language mean? Constructing a definition from the literature. *Journal of Reading Behavior, 22,* 301–329.

Blachman, B. A. (1994). Early literacy acquisition: The role of phonological awareness. In G. Wallach & K. Butler (Eds.), *Language learning disabilities in school-age children and adolescents: Some underlying principles and applications.* Columbus, OH: Charles Merrill.

Bloomfield, L. (1942). Linguistics and reading. *Elementary English Review, 19,* 125–130.

Chall, J. S. (1967). *Learning to read: The great debate.* New York: McGraw-Hill.

Clay, M. M. (1979). *Reading: The patterning of complex behavior.* Portsmouth, NH: Heinemann.

Ehri, L. C. (1992). Reconceptualizing the development of sight word reading and its relationship to recoding. In P. B. Gough, L. C. Ehri, & R. Treiman (Eds.), *Reading acquisition* (pp. 107–144). Hillsdale, NJ: Erlbaum.

Foorman, B. (1995). Research on "The Great Debate": Code-oriented versus whole language approaches to reading instruction. *School of Psychology Review, 24*(3), 376–392.

Fox, M. (1993). Hattie and the Fox. In *Goodness gracious me!* (pp. 82–113). New York: Macmillan.

Freppon, P. A., & Headings, L. (1996). Keeping it whole in whole language: A first-grade teacher's phonics instruction in an urban whole language classroom.

In E. McIntyre & M. Pressley (Eds.), *Balanced instruction: Strategies and skills in whole language* (pp. 65–82). Norwood, MA: Christopher-Gordon.

Fries, C. C. (1962). *Linguistics and reading.* New York: Holt.

Gough, P. (1996). *Integrated direct instruction: Balancing phonics and whole language.* Paper presented at the meeting of the Language Arts Foundation, Oklahoma City.

Gough, P. B., & Hillinger, M. L. (1980). Learning to read: An un-natural act. *Bulletin of the Orton Society, 30,* 179–196.

Haskell, D. W., Foorman, B. R., & Swank, P. (1992). Effects of three ortho-graphic/phonological units on first-grade reading. *Remedial and Special Education, 13,* 40–49.

Iversen, S., & Tunmer, W. E. (1993). Phonological processing skills and the reading recovery program. *Journal of Educational Psychology, 85,* 112–126.

Juel, C. (1988). Learning to read and write: A longitudinal study of fifty-four children from first through fourth grade. *Journal of Educational Psychology, 80,* 437–447.

Juel, C., & Roper-Schneider, D. (1985). The influence of basal readers on first grade reading. *Reading Research Quarterly, 22,* 134–152.

Just, M. A., & Carpenter, P. A. (1987). *The psychology of reading and language comprehension.* Boston: Allyn & Bacon.

Kiss, G. R., & Savage, J. E. (1977). Processing power and delay—limits on human performance. *Journal of Mathematical Psychology, 16,* 68–90.

Mason, J. M., Anderson, R. C., Omura, A., Uchida, N., & Imai, M. (1989). Learning to read in Japan. *Journal of Curriculum Studies, 21,* 389–407.

Moats, L. C. (1995). *Spelling development disability and instruction.* Baltimore: York Press.

Perfetti, C. A. (1985). *Reading ability.* New York: Oxford University Press.

Perfetti, C. A. (1992). The representation problem in reading acquisition. In P. Gough, L. Ehri, & R. Treiman (Eds.), *Reading acquisition* (pp. 145–174). Hillsdale, NJ: Erlbaum.

Perfetti, C. A., & Zhang, S. (1996). What it means to learn to read. In M. F. Graves, P. van den Broek, & B. M. Taylor (Eds.), *The first R: Every child's right to read* (pp. 37–61). New York: Teachers College Press.

Plaut, D. C., McClelland, J. L., Seidenberg, M. S., & Patterson, K. (1996). Understanding normal and impaired word reading: Computational principles in quasi-regular domains. *Psychological Review, 103*(1), 56–115.

Scarborough, H. S., & Dobrich, W. (1994). On the efficacy of reading to pre-schoolers. *Developmental Review, 14,* 245–302.

Seymour, P. H. K., & Elder, L. (1986). Beginning reading without phonology. *Cognitive Neuropsychology, 3,* 1–36.

Share, D. L. (1995). Phonological recoding and self-teaching: sine qua non of reading acquisition. *Cognition, 55,* 151–218.

Share, D. L., & Stanovich, K. E. (1995). Cognitive process in early reading development: Accommodating individual differences into a model of acquisition. *Issues in Education, 1*(1), 1–57.

Stanovich, K. E. (1986). Matthew effects in reading: Some consequences of individual differences in the acquisition of literacy. *Reading Research Quarterly, 21,* 360–406.

Stanovich, K. E. (1988). Explaining the differences between dyslexic and the garden-variety poor reader: The phonological-core variable-difference model. *Journal of Learning Disabilities, 21,* 590–612.

Strickland, D., & Cullinan, B. (1990). Afterword. In M. J. Adams *Beginning to read: Thinking and learning about print* (pp. 425–434). Cambridge, MA: MIT Press.

Treiman, R. (1992). The role of intrasyllabic units in learning to read. In P. Gough, L. Ehri, & R. Treiman (Eds.), *Reading acquisition* (pp. 65–106). Hillsdale, NJ: Erlbaum.

CHAPTER TWO

Family Cultures and Literacy Learning

VIVIAN L. GADSDEN
University of Pennsylvania

During the past decade, we have learned a great deal about children's literacy development in the early school years and about the social and cultural contexts in which they learn (Bloome & Greene, 1982; Moll & Gonzalez, 1994; Taylor & Dorsey-Gaines, 1988). Despite considerable attention to these issues, researchers and practitioners still are caught between an apparent desire to improve children's literacy (because we think strong literate abilities will improve their life chances and personal success) and perplexity about how to translate into practice what we know works for children, particularly those children who differ in income, ethnicity, and life experiences from each other or from us.

Current discussions about social and cultural contexts in literacy learning are filled with controversy and with stated commitment to issues of diversity (Au, 1995). Most literacy studies have touched only minimally upon complex issues of diversity among students; questions of race, racism, and class; or the increasing hardships facing a growing number of families who are disproportionately ethnic minority and poor. In some cases, we barely have moved past generic approaches to understanding these contexts or to exploring issues from the multiple perspectives of children and families; in other cases, we have been marginally successful in using knowledge about or from children and families to improve instruction and literacy support. Yet both our empirical knowledge and our intuitive sense of the world suggest that these contexts are the spaces in which children, along with their parents and other family members, can privilege their own collective and diverse experiences, irrespective of hardship. In them, they make plans, talk about hopes, share knowledge and expectations, and participate in acts of literacy—reading, writing, talking, listening, and problem solving.

The relative absence of a critical discourse about diversity and culture, above and beyond the recognition of differences alone, requires a reanalysis of the approaches used to teach reading and writing and assessment of instructional tools and artifacts used to convey the meaning of literacy within different contexts. It necessitates a discussion of what counts as knowing and knowledge. Do the cultural and literate experiences of a Latino boy from a low-income home in North Philadelphia count as much as the experiences of a white or Latino boy from a middle-class home in Bloomfield Hills, Michigan? What is the nature of each boy's prior knowledge? When and how do we achieve access to this knowledge or use it on behalf of children's literacy development? These questions invite us to reexamine a range of concepts that have aided literacy learning and teaching over the past decade (e.g., collaboration and classroom interaction, relationships between home and school, and prior knowledge). Our responses to these questions can serve as frames of reference to identify whether some sociocultural knowledge is more valued than other knowledge, who determines its value, and what criteria are used.

In this chapter, I focus on children's literacy development and the valuing of family and home contexts in that development, particularly for low-income children of color. Using an intergenerational learning framework, I address two broad issues: (1) how we understand the family as a social context that can contribute to children's literacy development and experiences in school; and (2) the ways in which classroom teachers can support the literacy development of children through knowledge of the family, its sociopolitical history, and the culture of the family itself. The intergenerational learning framework upon which the discussion is based is *family cultures,* a concept that has emerged from my literacy research with low-income families, adult parents in literacy programs, and schools.

This chapter is divided into four sections. In the first section, I offer a context for the discussion of family culture and literacy by focusing on parents' perceptions of literacy's value and the role of schools in promoting literacy. In the second section, I describe family cultures as a source of knowledge that elaborates upon or expands the literacy experiences of children within school and home. In the third section, I present a vignette to show how one teacher, her students, and their parents are beginning to explore family cultures as part of the social process of literacy learning. In the fourth section, I summarize the issues and the implications of family culture for literacy instruction and collaboration.

PARENTS' PERCEPTIONS OF LITERACY'S PURPOSE AND VALUE

A variety of educational and literacy studies have urged us to focus on the diversity and richness of families and communities as contexts for literacy learning (Heath, 1983; Leichter, 1984; Taylor & Dorsey-Gaines, 1988). In 1966, Durkin's work with low-income African American parents and children in Chicago spurred a series of studies that focused on the ways that poor parents engage and work with their children to promote literacy and how they contribute to their children's literacy development. Since Durkin's research, several explanations have been offered for the literacy problems that some children experience in the early grades, particularly children whose learning and language differences pose challenges to teachers.

One explanation focuses on parent–child book reading and suggests that how and when children use or practice specific literate abilities depend in large measure on the kind, quality, and quantity of literacy events and activities within the home (Edwards, 1991; Morrow, 1993). Children's early experiences with books and reading itself are thought to contribute to their later success or failure in learning to read. Parents with poor reading skills are described as infrequent readers who do not read to their children often and who expose their offspring to fewer literacy activities than parents who are better readers.

Several assumptions are embedded in this argument. Fitzgerald, Spiegel, and Cunningham (1991) identify two that are noteworthy because of what appear to be their oppositional stances. First, if children of poor readers are impeded in their acquisition of reading-related knowledge, such experiential differences may contribute to the well-established tendency for reading problems to aggregate in families. Second, children in homes in which parents have limited reading and writing are exposed to a range of literate and other problem-solving activities, behaviors, and events that enable them to develop literate abilities, some of which are not measurable through traditional assessments.

Each of these assumptions is developed around an expectation that parents hold certain ideas or beliefs about literacy, are engaged or are not engaged in children's school experiences, or have substantial influence on children's literacy development. Parental influences on children's school behaviors and achievement have long been an area of interest in literacy research, with most of the attention focused on how parents' literate behaviors and education affect children's acquisition of reading and writing. Many of these studies on parents' influences have either examined how middle-class parents expose their children to print and support their literacy or how low-income parents do not. In other words, most of the existing discourses in the field dichotomize the family and the literacy experiences of children into assets and deficits (Taylor, 1983; Strickland, 1995).

A small strand of studies, within traditional domains of school literacy and in adult and family literacy, focus on the potential contributions that poor parents, poor parents of color, and nonnative speakers of English can make to their children's development. This work suggests that parents and families across income levels and cultural and ethnic groups engage their children in a variety of critical literacy experiences and seek support to strengthen that engagement (Hartle-Schutte, 1993; Pellegrini, 1991; Purcell-Gates, 1993; Taylor, 1983). Such studies argue against deficit models in which children and families are portrayed as needing to be "fixed" and minimize false dichotomies that separate cognitive abilities from social processes and cultural contexts (Strickland, 1995).

Compared to the body of work on parents' influences, only a few literacy studies focus on parents' perceptions of children's literacy knowledge or understanding of their early literacy (e.g., Hiebert & Adams, 1987). Wong-Fillmore (1990) provides interesting accounts from parents about the importance of sound early educational programs that are also culturally sensitive. Delgado-Gaitan (1987) shows that Mexican American parents wanted a better life for their children but often used systems of support that did not mirror those of the dominant American culture. Weinstein-Shr (1991), referring to her work with Cambodian families, focuses on the degree to which the western-centered, time-honored view of history and culture constrains the opportunities for children and parents of other cultures to develop literacy. Eager to improve their children's literacy, African American and Puerto Rican Head Start parents in Philadelphia described school learning and schooling itself in relationship to its socially enabling qualities—to empower children and adults and to combat societal inequities (Gadsden, 1994).

From our intergenerational and family life-course research with low-income African American and Puerto Rican parents, my research team and I have found that parents' views about literacy, the ways that they construct definitions of literacy, their ability to understand their children's literate behaviors, the literacies they value most, and the value they assign to literacy in general are critical indicators of how they make meaning out of the developmental and literacy activities of their preschool and school-age children. Adolescent and young adult parents, particularly those with limited access to educational support and those who have had marginal school experiences, may have few resources and opportunities to explore their children's early literacies.

We have identified four categories of parents' assumptions or assertions about literacy. These data are extracted from interviews with approximately 100 mothers and fathers participating in three studies based in the urban and rural south and in the urban north. For every category of response listed in Table 2.1, at least 50% of the parents reported assumptions and made assertions that can be coded under the designated subheadings.

TABLE 2.1. Parents' Assumptions and Perspectives on Literacy's Accessibility and Power

Literacy as access and opportunity within and outside of racial limits

Literacy creates opportunity and reduces poverty.

"If I had been a better student, I wouldn't be poor, at least not as poor, I don't think. . . . I do think that if you have reading and writing you have a better chance, but if you are poor, no one seems to take you seriously."

Parents want success for their children and believe that opportunities exist (in a letter from mother to daughter).

"I want you to know I love you. I want you be a good student. I want you to make it. I don't want you to become pregnant like me. You have opportunities. I want you to go to college. I want you . . . to be happy."

Literacy's power is reduced in the face of race.

"But, you know, my husband, he finished school, and he has been laid off, laid off, more than once, and he is poor and black. He might not have been laid off so many times if he hadn't been black—last hired, first fired, no matter how well you're doing."

Literacy as school and classroom engagement

Schools and classrooms are not necessarily viable places that engage children in literacy learning.

"In school, the way teachers teach makes you not want to learn [and] makes reading seem hard. Then [the stories] weren't even interesting."

Possibilities exist to engage and sustain engagement. These possibilities exist when and if the diversity and interests of students are recognized.

"It would have been nice to read that a girl like me made it out of the ghetto and be able to understand what I had read. I am going to go and take some classes to improve my reading—as soon as my baby goes to Head Start."

Parents need access to teachers, and teachers need to know more about families.

"When my child left Head Start, he seemed like he was doing good [sic]. Then, he went to first grade; he liked school. Then he started messing up. The teacher wouldn't talk to us. She looked at us as Puerto Ricans with accents and didn't seem to know that our child could make it. You can see the difference this year. His teacher uses books with all kinds of different ideas and children, and she talks to us with respect."

Literacy as parent-supported

Parents can only contribute to their children's literacy through reading; literacy is a way out.

"Maybe if they [her children] see me reading, they will want to read, too, and make it out of this neighborhood. But education gives you one way out, and some people do it."

(continued)

Parents who have little income or poor reading and writing are often powerless in helping their children mediate the problems they will confront, particularly around inequity and inequality.

"What I would like my children to understand is that they don't have to be poor—that literacy is theirs for the tryin'. The problem isn't that I don't know what to say to them; it's that I don't know how to back up what I'm saying. Old people use to tell us to work hard in school, but [in truth], some of us weren't taught much reading in school. People who are literate and well educated, they run the world. But how many of them started off poor? I don't mean their white grandparents, I mean them."

Literacy as family and community imbued

Family life and schooling are domains that are imbued with responsibility of parents, teachers, and students.

"Family life isn't just about having children; no, it's about planning for them and them planning for themselves, *too*. Well. . . . and being black, a mother, and having children. When I was a child, well, things were a lot harder [than today]. But, despite the hard times, my parents talked about the future as though things were really going to be different for me! They had absolutely no idea how it would happen or what it would take exactly, but they knew it would take *hard work*! School was one place where I was going to be prepared, not only to help myself but to help the family."

Literacy is metacognitive and communal.

"So, you had to figure out what you wanted to achieve, how to get there, and what to do when you got there. There was no confusion about the fact that when you learned to read and write and if you became highly educated you were supposed to share the knowledge and the struggle so that children and families understood not only that you got to where you were but what it took—that you needed to continue the struggle as a black person, primarily for your family, and to make sure you were learning what you needed to improve the community. Parents prepared you to think about the struggle in the long-term, prepare for the [hurtles], and for what you needed to do if you didn't jump them. I don't know if you understand what I am talking about! In some ways, what children and parents are experiencing today is not that different from my childhood and my early years as a parent, and I tell my children, grands, and great-grands that."

Literacy is public knowledge.

"The other thing was that our parents expected us to demonstrate that we were learning something and what we were learning. Educated or not, many parents wanted to hear children read and made them read; they trusted schools in a way that their children find hard to do. The encouragement they gave us said that we had to persist in the face of difficulty and that persistence was tied to the struggle of . . . not black people in general but to the values of our small community."

First, some parents see literacy within the context of the power it can command and the power it gives; literacy and the power it provides are conceptualized in relationship to race and perceptions of race, as the statements in Table 2.1 suggest. Parents, for example, stated that they and members of their families encouraged children to achieve literacy but that they were realistic about the limitations of literacy in the face of race. In describing this tension between power and powerlessness, one Head Start mother noted, "But, you know, my husband finished school, and he has been laid off, laid off, more than once, and he is poor and black. He might not have been laid off so many times if he hadn't been black—last hired, first fired, no matter how well you're doing."[1]

Second, several parents described literacy as being entirely related to school and classroom engagement, although they recognized that literacy is developed in other contexts. Parents not only expect that children will learn literacy in school but they also seek a strong, reciprocal relationship between home and school that can encourage learning. They hope for an upward spiraling of literacy competence and are disappointed and angry when their expectations are not fulfilled. One couple closely observed the experiences of their child and the changes that occurred from year to year within different classrooms:

> "When my child left Head Start, he seemed like he was doing good [sic]. Then, he went to first grade; he liked school. Then he started messing up. The teacher wouldn't talk to us. She looked at us as Puerto Ricans with accents and didn't seem to know that our child could make it. You can see the difference this year. His teacher uses books with all kinds of different ideas and children, and she talks to us with respect."

Third, these parents acknowledge their responsibilities, strengths, and weaknesses in supporting children's literacy development within and outside of school. They aim to provide children with modeling for reading and want to be good role models for literacy and learning, education, and persistence. There are also contradictions and masked fears among some parents. After one parent in a full group minimized the effects of literacy, she privately talked about literacy's importance and the significance of her investing in her children's literacy development: "Maybe if they [her children] see me reading, they will want to read, too, and make it out of this neighborhood. But education gives you one way out, and some people do it."

Fourth, literacy is projected within the context of the family and community. Families and the home itself are seen as primary sites for the development of, appreciation of, and motivation for literacy. That is, the purposes of literacy are planful and monitored. They are also communal, as this 53-year-old father connotes:

"The other thing was that our parents expected us to demonstrate that we were learning something and what we were learning. Educated or not, many parents wanted to hear children read and made them read; they trusted schools in a way that their children find hard. The encouragement they gave us said that we had to persist in the face of difficulty and that persistence was tied to the struggle of . . . not black people in general but to the values of our small community."

The parents whom we interviewed attach their ideas, beliefs, and perceptions about literacy to a range of other family-based views about the intergenerational impact of learning, the meaning of success, and the values of the family itself. If we were to examine the convergences and differences in these parents' assumptions about, perspectives on, and expectations of literacy and schooling within a cultural difference analysis, we would argue for the importance of everyday experiences in relation to literacy. How these ideas are spoken or shared and how they are used were part of the family portraits painted, the intergenerational hopes described, and the family cultures that developed in different communities of parents, children, and families with whom we have worked.

FAMILY CULTURES

Although educators accept the premises of intergenerational literacy, some ask, "Why should we concern ourselves with the cultural and social practices of children and their families?" One immediate response might be that these practices tell us something worth knowing about the strengths of the families that nurture children and prepare them for school. Teachers and schools themselves, stretched by a variety of needs, can benefit from understanding families' strengths to build instruction rather than belaboring the weaknesses of families. Research and educational reports on literacy, schooling, and family support suggest that family-focused efforts that do not build on the strengths of families may succeed for parents and children in the short term but fail on a long-term basis. These reports encourage researchers and practitioners to approach the work on literacy and schooling from models that enable families to access and utilize resources effectively.

In our research with African American families and families from diverse ethnic groups, we have found that the families themselves create cultural frameworks, or what I have labeled "family cultures," within and across different generations (see Figure 2.1). Family cultures connect the cumulative life experiences of an individual family member with the life goals of the family. They are built upon intergenerational practices and learning within families and are formed around several factors: accepted ethnic traditions, cultural rituals, sociopolitical histories, religious practices

FIGURE 2.1. Family cultures (Gadsden, 1995).

and beliefs, and negotiated roles within families over time. Talk and problems about race, discrimination, and culture are deeply embedded in family cultures which are manipulated by societal events and affected by shifts in family mobility.

Family cultures often influence, if not dictate in many instances, the ways that individual family members think about, use, and pursue literacy and how they persist in educational programs. In most cases, family cultures seem to revolve around a premise that family members define and hold as central to their purpose and to the life trajectory of children. Families vary in their level of desire to adapt these cultures, which may be fluid or static, depending on the degree to which family members accommodate change. Family members construct traditions, practices, and behaviors that they consider critical to survival and achievement and that are linked to a sense of their own family histories. In conceptualizing a framework for instruction, educators weigh family expectations and the social and cultural practices in which the family currently engages or hopes to develop.

The concept of family cultures fits into several other concepts that allow us to see the strengths of families and understand better the ways in which family members construct their lives. For example, Reiss (1981) refers to "family paradigms." He writes that "the family, through the course of its own development, fashions fundamental and enduring assumptions about the world in which it lives. The assumptions are shared by all family members, despite the disagreements, conflicts, and differences that exist within the family" (p. 1). Paradigms are influenced by family history, culture, and the values and meanings assigned to experiences and perceptions. When families face stresses, they may move from implicit assumptions to stated alternatives to individual and family survival.

A second example is Stack and Burton's (1993) "kinscripts," which are developed upon the premise that families have their own agendas, their own interpretations of cultural norms, and their own histories. Stack and Burton's model focuses on the temporal nature of the life course (e.g., lifetime, social time, family time, and historical time) and life-course independence (e.g., the ways that individual transitions and trajectories are affected by or are contingent upon the life stages of others).

Intergenerational Learning

Family cultures, paradigms, and kinscripts all have a common theme of families operating with a shared or implicit assumption and view of the world. However, family members are not hopelessly bound by this world view. Each concept—family cultures, paradigms, and kinscripts—is housed within the larger framework of intergenerational learning. In educational research, the study of intergenerational learning focuses on the ways in which parents, grandparents, and other family members contribute to or affect children's academic performance, school attendance, discipline, and valuing of schooling and education.

A range of studies about intergenerational learning within families focus on the transmission of beliefs and practices and the modeling of behaviors from generation to generation. These studies typically aim to understand better the impact of families-of-origin on children's individual behaviors and family practices throughout the life span. However, intergenerational learning may include more than the biological family, although families create an obvious intergenerational connection. It may include a wide array of participants learning and teaching each other—parents, grandparents, teachers, and children.

The most common view of intergenerational learning shows children learning from adults within and outside of biologically connected families. Children and adults have opportunities to interact over periods of time. Adults transmit knowledge, beliefs, and practices to children either through direct teaching or informal activities. The transmission and learning may take place in formal settings such as schools where adult teachers share with children the strategies for reading and writing and facilitate the development of these abilities using a set of accepted approaches. It also takes place within homes—between parent and child, grandparent and grandchild, and other adult–child configurations. It may include an adult relative modeling a variety of behaviors, talking, or demonstrating the value and importance of beliefs, attitudes, and practices (Gadsden & Hall, 1996). In addition, intergenerational learning is an active part of relationships established in community settings, such as churches, in which an adult helps a child to understand the written ritual of the church or to participate in church or community activities.

On the other side, parents learn from children. Thus, intergenerational learning is often said to be bidirectional, particularly once children enter school (Bronfenbrenner, 1986). Examples of this bidirectionality may be found in programs such as Head Start, which is designed for young children but can result in significant changes in parents' behaviors and choices (Slaughter, Lindsey, Nakagawa, & Kuehne, 1989). Parents have differential responses to each of their children, and children shape the behavior of their parents.

Family Portraits: A Practical Approach

Family portraits comprise an intergenerational artifact that has uses in identifying familial themes and literacy categories. The family portrait or photograph offers one venue for examining family members' roles in the culture of the family. In one second-grade classroom, we asked the students to paint or draw their own family portraits with the help of a parent or other family member or to bring in a family picture. We used the family pictures as a way to begin talking about the family cultures of the teacher, the students, and the research team—to imagine what the possible uses of literacy were within the family and how these uses have changed over time.

Students were assigned literacy tasks of identifying and assigning the names and positions of different family members and of making connections between and among family members. They narrated the process by which they drew the pictures and shared problem solving around who was included in the picture and who was left out. This activity led to a series of questions from the students and to other tasks that required students to construct texts with their parents and required parents to assist their children in investigating their family constellation and cultural legacies. Students engaged with their parents and teacher in a variety of reading and writing episodes that enlightened them about their family culture and ethnic heritage as they developed the literacies of reading, writing, computing, and problem solving.

Family portraits are not a new source of information in research on family culture but have a less venerable history in literacy learning. More than 20 years ago, Philippe Aries (see Rutkowski, 1977) used portrait paintings to demonstrate or indicate the changes that occurred in European families, beginning in the 1700s. The portraits provided the most basic context for knowing the family. Anyone looking at the portraits recognized that the portraits themselves exhibited certain traits, and these served as a basis to interpret, for example, the number of family members portrayed, the posture and attitude of each, associated material artifacts such as dress and toys, and relationships between the people sitting in the portraits. Any observer could predict the relationships from examining specific characteristics such as proximity, physical contact, and focus of attention of the portrait sitters.

The portraits that Aries discusses were painted by artists, typically from outside the family. (Today we are more likely to have family photographs.) When portraits are painted by someone outside the family, they are problematical as a family source, primarily because they are heavily influenced by artistic considerations, in much the same way that a researcher or teacher influences the portrayals and expectations of students. Observers argue that the style and limitations of individual artists, prevailing artistic styles, and the demands on the sitters may well alter the images the families wish to display. Consider these limitations that Aries noted: The artists situate the sitters according to size, coloration of clothing, and so forth; the composition and presentation of the portrait are influenced by the inability of young children and older adults to stand for long periods of time; the presentation is positively or negatively affected by the popularity of neoclassical and romantic styles; or artist representation of the family is in a form that is more similar to his or her own experiences than those of the sitters.

These constraints are less true of photographers who take family pictures. How a person presents him- or herself is a combination of the image he or she wants to project and the photographer's intervention to ensure a clearly captured image of the whole family. When we draw our own portraits (and when children write stories) we offer to another the images of our family culture, a personal lens onto who is included and often what features and traits of the individual are valued most. The observer sees not simply the composition of the family but frequently gains a sense of how the artist places him- and herself within the family and contributes to the family's culture.

Self-designed family portraits present a perspective on family structure, culture, and behavior. They represent valuable artifacts that supply information about the norms and behaviors of families. The portraits suggest several interesting hypotheses about family type and interrelations. They can be used as a noninvasive approach and a point of entry to explore our own family cultures and those of our students as well as to explore the uses of children's prior knowledge and experiences in classroom literacy learning. Such family portraits serve as a point of entry for a teacher, Miss Poprow,[2] her 34 students, and 25 of their parents.

FAMILY CULTURES WITHIN ONE CLASSROOM

When we met Malik,[2] he was a second-grader in the New York City public schools living with his mother and father in a lower-middle-income neighborhood. He is the third of four children; he has two sisters and a brother. His family has lived in New York City for two generations—his parents having moved there from the South when they were young children. Both of Malik's parents work but have been laid off from several jobs because of downsizing. His family has never been on public assistance, in large part, because of their ability to depend on family members in the short term. Malik is a member of a closely knit, African American family whose members have supported each other in crisis. The family makes periodic pilgrimages to their southern home of origin, and the children are familiar with, if not close to, their extended family members. Within Malik's larger family community, parents give children what they call family legacies upon which they are expected to build. Education is seen as central to this legacy.

Malik is one of 20 boys in a class of 34 African American, Caribbean, and Latino children. His teacher, Miss Poprow, is white and has been teaching for 10 years. She describes Malik as bright, enthusiastic, and hardworking, while noting consistently his high level of energy. She is well liked by the children and by Malik's parents, whose experiences with his first-grade teacher were, at best, negative.

Miss Poprow is one of several teachers I interviewed as part of my intergenerational research with four generations of African American families. I interviewed Malik's great-grandparents in the South; then his grandparents who have returned to the South; his parents; and Malik. Miss Poprow became interested in my study and in the notion of "family legacies," which I described from my work. After a long conversation, she confided that she often felt uneasy with her students: "I don't know how to help them all. I try to understand their needs, but I know so little about their worlds, really. I just resort to being nice Miss Poprow when I feel that I am not giving them what they need. I teach them, but I want school to be a part of their lives, not this distant experience."

Throughout the research, I had been exploring approaches to using family cultures and histories as an effective literacy tool. As Miss Poprow and I talked about working together to develop a stronger relationship between her and her students and between her and her students' families, I proposed using the work around family legacies and family cultures that we had discussed to determine the uses for the concept and to engage the parents and students around a common literacy task. Miss Poprow responded with enthusiasm and commented, "I want to be a good teacher. I want to know about my students' cultures and their community." I asked her whether it was necessary for a teacher to know her students' cultures and community. She responded, "Well, not necessarily, but you know, if you have the content and you know what the important concepts are to share with children, you can really make a difference if you can involve parents rather than make them feel excluded. I don't want to be an expert . . . just want to help my kids."

Miss Poprow and I talked several times by telephone and face-to-face about how she might learn more about the family cultures of her students and share her own with them. She understood that such learning should be used to strengthen her instruction, not simply to expose the lives of her students to outsiders. She asked whether I would support her in this effort and co-record the development of this new experience for her and her students. I understood the importance of this experience for Miss Poprow and for me.

Because it was close to the end of the school year, we decided that we would spend the summer developing the plan and implement it in the fall. (Miss Poprow was going to stay with her students for their third-grade year.) Over the summer, Miss Poprow focused as much on her own family culture and family portrait as on the work with the students. She interviewed family members, read materials in her family records, and kept a journal of relevant ideas. She began the school year by visiting or meeting with her students' parents individually, then as a group. Together, we described to 28 parents present (most of whom were mothers) at an informal get-together that Miss Poprow wanted to involve the students and their families more deeply in the process of school learning and to build *real* home–school connections around literacy. Twenty-five parents agreed to participate in monthly meetings and weekly exchanges of information. They decided that the teacher, students, parents, and other family members would create a learning project that would span their shared interests in promoting children's and family members' literacy.

Although it is not possible to describe the project in detail here, I offer an overview of the nature and scope of the rich, year-long activities. Miss Poprow, her students, and their families used family cultures as a framework to identify, locate, and categorize literacy events and experiences and as an instructional tool. The students and Miss Poprow along with the parents developed expeditions, reading activities, and problem-solving tasks that centered on their own family cultures and those of other students. They used what they were learning as a historical exercise and a journal of their present-day interests and goals. Perhaps the greatest or most obvious changes occurred in the quantity of materials read by students (particularly those students labeled poor readers), the willingness of students to read, and the modest improvements in reading fluency and comprehension that occurred over the year.

How Miss Poprow came to seek out information about family systems or cultures was in large part a function of her desire to do so. In the early meetings, Miss Poprow and the parents talked about their mutual and different experiences—their common and not-so-common issues. Miss Poprow then spoke with individual parents alone. The parents organized into small focus groups in which they talked about the relationships between their cultural expectations and their family expectations, their hopes connected to literacy and schooling, and the contributions that they were willing to make. Parents were engaged in realistic ways and were asked to provide commentaries on selected items. They were welcomed in the classroom, but as a result of the talk between them and the teacher, one person stated, "[Miss Poprow] doesn't need to have a million parents in her face every day." There is a deeper understanding by all of the processes of reading and writing, the ways that parents can assist their children and the teacher, and the role of classroom interactions.

Parents and children participated in several activities within and outside of school. Children conducted investigatory tasks about family history and developed frameworks. With parents, community members, siblings, and peers, they developed family stories and compared these stories with those of other groups. They used these stories as a source of knowledge. They read unfamiliar, standard school texts, and they were able to incorporate their prior knowledge in critical ways to the text. In other words, they did not sacrifice the cognitive part of schooling. Rather, it was an essential part of the social process of learning.

The work with family cultures as a literacy framework within classrooms is in its early stages. The project allowed some parents to reminisce about stories and to write about and share a history that they had not experienced directly. Malik's parents commented:

"You know, we don't want everything to be like it was a long time ago. But, you know, some things were good. Like a long time ago, down South, teachers seemed like they cared whether you learned something or not, learned to read . . . and you didn't have to be ashamed of who you were. The teacher knew your family or lived in your community."

What is striking is that Malik's parents never lived in the South for more than a year and never attended school there. However, they have continued to map their images of past relationships between the black teachers in their parents' southern community against not only documented low literacy among black, urban youth but also undocumented low expectations of urban black youths' ability to achieve in school.

Miss Poprow, the parents, and children have struggled with several issues. They have discussed differences and similarities in their roles and life experiences, fears and anxieties about expectations, questions about the needs and successes of their children, subtle distrust about the purposes of the project, and issues related to race and culture. Of the 25 parents who committed to the project, 20 parents still are engaged actively in the activities; the others participate sporadically. In some cases, they have revealed their concerns; in others, they obviously wrestle with both personal feelings about and the intensity and sometimes complexity of the work they are asked to complete.

Miss Poprow has been challenged not only by the parents but also by her desire to improve her pedagogy. She has needed to revise her status as "the knower," and the power that status assumes, so as to create opportunities for mutual exchanges, to confront her own assumptions, to assess the process and curricula critically, and to chart the need for and effects of change. The parents similarly have been challenged to assume the role of knower, to explore their own cultural and familial histories, and to build their own literacies. Miss Poprow, the parents, and children have committed to the ideas and the process of collaboration to improve the children's literacy possibilities and relationships around learning. Miss Poprow's experiences with her students and their families offer insights into a variety of uses for the concept of family cultures as a way to locate children's interests, understand family ideologies, and construct new and innovative curricula that respond to the multicultural histories of students and strengthen cognitive abilities.

ISSUES FOR CONSIDERATION

The literacy instruction and learning that is occurring within Miss Poprow's classroom and in other classrooms throughout the country acknowledges and attempts to bridge the dual expectations of literacy learners, particularly those who are assigned "minority" status. Literacy learning, as Au (1995) points out, places potentially conflicting demands upon students. She suggests that, one, "Students must understand the history and culture of their own immediate environment;" and, two, "They must appropriate the culture and code of the dominant group in order to transcend their environment" (p. 88). Dyson (1992) reinforces the issue of diversity as a problem for teachers and learners. She suggests that stories of teaching and learning often make invisible the sociocultural diversity of children, the sociocultural consequences of teaching, and the ways in which instructional decisions may constrain or deny children's language, experiences, and intelligence. Miss Poprow, her students, and their parents aim to make these stories and the pleasures and struggles that accompany their (re)construction public.

In developing instructional goals, educators might question the degree to which instructional practices and goals represent and integrate learners' expectations and goals—sometimes different within the same family. In some cases, parents' goals may appear to be consistent with those in the instructional program or may be a subset of the program's purposes; in other instances, they may bear no resemblance to the program's mission. School programs that consider the family as a social unit place families at the center of educational change and must have the knowledge and tools to identify when, where, and how change can or should occur.

What is needed is a rigorous research- and practice-focused approach to understand social and cultural contexts—whether in school, home, or community—and the attendant issues of race and class. This would be a fluid and planful approach to obtain and use knowledge about or from children, parents, and other family members to improve literacy instruction and learning, to create new frameworks, or to refine old ones. At the center of the approach would be teachers, students, parents, and other family members who would be involved in the development, implementation, and critique of these new and refined frameworks.

From studies that chronicle the changing demographics of schools to research on families and literacy, we know that children in schools throughout the United States and their families are increasingly diverse in cultural and ethnic background, income, religious beliefs, family practices, and learning needs (Strickland, 1995). Such diversity may not respond well or immediately to a single instructional approach designed to fit the needs of all children. Nor will it be addressed appropriately or sufficiently by narrow perspectives on social processes that focus on school contexts ignoring or minimizing all other contexts that contribute to children's school learning. In addition, the diversity of children and children's literacy needs in classrooms require more than modestly informed assumptions about different cultural contexts and are not captured neatly or easily within existing frameworks.

It is unlikely that educators peering into their own world will engage in the directed analysis that is necessary to envision and to effect change within the walls of the school. Self-analysis is a particularly difficult and innovating task, and educators are no more or less capable than others in conducting it. However, it is this very kind of self-analysis, of introspection, that multiculturalists and antiracist pedagogues suggest is fundamental to recognize and respond to the needs of children learning literacy and that calls for approaches that complement the sociocultural experiences of students. It is central in removing unnecessary risks from the acts and stories of teaching and learning. In this way, Dyson (1992) suggests, we need to turn our attention to the approaches widely assumed to be the best we have to offer our young and interrogate them more incisively.

Research on the bidirectionality of learning suggests that we understand more deeply the nature of home and community contexts, the literacies of parents and their potential contributions to children's literacies, and the interplay between the primary contexts of home and school that affect whether and how children become engaged and sustain their engagement in literacy learning and how they themselves construct images of possibilities as learners. As researchers such as Delpit (1995), Foster (1996), and Harris (1995) note, teaching other people's children, whether they share a history or differ in experiences, is slippery and difficult work. However, when the ante is the literacy development of children, the investment is more than worth the work.

NOTE

1. The spoken commentaries of the parents have been edited in most cases, at the requests of the parents themselves.

2. "Miss Poprow" and "Malik" are pseudonyms.

REFERENCES

Au, K. (1995). Multicultural perspectives on literacy research. *Journal of Reading Behavior, 27,* 85–100.

Bloome, D., & Greene, C. (1982). Literacy learning, classroom processes, and race: A microanalytic study of two desegregated classrooms. *Journal of Black Studies, 13,* 207–226.

Bronfenbrenner, U. (1986). Ecology of the family as a context for human development: Research perspectives. *Developmental Psychology, 22,* 723–742.

Delgado-Gaitan, C. (1987). Mexican adult literacy: New directions for immigrants. In S. R. Goldman & H. Trueba (Eds.), *Becoming literate in English as a second language.* Norwood, NJ: Ablex.

Delpit, L. (1995). *Other people's children: Cultural conflict in the classroom.* New York: New Press.

Durkin, D. (1966). *Teaching young children to read.* Boston: Allyn & Bacon.

Dyson, A. H. (1992). Whistle for Willie, lost puppies, and cartoon dogs: The sociocultural dimensions of young children's composing. *Journal of Reading Behavior, 24,* 433–462.

Edwards, P. A. (1991). Fostering early literacy through parent coaching. In E. H. Hiebert (Ed.), *Literacy for a diverse society: Perspectives, practices, and policies* (pp. 199–212). New York: Teachers College Press.

Fitzgerald, J., Spiegel, D. L., & Cunningham, J. W. (1991). The relationship between parental literacy level and perceptions of emergent literacy. *Journal of Reading Behavior, 23,* 191–213.

Foster, M. (1996). *Black teachers on teaching.* New York: New Press.

Gadsden, V. L. (1994). Understanding family literacy: Conceptual issues facing the field. *Teachers College Record, 96,* 58–96.

Gadsden, V. L. (1995). Representations of literacy: Parents' images in two cultural communities. In L. M. Morrow (Ed.), *Family literacy: Connections in schools and communities* (pp. 287–303). New Brunswick, NJ: Rutgers University Press.

Gadsden, V., & Hall, M. (1996). *Intergenerational Learning: A review of the literature.* Philadelphia: National Center on Fathers and Families, University of Pennsylvania.

Harris, V. J. (1995). Using African American literature in the classroom. In V. L. Gadsden & D. A. Wagner (Eds.), *Literacy among African American youth* (pp. 229–260). Creskill, NJ: Hampton Press.

Hartle-Schutte, D. (1993). Literacy development in Navajo homes: Does it lead to success in school? *Language Arts, 70,* 642–654.

Heath, S. B. (1983). *Ways with words: Language, life, and work in communities and classrooms.* New York: Cambridge University Press.

Hiebert, E., & Adams, C. (1987). Fathers' and mothers' perceptions of their preschool children's emergent literacy. *Journal of Experimental Child Psychology, 44,* 25–37.

Leichter, H. J. (1984). Families as environments for literacy. In H. Goelman, A. Oberg, & F. Smith (Eds.), *Awakening to literacy* (pp. 38–50). Portsmouth, NH: Heinemann.

Moll, L., & Gonzalez, N. (1994). Lessons from research with language-minority children. *Journal of Reading Behavior, 26,* 439–456.

Morrow, L. M. (1993). *Literacy development in the early years: Helping children read and write.* Boston: Allyn & Bacon.

Pellegrini, A. D. (1991). A critique of the concept of at risk as applied to emergent literacy. *Language Arts, 68,* 380–385.

Purcell-Gates, V. (1993). Focus on research issues for family literacy research: Voices from the trenches. *Language Arts, 70,* 670–677.

Reiss, M. W. (1981). *The family's construction of reality.* Cambridge, MA: Harvard University Press.

Rutkowski, E. (Ed.). (1978). Papers and proceedings of the annual meeting of the Midwest History of Education Society (13th, Chicago, Illinois, October 28–29, 1977). *Journal of the Midwest History of Education Society, 6.*

Slaughter, D. T., Lindsey, R. W., Nakagawa, K., & Kuehne, V. S. (1989). Who gets involved? Head Start mothers as persons. *Journal of Negro Education, 58*(1), 16–29.

Stack, C. B., & Burton, L. M. (1993). Kinscripts. *Journal of Comparative Family Studies, 24*(Summer), 157–170.

Strickland, K. (1995). *Literacy not labels: Celebrating students' strengths through whole language.* Portsmouth, NH: Boynton/Cook.

Taylor, D. (1983). *Family literacy.* Portsmouth, NH: Heinemann.

Taylor, D., & Dorsey-Gaines, C. (1988). *Growing up literate: Learning from inner city families.* Portsmouth, NH: Heinemann.

Weinstein-Shr, G. (1991). *Literacy and second language learners: A family agenda.* Paper presented at the annual meeting of the American Educational Research Association, Chicago.

Wong-Fillmore, L. (1990). *Latino families and the schools.* Unpublished manuscript.

CHAPTER THREE

Growing Successful Readers: Homes, Communities, and Schools

VICTORIA PURCELL-GATES
Harvard University Graduate School of Education

> To Begin at the Beginning . . .
> "We want *all* children to be reading at grade level by the end of third grade."
> "By the end of third grade, *all* children should be reading."
> "All children will begin school *ready to learn!*"

In the past few years, politicians, policy experts, and public-interest groups have declared goals such as these for the literacy development of America's children. The general perception is that too many of our citizens are not learning to read and write well enough to participate fully in a rapidly growing technological society. The consensus is that all attempts to remedy this problem must start at the beginning. Thus the issue that needs careful and scholarly examination is: *Where* is the beginning? Where do we need to *start*?

My experience is that, overall, it is still assumed that young children *begin to learn* to read and write in kindergarten and/or first grade. I have drawn this conclusion from years of discussions with parents, teachers, colleagues, city commissions, and the like. Most people interpret the term *beginning reading* as referring to that "stage" in literacy development during which learners intentionally direct their energies to the decoding of print—learning the rules and conventions needed to "really read" on their own. This stage inevitably requires a "teacher" either to "direct" or "facilitate" this learning through a previously set curriculum.

This is not to say that many enlightened people do not acknowledge the importance of the early years; that is, the years *before* formal literacy

instruction. Increasingly, concerned educators, policy experts, and politicians have affirmed the importance of good preschool experiences, including adequate nutrition, health care, and nurturing. Generalized cognitive
benefits from programs such as Head Start have been proven, and legisla-
tures have succeeded in maintaining and increasing funding for these
programs. However, I do believe that, for the most part, people do not
think that children begin to learn to read until they are taught in some type
of school, and that those who are *taught* to read before kindergarten or
first grade are being taught to read *early,* suggesting that the beginning
reading stage, time, or level, is at age 5 or 6—that is, in kindergarten and/or
first grade.

Further confirmation of this conclusion comes from the discussions of
Goals 2000, particularly the goal proclaiming that all children will begin
school "ready to learn." Implicit in this proposition are the following
presuppositions: (1) What children are doing prior to school entrance is
not "learning" in the same sense as we mean it for school learning; (2)
there are things that render one "ready" to "learn" once formal schooling
commences; (3) it is possible to be "not ready" to learn at school entrance;
(4) because the main thing that children learn at school entrance is to read,
then the optimal situation is to be "ready" to learn to read; and finally, (5)
unless you are one of the "early readers" studied by Durkin (1966), who
historically constitute about 2% of school entrants, you have not been
learning to read up to the time of school entrance.

There is an impressive body of research into what is referred to as
"emergent literacy" that concludes that what takes place in schools in
kindergarten and first grade in the name of beginning reading is really just
the very *end* of a long period of learning to read, not the beginning of this
process. By documenting the acquisition of concepts and knowledge specific
to reading/writing, researchers have demonstrated that what was once
believed to be a "readiness" period for learning to read is actually a period
of developmental learning specifically about print and how one goes about
reading and writing it. In other words, young children who experience print
use in their lives are not just *getting ready* to learn to read; they *are* learning
to read. They are acquiring the concepts, skills, and knowledge, in a
developmental fashion, that will result in full literacy several years down
the road.

So, my intention in this chapter is to map out the learning-to-read
process from the true beginning and in its wholeness. I describe this process
for those learners who are successful readers and writers and talk about
ways in which the process is truncated, or short-circuited for those children
who are not as successful. After describing the learning-to-read process, I
address ways in which schools and communities can respond to learners
from different backgrounds and experiences to ensure that the process is
not adulterated for some children, and that equity in opportunity is
achieved for all.

CRITICAL PREINSTRUCTION EXPERIENCES: COGNITIVE, LINGUISTIC, AND AFFECTIVE CONSEQUENCES

Written Language Is Not Speech Written Down

Basic to my take on the critical nature of children's preinstruction learning about reading and writing is the fact that written language is crucially different from speech in many ways besides its mode of delivery. And it is *written language,* not speech, that we learn to read and write. Linguistic research has confirmed and described many of these differences. If you have ever tried to read and comprehend a transcript of an oral event such as a conversation or even a lecture, this difference is apparent to you. These differences are due to such pragmatic factors as psychological and physical distance from audience, amount of time people have to produce the language, and the degree of permanence of the language. The vocabulary, syntax, and cohesive conventions of written language differ in shifting degrees, depending upon genre, in response to these pragmatic factors (Chafe & Danielewicz, 1987; Horowitz & Samuels, 1987; Perfetti, 1987).

Written language tends to employ word choices that have been termed "literary" as compared to "colloquial" (e.g., *entrance* rather than *door*), more embedded and transformed syntax (e.g., "Down the hill ran the green, scaly dragon"); and references that are termed "endophoric" (within text) rather than "exophoric" (outside of text). This latter featural contrast reflects a basic difference between oral and written language: Oral language is contextualized in that the producer and receiver share the same physical space, whereas written language is decontextualized in that writers shape their language under the assumption that they will not be present physically when the readers process it for meaning. Thus all meaning must be retrievable from the linguistic text, eliminating exophoric references (e.g., "He was cold and hungry"—without a previous mention of a referent for "He"), prosodic cues (Schrieber, 1987), and other metalinguistic aids to meaning construction such as gesture, facial expression, and body language (Rubin, 1977).

Emergent Literacy or Beginning Reading

Given that written language is not simply oral language (speech) written down, learning to read and write is not simply a process of learning a written code for speech. Rather it involves learning to use a different, in many ways "new," language, with all of the complexities of language acquisition that this implies. And this learning begins with a child's initial experience with print use in the environment.

Assuming that children begin constructing knowledge about reading and writing long before formal instruction commences, emergent literacy researchers have examined literacy events in contexts other than schools—

in homes, grocery stores, churches, and other community gathering places. "Literacy events" refer to any activities that involve the reading or writing of print. A review of this research results in the following schematic description of the organization of the knowledge acquired by young children about print, given the requisite experiences (see Figure 3.1).

Young children appear to learn (implicitly, not necessarily explicitly) about written language within roughly three dimensions, each constraining and defining the other (Purcell-Gates, 1986, 1995). Figure 3.1 portrays this relationship. First, everything children learn about written language is constrained by what they learn through experience with its functions and the values placed on its various forms within their particular sociolinguistic communities and cultures (Anderson & Stokes, 1984; Taylor, 1982; Taylor & Dorsey-Gaines, 1988). This dimensional frame to learning about print has led me to refer to literacy as "cultural practice." In the United States, where the abilities to read and write are essential to economic and social success, many children are born into a world of written language. Their worlds abound with print: signs, menus, forms, directories, newspapers, regulations, instructions, memos, letters, calendars, bills, schedules, and books.

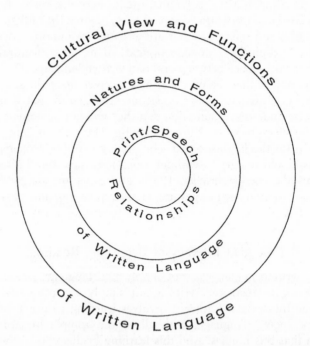

FIGURE 3.1. Dimensions of written language learned by young children as they experience print use in their environments. From Purcell-Gates (1995). Copyright 1995 by the President and Fellows of Harvard College. Reprinted by permission of Harvard University Press.

In her seminal family literacy study, Taylor (1982) described children who were growing up in families where "literacy is a part of the very fabric of family life." Reading and writing were interwoven into virtually all of the families' activities. The children learned reading as one way of listening and writing as one way of talking. Literacy gave them both status and identity within their families and their communities.

The children in Taylor's study were read to from birth. They were exposed to notes written by parents to siblings and by siblings to parents. They played games that involved printed directions; they created play that required the printing of such items as a label for a lemonade stand or a list of rules for a newly formed club. They observed their parents reading books, newspapers, notes from school, and letters from relatives, and daily encountered store signs and advertisements both in the immediate environment and on television. Other researchers, describing their own children, have documented similar experiences with print.

In a recent book (Purcell-Gates, 1995), I describe the opposite of this scenario, a home within which no one read or wrote because both parents were illiterate. I concluded that the two young children in this home, Timmy and Donny, were not growing up in a literate environment at all. Although they lived in a home that was in a city and a country that contained many forms and functions for print, they did not experience its use. They did not notice print around them, nor did they perceive any of its uses.

In another, larger observational study (Purcell-Gates, 1996), I document the uses of print in the homes of 20 low-socioeconomic-status (low-SES), mixed ethnicities families and measured the written language knowledge of 24 children from these homes between the ages of 4 and 6. I found that, in terms of frequency, print use overall was rather low. The frequency and the types of literacy events—the functions for print use such as reading books and magazines for entertainment and information as well as clipping and using coupons for grocery shopping—varied widely among the 20 homes. Some families rarely read or wrote anything and others used print very much like Taylor's highly literate middle- to upper-middle-class families.

A very important point for us to take from this, I believe, is that our school children—our kindergartners and first-graders—come from widely different and varying print environments. Without assigning value-laden labels to these different environments such as "rich" or "deficit-ridden," we must acknowledge these print–experience differences and account for them in our reading and writing instruction from the very beginning of formal instruction.

Within the functional frame, emergent literacy research has shown that as children experience and use written language to serve different functions, they begin to sort out the varying forms print can take (Butler & Clay, 1979; Holdaway, 1979; Snow & Ninio, 1986). In their classic study,

Harste, Woodward, and Burke (1984) describe children as young as 3 years demonstrating that they know that a grocery list is made up of a vertical list of nouns, representing items to be found in a grocery store, whereas a letter to grandma is composed of sentences that both inquire about grandma and report on personal activities. Sulzby (1985) has demonstrated a clear developmental path from oral to written forms of language produced by children rereading favorite storybooks. I (Purcell-Gates, 1988) have shown that well-read-to 5-year-olds know implicitly the syntax, vocabulary, and decontextualized nature of written stories before they have ever read such text on their own. When they were asked to pretend to read to a doll, the children all produced stories that were judged, through linguistic analysis, to be written in nature as compared to the oral narratives they produced. The children "sound" as if they are actually reading a book.

Further validation that the knowledge of the nature and forms that written language can take comes from extended experiences with print comes from studies of children who do not experience these forms in their home and community lives. When asked to "pretend read," children who were not read to often, if at all, exhibited statistically significant less knowledge of literate vocabulary and of the more complex syntax of book language (Dahl & Freppon, 1995; Purcell-Gates & Dahl, 1991; Purcell-Gates, McIntyre, & Freppon, 1995). Donny and Timmy, the children growing up in the nonliterate home (Purcell-Gates, 1995), had absolutely no knowledge of any forms of written language. They did not "know" how a book would "sound" as compared to a letter or an environmental sign. A telling example of this lack of knowledge and how it must be learned through experience or with direct explanation from a teacher/guide is found in the following excerpt from my book. This incident in the literacy center, where I was teaching him was precipitated by Donny's stated desire to "write notes" to his father who was in prison (Donny was 8 years old at this time and in the second grade):

> I pointed out the choices of stationery and envelopes available in the writing area, and he chose his favorite colors, green and yellow. He proceeded to print and soon asked me how to spell "like." After I spelled the word for him, he read to me:
> "Do you like it?"
> I looked at his letter and saw he had first written "I love you." I prodded, "What is it that he likes? This? When you say, 'I love you,' is that what you mean by, 'Do you like it?' "
> "No. Does he like it there? He'll say, 'no.' 'n,' 'o.' "
> "O.K. So then what would you say?" I continue.
> "Did you break any dishes? Cuz he washes dishes."
> As Donny proceeded through his short letter to his dad, I provided spelling when asked and helped with formulating language that could be understood by his father who would not be able to question and negotiate meaning with Donny when he received it—as in an oral situation. When

Donny indicated that he was finished, I asked, "Do you want to sign it so he knows who it's from?"

"How do you sign it?"

"Say, 'Love, Donny' at the very bottom so he knows it's the end," I directed.

As he placed the letter in the envelope, he asked what side to put "that stamp."

I showed him which side was the front and where the stamp would go. He picked up the scissors and began to cut slashes into the side of the envelope.

"What are you doing, Donny?" I said, quickly intervening. "Why are you cutting the envelope?"

"So he's know it's from me!"

I explained to him that an alternative to this was to sign his name up in the corner. "Whenever someone sends a letter, that's where they sign their name." We finished the letter writing event as I helped him address the letter. I told him I would mail it for him. (pp. 136–137)

Interacting with written language within the forms present in their lives, young children begin to sort out and learn about the print itself. They learn about the alphabetic nature of the relationship between speech and print (in written English). They also learn the various conventions of print such as linearity, directionality, and word boundaries. And they learn print-related terms such as *word* and *letter.* The emergent literacy research has consistently concluded that it is the interaction with print by children that enables this learning. Reading and writing attempts constitute the forms of this interaction. In other words, being allowed to "mess around" on one's own with writing and reading results in significant knowledge growth about how print works, how one encodes language and reads it back. As young children attempt to "read" familiar signs, recurring print in favorite books, and their names, they work toward an understanding of print as a code. As they engage in writing attempts from scribble writing to invented spelling, they become aware of letter features, letter sequences, and the ways in which certain letters map onto speech units.

Read's (1971) landmark study of what later became known as invented spelling demonstrated that children as young as 3 years, from highly literate homes, could intuitively categorize and represent English phonemes in print. Harste et al. (1984) cite evidence that young children in Israel will "scribble-write" from right to left, using marks that include the various script features typical of written Hebrew. Other researchers have documented children from English-speaking countries pretend writing from left to right with English letterlike forms (Clay, 1975).

Again, studies of children with fewer experiences with reading and writing attempts document the obverse of this (Dahl & Freppon, 1995; Purcell-Gates, 1995; Purcell-Gates & Dahl, 1991). When asked to "Write anything you can," these children draw borders around the paper, draw pictures, or simply make random slash marks. Or, like Donny, they simply refuse to respond or copy from existing print. They do not know the difference between a word, a letter, or a number. The graphophonemic nature of language representation in printed English is totally opaque to them, and they try to "read" by remembering shapes, guessing from the pictures, or simply "puttin' in your own words" (as Donny learned to do from his parents).

Relationships between Emergent Literacy Knowledge and Success at School

What do we know about the relationship between these dimensions of knowledge about written language that young children acquire to varying degrees before their formal instruction commences and their degree of success at learning to read and write from such instruction? For years now, it has been the conventional wisdom, supported by broad surveys and data sweeps, that the children of professional, educated parents are more successful at school and score higher on all tests of achievement than do children whose parents are less educated and hold lower-skilled jobs. The children who are the least successful on test scores and on measures such as tracking, high school completion, and so forth, for the most part grew up in homes with nonliterate or low-literate parents who had little or no formal education. These broad findings hold for children who experience the very same beginning literacy instruction, whether it be phonics-based, sight-word based, basal-based, skills-based, or whole-language-based. Looking at these data, I think we can conclude that home/community factors are key, and I want to argue—while acknowledging the critical role of adequate health care, nutrition, and other factors, the absence of which are often associated with poverty—that two of the critical operative factors in this relationship between parent educational level and children's literacy development are written language experiences and the subsequent learning from these experiences that takes place prior to schooling. I now sketch the operational relationships that exist between emergent literacy knowledge and success in school literacy and then discuss ways in which schools can respond to the challenge of ensuring success for all children.

CONNECTION BETWEEN AT-HOME LEARNING AND AT-SCHOOL LEARNING

To operationalize the connections between knowledge about written language that is learned in homes and communities prior to formal instruction and success at learning to read and write in school, I and others have used several measures intended to highlight different aspects of this knowledge (Dahl & Freppon, 1995; Purcell-Gates, 1996; Purcell-Gates & Dahl, 1991).

We hypothesized five dimensions of written language knowledge to be predictive of future school success: (1) intentionality, (2) written register knowledge, (3) alphabetic principle knowledge, (4) concepts of writing, and (5) concepts about print.

Intentionality

Do children beginning kindergarten understand that written language is a symbol system with linguistic meaning accessible to them (Harste et al., 1984) and that it functions for people in different ways? To assess intentionality, each child is presented with a sheet of 8½" × 11" paper, on which is typed in primary type the following sentence from a children's book: "A long time ago there was an old man." The children are asked the following questions: (1) Is there something on this paper? (2) What do you think it is? (3) What do you think it could be for? (4) Why do you think it could be there? If the child answers the first question with "writing," "words," or "letters" but does not answer the other questions, the researcher probes with "Have you ever seen writing (or words or letters) before? What do you think it was for? Why do you think we have writing?"

The domain of intentionality includes the conceptual understanding that *print* is a "semiotic system," signifying meaning linguistically. Children who know this, know that print "says something." They do not have to know *what* it says; they only have to know that it says something. Thus, when a young child tugs on her mother's sleeve, points to a printed sign (e.g., *Exit*) over the door in the store and asks, "What does that say?" you may conclude that this child knows that print is a linguistically meaningful system.

In a study of 35 randomly selected low-SES children from three different schools, results indicated that grasp of the intentionality concept at the beginning of kindergarten was highly related to success in reading and writing at the end of first grade (Purcell-Gates & Dahl, 1991). Results from the later study of 20 low-SES homes revealed that children in homes with fewer instances of print use scored lower on this task than did children in homes with more instances of print use. Further, these were all children with low-literate parents.

Again, this is not knowledge with which children are born. Without experiencing people in their lives reading and writing this semiotic system, using it, taking and giving meaning with it, the children would not suspect that those particular marks signify, as demonstrated in the case study of the nonliterate family. Without this understanding, instruction in reading and writing this system is meaningless nonsense to children. Learners must bring this concept to the tasks of learning (1) language, for English, maps onto printed symbols at the phoneme/grapheme level, and (2) the different concepts of print/writing. It is not possible, for example, for children to understand that the comma mark signals an oral intonation when speaking if they do not know that print and its conventions encode language.

Written Register Knowledge

Do children possess implicit schemas for the syntax, vocabulary, and reference characteristics of written narrative (Purcell-Gates, 1988) that are distinct from those they hold for oral speech? To determine this, children are asked to provide two types of language samples: (1) an oral narrative that results from telling the researcher all about their latest birthday or other event, and (2) a written register narrative resulting from pretend reading of a wordless picture book to a doll who is imagined to be a 5-year-old child being read to by the parent (the participant child). The children are offered a choice of two dolls, one male, one female. They are allowed to look through the book first to see what the story is as portrayed by the pictures. The researcher always reads the title of the book to the children and helps them to begin their pretend reading with the prompt, "Once upon a time. . . . " The children are reminded several times to "make it sound like a book story."

Results from three studies (Dahl & Freppon, 1995; Purcell-Gates, 1996; Purcell-Gates & Dahl, 1991) indicate that the domain of written register as measured is more or less independent of the other dimensions of written language measured. Knowledge of written storybook register is knowledge of vocabulary and syntax, and of linguistic ways to maintain meaning within text without reference to the physical world via gesture, intonation, or shared background knowledge. It is possible to possess this knowledge—how the text of a storybook "sounds"—without any under-standing of the alphabetic principle or concepts about print and writing as a system. Put another way, one can learn that written English words map onto speech at the phoneme level and about directionality, eye–voice match, and other concepts of print without being familiar with the vocabulary and syntax specific to written language.

Some research findings (Leu, 1982) lend weight to the strongly held hypothesis that this linguistic knowledge of written register facilitates the development of learners as readers and writers. However, this knowledge of syntax, vocabulary, and within-text reference conventions may not really affect literacy development until the learners are past the beginning-to-read stage. Formal literacy instruction generally begins by focusing on gaining control of the encoding and decoding aspects of print—those very domains of knowledge measured by the alphabetic principle, concepts about print, and concepts of writing tasks. Once learners have mastered these concepts, literacy skills then develop mainly through extensive reading/comprehen-sion of written language (Chall, 1983). It is at this point that children with superior knowledge of written-language-specific vocabulary, syntax, and reference conventions use this knowledge to more easily comprehend and learn from written text. It is also at this point that those children without this knowledge will founder seriously and fall further behind.

Again, this is knowledge that is acquired through experience, in this case with written stories. The only possible way in which young children can acquire this implicit knowledge is through hearing stories read to them. I have confirmed (Purcell-Gates, 1988) that children from all economic/social levels who were read to extensively during their preschool years did possess a describable written narrative register. My later studies of low-SES children strengthened the inference that the knowledge came from being read to by measuring it in randomly selected low-SES children (who, it was assumed were not read to so extensively). Findings across three studies revealed significantly lower scores on this measure (Dahl & Freppon, 1995; Purcell-Gates, 1996; Purcell-Gates & Dahl, 1991). The one study of these three that looked at the relationship between written register knowledge and home print experience found a significant correlation for preschoolers between being read to in the home and scores on this pretend reading task (Purcell-Gates, 1996).

Alphabetic Principle Knowledge

Do children understand that written English maps onto oral language alphabetically (embodies a grapheme/phoneme relationship)? For the studies referenced in this report, this knowledge was measured by a variety of reading and writing tasks. A version of an environmental print reading task (Harste et al., 1984) was administered. Ten words were selected from salient environmental print in the homes and neighborhoods of the children and prepared in three different conditions: (1) full context (i.e., an actual box of Tide laundry detergent); (2) two-dimensional, partial context (a photo of the stylized print with immediate context of logo); and (3) completely decontextualized and typed onto a 5" × 8" index card in primary type. The three conditions of presentation were presented on separate days and in different orders. The words used for this task varied by study to reflect the different neighborhoods but included such words as *Band-Aid, Burger King, Coca-Cola, Crest, Doritos, For Rent, Hershey's, Ivory, Milk,* and *Tide.*

Alphabetic principle knowledge was also measured through a "Write Your Name and Anything Else You Can" task. The children were asked to write their names and anything else they could by the researcher, who provided paper and pencil. They were then asked to read what they had written to the researcher, who made note of their responses.

Finally, alphabetic principle knowledge was also measured via a short spelling task. The children were asked to spell 10 words reflecting simple consonant and vowel correspondences on paper provided by the researcher. The words they were asked to spell were *bump, pink, drip, ask, bend, trap, net, chin, flop,* and *last.*

When one "gets" the alphabetic principle, he or she understands that when encoding and decoding the words of English (making it written), the code is at the phoneme/grapheme level. That is, letters generally stand for isolable "phonemes" (speech sounds). Whether one can do this accurately (conventionally map the correct letter to the sound) is beside the point at this stage. Understanding the alphabetic principle is knowing that one *should* do this to read and write English. A plethora of data exist (Adams, 1990) to affirm the crucial need for this understanding for learning to read and write.

However, one is not born knowing about the alphabetic principle. One can acquire oral language to a high degree of fluency and never understand that, for English, the written system is based on a grapheme/phoneme match. Studies show, actually, that the *perception* of the phoneme is not "natural" (Gleitman & Rozin, 1973); rather, the smallest, easily achieved, perceptual unit (a unit that can be "recognized" or "heard" as a unit) is the syllable. In fact, several written systems in the world use syllabaries; they represent syllables, not phonemes, with individual written symbols.

Several influential studies (Adams, 1990; Ehri, 1980; Ehri & Wilce, 1983; Richgels, 1995) have shown that children come to a complete grasp of the alphabetic principle in the process of learning to read and write when it is either pointed out to them as part of instruction or when they deduce it from exposure to written words in school. However, the evidence is strong that many young children *begin* school with the beginnings of this understanding, and some having achieved it totally. Read's study (1971) demonstrated that some 3- and 4-year-olds can perceive individual phonemes and encode them in a nonconventional but systematic way as they "invent spell." Having received no formal spelling or reading instruction, these children, it is hypothesized, must have achieved this alphabetical principle knowledge by deducing it from their environment filled with many instances of print as well as their active involvement in encoding and decoding it. Looking at the results of the three studies in which the above task was used with young children helps us explore this further.

The children's performances were scored on a 3-point scale and averaged across tasks. On the scale, the scores indicated the following: 1 = no evidence of alphabetic principle; 2 = some evidence of alphabetic principle; 3 = a consistent pattern of evidence of alphabetic principle. Across all three studies, the average score for this concept fell between 1 and 2 (1.28, 1.09, and 1.46). The at-home study revealed some interesting insights into acquisition of this concept. As the frequency of literacy events increased in the child's home, so did the likelihood that the child would know more about the alphabetic principle. Further, children whose parents focused them on print knew more about the alphabetic principle than did those whose parents did not. This was true for a focus at the letter and word level (e.g., helping a child to spell a word or to make a letter) as well as at the discourse level by parents reading children's books to them.

Children whose parents read and wrote proportionately more at the higher discourse levels (beyond simple clauses and phrases) knew more about the alphabetic principle. Children whose parents included literacy events more (1) as part of their entertainment activities, (2) to learn/teach about literacy, (3) for storybook time, and (4) to participate in information networks knew more about the alphabetic principle. And, finally, in those homes with more mother/focal child interactions, the children knew more about the alphabetic principle.

Concepts of Writing

How do children conceptualize writing as a system (i.e., when asked to write anything they can, do they draw lines around the edges of the paper, draw pictures, write letters, or write words)? Data for measurement of this concept came from the Write Your Name and Anything Else You Can task. On a 6-point scale (with 1 = writing as drawing line borders, picture-like scribbles, pictures, shapes; and 6 = writing is making words–pseudowords, words), the low-SES children across the three studies fall about in the middle, writing letter-like and number-like forms or letters mixed with numbers in response to the direction to "write anything you can."

The at-home study again found revealing relationships between at-home experiences with print and acquisition of this concept. The literacy events recorded in the home for this story were categorized according to the social domains they mediated for the families. These domains were taken from Teale's (1986) study of low-income families in San Diego. These included the following: *daily living routines* (e.g., shopping, cooking, paying bills); *entertainment* (e.g., reading a novel, reading ads for a movie; reading rules for a game); *work* (literacy for performing a job or for maintaining or securing a job); *religion* (e.g., *Bible* reading or reading church pamphlets); *interpersonal communication* (e.g., writing on greeting cards or reading/writing personal letters); *participating in an information network* (e.g., reading baseball scores to talk about them later with friends); *storybook time* (e.g., reading a book to a child); and *literacy for the sake of teaching/learning literacy* (e.g., teaching a child how to write her name or how to read a word).

Parents who read and wrote at a higher discourse level in terms of sheer frequency had children who knew more about writing as a system. This relationship was especially strong for preschoolers (schooling erased much of the variation in the scores). Also, children whose parents used print in the course of entertainment activities, learning and teaching about literacy, reading to their children, and reading to share information with other adults scored higher on this task. Those print-mediated activities that did not show this relationship included (1) daily living routines, (2) school-related activities, (3) interpersonal communication, (4) religion, and (5) work-related activities.

Concepts about Print

Do children know the various conventions for reading and writing such as (1) the front of book; (2) that print, not pictures, tells the story; (3) the first letters in a word; (4) big and little letters; (5) directionality; (6) concepts of *letter* and *word*; and (7) the identification and functions of punctuation marks? Clay's Concepts about Print test (1979) was administered to measure this knowledge. For this task, the children sat by the researcher, who read a simple children's book to them, asking them questions relevant to the various concepts about print during the course of the reading.

Again, the scores of the children were similar on this task across all three studies, falling in the 3rd stanine (below average). Our 1991 study (Purcell-Gates & Dahl) that followed the children through kindergarten and first grade found a strong relationship between scores on this task at the beginning of kindergarten and success at reading and writing at the end of first grade. The successful students averaged 4.2 (stanine), whereas the less successful ones averaged 2.8 (stanine). Looking at the children in the at-home study, we find print experiences related to performance on this task similar to those for the Alphabetic Principle and Concepts of Writing. Children whose parents read to them more and who focused them on letters and words more knew more about concepts of print. Also, children whose parents engaged in literacy events more as part of their entertainment activities (1) to help their children read and write; (2) for storybook time, and (3) to participate in information networks scored higher on this task. And finally, children whose mothers engaged them directly in interactions around print knew more concepts of print.

These two domains involving the physical manifestations of the ways in which print encodes meaning, Concepts about Print and Concepts of Writing, are closely related to the alphabetic principle in that they include the conventions for encoding written English. So when one knows the concepts of print and the concepts of writing as a system, one knows that marks called *letters* make up *words,* and *words* make up *sentences* that are marked by *periods, question marks,* and *exclamation marks.* One knows that these marks are written, and read, beginning at the top left corner of the block of print and across horizontally to the top right corner, at which point one returns to the left end of the line underneath the one just finished, and so on. One knows that *letters* are different from *numbers* and *pictures,* and that their shapes, orientations, and identities are stable across time and across contexts. Again, research has shown that while much of this knowledge is learned in the process of learning to read and write in school, many children have learned it "naturally" in the home context before beginning formal instruction. These children begin school with a clear advantage over those children who do not know these concepts.

WHAT SCHOOLS MUST DO

Concepts Inappropriately Assumed by Curricula

The research I have just cited builds on decades of previous work that documents the fact that entering kindergartners or first-graders begin what is formally known as beginning reading instruction with differing states of knowledge, or "readiness" about print (Clay, 1975; Downing, 1979; Ferriero & Teberosky, 1982; Mason, 1980). What this newer emergent literacy research does is to explore this disparity in knowledge and document its formation as it happens. As a result, we can now see where and how print knowledge is developed in the years before school and begin to make some inferences about ways to ensure that all children are given opportunities to engage in the same critical concept formations. Clearly, implications for family literacy programs are enormous and are presently the focus of many programs around the country. For the remainder of this chapter, though, I focus on the "end" of the beginning to read/write process: schools, classrooms, teachers, and formal beginning literacy curricula.

One only needs to look at formal beginning literacy instruction in light of children's entering knowledge to recognize the terrifying mismatch. In the process of conducting several of the studies discussed above, I analyzed several widely known, highly respected basal reading series for the skills taught at the kindergarten and first-grade levels and the assumed concepts on which these skills were based. Skills taught in kindergarten included letter formation, sight words, and letter sounds. These skills all assumed that all of the entering 5-year-olds knew that print was linguistically meaningful and functioned in different ways in the world outside of school; that written English is coded at the phoneme level; the differences between letters, words, and numbers; and many of the concepts of print and writing discussed above. We know that these concepts were assumed because they were never taught. The only concepts about print that were explicitly included in the curricula were those of punctuation.

The first-grade curriculum built on the kindergarten one and included word decoding (consonant sounds—beginning, final, and medial; vowel sounds—short, long, diphthongs, r-controlled, and variant forms); word identification using context and phonics; letter names, rhyming words; phonograms; inflected forms; possessives; contractions; and base words. In addition, sight words were presented with each new lesson and were cumulative. Basic comprehension skills involving direct recall, inferencing, and predicting were also taught with simple stories and texts. Again, learners were assumed to know that, in English, the print code is alphabetic, with individual letters representing isolable phonemes. They were also assumed to know many conventions of print, including the left-to-right eye sweep with return to left margin of the following line; the top-to-bottom ordering of lines of print; the eye-to-voice match with individual words;

and the concepts of *word, letter,* and *sound.* And, to read even the simple texts, they were assumed to know about the decontextualized nature of written language and the ways that it is operationalized through word choice, referencing conventions, and syntax (the concept of "written register," discussed previously). We can conclude that these concepts were assumed by the curriculum because the curriculum included no assessment of or instruction in them.

Explicit Guidance Needed for Unfamiliar Territory

So it becomes clearer, given what we know about different levels and types of written language concepts held by different children and the homogeneous nature of the concepts assumed for beginning formal literacy instruction, why some children "catch on" easily and quickly to reading and writing and others do not. What start out as clear but relatively small differences in achievement among children in kindergarten grow exponentially over the primary grades until it is not uncommon to see achievement differences of more than 5 years by the middle of third grade. The crucial issue, then, is what can we do in kindergarten and first grade to close these gaps before they grow wider? What can teachers and schools do to ensure that the goals being set forth across the nation and with which this chapter began have a chance of being met? I set forth the following four broad recommendations that I believe can move us toward successfully addressing this issue:

Begin with assumption that all children are learners. The notion that some children, because they hold different concepts about written language, are *not ready to learn* is nonsense. All children are not only *ready* to learn, they have been learning from birth. What this not-ready-to-learn dictum is really about is the fact that not all children are ready to learn from, or can make sense of, the curriculum presented to them in schools. Thus the issue becomes one of curriculum, not children. I will discuss that later.

This assumption of ability is a basic, prerequisite to effective teaching, and although it is given wide lip service, it is more often than not absent, especially as it relates to minority children and/or children from low-literate or differently literate homes. Stereotypes of different minority groups that are widely held by society and many middle-class teachers persist to cast a pall over the academic opportunities for all but middle-class, mainstream children. Uninformed, cultural-outsider assumptions about the inability of minority (including poor white), low-SES children to learn and achieve in school result in lowered expectations and standards, inappropriate instructional decisions and placements, and misinterpretation of student behaviors and performances (Delpit, 1993; Foster, 1990; Purcell-Gates, 1995).

Be diagnostic and proactive from a solid knowledge base. Simply put, teachers of beginning reading and writing need to be able to observe their students through an emergent literacy lens, note what they know and what they do not know about the ways in which written language works, and then teach what is unknown as quickly as possible. Although this sounds simplistic, in operation it requires a deep and solid knowledge of emergent/beginning reading and writing from cognitive, linguistic, and cultural perspectives. It requires the ability to infer ability and knowledge from performance. It requires the ability to teach responsively and reciprocally on an individual basis. And it requires the ability to assess the outcomes of that teaching/learning and plan for future instruction in a recursive manner that insures successful literacy development for individual learners. All of this requires proactive and empowered teachers who are not hamstrung by district and curricular scopes and sequences and who take on the ultimate responsibility for the learning of their students.

Be explicit and direct. All children do learn in school. Studies have shown repeatedly that all of the crucial emergent literacy concepts discussed in this chapter can be learned in school by children who start school not knowing them (Clarke, 1988; Dahl & Freppon, 1995; Purcell-Gates, 1996; J. Kagan, personal communication, August 28, 1996; Purcell-Gates & Dahl, 1991; Purcell-Gates et al., 1995; Richgels, 1995), given several conditions.

First of all, the experiences children encounter in school must be such that the concepts to be acquired are present and included. Thus if we want children to learn the span of concepts about print, including directionality, eye–voice match, and so forth, we need to have children involved in reading and writing attempts of actual, connected text. If we want children to learn about the phonemic base of written English, we must involve them in reading and writing attempts that focus them on discovering it through "sounding out" and with the help of teachers who help them do this. Many believe that this is best done at first with phonetically regular words and text (Juel & Roper/Schneider, 1985), and lots of opportunities to read such text in order to internalize the regularities and promote automaticity of word recognition and processing. If we want children to learn about the vocabulary, syntax, and decontextualized natures of different forms of written discourse, then we must read aloud to them from text that is too difficult for them to read on their own. We must read from storybooks, information books, lists of directions, computer manuals, game boards, and so on. If we want children to learn how writing works as a system, we must provide multiple opportunities for them to see proficient writers writing, physically creating written texts.

Embedded in all of these activities around print use, direct and explicit explanations must be given to children who are attempting to learn to read and write. As we, as teachers, write for children and help them to write, we must point out for them and name such written language concepts as *letters, words, sentences,* and so on. We need to tell children the difference between letters and numbers, for example. We need to tell them what "sounds" different letters "make" in a given word. We need to tell them the ways in which stories are different from reports, personal letters are different from stories, *b* is different from *p*. My own work (Purcell-Gates & Dahl, 1991; Purcell-Gates, 1995) and that of others (Cazden, 1993; Chall, Jacobs, & Baldwin, 1990; Delpit, 1993, Richgels, 1995) support strongly the notion that children who do not bring the complex of written language concepts to school with them benefit most from direct, explicit explanation of these concepts embedded in meaningful and purpose-driven literacy experiences.

Arguably, the most difficult, and last to be learned "naturally" concept and skill is that of the alphabetic principle and knowledge of the phoneme/grapheme nature of written English and other alphabetic print languages. This crucial knowledge is best taught explicitly and intentionally in a way that its function in decoding and encoding print for meaning is clear. Whereas many may argue for teaching these phonic skills incidentally, I strongly suspect that this is only safe to do with children who are about to learn to read on their own, no matter the instruction. These skills are too important to leave to chance—that the child will know what he or she does not know and ask; that the teacher will notice at the "teachable moment" what is needed; that the child will grasp what is being taught at any given time, retain it, and apply it to new situations. Rather, the sound–symbol system of print needs to be systematically and explicitly taught to beginning readers and writers in school. This does not preclude engaging learners in reading and writing attempts that allow them to come to these understandings for themselves, as this is the most effective type of learning. Rather, it is an argument for not restricting the learning activities to this self-exploration but for the inclusion of explicit and systematic instruction in "phonics." At all times, the teachers of beginning readers and writers need to keep in mind the variant ways that their learners speech dialects will map onto print and to allow for this in their instruction.

Even the playing field as fast as possible. Let us go back to the current literacy demands being shouted by politicians in the nation's newspapers with which I began. And let us really take them seriously for a moment. *All* children reading at a third-grade level by third grade (we ignore for the moment that the construct of *grade level* is a normative one, based on a normal distribution of scores/ability, and it merely reflects the *average* or 50th percentile). If we are to operationalize this in some half-way reasonable way, this could be taken to mean that all children need to be reading, with comprehension from texts deemed readable by third graders. What do we need to do to accomplish this?

Well, one way to think about this is to imagine a track race. We have runners of whom it is demanded that they all finish the race (wherever we set the finish line) within the same range of time. What sense would it make if in setting up this race, we made some runners begin further away from the finish line? Or, if we designated certain runners to wait until the others had begun their runs before they started? Assuming this was not a case of handicapping to even the odds for superior talent, we would have to conclude that we had programmed ourselves for failure; there would be no way that our goal of all runners finishing within the same range of time could be met if some did not start with the others. Those who started later, or crossed the beginning line later, would lose.

So it is for learning to read. If some groups of children begin this process *conceptually* later than others, then it is unreasonable to expect them to be at the same place at the end of 4 years. It does not make sense, and it will not work. To stand a half-way decent chance of meeting our goal, we must even the playing field as fast as possible. This means that by first grade at the latest, all children must have in place all of these emergent literacy concepts discussed in this chapter if they are to stand a chance of running the same race as those children who began kindergarten with the concepts. Kindergartens need to be focused on emergent literacy concepts, incorporating the suggestions already discussed: assessing what children know and do not know about reading and writing on all the dimensions of knowledge (not just pieces of it such as phonemic awareness; letter–name knowledge); intentionally setting out to teach that which is not known through concept-laden reading and writing experiences while being direct and explicit about pointing out and explaining that which is not known; and doing this with the conviction that *all* children are learners and are ready to learn *now*. The goal for the end of first grade for all children then should be the ability to read independently simple text with comprehension. To accomplish this, all first graders need to learn the sound–symbol correspondences of print from explicit and systematic phonics instruction that is embedded in authentic reading and writing activities that make clear the communicative goal of written language. And first-grade children need to have been given countless opportunities to practice their reading and writing skills in the context of actual reading and writing. Time spent reading and writing is the only way they will move toward the automaticity demanded of skilled readers. By the end of first grade, then, all children need to have *emerged*, as most of us define the concept of "emergent literacy." Second-grade literacy instruction should build on this and move children into increasingly complex patterns of written language, both for reading and writing.

Every study I have done or read about (Purcell-Gates, 1995; Purcell-Gates et al., 1996; J. Kagan, personal communication, August 28, 1996) has shown that all children, no matter what their degree of print experience in their preschool years, have learned quickly these emergent literacy concepts in kindergarten/first grade if they have been given the experiences and teaching I have just described. But what many of us have heard about through anecdote or documentation is that too many children are left to languish in either (1) a "garden of print" and expected to emerge on their own eventually with no direct, systematic explanations or teaching; or

(2) subjected to relentless drill and practice in remedial or special education classrooms on pieces of the emergent literacy whole (usually the sound–symbol piece) with no opportunity to build a complete and complex understanding of reading and writing as a communicative system through engaging in actual reading and writing events.

In summary, I urge those concerned with these admirable goals being set forth for young children's literacy development to keep the whole picture in mind, approach instructional and curricular decisions with a diagnostic mindset and with the assumption that *all* children are learners, and to work as quickly and effectively as possible to even the playing field at the beginning so that we do not continue to create a condition of inevitable failure for a significant portion of our population.

REFERENCES

Adams, M. J. (1990). *Beginning to read: Thinking and learning about print.* Cambridge, MA: MIT Press.

Anderson, A., & Stokes, S. (1984). Social and institutional influences on the development and practice of literacy. In H. Goelman, A. Oberg, & F. Smith (Eds.), *Awakening to literacy* (pp. 24–37). Exeter, NH: Heinemann.

Butler, D., & Clay, M. M. (1979). *Reading begins at home.* Exeter, NH: Heinemann.

Cazden, C. (1993, March). *Immersing, revealing, and telling: A continuum from implicit to explicit teaching.* Plenary address to the International Conference on Teacher Education in Second Language Teaching. (ERIC Document Reproduction Service No. ED 365134)

Chafe, W., & Danielewicz, J. (1987). Properties of spoken and written language. In R. Horowitz & S. J. Samuels (Eds.), *Comprehending oral and written language* (pp. 83–112). San Diego: Academic Press.

Chall, J. S. (1983). *Stages of reading development.* New York: McGraw-Hill.

Chall, J. S., Jacobs, V., & Baldwin, L. E. (1990). *The reading crisis: Why poor children fall behind.* Cambridge, MA: Harvard University Press.

Clarke, L. K. (1988). Invented versus traditional spelling in first graders' writing: Effects on learning to spell and read. *Research in the Teaching of English, 22,* 281–309.

Clay, M. M. (1975). *What did I write?* Auckland, New Zealand: Heinemann.

Clay, M. M. (1979). *Early detection of reading difficulties.* Portsmouth, NH: Heinemann.

Dahl, K. L., & Freppon, P. (1995). A comparison of innercity children's interpretations of reading and writing instruction in the early grades in skills-based and whole language classrooms. *Reading Research Quarterly, 30,* 50–76.

Delpit, L. D. (1993). Skills and other dilemmas of a progressive black educator. *Harvard Educational Review, 56,* 379–385.

Downing, J. (1979). *Reading and reasoning.* New York: Springer-Verlag.

Durkin, D. (1966). *Children who read early.* New York: Teachers College Press.

Ehri, L. C. (1980). The development of orthographic images. In U. Firth (Ed.), *Cognitive processes in spelling* (pp. 311–338). London: Academic Press.

Ehri, L. C., & Wilce, L. S. (1983). Development of word identification speed in skilled and less skilled beginning readers. *Journal of Educational Psychology, 75,* 3–18.

Ferriero, E., & Teberosky, A. (1982). *Literacy before schooling.* London: Heinemann.

Foster, M. (1990). The politics of race: Through the eyes of African-American teachers. *Journal of Education, 172,* 123–141.

Gleitman, L., & Rozin, P. (1973). Teaching reading by use of a syllabary. *Reading Research Quarterly, 11,* 447–483.

Harste, J., Woodward, V., & Burke, C. (1984). *Language stories and literacy lessons.* Exeter, NH: Heinemann.

Heath, S. B. (1982). *Ways with words.* New York: Cambridge University Press.

Holdaway, D. (1979). *The foundations of literacy.* Auckland, New Zealand: Heinemann.

Horowitz, R., & Samuels, S. J. (1987). Comprehending oral and written language: Critical contrasts for literacy and schooling. In R. Horowitz & S. J. Samuels (Eds.), *Comprehending oral and written language* (pp. 1–46). San Diego: Academic Press.

Juel, C., & Roper/Schneider, D. (1985). The influence of basal readers on first grade reading. *Reading Research Quarterly, 20,* 134–152.

Leu, D. (1982). Differences between oral and written discourse and the acquisition of reading proficiency. *Journal of Reading Behavior, 15,* 111–125.

Mason, J. M. (1980). When do children begin to read? An exploration of four-year-old children's letter and word reading competencies. *Reading Research Quarterly, 15,* 203–227.

Perfetti, C. A. (1987). Language, speech, and print: Some asymmetries in the acquisition of literacy. In R. Horowitz & S. J. Samuels (Eds.), *Comprehending oral and written language* (pp. 355–368). San Diego: Academic Press.

Purcell-Gates, V. (1986). Three levels of understanding about written language acquired by young children prior to formal instruction. In J. Niles & R. Lalik (Eds.), *Solving problems in literacy: Learners, teachers and researchers.* Rochester, NY: National Reading Conference.

Purcell-Gates, V. (1988). Lexical and syntactic knowledge of written narrative held by well-read-to kindergartners and second graders. *Research in the Teaching of English, 22,* 128–160.

Purcell-Gates, V. (1995). *Other people's words: The cycle of low literacy.* Cambridge, MA: Harvard University Press.

Purcell-Gates, V. (1996). Stories, coupons, and the *TV Guide*: Relationships between home literacy experiences and emergent literacy knowledge. *Reading Research Quarterly, 31,* 406–429.

Purcell-Gates, V., & Dahl, K. (1991). Low-SES children's success and failure at early literacy learning in skills-based classrooms. *Journal of Reading Behavior, 23,* 1–34.

Purcell-Gates, V., McIntyre, E., & Freppon, P. (1995). Learning written storybook language in school: A comparison of low-SES children in skills-based and whole language classrooms. *American Educational Research Journal, 32,* 659–685.

Read, C. (1971). Preschool children's knowledge of English phonology. *Harvard Educational Review, 41,* 1–34.

Richgels, D. J. (1995). Invented spelling ability and printed word learning in kindergarten. *Reading Research Quarterly, 30,* 96–109.

Rubin, A. D. (1977). *A theoretical taxonomy of the differences between oral and written language* (Technical Report No. 335). Champaign–Urbana: Center for the Study of Reading, University of Illinois.

Schieffelin, B., & Cochran-Smith, M. (1984). Learning to read culturally: Literacy before schooling. In H. Goelman, A. Oberg, & F. Smith (Eds.), *Awakening to literacy* (pp. 3–23). Victoria, British Columbia, Canada: University of Victoria.

Schrieber, P. A. (1987). Prosody and structure in children's syntactic processing. In R. Horowitz & S. J. Samuels (Eds.), *Comprehending oral and written language* (pp. 243–268). San Diego: Academic Press.

Snow, C., & Ninio, A. (1986). The contracts of literacy: What children learn from learning to read books. In W. H. Teale & E. Sulzby (Eds.), *Emergent literacy: Writing and reading* (pp. 116–138). Norwood, NJ: Ablex.

Sulzby, E. (1985). Children's emergent abilities to read favorite storybooks, a developmental study. *Reading Research Quarterly, 20,* 458–481.

Taylor, D. (1982). *Family literacy: Children learning to read and write.* Exeter, NH: Heinemann.

Taylor, D., & Dorsey-Gaines, C. (1988). *Growing up literate: Learning from inner city families.* Portsmouth, NH: Heinemann.

Teale, W. H. (1986). Home background and young children's literacy development. In W. H. Teale & E. Sulzby (Eds.), *Emergent literacy: Writing and reading* (pp. 173–206). Norwood, NJ: Ablex.

CHAPTER FOUR
The Three-Cueing System

MARILYN JAGER ADAMS
Harvard University Graduate School of Education

The meaningfulness of a text depends no more on the knowledge and thought with which it has been written than it does on the knowledge and thought with which it is read. Indeed, readers can interpret and evaluate an author's message from the print on the page only to the extent that they possess and call forth the vocabulary, syntactic, rhetorical, topical, analytic, and social knowledge and sensitivities on which the meaning of the text depends.

Over the last several decades, cognitive scientists have energetically investigated the extent to which such dimensions of background knowledge and responsiveness might explain individual differences in reading proficiency. As expected, children do contrast along such dimensions, both with each other and with the demands of their texts. Also as expected, instructional support of such knowledge and strategies generally does result in increases in the productivity of their reading. Yet research also has shown that as children's reading experience grows, these sorts of capabilities tend to grow alongside. That is, to the extent that children do read, they generally do learn new words, new meanings, new linguistic structures, and new modes of thought through reading (Stanovich, 1993).

The wisdom of the popular dictum, that reading is best learned through reading, follows directly. So, too, however, does the seriousness of its most nettlesome caveat: Where children find reading too difficult, they very often will not do it—or at least not with the sort of engagement that best fosters learning. Fortunately, with respect to the language and meaning of text, finding selections that are within a child's comfort level is rarely a problem. However, the same is not true with respect to the wording of text. Until well into the middle grades, children's ability to understand text that is read aloud to them significantly exceeds their ability to understand the same text when reading on their own (Curtis, 1980). The bulk of this difference is traced to their difficulties in reading the words. Moreover, poorly developed word recognition skills are the most pervasive and debilitating source of reading difficulty (Adams, 1990; Perfetti, 1985; Share & Stanovich, 1995).

Words, as it turns out, are the raw data of text. It is the words of a text that evoke the starter set of concepts and relationships from which its meaning must be built. Research has shown that for skillful readers, and regardless of the difficulty of the text, the basic dynamic of reading is line by line, left-to-right, and word by word. It is because skillful readers are able to recognize words so quickly that they can take in text at rates of approximately five words per second or nearly a full type-written page per minute. It is because their capacity for word recognition is so overlearned and effortless that it proceeds almost automatically, feeding rather than competing with comprehension processes. Most surprising of all, research teaches us that what enables this remarkably swift and efficient capacity to recognize words is the skillful reader's deep and ready knowledge of the words' spellings and spelling–speech correspondences. During that fraction of a second that the eyes are paused on any given word of a text, its spelling is registered with complete, letterwise precision even as it is instantly and automatically mapped to the speech patterns it represents.

Although scientists are only beginning to understand the various roles of these spelling-to-speech translations, they are clearly of critical importance to the reading process. To the extent that knowledge of spelling-to-speech correspondences is underdeveloped (as evidenced, for example, by subnormal speed or accuracy in reading nonsense words), it is strongly and reliably associated with specific reading disability (Rack, Snowling, & Olson, 1992). Moreover, research affirms that except as children have internalized the spelling-to-speech correspondences of the language, learning to recognize an adequate number of words with the speed and accuracy on which fluent reading depends is essentially impossible.

Useful knowledge of the spelling-to-speech correspondences of English does not come naturally. For all children, it requires a great deal of practice, and for many children, it is not easy. The acquisition of this knowledge depends on developing a reflective appreciation of the phonemic structure of the spoken language; on learning about letter–sound correspondences and spelling conventions of the orthography; and on consolidating and extending this knowledge by using it in the course of one's own reading and writing. Each of these accomplishments depends, in turn, on certain insights and observations that for many if not most children are simply not forthcoming without special instructional guidance and support (for a review, see Adams, 1990). As researchers have gained appreciation of the critical importance of able word recognition within the reading complex, they have also uncovered reasons for its difficulty (e.g., Juel, 1994;

Liberman & Liberman, 1990; Stanovich, 1986) and a variety of instructional strategies for easing, speeding, and assessing its acquisition (e.g., Ball & Blachman, 1991; Byrne & Fielding-Barnsley, 1989, 1991; Henry, 1989; Lundberg, Frost, & Petersen, 1988; Uhry & Shepard, 1993). Moreover, it is *because* there is far, far more to literacy development than recognizing the words that these lessons are of such crucial importance to everyone in reading education.

WHAT IS THE THREE-CUEING SYSTEM?

Over the last few years, I have spent much time in schools around the country, working with teachers and administrators. My challenge has been to tell them about these lessons from research and their implications with respect to instruction. At some point during such sessions, I am almost inevitably asked how what I have said relates to the three-cueing system.

The first time I was hit with this question, I naively asked what, specifically, my audience meant by "the three-cueing system." Whose three-cueing system? Although nobody could provide a reference, someone in my audience graciously drew a schematic of the three-cueing system for me (see Appendix 4.1).

I was greatly relieved. I understood this schematic. It looked to be nothing more or less than a Venn diagram. As such, its interpretation was straightforward. The intersection or overlap of the circles of a Venn diagram correspond to a logical "and" between the sets its circles respectively represent. In logic, when an outcome depends on any number of elements linked by "and," it means that if any of those elements is missing, the outcome will not follow. Thus by depicting the *meaning* of a text in the intersection of its *semantic, syntactic,* and *graphophonic* cues, the Venn diagram succinctly asserts that the meaning of a text depends on all three; all three of these types of information are necessary, all three must be properly processed, and not one of them can be safely ignored or finessed except at the risk of forfeiting or distorting the meaning of the text. Sometimes, as shown in Figure 4.1, a fourth cueing system, *pragmatics,* is included in the schematic to indicate that, in addition, getting to the author's point from what she or he has literally written depends on the application of practical knowledge and good sense.

Not only was the logic of this schematic clear to me, its evident message was thoroughly familiar as well. That the meaning of text is constructed by the reader as jointly determined by its lexical, semantic, and syntactic constraints had been a central theme of the reading literature in the late 1970s and early 1980s (examples include Anderson & Pearson, 1984; Bransford, Barclay, & Franks, 1972; Brown, Bransford, Ferrara, & Campione, 1983; Perfetti & Roth, 1977; Rumelhart, 1980; Rumelhart & Ortony, 1977; Sanford & Garrod, 1981; Smith, 1971; Stanovich, 1980). It

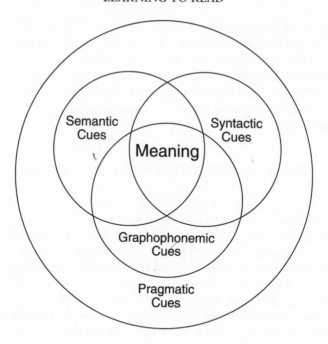

FIGURE 4.1. The three-cueing system.

was, as a matter of fact, a literature to which I, too, had contributed (Adams, 1980, 1982; Adams, Anderson, & Durkin, 1978; Adams & Bruce, 1982; Adams & Collins; 1979; Huggins & Adams, 1980). I was delighted to find that the essence of the researchers' collective effort had so enduringly impressed the practitioners before me.

Feeling thus endorsed, I turned attention to how each of the three "cueing systems" could mislead a reader except as used in coordination with the others. To make the point, I presented a number of examples and linguistic surprises; I showed how the system explained a variety of confusions rooted in developmental difficulties and cross-linguistic differences; and I led my audience to share examples from their own classrooms and discuss their instructional implications. This was happy, familiar territory, and I carried on for nearly an hour. My audience was clearly interested. Yet they also seemed a bit uncomfortable. It was evident from their faces and posture that what I was saying differed from what they were expecting in some fundamental way. Whatever they saw as the main point of this schematic, I knew I was somehow missing it.

In fact, I understate the dissonance in the room that day. When I asked these people what they meant by the three-cueing system, they looked at me as though I were from Mars. They were at least as embarrassed as I was. For indeed, how could I *not* know? How could I present myself to them as an expert on early literacy and *not* know? What was at issue here was clearly *not* any general notion of the interplay of syntax, semantics, and graphophonemics but, rather, some particular, specific version of this notion—one with which I was frankly unfamiliar.

THE SOURCE OF THE THREE-CUEING SYSTEM

From that day on, it seemed that I encountered the three-cueing system at every turn. Not only was I asked about it again and again, but I also found pictures of or allusions to it in inservice materials across the country and at the center of a surprising number of state and district reading/language arts documents. Though the schematic differed slightly from one source to the next, the common ancestry was apparent. Casually, at first, I began to collect examples (see Appendix 4.1).

My interest might have remained idle curiosity, except that I soon found the three-cueing system getting in the way of my efforts to communicate with practitioners more often than it helped. The problem, to my mind, was not the schematic but some of the interpretations that had become attached to it. Given the widespread familiarity of the schematic in the community of practice, I wanted to correct and clarify its intent. To do so, I needed to find the original. I was confident of the original author's logical leanings and scholarship from the very fact that she or he had chosen a Venn diagram as means of expression.

I began to search in earnest. In addition to tackling the literature, I began asking audiences everywhere if they had encountered this schematic and if they could give me a source. People gave me copies of the schematic instead, and my collection grew. Still, in not one single instance did the graphic include a citation of its source.

Turning to the internet, I posted a query to the Teachers Applying Whole Language (TAWL) listserve. A number of people responded, indicating their familiarity with the schematic ("I'm looking at it right now," wrote one). Some had hypotheses as to its original author. Most prominently, these suggestions included Ken and Yetta Goodman, Marie Clay, Don Holdaway, and Brian Cambourne. However, nobody was sure. Notably, Ken Goodman, who is himself a frequent participant on the TAWL listserve, seemed most perplexed of all.

In addition to asking practitioners, I quizzed my colleagues in educational research, beginning with those whom I have long revered as having near-encyclopedic knowledge of the literature. As it turns out, the schematic was unfamiliar to most of them, as it had been to me. Their best guesses as to its origin were by and large the same as those offered by the TAWL subscribers. A few were certain they had seen it before; they reached back into their minds with that pained look of arduous recall. I became hopeful. But again, to no avail. In every one of these cases, interestingly, what I ultimately got back was a pointer to work by Lois Bloom. Indeed, Bloom did publish such a Venn triplet, twice. In the first case (Bloom, 1970, p. 232), the circles are labeled "Cognitive–Perceptual Development," "Linguistic Experience," and "Nonlinguistic Experience," and their overlap is labeled "Linguistic Competence." In the second (Bloom & Lahey, 1978, p. 22), the three circles are labeled "Form," "Content," and "Use," and their overlap as "Language." In other words, Bloom's graphic was similar, but her topic was not. Bloom was not the source I was seeking, but her repeated citation did affirm my faith in these people's mental inventory of the literature they had read. Whatever the true source of the three-cueing schematic, I was increasingly convinced that it was not part of the mainstream academic repertoire.

As I continued my search, several people suggested that the schematic's original printing had been in a publication of the New Zealand Ministry of Education. Brian Cutting, now Educational Director of the Wright Group/Sunshine Reading Programme and who has long been centrally involved in reading practice, policy, and research in New Zealand, valiantly volunteered to help me out on this front, but again to no avail.

Among sources of consternation in this quest was the frequency with which the schematic was used and the similarity with which it was described in state and district reading documents. Pushing this angle, I was told by several people that the schematic came from the Frameworks group. This group operates through the Wayne–Finger Lakes Board of Cooperative Educational Services (BOCES) in New York with funding from Rigby Education and the Children's Literacy Foundation, a video-disc literacy inservice enterprise started by Ben Brady, founder of Rigby of America. Featuring Jan Turbill, Andrea Butler, and Brian Cambourne, the Frameworks group is an outgrowth of Australia's Early Literacy Inservice Course (ELIC), and offers inservice throughout the country on staff development and, in particular, on how to write a reading framework document. Working from an advertisement in the International Reading Association's newspaper, *Reading Today*, I called the Frameworks office and requested information. They were very cordial, but the information never came.

Turning again to the internet, I submitted a query to the Reading Specialists Online at the Wright Group's website. In response, one of the specialists, Katy Kane, posted a very nice explanation of the origin and interpretive intent of the schematic on the Wright Group's online Question and Answer page:

> The term "cueing systems" comes from Ken and Yetta Goodman, Carolyn Burke, Marie Clay, Brian Cambourne, and New Zealand's Reading in Junior Classes. Cueing systems are assessed with running records (Clay) and reading miscue analysis (Goodman, Watson, Burke, et al.) to illustrate the strategies that readers have at their disposal when confronting [unfamiliar words], how these strategies are integrated, what

readers do when they come to something they don't know, what patterns emerge, how well readers self-correct, and always and ever, what does what they have read mean to them. The Venn diagram is used and explained in *Invitations* (1994) by Regie Routman.

The version of the three-cueing schematic that appears in Routman's (1988, 1994) books is included in Appendix 4.1. Of note, it is one of only two that I have been able to find in archival journals or books as opposed to, for example, inservice handouts, framework documents, and advertising copy. The other, which is also the oldest in my collection, is from an article by Pearson that first appeared in *Language Arts* in 1976 and was later reprinted in the International Reading Association volume *What Research Says to the Teacher* (Samuels, 1983). I did not find this article on my own. Instead, it was sent to me by Pearson himself, in response to one of my end-of-talk queries. He assures me that he created it on his own in 1976. Nevertheless, he, too, had been unaware of the schematic's present-day ubiquity—and seemed wholly bemused by the thought that it might have been he who started it. In any case, if this article by Pearson (1976) is the original source for the three-cueing schematic, then, insofar as I can tell, it lay dormant for over a decade.

THE SIGNIFICANCE OF THE THREE-CUEING SYSTEM

Again, my concerns with the three-cueing system relate not to the schematic, which I find wholly sensible insofar as it goes. My concerns relate instead, and in two major ways, to the interpretations so broadly attached to the schematic.

First, the three-cueing schematic is sometimes presented as rationale for subordinating the value of the graphophonemic information to syntax and semantics and, by extension, for minimizing and even eschewing attention to the teaching, learning, and use of the graphophonemic system. This interpretation directly contradicts the logical import of the Venn diagram which, by virtue of its structure, asserts that productive reading depends on the interworking of all three systems. More importantly in the context of instructional guidance for teachers and school districts, such marginalization of the role of spelling-to-speech correspondences is alarmingly discrepant with what research has taught us about the knowledge and processes involved in learning to read.

My second major concern is that discussion of the remaining two or three systems—syntax, semantics, and pragmatics—tends to be unproductively superficial in the discourse surrounding the three-cueing schematic. Given the extreme, if inappropriate, share of the reading load that is ascribed to these sophisticated systems, this lack of guidance with respect to the instructional support that each warrants is all the more troubling.

THE DEMISE OF THE GRAPHOPHONEMIC SYSTEM

Pearson's 1976 article might well have been the original source not just of
the three-cueing schematic but also of the de-emphasis of spelling–sound
instruction that so often attends it. With respect to graphophonemic
instruction, Pearson proposes that teachers should "value most highly those
phonics skill activities which allow children to utilize the most semantic
and syntactic information while they are "cracking the code,'" and,
conversely, "value least highly those phonics skill activities which are most
isolated from context" (Pearson, 1978, p. 90). To anchor this argument,
he writes:

> Efficient readers maximize their reliance on syntactic and semantic
> information in order to minimize the amount of print to speech process-
> ing (call this decoding, phonic, or grapho-phonemic analysis) they have
> to do. . . . For example, it doesn't take much visual or grapho-phonemic
> information to confirm the hypothesis that telescope fits into the sentence,
> "The astronomer looked through the _____." (p. 86)

Presented in excerpt, however, the force of such quotes may be
misleading; in journal articles as in children's literature, context matters. A
full read of the paper assures that Pearson's goal is one of promoting
classroom support of semantic and syntactic factors *not* instead of but
relative to phonics. Thus, he clarifies, although initial phonics instruction
may need be conducted "in isolated contexts, we will always require the
intermediate phonics-in-context step *prior to* the attempt to have children
transfer the skill to a *real reading* situation" (Pearson, 1978, p. 90). To
illustrate this intermediate, phonics-in-context step, he provides examples
that look very much like traditional skills worksheets and very little like
the whole-language activities of today; the suggested activities are primarily
designed to teach phonics, albeit with semantic and/or syntactic support
(e.g., given a picture of a can, choose the label: *can, cane*). In overview,
Pearson's intention seems not in the least to dismiss or even diminish the
teaching or learning of the graphophonemic system. It is instead to criticize
texts and activities that are made abstruse or incomprehensible through
emphasis of phonics elements to the exclusion or at the expense of the
other, potentially supportive dimensions of language and learning. At the
same time, he strives to emphasize the pedagogical importance of providing
enlightened instructional support for the other two systems.

Pearson (1976, 1978) attributes the inspiration for his three-cueing
system graphic—or at least the ideas that the graphic was intended to
capture—to a book by Smith (1975). Smith, I would agree, deserves
singular credit for the philosophy that spellings and spelling–sound correspondences are essentially irrelevant to reading or learning to read (see
Adams, 1991). On the other hand, insofar as I can determine, in neither

that book nor any of his others, has Smith discussed reading in terms of semantic, syntactic, and graphophonemic cueing systems.

Rather, the description of reading in terms of semantic, syntactic, and graphophonemic cueing systems seems best attributed to early work by Goodman (e.g., 1970a, reprinted in Smith, 1973; Goodman, 1970b, reprinted in Singer & Ruddell, 1976). Each of the systems, Goodman explains, is necessary and used simultaneously in the reading process.

The graphophonic system, Goodman continues, is particularly useful for beginning readers as they are developing control over written language. Drawing on their oral language competence, children "recode graphic input as speech" such that "the alphabetic character of the writing system makes it possible to match sound sequences already known with less familiar graphic sequences" (Goodman, 1976, p. 481). The print-to-speech route, he suggests, falls to secondary or back-up status only as the reader becomes proficient and, even then, he points out, "there is some echo of speech involved as the reader proceeds even in silent reading. At times, the reader may find it helpful to recode print as speech and then [construct its meaning]" (p. 482).

Meanwhile in his model, which Goodman emphasizes "represents the *proficient* reader" (1976, p. 483), the process of rapidly sampling, predicting, and comprehending the text is continually monitored and adjusted through instant, easy access to words from their spellings and, as needed, spelling–sound correspondences. Given that the model "also represents the competence which is the goal of reading instruction" (p. 483), he quite reasonably cautions that restricting children's early instruction to isolated words and meaningless phonic elements is, at best, shortsighted. Goodman's thesis, in short, is that instruction should be designed with sensitive awareness that as readers gain in skill, their active attention is devoted less and less to sounding out words and more and more to the higher-order nuances and import of the text. In this spirit, he also provides more insightful and sophisticated discussion of the kinds of support warranted than I have seen in any recent text. Within the present discussion, however, the point is that neither can contemporary dismissal of spelling–sound instruction be traced to Goodman's early work.

If Routman (1988, 1994) borrowed the three-cueing system schematic from Pearson (1976), she does not mention him. Nor does she credit Goodman. Instead she attributes her inspiration to Holdaway (1979) and, indeed, Holdaway's express view of the utility of graphophonemic information is extreme.

Holdaway begins his discussion of graphophonemic cues with an example: "An illuminating exercise to place oneself in a similar position to the beginning reader . . . by using our own alphabetic code with deprived cues" (1979, p. 91). Through an exercise suitable to *The London Times,* he therewith purports to demonstrate the superfluity of letters and spelling–sound correspondences. He then walks us, insight by insight, through an explanation of how it is that the full and complete wording of the following sentence leaps to mind, almost instantly and with incontestably clarity:

Lxttxxx xxx xxt xxx xxly clxxx xo xxkxxxn xxxdx.

The exercise is intended to demonstrate not merely our scant dependence on letters while reading—only 12 of the 39 letters of this sentence are available—but, further, that what letter information we do use, need entail "no necessary phonic involvement" (Holdaway, 1979, p. 93). Instead, he assures us, our ready success in understanding the sentence is the product of nothing more than our deep and ready knowledge of the semantic and syntactic constraints of text. *Plus* our faith that the author would not write so as to foil or confuse our initial expectations. *And* solid sense of the informational value of word length and configuration cues. *Along with* an ability to parse words into roots and affixes given the scantiest visual cues. *Complemented by* a prodigious sense of the distributional properties and redundancies of English spelling.

Holdaway's exercise is fun. It sparkles with energy and intelligence as does his text throughout. His encrypted sentence (which, by the way, is intended to read, "Letters are not the only clues to unknown words") is a clever springboard for discussing the layers upon layers of redundancy that characterize written language. As a developmental analogy, however, it is unconvincing at best: The knowledge and processes he leads us to use in its decryption are not remotely available to the beginning reader. Nevertheless, this exercise is the departure point from which Holdaway builds his theory of how the reading process works and the instructional recommendations on which Routman, in turn, builds hers.

Routman's books *Transitions: From Literature to Literacy* (1988) and *Invitations: Changing as Teachers and Learners, K–12* (1994), in which she shares the attitudes and process of becoming a whole-language teacher, are extremely popular among practitioners. Her treatment of phonics in her first book, *Transitions,* is full of angst and ambivalence. On one hand, she acknowledges the pressure, from both within the educational community and without, that phonics be taught first and well; on the other, she is concerned that this pressure is misguided. On one hand, she reports that the teaching of phonics had been the main emphasis of her preservice and graduate training; on the other, she has just read, and been strongly impressed with, Holdaway's 1979 book, *The Foundations of Literacy.* On one hand, she cites the validation of phonics instruction by the then-recent report of the National Commission on Reading, *Becoming a Nation of Readers* (Anderson, Hiebert, Scott, & Wilkinson, 1985); on the other, she does not see how such phonics emphasis can be reconciled with the report's tandem recommendation for the use of more meaningful, memorable stories with beginners. Although she has heard "enthusiastic talk by salesmen of 'predictable text,' 'meaningful story,' and 'real literature,'" the basal text-books she has seen are still "driven by skills and phonics" (1988, p. 23). She disdains the detailed teacher manuals that accompany the basals as "demeaning to teachers and to children. They discourage independent thought and imply that teachers and students are not to be trusted" (p. 24). Yet she also reports with satisfaction her past pleasure and success in using *Recipe for Reading* (Traub & Bloom, 1975), a phonics supplement in which skills are taught explicitly, systematically, and in isolation.

Routman observes that good readers both know and use phonics well. In contrast, nearly all poor readers struggle with phonics and, when reading meaningful text, this struggle directly detracts from their capacity for comprehension. The epiphany came, she claims, in the course of her experience as a Reading Recovery trainee. There she has witnessed beginners who "became competent readers by relying primarily on meaning—especially picture cues—and memory for text" and "without ever having mastered short vowels and other phonics generalizations" (1988, p. 45). The paradox, to her mind, was resolved. "Effective readers," she concludes, "use all three cueing systems interdependently. Ineffective readers tend to rely too heavily upon graphophonic cues" (p. 41). Moreover, she explains, "It has become crystal clear to me—and it has taken about ten years to come to this understanding—that children learn phonics best *after* they can already read. I am convinced that the reason our good readers are good at phonics is that in their being able to read they can intuitively make sense of phonics" (p. 44).

Thus in her second book, *Invitations* (1994), Routman presents the three-cueing schematic with the following introduction:

> Proficient readers function with an interdependence between the three cueing systems: semantics, syntax, and grapho-phonics. Semantic cues (context: what makes sense) and syntactic cues (structure and grammar: what sounds right grammatically) are strategies the reader needs to be using *already* in order for phonics (letter–sound relationships: what looks right visually and sounds right phonetically) to make sense.... While phonics is integral to the reading process, it is subordinate to semantics and syntax. (p. 147)

(This is apparently why the graphophonic system is depicted *beneath* the other two in her version of the diagram. Note, however, that the position of the circles is formally of no significance to the logic of a Venn diagram. What matters is only whether they overlap partly, totally, or not at all with each other and the outcome of interest.)

The major reason for poor readers' overreliance on graphophonic cues, Routman surmises, is its instructional overemphasis by their parents and teachers. To help teachers discourage parents from asking their children to sound words out, she provides a reproducible letter (see Appendix 4.2), entitled, "Ways to Help your Child with Reading at Home" (1994, p. 200b). I ask that you read through the recommendations in this letter to parents: Phonics truly seems the last resort.

To help teachers deal with unknown words without directing attention to graphophonemic cues, Routman provides a similar reproducible set of guidelines for the classroom (1994, p. 226b). In addition, she describes a few ways of introducing various phonic elements in what she deems proper subordination to other literacy goals. Although some of these activities are similar to those proposed by Holdaway (1979), the differences are also noteworthy. First, Holdaway's recommendations were intended principally for kindergarten children and motivated by his experience with Maori children who approached the challenge of learning to read with much trepidation and little notion of what reading was all about. Routman's recommendations are directed to teachers across the kindergarten and primary grades. Second, although Holdaway uses context for motivation and support, he gradually does expose and exercise the full logic of the alphabetic system, if somewhat haphazardly. Routman's (1994) activities, in contrast, are focused on initial and final consonants: The vowels, she submits, are generally unnecessary for printed word recognition, and their evident difficulty should convince us that beginning readers are not developmentally ready for them anyhow. In refusing the vowels and focusing instead on bits and pieces of occasional words, Routman's approach not only denies the utility of the alphabetic principle but fails to reveal its basic logic and structure.

Routman frequently acknowledges the difficulty of pursuing her avowed instructional course:

> It has taken me well over ten years to feel completely comfortable with this approach. One thing that eased my further transition was holding onto the spelling workbooks for a while after I had long given up phonics worksheets. Knowing that the skills were still being covered relieved my conscience and helped my comfort level. Like many teachers, I did not believe children would really learn to read without a heavy dose of phonics first. (1994, p. 149)

As I encountered such remarks again and again, I kept wondering if the reason she was able to make the switch complete was because she had become a resource teacher. Visiting classrooms only "by invitation" to give demonstration lessons, she was no longer responsible for monitoring the children's larger developmental progress. In any case, here is a note Routman received from a regular first-grade teacher:

> I did more phonics in context this year, noting beginning and ending sounds and digraphs in chart poems and Big Books. The kids really like the big charts we made where they could add their own words, but I am

still struggling to find a balance in teaching phonics. I find myself feeling pressure from some of the second-grade teachers who expect kids to arrive with solid word-attack skills. Also, I feel guilty for not giving spelling tests. When I'm teaching all the phonics sounds, I feel as through I'm teaching spelling too. I still teach phonics separately even though I don't see kids transferring the skills. I notice that every time I pull a sound out of context, two or three kids give me an example of a word that doesn't fit the rule at all. I'm still not comfortable with the way I handle phonics. (1994, p. 157)

Having reprinted this letter so as to encourage others to take heart, Routman consoles, "Most of us seem to find the transition from prescribed phonics in isolation to teaching meaningful phonics in the context of literature very difficult and slow going. It may be reassuring to know that most teachers are struggling with making phonics teaching more relevant and applicable to reading and writing" (1994, p. 157).

Whether Routman's text is its source or echo, this attitude about the disruptiveness of phonics and its instruction is one that is very broadly held in the field. Indeed, I have collected several renditions of the three-cueing system that are boldly headed with the admonition: "Let's all work together to avoid the phrase, 'sound it out'!" According to Pesetsky, a professor in the linguistics department at the Massachusetts Institute of Technology, it was an in-school poster very like Routman's letter to parents, along with his first-grade son's steadfast insistence that he was not to sound words out, that initially triggered his own concern about how reading was being taught. Seeking an audience for that concern, first in his son's classroom, then in his son's school, then at the district level, he was ultimately given a copy of the proposed Reading Curriculum Framework for the State of Massachusetts—only to find the phonics-last philosophy promoted in that document as well.

The result was the famous letter from 40 linguists and psycholinguists to the Massachusetts Commissioner of Education (see Appendix 4.3). The focus of the linguists' protest is the document's promotion of the view that "the decoding of written words plays a relatively minor role in reading compared to strategies such as contextual guessing. This treats the alphabetic nature of our writing system as little more than an accident, when in fact it is the most important property of written English." They conclude:

We are concerned that the Commonwealth, through its powers to set standards for schools, should presume to legislate an erroneous view of how human language works, a view that runs counter to most of the major scientific results of more than 100 years of linguistics and psycholinguistics. We are even more concerned that uninformed thinking about language should lie at the heart of a "standards" document for Massachusetts schools. (Pesetsky et al., 1995)

Broadly circulated via the internet, and in part, no doubt, because of the world renown of many of its individual signers, this letter quickly found its way into policy forums on reading across the country. In Massachusetts, it was singularly responsible for the retraction and rewriting of the state's language arts framework to include due acknowledgment of the importance of teaching children how to understand and use phonics.

Routman's observation that good readers, as a group, are quite facile with phonics is correct. Yet her conjecture that this is *because* they are good readers is backwards. Again, scientific research argues incontrovertibly that becoming a good reader depends on understanding and using spellings and spelling–sound correspondences and, conversely, that poorly developed knowledge or facility with spellings and spelling–sound correspondences is the most pervasive cause of reading delay or disability (Rack et al., 1992; Stanovich, 1986). Research further demonstrates that, with the exception of no more than 1–3% of children, reading disability can be prevented through well-designed, early instruction (Vellutino et al., 1996). However, such instruction must include attention to phonics, and it is most effective when it includes explicit, systematic instruction on the alphabetic principle, including phonemic awareness and on the spelling–sound patterns and conventions of English, as well as an active emphasis on practicing and using that knowledge both in isolation and in the context of meaningful reading and writing (Bond & Dykstra, 1966; Brown & Felton, 1990; Chall, 1967; Foorman, Francis, Fletcher, Schatschneider, & Mehta, in press).

THE DIMINUTION OF THE OTHER CUEING SYSTEMS

Given that the principal argument for the de-emphasis of phonics instruction has been that children are in greater need of developing their sensitivity to the syntactic, semantic, and pragmatic cues of text, one might expect an attendant surge in the amount and rigor of instruction on the latter. Yet, quite the opposite has happened. I had struggled with resulting problems a number of times from a number of angles and in a number of different situations before I realized them as part of the same "elephant."

One such encounter occurred as I was reviewing a draft language arts framework for one of the state departments of education. The topic was that of supporting vocabulary knowledge. The text did a laudable job of explaining the importance of ensuring that children possessed the background knowledge on which productive understanding of a word's meaning depended. However, the text neglected to mention anything about helping the children add the words per se to their vocabularies. I wrote a comment to this effect. But it went unheeded. On the next draft, I provided a carefully worded insert to the same effect. Still it was not accepted.

I confronted this same lapse again as I worked on the reading advisory for another state. This time I was a legitimate co-author of the document, so I exercised the prerogative of adding the point: Written language places far greater demands on people's vocabulary knowledge than does casual spoken language. Indeed, more advanced texts depend so heavily on precise wording to build meaning and message that, from the middle grades on, students' reading comprehension can be closely estimated by measures of their vocabulary. Students will be able to learn from these texts only if they approach them with most of the vocabulary they require (California Department of Education, 1996, p. 9).

The text goes on to discuss both the prospects of expanding one's vocabulary through reading, as explored by Nagy, Anderson, and Herman (1987), as well as the potency of Matthew effects (the rich get richer) in understanding and retaining new vocabulary items (e.g., Robbins & Ehri, 1994), and suggests, quite sensibly I thought, that "Beginning in kindergarten, vocabulary growth should be actively supported in the classroom" (p. 10). Not long thereafter, I received an unauthorized copy of an e-mail that had been circulating through the state internet referring to "Marilyn Adams's pernicious use of Nagy's vocabulary data." I didn't get it. I wrote to Bill Nagy. He didn't get it either.

I had a similar experience in critiquing the explanation of semantic cues in one of these draft frameworks. The text explained that semantic cues "are meaning cues used as readers bring their knowledge of the world, feelings, attitudes, and beliefs to the printed page." Correcting what again seemed to me to be nothing more than an oversight, I suggested the most minor edit: Semantic cues "are meaning cues used as readers bring their knowledge of the meanings of words and of the world, feelings, attitudes, and beliefs to the printed page." Again, the insert was rejected. How strange. After all, in cognitive psychology, the distributed semantics of words are held to be the starting points from which the meaning of text is constructed.

One of the fundamental tenets of the three-cueing rhetoric is that readers must learn to monitor their comprehension as they read. Thus in the typical exposition of the three-cueing system, a question is provided with each system. For the semantic cues, readers are to ask, "Does it make sense?" For the syntactic system, they are to ask, "Does it sound like language?" And for the pragmatic system, they are to ask, "Is this the language that should be used in this situation?" As I encountered each of these questions in the draft framework on which I was working, it seemed to me that each could be augmented so as to give teachers better guidance as to comprehension difficulties associated with its system. With this thought in mind, I added to the semantic question, "Do I understand to what the author is referring?" To the syntactic question, I added, "Do I understand how the author wants me to interrelate the concepts s/he has named?"

But I balked at the question provided for the pragmatic system. Pragmatic sensitivity is about the larger meaning and message of the text.

It is about understanding why the author chooses to say what she or he says and how she or he chooses to say it. It is about the author's point and point of view. In Goodman's words, it is about "the subtle differences between the straightforward and the sarcastic, the profane and the profound, the humorous and the serious" (1976, p. 832). Pragmatic processing, in short, is just another term for metacognitive processing. As such, and more so than for any of the other systems, sensitivity to pragmatics depends on readers' willingness and ability to examine the language, the cohesion, and the nuances of the text and to bring their own background knowledge actively and critically to bear. Of all the questions one might provide to clarify the role and importance of pragmatic processing, why in the world would the first choice be: "Is this the language that should be used in this situation?"

And then it hit me. In discussions of pragmatics within the three-cueing rhetoric, the standard explanation is that proficient readers, having experienced language in many contexts, are familiar with the kinds of words and language that are used in informal versus formal situations, in literature versus science, and so on. In other words, the question, "Is this the language that should be used in this situation?" is not intended to guide readers' pragmatic understanding of the text at all. It is instead intended exactly and only to remind them to use any such understanding they might have as means of assessing whether they have misidentified a word.

I was stunned. Yet, when I looked again, the questions attached to the other systems had the same character. None of these questions was directed toward supporting or strengthening the children's comprehension skills. The semantic question had nothing to do with prodding readers to monitor or extend their understanding of the text. The question is not "Does the text make sense given the words I've read?" but, instead, "Does this word make sense given my understanding of the text?" In view of this, the strong emphasis on choosing literature that matches students' prior knowledge and interests is understandable. However, the converse message—that comprehension instruction integrally involves building students' background knowledge and vocabulary so as to meet the demands of new texts—tends to get lost. The latter message was among the focal points of both Pearson's (1976) and Goodman's (1970b) works. It was, moreover, among the central and critical lessons of schema theory.

Similarly, the syntax of written text is important and tricky. Syntax is language's formal means of communicating the intended relations between concepts and events, as in the difference between "Students who like school get good grades" versus "Students who get good grades like school." In reading essays and informational texts, where the motive is to create new understandings and knowledge by building new relationships between familiar concepts, syntax is vital. In understanding algebra problems, syntax is almost all that matters; whether the problem is about a plane in the wind or a riverboat in a current is only incidental with respect to the mathematics at issue. Learning to use the syntactic cues of text well is not easy. Yet, the syntactic issue in focus with the question "Does is sound right?" is only that some strings of words are permissible in English and some are not. The purpose of the question is only to alert the reader to syntactically anomalous word recognition errors.

I finally understood why my audience looked so puzzled on that first run-in with the three-cueing system. They had been operating on the belief that the semantic, syntactic, and pragmatic cues were straightforward and familiar to children, and, because of this, were wholly available for use in finessing the graphophonemic system, which was complicated and unfamiliar. It had never occurred to them that there was much to teach or learn about the semantic, syntactic, and pragmatic cues involved in skillful reading. What I was saying must have been totally disorienting to these people.

SUMMARY

If the intended message of the three-cueing system was originally that teachers should take care not to overemphasize phonics to the neglect of comprehension, its received message has broadly become that teachers should minimize attention to phonics lest it compete with comprehension. If the original premise of the three-cueing system was that the reason for reading the words is to understand the text, it has since been oddly converted such that, in effect, the reason for understanding the text is in order to figure out the words. How did this happen?

My reason for quoting so extensively from Routman's (1988, 1994) text was to convey a sense of how the three-cueing belief system is realized in the field—in terms of both its classroom practice and the arduous commitment of its practitioners. Although Routman is extremely influential among practitioners, I do not believe her books to be the source of this widespread belief system. First, if they were, more people would have cited Routman as a source of the schematic. Yet, of the many, many people I asked, only one did so. Second, the very fact that there are so many slightly different versions of the schematic around suggests that people's knowledge of it is not coming from a book. Given the option, after all, it is much easier to cut and paste than to draw a graphic anew. Third, marginal interpretations of the three-cueing schematic are also too scattered for me to believe they are a product of book-learning. For example, in the core curriculum of one district with which I worked, cursive writing and spelling conventions are given as instances of the syntactic cueing system. Inasmuch as the syntactic cueing system was explained as knowledge about the order and structure of language, these errors were understandable—except for the fact that syntax has nothing to do with the order or structural properties of letters.

Again, the simplifications and distortions that the three-cueing system has suffered are uncharacteristic of the fate of written information. My

hypothesis is, instead, that the three-cueing system principally has prolifer-
ated through inservice sessions, workshops, and conferences, and that it is
through that process that its interpretation has been changed and its
heritage forgotten. Such forums have become a common mode of inservice
education in recent years:

> With some exceptions, university- and college-level literacy courses have
> not kept pace with the widespread implementation of process instruction.
> Instead, process instruction has been largely a grassroots movement
> spreading from coast to coast. Organized teacher groups, known as
> Teachers Applying Whole Language (TAWL), have sprung up everywhere.
> . . . and have served as support groups for those implementing whole
> language. The majority of teachers not involved in these groups, however,
> has relied primarily on information learned from institutes, workshops,
> and conferences conducted by whole language and writing process
> advocates. In many cases, teachers attending these meetings have taught
> other teachers in their school districts.
>
> While the enthusiasm of teachers teaching teachers is commendable,
> the short-term nature of such training presents a unique problem; it
> virtually assures that only the rudimentary elements of these theories can
> be presented. (Reyes, 1992, p. 429)

Consistent with Reyes's (1992) lament, the sobering revelation of this
story is the profound breach in information and communication that
separates the teaching and research communities. In the world of practice,
the widespread subscription to the belief system that the three-cueing
diagram has come to represent has wreaked disaster on students and
hardship on teachers. At the same time, it is the underlying cause of not
insignificant distrust and ill-will among teachers, teacher educators, and
researchers. Yet whereas teachers widely believe that the lore of the
three-cueing system is based on the best of current research, researchers are
barely aware of its existence, nature, or influence. The lesson of the story
is thus clear and urgent. We must work together to rebuild the bridge,
socially and intellectually, between those involved in research and practice.
Toward regaining respect for as well as the productivity, morale, and
forward momentum of our educational system, there may be no more
important effort we can undertake.

APPENDIX 4.1. Schematics of the Three-Cueing System

The Three Reading Cue Systems

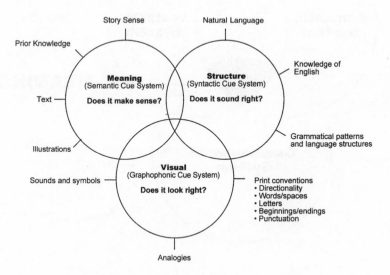

Source unknown.

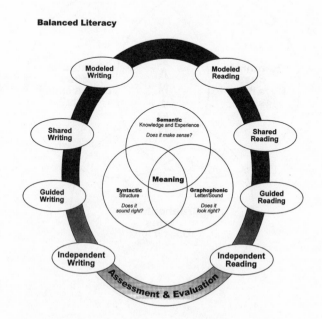

Sacramento, California, City Unified School District, 1995.

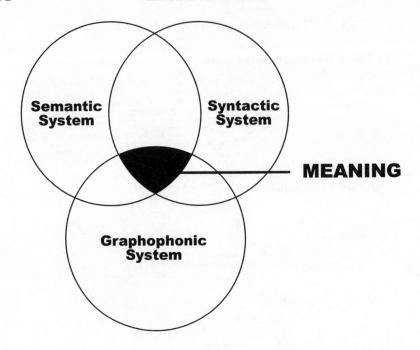

Frameworks Inservice Manual, 1991.

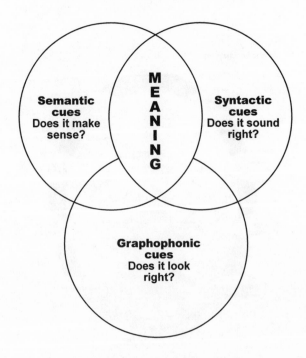

North Carolina Public Schools, 1992.

Reading Cueing System

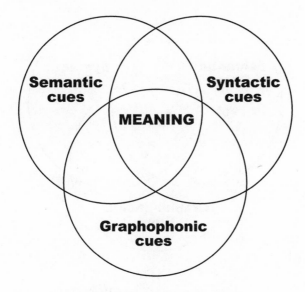

Dallas, Texas public schools, 1996.

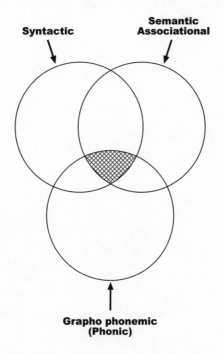

David Pearson, 1976-1978.

The Three Cueing Systems

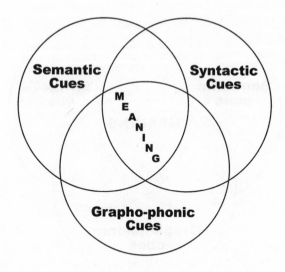

Regie Routman, 1988-1994.

APPENDIX 4.2. Ways to Help Your Child with Reading at Home (Routman, 1994, p. 200b)

Setting the atmosphere
Help your child find a quiet, comfortable place to read.
Have your child see you as a reading model.
Read aloud to your child. Reread favorite stories.
Read with your child.
Discuss the stories you read together.
Recognize the value of silent reading.
Keep reading time enjoyable and relaxed.

Responding to errors in reading
Based on the way most of us were taught to read, we have told the child to "sound it out" when he comes to an unknown word. While phonics is an important part of reading, reading for meaning is the primary goal. To produce independent readers who monitor and correct themselves as they read, the following prompts are recommended *before* saying "sound it out."

- Give your child wait time of 5 to 10 seconds. See what he attempts to do to help himself.
- "What would make sense there?"

- "What do you think that word could be?"
- "Go back to the beginning and try that again."
- "Skip over it and read to the end of the sentence (or paragraph). Now what do you think it is?"
- "Put in a word that would make sense there."
- "You read that word before on another page. See if you can find it."
- "Look at how that word begins. Start it out and keep reading."
- Tell your child the word.

Most important, focus on what your child is doing well and attempting to do. Remain loving and supportive. When your child is having difficulty and trying to work out the trouble spots, comments such as the following are suggested:

- "Good for you. I like the way you tried to work that out."
- "That was a good try. Yes, that word would make sense there."
- "I like the way you went back to the beginning of the sentence and tried that again. That's what good readers do."
- "You are becoming a good reader. I'm proud of you."

APPENDIX 4.3. The Letter from 40 Linguists to the Massachusetts Commissioner of Education

From: Forty Massachusetts specialists in linguistics and psycholinguistics
To: Dr. Robert V. Antonucci
    Commissioner of Education, Commonwealth of Massachusetts
cc: Linda Beardsley, Curriculum Frameworks Coordinator, Dept. of Education
    Dr. Michael Sentance, Secretary of Education
    His Excellency, William F. Weld, Governor of Massachusetts
Date: July 12, 1995
Subject: Standards for Reading Instruction in Massachusetts

Dear Dr. Antonucci:
    We are researchers in linguistics and psycholinguistics—and Massachusetts residents. We are writing to raise certain questions about the inclusion of contentious and, in our view, scientifically unfounded views of language in the sections on reading instruction of the draft Curriculum Content Chapter on Language Arts ("Constructing and Conveying Meaning"), recently circulated by the Massachusetts Department of Education. These views are presented as a principal support for the reading curriculum advocated as an instructional "standard" in this document.
    The proposed Content Chapter replaces the common-sense view of reading as the decoding of notated speech with a surprising view of reading as directly "constructing meaning." According to the document, "constructing meaning" is a process that can be achieved using many "strategies" (guessing, contextual

cues, etc.). In this view, the decoding of written words plays a relatively minor role in reading compared to strategies such as contextual guessing. This treats the alphabetic nature of our writing system as little more than an accident, when in fact it is the most important property of written English—a linguistic achievement of historic importance.

The authors of the draft Content Chapter claim that research on language supports their views of reading. The document asserts that research on language has moved from the investigation of particular "components of language—phonological and grammatical units" to the investigation of "its primary function— communication." These supposed developments in linguistic research are used as arguments for a comparable view of reading. We are entirely unaware of any such shift in research.

We want to alert the educational authorities of Massachusetts to the fact that the view of language research presented in this document is inaccurate, and that the claimed consequences for reading instruction should therefore be subjected to serious re-examination.

The facts are as follows. Language research continues to focus on the components of language, because this focus reflects the "modular" nature of language itself. Written language is a notation for the structures and units of one of these components. Sound methodology in reading instruction must begin with these realities. Anything else will shortchange those students whom these standards are supposed to help.

As linguists, we are concerned that the Commonwealth, through its powers to set standards for schools, should presume to legislate an erroneous view of how human language works, a view that runs counter to most of the major scientific results of more than 100 years of linguistics and psycholinguistics. We are even more concerned that uninformed thinking about language should lie at the heart of a "standards" document for Massachusetts schools.

REFERENCES

Adams, M. J. (1980). Failures to comprehend and levels of processing in reading. In R. J. Spiro, B. C. Bruce, & W. F. Brewer (Eds.), *Theoretical issues in reading comprehension* (pp. 87–112). Hillsdale, NJ: Erlbaum.

Adams, M. J. (1982). Models of reading. In J. F. Leny & W. Kitsch (Eds.), *Language and comprehension* (pp. 193–206). Amsterdam: North Holland.

Adams, M. J. (1990). *Beginning to read: Thinking and learning about print.* Cambridge, MA: MIT Press.

Adams, M. J. (1991). Why not phonics and whole language? In W. Ellis (Ed.), *All language and the creation of literacy* (pp. 40–53). Baltimore: Orton Dyslexia Society.

Adams, M. J., Anderson, R. C., & Durkin, D. (1978). Beginning reading: Theory and practice. *Language Arts, 55,* 19–25.

Adams, M. J., & Bruce, B. C. (1982). Background knowledge and reading comprehension. In J. A. Langer & M. T. Smith-Burke (Eds.), *Reader meets author/Bridging the gap* (pp. 2–25). Newark, DE: International Reading Association.

Adams, M. J., & Collins, A. M. (1979). A schema-theoretic view of reading. In R. Freedle (Ed.), *New directions in discourse processing* (pp. 1–22). Norwood, NJ: Ablex.

Anderson, R. C., Hiebert, E., Scott, J., & Wilkinson, I. (1985). *Becoming a Nation of Readers.* Washington, DC: National Institute of Education; Champaign, IL: Center for the Study of Reading, University of Illinois.

Anderson, R. C., & Pearson, P. D. (1984). A schema-theoretic view of basic processes in reading. In P. D. Pearson, R. Barr, M. Kamil, & P. Mosenthal (Eds.), *Handbook of reading research* (Vol. 1, pp. 255–292). New York: Longman.

Ball, E. W., & Blachman, B. A. (1991). Does phoneme awareness training in kindergarten make a difference in early word recognition and developmental spelling? *Reading Research Quarterly, 26,* 49–66.

Bloom, L. (1970). *Language development: Form and function in emerging grammars.* Cambridge, MA: MIT Press.

Bloom, L., & Lahey, M. (1978). *Language development and language disorders.* New York: Wiley.

Bond, G. L., & Dykstra, R. (1967). The cooperative research program in first-grade reading instruction. *Reading Research Quarterly, 2,* 5–142.

Bransford, J. D., Barclay, J., & Franks, J. (1972). Sentence memory: A constructive versus interpretative approach. *Cognitive Psychology, 3,* 193–209.

Brown, A. L., Bransford, J. D., Ferrara, R. A., & Campione, J. C. (1983). Learning, remembering, and understanding. In J. H. Flavell & E. M. Markman (Eds.), *Handbook of child psychology: Vol. 3: Cognitive development* (pp. 77–166). New York: Wiley.

Brown, I. W., & Felton, R. H. (1990). Effects of instruction on beginning reading skills in children at risk for reading disability. *Reading and Writing: An Interdisciplinary Journal, 2,* 223–241.

Byrne, B., & Fielding-Barnsley, R. (1989). Phonemic awareness and letter knowledge in the child's acquisition of the alphabetic principle. *Journal of Educational Psychology, 81,* 313–321.

Byrne, B., & Fielding-Barnsley, R. (1991). Evaluation of a program to teach phonemic awareness to young children. *Journal of Educational Psychology, 83,* 451–455.

California Department of Education. (1996). *Teaching reading: Program advisory.* Sacramento: Author.

Chall, J. S. (1967). *Learning to read: The great debate.* New York: McGraw-Hill.

Curtis, M. E. (1980). Development of components of reading skill. *Journal of Educational Psychology, 72,* 656–669.

Foorman, B., Francis, D. J., Fletcher, J. M., Schatschneider, C., & Mehta, P. (in press). The role of instruction in learning to read: Preventing reading failure in at-risk children. *Journal of Educational Psychology.*

Goodman, K. S. (1970a). Psycholinguistic universals in the reading process. *Journal of Typographic Research, 4,* 103–110.

Goodman, K. S. (1970b). Behind the eye: What happens in reading. In K. S. Goodman & O. S. Niles (Eds.), *Reading process and program* (pp. 3–38). Urbana, IL: NCTE.

Goodman, K. S. (1976). Behind the eye: What happens in reading. In H. Singer & R. B. Ruddell (Eds.), *Theoretical models and processes of reading* (2nd ed., pp. 470–496). Newark, DE: International Reading Association.

Henry, M. K. (1989). Children's word structure knowledge: Implications for decoding and spelling instruction. *Reading and Writing, 2*, 135–152.

Holdaway, D. (1979). *The foundations of literacy.* Sydney, Australia: Ashton Scholastics.

Huggins, A. W. F., & Adams, M. J. (1980). Syntactic aspects of reading comprehension. In R. J. Spiro, B. C. Bruce, & W. F. Brewer (Eds.), *Theoretical issues in reading comprehension* (pp. 87–112). Hillsdale, NJ: Erlbaum.

Juel, C. (1994). *Learning to read and write in one elementary school.* New York: Springer-Verlag.

Liberman, I. Y., & Liberman, A. M. (1990). Whole language vs. code emphasis: Underlying assumptions and their implications for reading instruction. *Annals of Dyslexia, 40*, 51–76.

Lundberg, I., Frost, J., & Petersen, O. P. (1988). Effects of an extensive program for stimulating phonological awareness in preschool children. *Reading Research Quarterly, 23*, 263–284.

Nagy, W. E., Anderson, R. C., & Herman, P. A. (1987). Learning word meanings from context during normal reading. *American Educational Research Journal, 24*, 237–270.

Pearson, P. D. (1976). A psycholinguistic model of reading. *Language Arts, 53*, 309–314.

Pearson, P. D. (1978). Some practical applications of a psycholinguistic model of reading. In S. J. Samuels (Ed.), *What research says to the teacher* (pp. 84–97). Newark, DE: International Reading Association.

Perfetti, C. A. (1985). *Reading ability.* New York: Oxford University Press.

Perfetti, C. A., & Roth, S. (1977). Some of the interactive processes in reading and their role in reading skill. In A. M. Lesgold & C. A. Perfetti (Eds.), *Interactive processes in reading* (pp. 269–297). Hillsdale, NJ: Erlbaum.

Rack, J. P., Snowling, M. J., & Olson, R. K. (1992). The nonword reading deficit in developmental dyslexia: A review. *Reading Research Quarterly, 26*, 28–53.

Reyes, M. (1992) Challenging venerable assumptions: Literacy instruction for linguistically different students. *Harvard Educational Review, 62*, 427–446.

Robbins, C., & Ehri, L. C. (1994). Reading storybooks to kindergartners helps them learn new vocabulary words. *Journal of Educational Psychology, 86*, 54–64.

Routman, R. (1988). *Transitions: From literature to literacy.* Portsmouth, NH: Heinemann.

Routman, R. (1994). *Invitations: Changing as teachers and learners K–12.* Portsmouth, NH: Heinemann.

Rumelhart, D. E. (1980). Schemata: The building blocks of cognition. In R. J. Spiro, B. C. Bruce, & W. F. Brewer (Eds.), *Theoretical Issues in reading comprehension* (pp. 1–34). Hillsdale, NJ: Erlbaum.

Rumelhart, D. E., & Ortony, A. (1977). The representation of knowledge in memory. In R. C. Anderson, R. J. Spiro, & W. E. Montague (Eds.), *Schooling and the representation of knowledge.* Hillsdale, NJ: Erlbaum.

Samuels, S. J. (1983). *What research says to the teacher.* Newark, DE: International Reading Association.

Sanford, A. J., & Garrod, S. C. (1981). *Understanding written language.* New York: Wiley.

Share, D., & Stanovich, K. (1995). Cognitive processes in early reading development: Accommodating individual differences into a mode of acquisition. *Issues in education: Contributions from educational psychology, 1,* 1–57.

Singer, H., & Ruddell, R. B. (Eds.). (1976). *Theoretical models and processes of reading* (2nd ed.). Newark, DE: International Reading Association.

Smith, F. (1971). *Understanding reading.* New York: Holt, Rinehart & Winston.

Smith, F. (1973). *Psycholinguistics and reading.* New York: Holt, Rinehart & Winston.

Smith, F. (1975). *Comprehension and learning.* New York: Holt, Rinehart & Winston.

Stanovich, K. E. (1980). Toward an interactive-compensatory model of individual differences in the development of reading fluency. *Reading Research Quarterly, 16,* 32–71.

Stanovich, K. E. (1986). Matthew effects in reading: Some consequences of individual differences in the acquisition of literacy. *Reading Research Quarterly, 21,* 360–406.

Stanovich, K. E. (1993). Does reading make you smarter? Literacy and the development of verbal intelligence. In H. Reese (Ed.), *Advances in child development and behavior* (Vol. 24, pp. 133–180). San Diego: Academic Press.

Traub, N., & Bloom, F. (1975). *Recipe for reading.* Cambridge, MA: Educators Publishing Service.

Uhry, J. K., & Shepherd, M. J. (1993). Segmentation/spelling instruction as part of a first-grade reading program: Effects on several measures of reading. *Reading Research Quarterly, 28,* 218–233.

Vellutino, F. R., Scanlon, D. M., Sipay, E., Small, S., Pratt, A., Chen, R., & Denckla, M. (1996). Cognitive profiles of difficult-to-remediate and readily remediated poor readers: Early intervention as a vehicle for distinguishing between cognitive and experiential deficits as basic causes of specific reading disability. *Journal of Educational Psychology, 88,* 601–638.

CHAPTER FIVE

The Prevention
of Reading Failure:
Teach Reading and Writing

JANET S. GAFFNEY

University of Illinois at Urbana–Champaign

Well over a decade ago, I read with interest a list Lewis (1983) made of recommendations for the reading instruction of students with learning disabilities. Her first recommendation, encapsulated in one word, was seared into my memory: "Teach." As I have shared this recommendation over the years, it has been received as heresy by some and as obvious by others. In 1992, following a presentation I made at a national research conference, I asked a colleague if the audience reacted to any of my comments. "Yes," she said, "they bristled when you said, 'teach.' " Modifying Lewis's original list, I offer an additional recommendation: Teach reading and writing.

POLICY ISSUES

Prevalence and Prevention

In 1995, the front page of *CEC Today* (Council for Exceptional Children, 1995a), the newsletter of the Council for Exceptional Children, featured an article with the following headline: "Record Number of Special Education Students Served in 1993–1994." The article highlighted data from the Office of Special Education Programs' *Seventeenth Annual Report to Congress on the Implementation of the Individuals with Disabilities Education Act (IDEA)*. The article heralded a 4.2% increase in the number of individuals receiving special education services in 1993–1994 as the largest since the inception of IDEA in 1975.

I was baffled by the banner headline and spoke with a few colleagues about the article. The idea that CEC was proud of the increase in the identification of students with handicapping conditions puzzled me. The growth of special education is due predominantly to the continued rise in the numbers of students with learning disabilities. The field has not had a major breakthrough in improved identification of students with learning disabilities, so it is doubtful that the rise results from better assessment practices. Perhaps the opposite is true. The ambiguity that plagues the identification of learning disabilities promotes this category as the "growth fund" in special education. Less tolerance for diversity in the general education may be a concomitant explanation for the increase in special education placements (Pianta & Walsh, 1996).

The article also noted that more students with disabilities (39.8%) were being served in general classrooms. General classroom placements for school-aged students (aged 6–21) have increased by almost 10% in the last 5 years, consistent with the trend of serving more children in inclusive settings. The Office of Special Education Programs (1995) report to Congress reflects that of the population of students (aged 6–21) with learning disabilities, nearly 80% receive all (35%) or some (44%) of their services in the regular classroom. Consistent with the trend of serving more children in inclusive settings, the data reflect a 10% increase in general classroom placements for these students over the last 5 years (Council for Exceptional Children, 1995a).

Since its inception, the field of special education has been in the process of defining, creating, and recreating itself in response to societal changes. The field has fluctuated between positions of exclusion such as limiting access of individuals with disabilities to public settings, to positions of inclusion such as testing individuals for eligibility for special placements and encouraging participation of individuals with disabilities in mainstream settings. In the 1990s, the notion of inclusion is a particular challenge for those concerned with students who have mild disabilities. Students must be evaluated for eligibility and found in need of specialized services to be included in a special education category. At the same time, the trend toward an inclusionary model of education provides that students with disabilities will be educated to the greatest extent possible within general classroom settings. An apparent contradiction lies in awarding *special* labels to students who, for the most part, are taught in classroom settings.

The field of special education has been defined variously by the population served, the certification of the teacher, the instructional setting, and the type of instruction. The work of educators and researchers is influenced by the definition to which they adhere. Public Law 94-142, now the Individuals with Disabilities Education Act (IDEA, PL 101-476, 1990) guarantees a child access to "specially designed instruction." This criterion supports the conclusion that instruction, not setting is the key variable for student achievement (Hocutt, 1996).

The classification of mild disabilities applies to individuals with specific learning disabilities, mild mental retardation, emotional disturbance, behavior disorders, and attention deficit disorders. The Office of Special Education Programs' (1995) most recent report to Congress indicates that of the 8% of children aged 6–21 who received special education services in 1993–1994, nearly 6% were served within these categories of mild disabilities. Indeed, more than 50% of all children served were identified within the single category of specific learning disabilities. The number of students classified as having learning disabilities has more than doubled over the past 10 years (National Center for Education Statistics, 1995). Of these students, 75–80% experience significant difficulties in basic language and reading skill (Ellis & Cramer, 1994). The National Center for Learning Disabilities (1996) reports that the incidence of reported learning disabilities is an underestimation of their prevalence and that national studies indicate that as many as one in six elementary students encounters reading problems.

Learning disability is most often determined by the use of a discrepancy standard, which requires that a student have a significant deficit in one or more basic abilities, such as reading, in comparison to the student's intelligence. Students often must experience school failure for 2 or more years to score sufficiently low on an achievement test to obtain a substantial discrepancy between ability and achievement. The majority of students with mild disabilities are identified, therefore, in third and fourth grades, at which time the 2-year discrepancy is possible. Longitudinal studies show that approximately 74% of students who are identified as having learning disabilities that are identified in third grade have reading difficulties that persist through ninth grade (Francis, Shaywitz, Steubing, Shaywitz, & Fletcher, 1994).

In another longitudinal study, Juel (1988) determined that poor readers in first grade, in the absence of intervention, are most likely to be poor readers in fourth grade. Delaying reading services to young children with low achievement scores is problematic whether or not these students are later identified as requiring special education services. The problems are only exacerbated by the ever-increasing gap between the reading achievement of the poor readers and their average-achieving peers as both groups proceed through the grades.

A major educational issue arises at the intersection of the requirements for identifying children as having mild disabilities and the need for early intervention. Given that most mildly disabling conditions are not noticed until a child enters school and that 2 or more years of failure typically go by prior to identification and access to special services, the optimum time for early intervention has passed.

Traditional Options

The traditional options available to address the needs of low-achieving students are grade retention, transitional placements, or remedial services through Title I. In transitional placements, the lowest students are heterogeneously grouped and assigned to pre-first or transitional rooms for an additional year of instruction between kindergarten and grade 1. Research, however, has not supported grade retention or transition programs as effective alternatives (Allington & McGill-Franzen, 1995; Shepard, 1991). As a result, retention and transitional placements are no longer widely used.

Title I (formerly Chapter 1) provides federal funding for supplementary or remedial services in language arts, reading, and math for approximately 10% of elementary and secondary students. Schools with a large percentage (50% or more) of low-income students are eligible for these federal funds. One of the requirements for use of the funds is that the Title I services are provided to children *in addition to* instruction provided to other children in their class, rather than replacing services that are already provided by the school.

Many primary-grade students with reading and writing difficulties receive Title I remedial services throughout their years in elementary school. For others, Title I functions as a "waiting area" in which students are provided interim services until they are performing far enough behind their peers to be eligible for special-education services. In recent years, Title I has been challenged to demonstrate effectiveness in terms of student progress. Interestingly, special education is only accountable in terms of the *number* of individuals who receive special education and related services and is not required to report on the effectiveness of these services.

Teacher Certification and Teacher Competencies

What is special about special education? Audette and Algozzine (1992) found little evidence that differentiated good teaching for students with disabilities from teaching for many other students. In addition, Marston (1987) found that categorical licensure of the teacher did not significantly influence gains made by students with learning disabilities or with educable mental retardation. Although there was extensive variability, observations of students receiving services through Chapter 1 and special education programs indicated that the Chapter 1 programs afforded students greater quantity and quality of reading instruction than did special education programs (Allington & McGill-Franzen, 1989). Particularly noteworthy is that students who were participating in Chapter 1 were favored with greater quantities of reading instruction in their classroom than were students with disabilities who were mainstreamed.

Also of note is the teacher preparation for Title I and special education teachers typically required for state certification at the elementary level. In

Illinois, for example, Title I teachers are required to earn a Reading Endorsement. This endorsement represents the completion of 18 semester hours of coursework beyond the elementary certification. Certification in special education, including learning disabilities, may be attained by the completion of a generic (all academic areas) course in special education methods. Allington and McGill-Franzen (1989) report a similar discrepancy in the educational preparation of remedial reading and special education teachers. In their study, special education teachers reported less preparation in reading than did remedial reading teachers. Long (1995) suggests that differential preparation of reading and special education teachers is one of the barriers to literacy instruction for students with learning disabilities. In the white paper disseminated by the International Reading Association, Long writes:

> Special education teachers are trained to teach special education students, and reading teachers are trained to teach students with reading problems. Special education teachers know how to respond to a student who has a problem processing information. In most cases, a special education teacher does not know how to handle a student who is having difficulty in a core content area. (1995, p. 6)

Generally, one would expect that children with the most severe problems would be taught by the most knowledgeable specialists. In the case of reading, this clearly is not the standard practice. The Division for Learning Disabilities and the CEC are making concerted efforts to highlight the need for increased competencies of learning disabilities teachers in reading and writing (Council for Exceptional Children, 1995b; Graves, Landers, Lokerson, Luchow, & Horvath, 1993). Despite these recent efforts, teacher-preparation programs in special education emphasize consultative/collaborative models. Although increased communication and closer working relationships between general and special education teachers are highly desirable outcomes, special educators need to bring to the partnership exceptional expertise in the teaching and learning of reading and writing. This is, after all, the most problematic area for the overwhelming majority of students who are experiencing failure in schools. As Darling-Hammond (1996) asserts, "Students' right to learn is directly tied to their teachers' opportunities to learn what they need to know to teach well" (p. 6).

CRITICAL DISTINCTIONS

Programs for the prevention of reading and writing failure have been variously incorporated into schools. Programs for preschool children and their parents have been the primary vehicles employed by schools for assisting children who might be at risk of failing to learn commensurate with their peers (e.g., Headstart and Even Start). Once children are school-aged, however, prevention efforts are scarce.

Caplan (1961) proposes a three-pronged system of prevention: *primary, secondary,* and *tertiary.* Pianta (1990) suggests that services in schools may be implemented using Caplan's organizational scheme.

Primary preventive actions are available to all students and are designed to strengthen all of them in a particular area. Comparable to inoculation of all school-aged children against measles, classroom instruction in reading and writing is an example of primary prevention.

Secondary preventions are designed for a select group of students who have a higher probability of experiencing problems in a designated area to eliminate the problem or diminish the anticipated negative effects. Flu shots for the elderly or persons with weak immune systems is an example of secondary preventive actions. Reading Recovery (Clay, 1993) is a school-based, secondary-prevention program for first-grade children who are experiencing difficulties in learning how to read and write. When a student is being considered for referral for a comprehensive evaluation with possible need of special education, school assistance teams design a variety of prereferral interventions. These prereferral interventions are also examples of secondary prevention programs (Gaffney, 1994).

Tertiary prevention consists of services provided once a negative outcome has occurred (i.e., reading and writing failure). Whereas persons who are high-risk for heart problems may exercise regularly, eat a low-fat diet, and require blood-pressure medication (secondary preventions), the onset of a heart attack requires tertiary prevention (e.g., by-pass surgery). The goal of services at this third level is to reduce the residual effects and adverse consequences of the problem. Long-term remedial and Title I programs and special-education services are the most common forms of tertiary programs in schools.

The distinctions among these forms of prevention emphasize that the nature of instruction will vary with the learning goals. Of particular interest is the distinction between conventional instruction and an intervention (Gaffney & Paynter, 1994).

Conventional Instruction and Interventions

Conventional instruction, offered to all students in regular classrooms, is intended to meet the needs of the students across wide-ranging ability levels in all content areas. Alternatively, interventions have a narrow content focus for a designated population. Additionally, conventional instruction is based on continuous service as children proceed through grade levels.

The nature of interventions requires that their duration be short term. Thus the expected outcomes of instruction in a regular classroom are very different from those of a specific intervention. The promise of an intervention is that it seeks to effect existing conditions in such a dramatic way as to change the subsequent course of events, whereas conventional instruction is designed to provide continuous help with a goal of consistent progress. A literacy intervention, therefore, is designed to produce accelerated change, facilitating rapid and dramatic increases in reading and writing performance that will be sustained over time (Gaffney & Paynter, 1994, p. 24).

Whereas all schools provide conventional instruction and special education, the availability of early-literacy interventions remains limited. The vast majority of students experiencing difficulties in learning to read and write are not afforded the opportunity to participate in an intensive intervention prior to placement in long-term remedial or special education programs. One reason that early interventions are not common may be that the concept lacks ownership in many schools.

A dual system of education persists in which classroom teachers maintain responsibility for general education and special education teachers garner the realm of specialized services (Skrtic, 1991). Unfortunately, the dual system has inherent appeal for both classroom and special education teachers. Classroom teachers defer responsibility for teaching students with significant learning and behavior problems to a specialist, which minimizes classroom teachers' need to alter their instruction. Even with the increase in the percentage of students with mild disabilities being *included* in regular classrooms, the teaching of the identified students falls to a Title 1 or special education teacher or teaching assistant who works in the classroom. The current trend is to prepare special education teachers to work cooperatively with class teachers in the classroom setting to meet the diverse needs of students rather than to provide part-time, specialized instruction in resource rooms. This cooperative teaching is often referred to as a collaborative/consultative model. A wide variety of ways have been proposed for general and special education teachers to co-teach in the class settings. Collaborative/consultative models are being enthusiastically encouraged, although no research on their impact on student progress has been reported.

Special education teachers, however, experience increased anxiety about their jobs in a unitary system, in part as a result of ambiguity regarding their changing roles as they shift away from direct teaching of students in resource rooms and self-contained classes. Special education teachers also have less of a control over the environment as they enter into the space domain of class teachers. Finally, special education teachers have expressed concern over a reduced sense of efficacy (i.e., information about the relationship between student learning and their teaching). Without sufficient skill for and time allocated to planning, special education teachers assume responsibilities similar to those of paraprofessionals such as teacher aides rather than professional educators.

Only when *all* educators claim responsibility for *all* students will they develop a systemic, unitary plan that comprises all forms of prevention. Significant and paradigmatic change is needed to make the shifts in educational organizations and practice that are required to impact student progress positively, particularly the progress of the lowest achieving students (Gaffney & Paynter, 1994). Numerous authors have contributed to a rich, research-based description of the kind of school organization and professional development schemes that are required to support teachers' work (see, e.g., Darling-Hammond, 1996; Fullan, 1993; Rosenholtz, 1989).

School cultures influence the important relationships among services. Even when classroom teaching is of the highest quality, some students will require extra support that is responsive to their unique repertoire of skills. Certified teachers with special preparation are necessary to achieve the anticipated results with the velocity expected of an intervention. The intervention itself must be sufficiently robust to meet the challenge of rapid increases in reading and writing performance and sufficiently adaptive to the variability of learning difficulties that are inherent in low-achieving students.

EARLY-LITERACY CURRICULUM THEORY

I have constructed four questions that may be used by teachers and researchers to reflect on their theories and teaching practices. These questions will stimulate discussions among educators as they plan how to implement the most effective conventional instruction, interventions, and long-term remedial and special education services. The goal is to provide optimal opportunities for young children to learn how to read and to write early in their school careers.

1. How do you decide what you will teach?
One's teaching generates from some sources. Identifying these sources may reveal one's theory of teaching and learning. The sources may be, for example, a blueprint of the districts and a curriculum guide to inform goals instructional planning. Sophisticated knowledge of learning progressions of typical students contributes to the information available to expert teachers.

Deep knowledge of the subject is another important source of information. Use of assessment tools influences teachers' decisions in ways that feed information both forward and back. In a feedforward mode, teachers align their instruction to assessment that will be administered in the future. In a feedback mode, teachers systematically collect useful information about student performance to evaluate their teaching effectiveness. In reality, teachers use a combination of sources to guide their teaching.

2. How do you sequence instruction?
Even if there were consensus about what was most important for children to learn to become competent readers and writers, the sequence of instruction may lead to unreconcilable differences. Decisions about sequence are made by teachers moment-by-moment as they attempt to facilitate forward moves by their students:

We blame the programs, the educational system, the material resources, or the children, but almost never do we attribute the result to the sequence of instruction itself creating in a particular child a set of behaviors that are self-limiting rather than self-extending. (Clay, 1979, p. 157)

3. How do you determine what a child has learned daily?

I clearly recall Johnston's (1987) statement that any teacher ought to be able to tell parents what their child learned in reading and writing that day. This question is an attempt to unravel the teaching–learning interaction to ask how we "know" what has been learned by individual children in order to separate it from what has been taught.

4. What are you willing to count as evidence?

Conversations among teachers, researchers, parents, and administrators about credible evidence may illuminate some of the variability in perspectives held in a single community, school, or classroom. Although some teachers and researchers consider decoding a list of nonsense items as the best measure of reading, others give greatest weight to the reading of continuous text. These two tasks may lead to disparate results and, therefore, leverage different teaching programs.

CONCLUSION

In general, research, teacher education, and practice in the area of mild disabilities have been dominated by concerns with definition and identification, especially in the case of learning disabilities. Although 85–90% of students with mild disabilities are experiencing reading and writing difficulties, preservice teachers in special education often are required to take only one course in reading. As teachers increase collaborative endeavors, understanding distinctions among the forms of prevention may assist them in advocating for system change and requesting additional, specialized staff development to add to their present competencies. Finally, discussions of the four questions posed at the end of the chapter by different configurations of teacher groups and community members may reveal areas of instructional strength as well as gaps in the instructional opportunities available to students.

REFERENCES

Allington, R. L., & McGill-Franzen, A. (1989). School response to reading failure: Instruction for Chapter 1 and special education students in grades two, four, and eight. *Elementary School Journal, 89,* 529–542.

Allington, R. L., & McGill-Franzen, A. (1995). Flunking: Throwing good money after bad. In R. L. Allington & S. A. Walmsley (Eds.), *No quick fix* (pp. 45–60). New York: Teachers College Press.

Audette, B., & Algozzine, B. (1992). Free and appropriate education for all students: Total quality and the transformation of American public education. *Remedial and Special Education, 13(6),* 8–18.

Caplan, G. (1961). *Prevention of mental disorders in children.* London: Tavistock.

Clay, M. M. (1979). Theoretical research and instructional change: A case study. In L. Resnick & P. A. Weaver (Eds.), *Theory and practice in early reading* (pp. 149–171). Hillsdale, NJ: Erlbaum.

Clay, M. M. (1993). *Reading recovery: A guidebook for teachers in training.* Portsmouth, NH: Heinemann.

Council for Exceptional Children. (1995a). *CEC Today, 2(6),* 1, 5.

Council for Exceptional Children. (1995b). *What every special educator must know: The international standards for the preparation and certification of special education teachers.* Reston, VA: Council for Exceptional Children.

Darling-Hammond, L. (1996). The right to learn and the advancement of teaching: Research, policy, and practice for democratic education. *Educational Researcher, 25(6),* 5–17.

Ellis, W., & Cramer, S. C. (1994). *Learning disabilities: A national responsibility* (Report of the Summit on Learning Disabilities in Washington, DC, September 20–21). New York: National Center for Learning Disabilities.

Francis, D. J., Shaywitz, S. E., Steubing, K. K., Shaywitz, B. A., & Fletcher, J. M. (1994). Measurement of change: Assessing behavior over time and within a developmental context. In G. R. Lyon, D. B. Gray, J. F. Kavanagh, & N. A. Krasnegor (Eds.), *Frames of reference for the assessment of learning disabilities: New views on measurement issues* (pp. 29–58). Baltimore: Paul H. Brookes.

Fullan, M. (1993). *Change forces: Probing the depths of educational reform.* Bristol, PA: Falmer Press.

Gaffney, J. S. (1994). Reading recovery: Widening the scope of prevention for children at risk of reading failure. In K. D. Wood & B. Algozzine (Eds.), *Teaching reading to high-risk learners: A unified perspective* (pp. 231–246). Needham Heights, MA: Allyn & Bacon.

Gaffney, J. S., & Paynter, S. Y. (1994). The role of early literacy interventions in the transformation of educational systems. *Literacy, Teaching, and Learning, 1,* 23–29.

Graves, A., Landers, M. F., Lokerson, J., Luchow, J., & Horvath, M. (1993). The development of a competency list for teachers of students with learning disabilities. *Learning Disabilities Research and Practice, 8,* 188–199.

Hocutt, A. M. (1996). Effectiveness of special education: Is placement the critical factor? *The Future of Children, 6(1),* 77–102.

Johnston, P. (1987). Teachers as evaluation experts. *The Reading Teacher, 40,* 744–748.

Juel, C. (1988). Learning to read and write: A longitudinal study of fifty-four children from first through fourth grade. *Journal of Educational Psychology, 80,* 437–447.

Lewis, R. B. (1983). Learning Disabilities and Reading: Instructional recommendations from current research. *Exceptional Children, 50,* 230–240.

Long, R. (1995). *Learning disabilities: A barrier to literacy instruction.* Washington, DC: International Reading Association.

Marston, D. (1987). Does categorical teacher certification benefit the mildly handicapped child? *Exceptional Children, 55,* 38–44.

National Center for Education Statistics. (1995). *The condition of education.* Washington, DC: U.S. Department of Education.

National Center for Learning Disabilities. (1996, Summer). Learning to read/reading to learn. *NCLD News.*

Office of Special Education Programs. (1995). *To assure the free appropriate public education of all children with disabilities* (Seventeenth Annual Report to Congress on the Implementation of the Individuals with Disabilities Act). Washington, DC: U.S. Department of Education.

Pianta, R. C. (1990). Widening the debate on educational reform: Prevention as a viable alternative. *Exceptional Children, 56,* 306–313.

Pianta, R. C., & Walsh, D. J. (1996). *High-risk children in schools: Constructing sustaining relationships.* New York: Routledge.

Public Law 94-142. (1975). Education for All Handicapped Children Act.

Public Law 101-476. (1990). Individuals with Disabilities Education Act.

Rosenholtz, S. J. (1989). *Teachers' workplace: The social organization of schools.* New York: Longman.

Skrtic, T. M. (1991). The special education paradox: Equity as the way to excellence. *Harvard Educational Review, 61*(2), 148–206.

Shepard, L. A. (1991). Negative policies for dealing with diversity: When does assessment and diagnosis turn into sorting and segregation? In E. H. Hiebert (Ed.), *Literacy for a diverse society: Perspectives, programs, and policies* (pp. 279–298). New York: Teachers College Press.

PART TWO

PURPOSES FOR READING
AND TALKING
ABOUT BOOKS

CHAPTER SIX

Comprehension Strategies Instruction

MICHAEL PRESSLEY
University of Notre Dame

Much of the discussion at the Wingspread Conference documented in this volume was concerned with basic decoding instruction. An important reason for this was that there were a number of state policy makers at the conference, many of whom were concerned with debates occurring in their states about beginning reading instruction. Several policy makers from California who attended the conference were hopeful that they could leave the meeting with a statement from the researchers present about the nature of effective beginning reading instruction. They were particularly concerned that the statement emphasize the criticality of phonemic awareness and systematic decoding instruction.

What happened at the conference well reflected the larger culture at the time. Many articles on beginning reading had appeared in mainstream periodicals in the several years preceding Wingspread. Indeed, a highly visible article appeared in *Parents* magazine just before the conference convened. This article, circulated at the meeting, examined the whole language approach to beginning reading, suggesting that recent failures in student achievement in reading were due largely to whole language (Levine, 1996). The popular media was especially on the minds of conferees because an education journalist, Richard Colvin of *The Los Angeles Times,* was present throughout the meeting. Like many at the conference, Colvin seemed more aware of the beginning reading debates than of other issues.

In short, the stage was set for the Wingspread Conference to be concerned more with beginning reading instruction, especially the development of word recognition skills, than with other aspects of literacy. Yes, the formal presentations, as reflected by the chapters in this volume, were more diverse, but word recognition was the topic of conversation at the meals, in the hospitality suite, and during walks and bicycle rides along the shore of Lake Michigan, adjacent to Wingspread's campus. Some of the scholars (including me) who made presentations on topics other than beginning reading felt marginalized. I fared better than others, however, because I have made contributions to the beginning reading debate (e.g., McIntyre & Pressley, 1996; Pressley, 1994; Pressley, Rankin, & Yokoi, 1996; Pressley, Wharton-McDonald, Rankin, et al., 1996; Wharton-McDonald, Pressley, Mistretta, & Echevarria, 1996). As a result, I was pulled into some of the many discussions concerning beginning reading.

Because comprehension received so little attention at the conference, I left Wingspread determined that this chapter would be a powerful statement about the need for getting beyond the beginning reading debate. Since the late 1970s, comprehension has been studied intensely by scholars interested in reading education. Researchers at the Center for the Study of Reading (CSR) at the University of Illinois were especially interested in how prior knowledge affects reading comprehension (e.g., Anderson & Pearson, 1984). The most visible work on comprehension strategies instruction to date, research on reciprocal teaching, was begun at the CSR in the early 1980s (Palincsar & Brown, 1984) and continued throughout that decade (Brown & Palincsar, 1989). That the CSR was involved so prominently in research on comprehension is a point that should be made in this context. Once again, CSR, as the organizer of the Wingspread Conference, was attempting to shape a reading instructional research and policy agenda for the nation. I am confident that as CSR researchers continue their work, more than beginning word-level instruction will be considered.

One policy maker who was interested in a broader range of literacy issues than were many of the other policy makers at the meeting, said to me before my talk, "Make certain they get the message about how important comprehension is." I did not succeed in doing that at the conference, given the overarching concern with beginning reading, I kept hearing them in my head as I left the meeting, headed home, and reflected on the events of the Wingspread weekend while sitting in my study. If what follows is convincing, part of the credit belongs to that policy maker; if it does not, the blame is mine.

RESEARCH ON COMPREHENSION STRATEGIES INSTRUCTION: BRIEF REVIEW

There have been three important waves of research on comprehension strategies instruction. The first was the evaluation of single comprehension strategies. The second featured the development of packages of a few strategies that students could be taught to coordinate as they read. These packages were evaluated by the researchers who developed them and generally involved short-term implementation (e.g., 20 lessons). The third wave of research examined what my colleagues and I have termed "transactional strategies instruction" (Pressley, El-Dinary, Gaskins, et al., 1992), which was largely an educator invention, the translation by educators in schools of previous research on comprehension instruction into long-term instruction.

Wave 1: Studies of Individual Comprehension Strategies

Much of the research on comprehension strategies instruction in the 1970s and early 1980s was of the following form: A researcher believed that if students constructed a particular type of representation (e.g., mental images representing the story told in a narrative or summaries) or reacted to texts in a particular way (e.g., relating it to prior knowledge or explicitly seeking clarifications when unsure of meaning), their comprehension and, hence, their long-term memories of text would be improved. The researchers testing these strategies usually had reasons to believe that students were not already engaging in such processing when they read, or that students were doing so less systematically and completely than they could. In these studies, the reading comprehension of students receiving instruction typically was measured by some type of objective test of understanding (e.g., multiple-choice items over literal and implied messages in text). The performances of students receiving comprehension strategies instruction on such tests were compared to the performances of control students who did not receive strategy instruction and who were permitted to read as they normally would in preparation for an objective test. If the strategy-trained students outperformed the control students on the test, there was support for two conclusions: The students (1) probably were not using the trained strategy on their own or were not using it systematically. More positively, (2) they could be taught to use the strategy. For detailed reviews of this work, see Haller, Child, and Walberg (1988), Pearson and Dole (1987), Pearson and Fielding (1991), and Pressley, Johnson, Symons, McGoldrick, and Kurita (1989).

A variety of individual strategies proved their worth in such studies, including prior knowledge activation (e.g., Levin & Pressley, 1981), identification of main ideas (e.g., Brown & Day, 1983; Brown, Day, & Jones, 1983), construction of mental images representing text content (e.g., Gambrell & Bales, 1986; Gambrell & Jawitz, 1993; Oakhill & Patel, 1991; Pressley, 1976), analyzing stories into their story grammar components such as identification of characters, settings, problems, attempts at problem resolutions, and resolutions (Idol, 1987; Idol & Croll, 1987; Short & Ryan, 1984); question generation (e.g., Oakhill, 1993; Rosenshine, Meister, & Chapman, 1996); and summarization (e.g., Armbruster, Anderson, & Ostertag, 1987; Bean & Steenwyk, 1984; Berkowitz, 1986; Taylor, 1982;

Taylor & Beach, 1984). In short, researchers validated strategies that can be applied before (e.g., making predictions based on prior knowledge), during (e.g., imagery generation), and after (e.g., summarization) reading (Levin & Pressley, 1981).

Wave 2: Instructional Studies of Repertoires of Comprehension Strategies

With the development of sophisticated models of thinking specifying that multiple strategies are articulated in making sense of text (e.g., Brown, Bransford, Ferrara, & Campione, 1983; Levin & Pressley, 1981), a theoretical point of departure for the development of comprehension strategies instruction was established that could promote the development of reading competence from the beginning to the end of a reading. A great deal of progress was made in the 1980s and 1990s in determining whether and how students could be taught repertoires of comprehension strategies. To be sure, not all attempts were successes (e.g., Paris & Oka [1986] failure to obtain any effects on standardized measures following 20 lessons), but the successes that occurred, which are summarized in this subsection, were visible and made an impact on educators.

Reciprocal Teaching

"Reciprocal teaching," as defined by Palincsar and Brown (1984), involved teaching students to use four comprehension strategies: prediction, questioning, seeking clarification when confused, and summarization. In Palincsar and Brown's (1984) Study 1, on each of 20 days of intervention, an adult teacher began by discussing the topic of the day's text with the grade-7 students who were the targets of the intervention. The targeted students were capable decoders, but they also experienced comprehension problems. If the passage was completely new, the teacher called for predictions about the content of the passage based on the title. For passages that had been begun the previous day, the teacher called for a review of main points covered thus far. The adult teacher then assigned one of the two students being taught to be the "teacher." Adult teacher and students then read the first paragraph of the day's reading silently. Following the reading, the student teacher posed a question about the paragraph, summarized it, and then either predicted upcoming content or sought clarification if she or he was confused about the ideas in the paragraph. If the student teacher faltered, the adult teacher scaffolded these activities with prompts (e.g., "What question do you think a teacher might ask?"), instruction (e.g., "Remember, a summary is a shortened version"), and modifying the activity (e.g., "If you're having a hard time thinking of a question, why don't you summarize first?"). Students were praised for their teaching and given feedback about the quality of it (e.g., "You asked that question well." "A question I would have asked would have been ... "). Students took turns as the student teacher, with a session lasting about 30 minutes.

Throughout the intervention, the students were explicitly informed that questioning, summarization, prediction, and seeking clarification were strategies that were to help them to understand better and that they should try to use these strategies when they read on their own. The students were also informed that being able to summarize passages and being able to predict the questions on upcoming tests were good ways to assess whether what was read was understood. At the end of each day, the reciprocal teaching participants read a 400- to 475-word assessment passage and then answered 10 questions about the content of the assessment passage.

Reciprocal teaching positively impacted all of the comprehension measures used in the study. The instruction affected processing as it was intended to do so, increasing summarization skills, question-generation competencies, and monitoring, as reflected by the detection of semantic anomalies (Markman, 1977). Importantly, for all six reciprocal teaching students, daily assessment performance jumped shortly after the onset of the reciprocal teaching intervention. For four of the six students in the reciprocal teaching condition, there were striking gains on a measure of standardized comprehension: 15, 17, 20, and 36 months growth for these students. In short, this study provided reason for enthusiasm about reciprocal teaching. Palincsar and Brown (1984, Study 2) also validated reciprocal teaching in a realistic classroom situation, again with middle-school-aged poor comprehenders.

More research on the method followed, summarized by Rosenshine and Meister (1994). There were consistent, striking effects on cognitive-process measures such as those tapping summarization and self-questioning skills. With respect to standardized comprehension, however, the effects were less striking, with an average effect size of 0.3 SDs. Perhaps the most important conclusion to emerge from the Rosenshine and Meister (1994) analysis was that reciprocal teaching was more successful when there was more direct teaching of the four comprehension strategies than when there was not. This conclusion is important in light of subsequent results presented in this section.

Bereiter and Bird's Approach

Bereiter and Bird (1985) collected verbal protocols of reading from good adult readers, who reported a variety of comprehension strategies as they read: restatement or rephrasing of a difficult portion of text, backtracking to seek clarification, demanding relationships (i.e., deciding to watch for causes for effects, reasons, links between topics, particular information that should be in text), formulating a problem and trying to solve it (i.e., by inference, closer examination of text, rejection of information), prediction, imagery, and recall of related information.

In a 6-hour instructional study that followed the verbal protocol study, 80 grade-7 and grade-8 average-achieving readers benefited from being taught to use four of the strategies observed in the first study (restatement, backtracking, demanding relationships, and formulating a problem to solve). The students were taught through teacher modeling and explanation. Increased use of trained strategies from pretest to posttest were clearly evidenced in verbal protocols in the modeling plus explanation condition but not in the control condition. Controls experienced a slight increase in standardized comprehension versus a 2.7 grade-equivalent increase in the modeling plus explanation condition.

Direct Explanation Approach

Roehler and Duffy (1984; Duffy & Roehler, 1989) proposed that effective strategies instruction begins with teacher explanations and mental modeling or by thinking aloud, showing students how to apply a strategy. Following this, students begin to practice the strategies in the context of real reading. Practice is monitored by the teacher, who provides additional explanations and modeling as needed. Feedback and instruction are reduced as students become more and more independent. That is, instruction is scaffolded. Teachers encourage transfer of strategies by pointing out when and where the strategies being learned might be used. They cue use of the new strategies when students encounter situations in which the strategies might be applied profitably, regardless of when these occasions arose during the school day. In other words, scaffolding continues throughout the school day. Cuing and prompting continue until students autonomously apply the strategies being taught.

Duffy et al. (1987) evaluated the effects of direct explanation strategy instruction on the reading of grade-3 students over the course of an entire academic year. All of the skills typically taught in grade-3 literacy instruction were taught as strategies. By the end of the year, students in the direct explanation condition outperformed control students on standardized measures of reading. These results had a profound effect on the reading education community, with direct explanation as Duffy et al. (1987) defined it used subsequently by many educators to implement comprehension strategies instruction in their schools.

Summary

The studies I have summarized compelled the conclusion that reading comprehension strategies can be taught to students. In these studies, direct explanations of strategies, including modeling, were followed by teacher-assisted student practice of the strategies. At least some of the time, the approach produced improvement in reading, including improvement as defined by standardized measures of reading achievement. Educators were inspired by this research to teach repertoires of comprehension strategies.

Wave 3: Studies of Educator-Devised Comprehension Strategies Instruction (Transactional Strategies Instruction)

Beginning in 1989, my colleagues and I set out to study effective, school-based, educator-developed comprehension strategies instruction. Our initial contacts with these programs made clear that comprehension strategies implementation was very different from instructional interventions such as reciprocal teaching. Thus we set out to document exactly how the instruction was being delivered.

Descriptive Studies

We used a variety of qualitative methods in this research, including ethnographies, ethnographic interviews, long-term case studies, and analyses of classroom discourse (Brown & Coy-Ogan, 1993; El-Dinary, Pressley, & Schuder, 1992; Gaskins, Anderson, Pressley, Cunicelli, & Satlow, 1993; Pressley, El-Dinary, Gaskins, et al., 1992; Pressley, El-Dinary, Stein, Marks, & Brown, 1992; Pressley, Gaskins, Cunicelli, et al., 1991; Pressley, Gaskins, Wile, Cunicelli, & Sheridan, 1991; Pressley, Schuder, SAIL Faculty and Administration, Bergman, & El-Dinary, 1992).

Although the instructional programs we studied differed in their particulars, we found that a number of conclusions held across programs. In all of the programs, a small repertoire of strategies were taught, typically including (1) prediction based on prior-knowledge activation, (2) question-generation, (3) seeking clarification when confused, (4) mental imagery, (5) relating prior knowledge to text content, and (6) summarization. In general, students were taught to use strategies to comprehend, interpret, and remember text.

There were also commonalities in the ways that the comprehension instruction occurred:

- Instruction was long-term, occurring optimally over a number of school years.
- Teachers initially explained and modeled the comprehension strategies, generally consistent with the direct explanation approach as described by Roehler and Duffy (1984).
- Following introduction of the strategies, teachers coached students to use them, on an as-needed basis, providing hints to students about when they might make strategic choices. There were many mini-lessons about when it was appropriate to use particular strategies.

- Students modeled use of strategies for one another, for example, thinking aloud as they read. Students explained to one another how they used strategies to process text.
- Throughout instruction, teachers emphasized the usefulness of strategies. Information about when and where various strategies can be applied was discussed often.
- Teachers consistently modeled flexible use of strategies, for example, when they read stories to students.

Much of the strategies instruction occurred in the context of small-group instruction. In particular, the strategies were used as vehicles for coordinating dialogue about text as students read aloud in groups (see especially Gaskins et al., 1993). That is, they were encouraged to relate text to their prior knowledge, talk about their summaries of text meaning as they read, report the images they experienced during reading, and predict what might happen next. As students read aloud, they engaged in and exchanged personal interpretations of and responses to text (Brown & Coy-Ogan, 1993).

Our group described such teaching as "transactional strategies instruction," because it emphasized reader transactions with texts (Rosenblatt, 1978), interpretations constructed by readers thinking about text together (*transacting*; e.g., Hutchins, 1991), and the teacher's and students' reactions to text affecting each other's individual thinking about text. That is, the interactions were transactional (see Bell, 1968). Effective strategies instruction largely occurred in small groups, with the intent being that students would internalize the procedural skills practiced in groups (Pressley, El-Dinary, Gaskins, et al., 1992). Consistent with Vygotskian thinking (Vygotsky, 1978), the assumption was that thinking skills can be developed by engaging in cognitively rich interactions with other people.

In summary, the descriptive studies of transactional strategies instruction established that it involved direct explanations and teacher modeling, followed by guided practice of strategies. Teachers provide assistance on an as-needed basis. That is, strategy instruction is scaffolded (Wood, Bruner, & Ross, 1976). There are lively interpretive discussions of texts, with students encouraged to interpret and respond to text as they are exposed to the diverse reactions of their classmates.

Validations of Transactional Strategies Instruction

The descriptive studies conducted by our group were in anticipation of a comparative evaluation of the educator-developed approach to comprehension strategies instruction. Brown, Pressley, Van Meter, and Schude (1996) conducted a year-long quasiexperimental investigation of the effects of transactional strategies instruction on grade-2 children's reading. Five grade-2 classrooms receiving transactional strategies instruction were matched with grade-2 classrooms taught by teachers who were well regarded as language arts teachers but who were not using a strategies instruction approach. In each classroom, a group of readers who were low-achieving at the beginning of grade 2 were identified.

In the fall of the year, students in the strategies instruction condition and control participants did not differ on standardized measures of reading comprehension and word attack skills. By the spring there were clear differences on these measures, favoring the transactional strategies instruction classrooms. In addition, there were differences favoring the strategies-instructed students on strategies use measures as well as interpretive measures (i.e., strategies-instructed students made more diverse and richer interpretations of what they read than controls).

One of the most compelling differences between the transactional strategies instruction students and control students was that the students who had learned strategies acquired more content from their daily lessons. This was documented when all children in the study read a particular story as part of their regular instruction. When tested later on what they remembered from the story, the strategies instruction students remembered more than did the controls. When students learned comprehension strategies and used them, they got much more from the texts they encountered than did students who were not taught to be strategic as they read.

In addition to the Brown et al. (1996) study, there are at least two other reports of experimental validations of instruction consistent with the transactional strategies approach. Collins (1991) produced improved comprehension in students in grades 5 and 6 by providing them with 3 days of comprehension strategies lessons a week for an entire semester. Her students were taught to predict, seek clarification when uncertain, look for patterns and principles in arguments presented in text, analyze decision making that occurs during text processing, problem solve (including the use of backward reasoning and visualization), summarize, adapt ideas in text (including rearranging parts of ideas in text), and negotiate interpretations of texts with others. Although the strategies-instructed students did not differ from controls before the intervention with respect to standardized comprehension performance, there was a very large difference on the posttest in favor of the treated condition over the control condition.

Anderson (1992; see also Anderson & Roit, 1993) conducted a 3-month experimental investigation of the effects of transactional strategies instruction on reading-disabled students in grades 6 through 11. Students were taught comprehension strategies in small groups, with nine groups of transactional strategies students and seven control groups. Although both strategies-instructed and control students made gains on standardized comprehension measures from before to after the study, the gains were greater in the trained group than in the control condition. Anderson (1992) also collected a variety of qualitative data that supported the conclusions that reading for meaning improved in the strategies-instructed condition: For example, strategies instruction increased students' willingness to read difficult material and attempt to understand it, collaborate with classmates to discover meanings in text, and react to and elaborate text.

Summary and Discussion

Some educators are providing effective comprehension strategies instruction in school. The educator approach to strategies instruction that has received most intensive study has been transactional strategies instruction. In quasiexperimental and experimental tests of the approach to date, transactional strategies instruction has fared well, proving to promote reading achievement.

A question that came up in informal discussions at the Wingspread Conference was how transactional strategies instruction differs from reciprocal teaching, the best-known of the researcher-developed approaches to comprehension strategies instruction. The answer is as follows:

- Both transactional strategies instruction and reciprocal teaching involve teaching of cognitive processes for coming to terms with text.
- Both include modeling and explanation of strategies.
- Both include much discussion of what is being read as students practice strategies.
- Both include teacher scaffolding of instruction—the teacher monitors what is going on and offers supportive instruction on an as-needed basis.
- Both cultivate cooperative, supportive relations during reading.
- The assumption in both approaches is that participating in the instructional group and receiving the scaffolded instruction will result in long-term internalization of the cognitive processes being fostered by the group, so that the teacher is progressively less involved as instruction proceeds.

Nonetheless, the differences between reciprocal teaching and direct explanations-based transactional strategies instruction are striking. Reciprocal teaching conveys four particular comprehension strategies—predicting, questioning, seeking clarification, and summarizing. Direct explanation can be applied with almost any set of strategies. The most important difference between reciprocal teaching and transactional strategies instruction, however, is with respect to the saliency of the teacher. Those committed to reciprocal teaching are committed to reducing quickly the adult teacher's control. The belief is that if students are to internalize decision making with respect to cognitive processes, they need to be controlling the cognitive processes. In contrast, as part of transactional strategies instruction, the teacher is much more visibly in charge—although always with the goal of reducing teacher input. That is, transactional strategies instruction is scaffolded in the sense intended by Vygotsky (1978), with the teacher pulling back as soon as it is possible to do so but not earlier.

An important consequence of the difference in saliency of the teacher in reciprocal teaching and transactional strategies instruction, in our view, favors the direct explanation approach. Reciprocal teaching involves a rigid sequence, with the strategies always executed in the same order. Each time after a portion of text is read, the student leader of the moment poses a question for peers. The peers attempt to respond. Then the student leader proposes a summary. Only then are the other students in the group invited into the conversation, to seek clarifications by posing questions or make predictions about upcoming text. Those who favor reciprocal teaching point out correctly that a great deal of flexible discussion of text and issues in text can be covered with this framework. Moreover, they correctly argue that the particular processes are ones that are critical to comprehension of text (e.g., Baker & Brown, 1984). The flexibility of discussion certainly is greater during transactional strategies instruction, however, with the direct explanation approach in no way restricting the order of strategies execution and less restrictive about which students participate and when. The transactional strategies instructional approach succeeds in stimulating interpretive, engaging discussions among students (see Gaskins et al., 1993).

Summary

Comprehension can be improved through teaching of comprehension strategies. The experimental literature I have reviewed provides plenty of support for explicit teaching of comprehension. In the next section, I make the case that such teaching orients young readers to process texts much as excellent readers do.

THE CONSCIOUS COMPREHENSION
PROCESSES OF SKILLED READERS

Much has been learned about conscious, active comprehension processes by having good adult readers think aloud as they read. That is, researchers have asked adults to read text, stopping every so often to tell exactly what they are thinking and what they are doing as they read. Such conscious decision making during reading often is more obvious when readers read demanding texts, ones difficult for them. Thus the texts read in verbal protocol studies often have been very demanding, requiring a good deal of thought if readers are to understand the messages in them.

Study of Professors Reading

I have some first-hand experience with the verbal protocol method because my students and I carried out a verbal protocol study of skilled reading (Wyatt et al., 1993). In that investigation, 15 professors from the University of Maryland thought aloud as they read articles in their areas of expertise. The articles they selected were ones the professors wanted to read. Although the professors and articles spanned a number of different academic disciplines, there were important similarities that could be identified in their reading.

First, all of the readers were exceptionally active as they read: (1) Based on information in the article they read and on their prior knowledge of the topic of the article, the professors anticipated what might be said later in the article. They were very aware of when their predictions were on target as opposed to when their predictions were in error. (2) In reading the article, they looked for information that was relevant to their personal interests and personal goals. Professors read information that was relevant to their personal goals in reading the text more slowly than they read information they considered to be not so important to their goals. (3) Although the professors generally read the articles from beginning to end, they also jumped ahead to look for information that they thought might be in the article. Sometimes they looked back for additional clarification about a point that seemed confusing at first. (4) The professors explained the ideas in the text to themselves, constructing summaries and reasoning about why what was stated in the text made sense, or in some cases, did not make sense. (5) The professors monitored their reading a great deal. They were aware of how difficult or easy the text was to read. They were aware of whether they already knew the ideas stated in the text. And, they were aware of the portions of text most pertinent to their personal reading goals.

Second, and even more striking than all the activity that occurred during reading, the professors were extremely passionate as they read. They constantly evaluated what they were reading. This was possible because of their extensive prior knowledge. Thus, when the text included ideas near and dear to their hearts, they reacted positively, saying aloud things such as, "Right on," "She's got it!" In contrast were those occasions when text contained ideas that clashed with the reader's thinking. The professors sometimes greeted such ideas with exclamations of disgust (including profanity) or nonverbal reactions, such as giving the article the raspberry. Throughout reading, the professors reported when they were interested and when they were bored. It was very clear that reading was anything but an affectively neutral experience for these readers.

The Many Verbal Protocols of Reading

The think-aloud study my colleagues and I conducted is one of about 50 that have been carried out and published in scientific journals. The exact types of activities reported by readers as they read have varied from study to study, probably reflecting variation in the directions given to participants in different studies as well as the variety of different texts read in different studies. Even so, when Afflerbach and I reviewed the various studies that had been published until 1994, we were able to construct a summary of good reading that cut across the various investigations (Pressley & Afflerbach, 1995).

The readers that Wyatt et al. (1993) studied were not unusual. Active reading is apparent in virtually every verbal protocol study in the research literature. Yes, there is evidence that some readers are more active than others, but, in general, conscious reading seems to be very common. Conscious processing begins before reading, continues during reading, and persists after reading is completed.

Before reading, good readers make certain that they know why they are reading the text and are clear about what they want to get from reading this text (e.g., information about the role of the Indians in the French and Indian War, an understanding of what the professor who wrote this article is doing in his current research, etc.). Rather than simply diving into a text and beginning to read a piece from beginning to end, good readers often overview a text. During the overview, they are sensitive to the structure of the text, especially noting parts of the text that might contain information that is particularly relevant to their reading goal. During overviewing, the good reader begins to relate what is in the text to prior knowledge and to get a summary idea of what is in the text. Good readers make a reading plan in light of the information they obtain during the overview. Often, they pick up enough from the overview to have some hypotheses about the ideas that will be presented and developed in the text. The information gained during overviewing permits the good reader to gauge which parts of the text should be read first, which parts of text should be read more carefully than others, and which parts should not be read at all. Sometimes, overviewing reveals that the text is entirely irrelevant to the reader's goals (e.g., there seems to be nothing new in it about the role of the Indians in the French and Indian War). In this case, a good reader might decide not to read the text any further.

Assuming, based on the overview, the reader does think the text is worthwhile, he or she begins to read from the beginning, varying reading speed from section to section of the text, sometimes skimming and sometimes skipping sections. Sometimes the reader stops and rereads a segment or pauses to think about what was just said. The reader gives much greater attention to information that she or he considers important relative to her or his reason for reading the text. The predictions based on overviewing are updated based on the information encountered in text (e.g., "I knew it, Professor X now realizes that his old approach to this problem was wrong, but he cannot really say it that boldly"). New predictions about upcoming content are also made continuously as the reader processes the text. That is, the good reader draws conclusions throughout reading, although the conclusions remain tentative, subject to change as reading continues.

Throughout reading, good readers make conscious inferences. They try to fill in information gaps in text, attempt to determine the meaning of unknown words, and relate ideas in the text to their prior knowledge (e.g., "That's just like . . . "). They make inferences about the author, for example, her or his intentions in writing the text or the particular sources that the author used. When reading fiction, readers make inferences constantly about the intentions of characters in the story.

Good readers consciously attempt to integrate ideas encountered in different parts of a text (e.g., how the actions of characters in a story are related to the larger story). When reading fiction, early in the reading, they think about the setting and how the characters who are being introduced relate to the setting. The setting is kept in mind as the action proceeds. Readers look for cause-and-effect connections between different parts of text (e.g., how one character's actions early in a story motivated another character's responses later in the story). As part of integrating ideas across text, a reader may review previous text or jump ahead.

Good readers make many interpretations as they read. Sometimes this is apparent in paraphrases (e.g., So this myth is like the Exodus story . . .). They form personal images of the events described in a text. When reading an expository text, they come up with summary comments (e.g., What Professor X really wants to say in this chapter is . . .). Prior knowledge plays a big role in making interpretations. Thus a gender-stereotyped story written in the early 20th century gets a more sympathetic reading from an ardent feminist reader than does a gender-stereotyped story written for the most recent issue of *The New Yorker.*

Processing of text does not conclude when the final word is read. Rather good readers sometimes reread sections or reskim parts that seem especially important. They might try to restate important ideas or state a summary of the text to themselves to make certain the ideas in the text can be recalled later. Sometimes they make notes. They often continue to reflect on a text and what it might mean long after reading is concluded.

The monitoring processes that my students and I witnessed in our study of college professors as they read articles were also apparent in many other verbal protocol studies. Readers are consciously aware of many characteristics of text, from the author's style to the tone of the messages in the text. They are especially aware of whether they are understanding the text and whether such understanding is easy or requires considerable effort. When good readers detect a problem, whether it is in understanding overall meanings in text or knowing the meaning of a particular word in a text, they do what they can to solve the problem.

Finally, just as evaluations were salient in the verbal protocols collected by my colleagues and me, they were salient in many other verbal protocol studies. Readers express feelings as they read. They consciously accept or reject the style of the text (e.g., quality of the writing) as well as the ideas expressed in the text.

Relevance to Elementary Reading Instruction

A great deal of evidence exists to show that good readers are very strategic as they read. Their strategies include overviewing, selectively reading, summarizing, and rehearsing information they want to remember for later. <u>Good readers are highly metacognitive</u>. They are aware of how reading is going and why, for example, when a text is difficult to read through because so many ideas in it are new compared to it being difficult to read through because it is poorly written. Good readers use their prior knowledge as they read to make predictions about what might be reported in text and to understand ideas as they are encountered in text. And, finally, good readers are motivated. They get a charge out of reading. For example, although I did not mention it earlier, the readers in the study conducted by my students and me all reported doing a great deal of reading to stay current in their fields. Those readers and readers in other verbal protocol studies consistently reacted emotionally as they read, agreeing and disagreeing with text, finding reasons for joy and reasons for despair.

So how does this work on skilled reading relate to comprehension strategies instruction? I invite you to recall the specific strategies reported earlier that are taught as part of transactional strategies instruction: prediction, question generation, seeking clarification, mental imagery, relating prior knowledge to text content, and summarization. Compare those strategies with the processes just summarized as exhibited by skilled readers. Skilled readers predict, ask themselves questions as they read, seek clarification when confused, generate mental images, react to text based on prior knowledge, and construct summaries of what they have read for themselves. That is, transactional strategies instruction teachers, in fact, are encouraging their students to process texts the way that good readers process them.

Part of the justification for the creation of the first comprehension instructional packages in the early 1980s was awareness of the processes used by skilled readers (in particular, Bereiter & Bird, 1985). Since that time, there have been many additional verbal protocol studies (Pressley & Afflerbach, 1995). There is now a great deal of evidence to support the assumption of comprehension strategies instruction researchers that encouraging use of comprehension strategies is encouraging children to be active as good readers are active. As crystal clear as this message is from reading the literature reviewed in this chapter, comprehension strategies instruction is still, however, not widespread.

COMPREHENSION INSTRUCTION
THAT IS NOT OCCURRING

Not so long ago, it was recognized that comprehension strategies were not taught in school. Durkin (1978–1979) observed grade-3 through grade-6 classrooms and students, watching for comprehension instruction during reading and social studies. What she observed was that teachers did not teach students how to comprehend. Rather, they asked students comprehension questions after reading to assess comprehension. Basal reader manuals provided little guidance about how to teach comprehension. They did provide much material, such as comprehension questions, to aid assessment of reading comprehension (Durkin, 1981).

All that testing of comprehension did heighten the awareness of reading teachers and researchers that children often do not comprehend well what they have read. For example, Wiener and Cromer (1967) observed that some child readers could decode but could not construct meanings that captured the overall messages in text. Developmental psychologists observed that children in the early elementary grades often did not make straightforward inferences from simple prose (e.g., Paris & Upton, 1976). Other developmentalists documented that young children sometimes missed the main ideas in texts (e.g., Brown & Smiley, 1977).

There were no effective solutions to these text-processing problems. There were, however, study skills procedures that were recommended at the time as means of increasing students' comprehension (Forrest-Pressley & Gilles, 1983). The best-known study skills approach for increasing comprehension was proposed by Robinson (1946), the *SQ3R* method: Students using this approach first *survey* (S) the text and then generate *questions* (Q) about it based on the bold-faced headers in text. They continue by *reading* (first R), *reciting* (second R), and *reviewing* (third R) the text, including attempting to recall it. Although SQ3R was widely recommended, its weaknesses were apparent by the late 1970s and early 1980s. Most notably, SQ3R did not reliably produce much better learning of text than simple reading and rereading (e.g., Johns & McNamara, 1980). Students who lacked background knowledge related to the topic of a reading particularly had difficulty carrying out the method, an evident bottleneck at the elementary level when children are confronted with many texts about unfamiliar topics (e.g., Bean, Smith, & Searfoss, 1980).

In short, by the late 1970s, there was a definite awareness of the need for comprehension instruction. There was also awareness of the need for research on comprehension strategies instruction that would work more certainly at the elementary level than approaches such as SQ3R. As I have documented in this chapter, the research that was needed occurred, and in some schools, comprehension strategies instruction became part of the classroom day.

Even so, when my colleagues and I systematically observed 10 grade-4 and grade-5 classrooms in upstate New York during the 1995–1996 school year, we observed little teaching of comprehension strategies (Pressley, Wharton-McDonald, Mistretta, & Echevarria, 1996). What we observed, instead, was students engaging in a steady diet of uninterrupted, sustained, silent reading, consistent with the whole language emphasis that the route to becoming a good reader is to read, read, read. The evidence reviewed in this chapter, however, is simply the tip of an iceberg of data and conclusions that can be marshaled against the simple practice of reading as a remedy for improving comprehension. In general, when children have been taught to use even one of the comprehension strategies that typify excellent readers, their reading improves (Pressley et al., 1989). When children have internalized repertoires of comprehension strategies, as occurred in the transactional strategies instruction studies, there have been notable improvements even on standardized test performances.

Although the need for comprehension instruction persists in the 1990s, we know better now how to meet that need than we did in previous decades. We also know better now that, in teaching children to use a repertoire of comprehension strategies, we are encouraging them to read as good readers read. There are reasons to doubt that it is a good thing to encourage children to read book after book, article after article, and story after story by starting at the beginning and reading straight through, which is the type of reading observed by Pressley, Wharton-McDonald, Mistretta, et al. (1996). Once the whole language versus decoding skills debate winds down, there is another heated debate on the horizon: Should reading instruction during the later elementary grades emphasize uninterrupted silent reading or should the instruction and encouragement of more active reading be a main focus in grades 3 through 6—and perhaps beyond that?

REFERENCES

Anderson, R. C., & Pearson, P. D. (1984). A schema-theoretic view of basic processes in reading. In P. D. Pearson, R. Barr, M. Kamil, & P. Mosenthal (Eds.), *Handbook of reading research* (pp. 255–292). New York: Longman.

Anderson, V. (1992). A teacher development project in transactional strategy instruction for teachers of severely reading-disabled adolescents. *Teaching and Teacher Education, 8,* 391–403.

Anderson, V., & Roit, M. (1993). Planning and implementing collaborative strategy instruction for delayed readers in grades 6–10. *Elementary School Journal, 94,* 121–137.

Armbruster, B. B., Anderson, T. H., & Ostertag, J. (1987). Does text structure/summarization instruction facilitate learning from expository text? *Reading Research Quarterly, 22,* 331–346.

Baker, L., & Brown, A. L. (1984). Metacognitive skills and reading. In P. D. Pearson, R. Barr, M. Kamil, & P. Mosenthal (Eds.), *Handbook of reading research* (pp. 353–394). New York: Longman.

Bean, T., Smith, C., & Searfoss, L. (1980). *Study strategies for the content classroom.* Paper presented at the 13th annual meeting of the California Reading Association, Newport Beach, CA.

Bean, T. W., & Steenwyk, F. L. (1984). The effect of three forms of summarization instruction on sixth graders' summary writing and comprehension. *Journal of Reading Behavior, 16,* 297–306.

Bell, R. Q. (1968). A reinterpretation of the direction of effects in studies of socialization. *Psychological Review, 75,* 81–95.

Bereiter, C., & Bird, M. (1985). Use of thinking aloud in identification and teaching of reading comprehension strategies. *Cognition and Instruction, 2,* 131–156.

Berkowitz, S. J. (1986). Effects of instruction in text organization on sixth-grade students' memory for expository reading. *Reading Research Quarterly, 21,* 161–178.

Brown, A. L., Bransford, J. D., Ferrara, R. A., & Campione, J. C. (1983). Learning, remembering, and understanding. In J. H. Flavell & E. M. Markman (Eds.), *Handbook of child psychology: Vol. III. Cognitive development* (pp. 77–166). New York: Wiley.

Brown, A. L., & Day, J. D. (1983). Macrorules for summarizing texts: The development of expertise. *Journal of Verbal Learning and Verbal Behavior, 22,* 1–14.

Brown, A. L., Day, J. D., & Jones, R. S. (1983). The development of plans for summarizing texts. *Child Development, 54,* 968–979.

Brown, A. L., & Palincsar, A. S. (1989). Guided, cooperative learning and individual knowledge acquisition. In L. B. Resnick (Ed.), *Knowing, learning, and instruction: Essays in honor of Robert Glaser* (pp. 393–451). Hillsdale, NJ: Erlbaum.

Brown, A. L., & Smiley, S. S. (1977). Rating the importance of structural units of prose passages: A problem of metacognitive development. *Child Development, 48,* 1–8.

Brown, R., & Coy-Ogan, L. (1993). The evolution of transactional strategies instruction in one teacher's classroom. *Elementary School Journal, 94,* 221–233.

Brown, R., Pressley, M., Van Meter, P., & Schuder, T. (1996). A quasi-experimental validation of transactional strategies instruction with low-achieving second-grade readers. *Journal of Educational Psychology, 88,* 18–37.

Collins, C. (1991). Reading instruction that increases thinking abilities. *Journal of Reading, 34,* 510–516.

Duffy, G. G., & Roehler, L. R. (1989). Why strategy instruction is so difficult and what we need to do about it. In C. B. McCormick, G. Miller, & M. Pressley (Eds.), *Cognitive strategy research: From basic research to educational applications* (pp. 133–154). New York: Springer-Verlag.

Duffy, G. G., Roehler, L. R., Sivan, E., Rackliffe, G., Book, C., Meloth, M., Vavrus, L. G., Wesselman, R., Putnam, J., & Bassiri, D. (1987). Effects of explaining the reasoning associated with using reading strategies. *Reading Research Quarterly, 22,* 347–368.

Durkin, D. (1978–1979). What classroom observations reveal about reading comprehension instruction. *Reading Research Quarterly, 15,* 481–533.

Durkin, D. (1981). Reading comprehension instruction in five basal reading series. *Reading Research Quarterly, 22,* 347–368.

El-Dinary, P. B., Pressley, M., & Schuder, T. (1992). Becoming a strategies teacher:

An observational and interview study of three teachers learning transactional strategies instruction. In C. Kinzer & D. Leu (Eds.), *Forty-first yearbook of the National Reading Conference* (pp. 453–462). Chicago: National Reading Conference.

Forrest-Pressley, D. L., & Gilles, L. A. (1983). Children's flexible use of strategies during reading. In M. Pressley & J. R. Levin (Eds.), *Cognitive strategy research: Educational applications*. New York: Springer-Verlag.

Gambrell, L. B., & Bales, R. J. (1986). Mental imagery and the comprehension-monitoring performance of fourth- and fifth-grade poor readers. *Reading Research Quarterly, 21,* 454–464.

Gambrell, L. B., & Jawitz, P. B. (1993). Mental imagery, text illustrations, and children's comprehension and recall. *Reading Research Quarterly, 28,* 264–273.

Gaskins, I. W., Anderson, R. C., Pressley, M., Cunicelli, E. A., & Satlow, E. (1993). Six teachers' dialogue during cognitive process instruction. *Elementary School Journal, 93,* 277–304.

Haller, E. P., Child, D. A., & Walberg, H. J. (1988). Can comprehension be taught? A quantitative synthesis of "metacognitive" studies. *Educational Researcher, 17*(9), 5–8.

Hutchins, E. (1991). The social organization of distributed cognition. In L. Resnick, J. M. Levine, & S. D. Teasley (Eds.), *Perspectives on socially shared cognition* (pp. 283–307). Washington, DC: American Psychological Association.

Idol, L. (1987). Group story mapping: A comprehension strategy for both skilled and unskilled readers. *Journal of Learning Disabilities, 20,* 196–205.

Idol, L., & Croll, V. J. (1987). Story-mapping training as a means of improving reading comprehension. *Learning Disability Quarterly, 10,* 214–229.

Johns, J. C., & McNamara, L. P. (1980). The SQ3R study technique: A forgotten research target. *Journal of Reading, 23,* 705–708.

Levin, J. R., & Pressley, M. (1981). Improving children's prose comprehension: Selected strategies that seem to succeed. In C. M. Santa & B. L. Hayes (Eds.), *Children's prose comprehension: Research and practice* (pp. 44–71). Newark, DE: International Reading Association.

Levine, A. (1996, October). *Parents* report on America's reading crisis: How the whole-language approach to teaching has failed millions of children. *Parents, 71*(10), 63–68.

Markman, E. M. (1977). Realizing that you don't understand: A preliminary investigation. *Child Development, 46,* 986–992.

McIntyre, E., & Pressley, M. (Eds.). (1996). *Balanced instruction: Strategies and skills in whole language*. Norwood, MA: Christopher-Gordon.

Oakhill, J. (1993). Children's difficulties in reading comprehension. *Educational Psychology Review, 5,* 223–237.

Oakhill, J. V., & Patel, S. (1991). Can imagery training help children who have comprehension problems. *Journal of Research in Reading, 14,* 106–115.

Palincsar, A. S., & Brown, A. L. (1984). Reciprocal teaching of comprehension-fostering and monitoring activities. *Cognition and Instruction, 1,* 117–175.

Paris, S. G., & Oka, E. R. (1986). Children's reading strategies, metacognition, and motivation. *Developmental Review, 6,* 25–56.

Paris, S. G., & Upton, L. R. (1976). Children's memory for inferential relationships in prose. *Child Development, 47,* 660–668.

Pearson, P. D., & Dole, J. A. (1987). Explicit comprehension instruction: A review of research and a new conceptualization of instruction. *Elementary School Journal, 88,* 151–165.

Pearson, P. D., & Fielding, L. (1991). Comprehension instruction. In R. Barr, M. L. Kamil, P. B. Mosenthal, & P. D. Pearson (Eds.), *Handbook of reading research* (Vol. 2, pp. 815–860). New York: Longman.

Pressley, G. M. (1976). Mental imagery helps eight-year-olds remember what they read. *Journal of Educational Psychology, 68,* 355–359.

Pressley, M. (1994). Commentary on the ERIC whole language debate. In C. B. Smith (Moderator), *Whole language: The debate* (pp. 155–178). Bloomington, IN: ERIC/REC.

Pressley, M., & Afflerbach, P. (1995). *Verbal protocols of reading: The nature of constructively responsive reading.* Hillsdale, NJ: Lawrence Erlbaum Associates.

Pressley, M., El-Dinary, P. B., Gaskins, I., Schuder, T., Bergman, J., Almasi, L., & Brown, R. (1992). Beyond direct explanation: Transactional instruction of reading comprehension strategies. *Elementary School Journal, 92,* 511–554.

Pressley, M., El-Dinary, P. B., Stein, S., Marks, M. B., & Brown, R. (1992). Good strategy instruction is motivating and interesting. In A. Renninger, S. Hidi, & A. Krapp (Eds.), *The role of interest in learning and development* (pp. 333–358). Hillsdale, NJ: Erlbaum.

Pressley, M., Gaskins, I. W., Cunicelli, E. A., Burdick, N. J., Schaub-Matt, M., Lee, D. S., & Powell, N. (1991). Strategy instruction at Benchmark School: A faculty interview study. *Learning Disability Quarterly, 14,* 19–48.

Pressley, M., Gaskins, I. W., Wile, D., Cunicelli, B., & Sheridan, J. (1991). Teaching literacy strategies across the curriculum: A case study at Benchmark School. In J. Zutell & S. McCormick (Eds.), *Learner factors/teacher factors: Issues in literacy research and instruction: Fortieth yearbook of the National Reading Conference* (pp. 219–228). Chicago: National Reading Conference.

Pressley, M., Johnson, C. J., Symons, S., McGoldrick, J. A., & Kurita, J. A. (1989). Strategies that improve memory and comprehension of what is read. *Elementary School Journal, 90,* 3–32.

Pressley, M., Rankin, J., & Yokoi, L. (1996). A survey of instructional practices of primary teachers nominated as effective in promoting literacy. *Elementary School Journal, 96,* 363–384.

Pressley, M., Schuder, T., SAIL Faculty and Administration, Bergman, J. L., & El-Dinary, P. B. (1992). A researcher–educator collaborative interview study of transactional comprehension strategies instruction. *Journal of Educational Psychology, 84,* 231–246.

Pressley, M., Wharton-McDonald, R., Mistretta, J., & Echevarria, M. (1996). *The nature of literacy instruction in ten grade-4/5 classrooms in upstate New York.* Manuscript under review. Albany, NY: State University of New York.

Pressley, M., Wharton-McDonald, R., Rankin, J., Mistretta, J., Yokoi, L., & Ettenberger, S. (1996). The nature of outstanding primary grades literacy instruction. In E. McIntyre & M. Pressley (Eds.), *Balanced instruction: Strategies and skills in whole language* (pp. 251–276). Norwood, MA: Christopher-Gordon.

Robinson, F. P. (1946). *Effective study* (2nd ed.). New York: Harper & Row.

Roehler, L. R., & Duffy, G. G. (1984). Direct explanation of comprehension processes. In G. G. Duffy, L. R. Roehler, & J. Mason (Eds.), *Comprehension instruction: Perspectives and suggestions* (pp. 265–280). New York: Longman.

Rosenblatt, L. M. (1978). *The reader, the text, the poem: The transactional theory of the literary work.* Carbondale: Southern Illinois University Press.

Rosenshine, B., & Meister, C. (1994). Reciprocal teaching: A review of nineteen experimental studies. *Review of Educational Research, 64,* 479–530.

Rosenshine, B., Meister, C., & Chapman, S. (1996). Teaching students to generate questions: A review of the intervention studies. *Review of Educational Research, 66,* 181–221.

Short, E. J., & Ryan, E. B. (1984). Metacognitive differences between skilled and less skilled readers: Remediating deficits through story grammar and attribution training. *Journal of Educational Psychology, 76,* 225–235.

Taylor, B. M. (1982). Text structure and children's comprehension and memory for expository material. *Journal of Educational Psychology, 74,* 323–340.

Taylor, B. M., & Beach, R. W. (1984). The effects of text structure instruction on middle-grade students' comprehension and production of expository text. *Reading Research Quarterly, 19,* 134–146.

Vygotsky, L. S. (1978). *Mind in society: The development of higher psychological processes.* Cambridge, MA: Harvard University Press.

Wharton-McDonald, R., Pressley, M., & Mistretta, J. (1996) *Outstanding literacy instruction in first grade: Teacher practices and student achievement.* Manuscript under review, State University of New York at Albany, Albany, NY.

Wiener, M., & Cromer, W. (1967). Reading and reading difficulty: A conceptual analysis. *Harvard Educational Review, 37,* 620–643.

Wood, S. S., Bruner, J. S., & Ross, G. (1976). The role of tutoring in problem solving. *Journal of Child Psychology and Psychiatry, 17,* 89–100.

Wyatt, D., Pressley, M., El-Dinary, P. B., Stein, S., Evans, P., & Brown, R. (1993). Reading behaviors of domain experts processing professional articles that are important to them: The critical role of worth and credibility monitoring. *Learning and Individual Differences, 5,* 49–72.

CHAPTER SEVEN

Balanced Instruction and the Role of Classroom Discourse

TAFFY E. RAPHAEL
Oakland University
Rochester, MI

The importance of understanding classroom discourse is underscored in the writings of sociocultural theorists such as Vygotsky (1986) and Wertsch (1991), in the research within sociolinguistic (e.g., Cazden, 1988; Wells, 1993) and sociocognitive (e.g., Almasi, 1995) traditions, and in the many books and chapters that describe effective instructional practices (e.g., Gambrell & Almasi, 1996; Short & Pierce, 1990; Paratore & McCormack, 1997). This combination of forces has highlighted the need for new roles for both teachers and students, particularly more opportunities for students to engage in talk with their teacher and among their peers. Cazden (1997, p. v) notes that student talk is, in fact, receiving more attention today, and "that teachers are trying to both talk less and to talk in different ways." However, Cazden cautions against the danger "that we will slide too easily into yet another pendulum swing, and replace a 'teacher-centered classroom' with a 'child-centered classroom.' ... " Any discussion about classroom discourse—the talk that teachers and students engage in during whole-class, small-group, and one-to-one settings—and its relationship to balanced instruction raises a fundamental question: What is to be "balanced" when we think about classroom talk? In this chapter, I suggest that balance refers to three aspects: (1) balance among those participating in classroom talk: the teacher and students; (2) balance across the content of what is talked about—the curricular areas within literacy as well as between literacy and subject matter; and (3) balance in conversational contexts— whole class, small groups, dyads, and individuals. I begin with a discussion of the theoretical lens that grounds my belief in the importance of classroom discourse. I then draw on my colleagues' and my work within the Book Club Program, laying out a curricular framework that captures the content of classroom talk about literacy. Having set a theoretical and curricular stage, I then turn to this question: What are the contexts and opportunities for teaching this curriculum through classroom discourse?

WHY "TALK"? A THEORETICAL PERSPECTIVE

My interest in classroom discourse grows out of the tenets of sociocultural theory. This theory places language in a central role for human learning to occur, suggesting that we learn through mediation by more knowledgeable others. Through social interactions, specifically sign-mediated interactions (i.e., mediation through symbol systems such as language), humans learn the knowledge base of their cultures. The emphasis this theoretical perspective places on both *language* and *the social construction of mind* is important to understanding today's focus on classroom talk, for it is through talk that learners make sense of their world, and it is through talk that teachers and students construct meaning (Vygotsky, 1978; Wertsch, 1985).

Vygotsky (1978) introduced his general genetic law of cultural development to describe this social- and language-based learning process: "every function in the child's cultural development appears twice: first, on the social level, and later, on the individual level; first, *between* people (*interpsychological*) and then *inside* the child (*intrapsychological*)." Harré (1984) visually represented Vygotsky's genetic law in a model he termed "the Vygotsky Space." Gavelek and Raphael (1996) adapted his model recently to focus on literacy instruction and learning. The Vygotsky Space is created by crossing two axes—public/private and social/individual—to form four quadrants (Q_I through Q_{IV}). Figure 7.1 (top) depicts the four quadrants, whereas 7.1 (bottom) conveys the iterative nature of the process across both quadrants and time.

The public/private vertical axis represents the continuum of *activities* from public (hence, observable or visible) to private (hence, unobservable and available only through inference). The individual/social horizontal axis represents a continuum of the *individuality* of how learned concepts are used from societal or conventional ways to those unique to an individual. Crossing these two axes creates the four quadrants and four processes—appropriation, transformation, publication, and conventionalization—involved in movement among quadrants. The process is iterative: It happens repeatedly, but not necessarily in a single direction or pattern; it is interactive, involving other learners as well as teachers; and it is, as represented in Figure 7.1 (bottom), continual, over time and across settings.

The four quadrants help underscore the importance of creating multiple contexts in which classroom discourse can occur. Some of these contexts

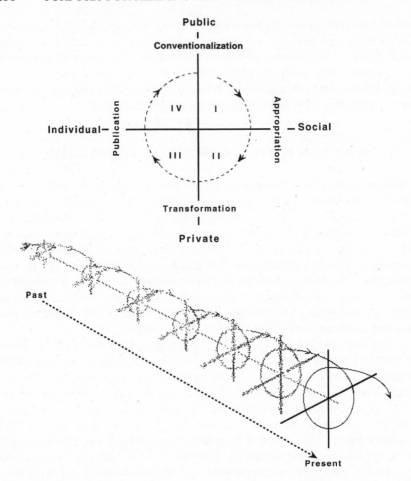

FIGURE 7.1. The Vygotsky Space. From Gavelek and Raphael (1996). Copyright 1996 by *Language Arts*. Reprinted by permission.

should provide sites for students to engage with others in public settings, as they are introduced to new ideas and concepts (in Q_I), or as they have a chance to "go public" (in Q_{IV}) with their ways of appropriating and transforming what they have experienced in these social settings. Further, contexts should allow for students to engage in private use of what they have experienced in the public settings, opportunities to appropriate the use of their experiences, in the social way in which they were introduced as well as to transform their experiences in their own unique ways. Across contexts, classroom talk becomes the means by which ideas are exchanged as well as an important information source for students as they individually construct meaning. A question that logically follows, then, concerns what classroom participants talk about, the focus of the next section.

TALK ABOUT "WHAT"? A CURRICULAR QUESTION

What do we want teachers and students to talk about during classroom talk? In the public quadrants of the Vygotsky Space, teachers and students engage in talk to promote students' literacy development. Teachers are responsible for introducing students to, and further developing their understandings of, the knowledge, strategies, and skills available to fluent readers and writers. Although the content of classroom literacy talk varies across grade levels, research about literacy instruction suggests that students need to understand how our language systems—written and oral—work, how to build upon what they know to construct meaning, and the nature of the literature they are reading.

My colleagues and I have been engaged in a line of research exploring alternative approaches to literacy instruction (see McMahon & Raphael, 1997; Raphael & McMahon, 1994; Raphael, Goatley, McMahon, & Woodman, 1995). In one of our studies, we examined what teachers and students in a fourth- and a fifth-grade classroom talked about during both formal instructional events as well as informal discussions about text. The study (see Raphael & Goatley, 1994) helped us identify four key curricular areas: (1) language conventions, (2) comprehension, (3) literary elements, and (4) response to literature, consistent with others' research (also known as our "common knowledge") related to literacy instruction (see Table 7.1).

The *language conventions* curricular area detailed in Table 7.1 emphasizes how our language works: the symbol system, written forms and genres, and oral language and rules for interacting around literary texts. For younger students, introducing them to the way in which our written symbols relate to their already familiar oral language is critical. For all students, learning conventional spelling and grammatical systems is helpful. The content may vary across grades, but the overall focus within this curricular area is helping demystify our written and oral language systems.

A second key curricular area detailed in Table 7.1 is *comprehension instruction*, which includes the knowledge, strategies, skills, and dispositions that help readers construct meaning and interpret text. Research in the 1970s and 1980s helped us understand that, just as we can demystify how our written language system works, we can demystify the processes skilled literacy users engage in when constructing meaning as they read and write (see Dole, Duffy, Roehler, & Pearson, 1991; Pearson, 1986; Pearson & Stephens, 1993; Tierney & Cunningham, 1984). In Table 7.1, I distinguish among three aspects of the comprehension curriculum: background knowledge, text-processing strategies, and monitoring or control strategies.

The third key curricular area, *literary elements*, draws from the extensive research within a literary theory tradition, detailing the craft that underlies text creation. With the increase in literature-based literacy instruction, teachers should honor the literature they are using to avoid turning "literature use" into "literature abuse." Eeds and Peterson (1995, p. 11)

TABLE 7.1. Book Club Curriculum Chart

Language conventions	Comprehension	Literary elements	Response to literature

Sound symbol
  Spells conventionally
  Reads with fluency
Grammatical conventions
  Uses appropriate
    language choices:
    Verbs
    Syntax
    Punctuation
  In oral reading,
  discussion, and
  writing
Interaction conventions
  Works with peers
    to set goals
  Interacts with peers
    in literacy contexts:
    Writing
      conferences
    Literary circles
    Author's chair
	Background knowledge
	  Prediction
	  Draws on prior
	    knowledge
	  Builds knowledge
	    if needed
	  Context clues
	  Intertextual
	    connections
	Text-processing strategies
	  Summarizing
	  Sequencing
	  Vocabulary
	  Organizing and
	    drawing on text
	    structure
	    knowledge
	  Analyze/develop
	    characters,
	    setting, plot
	    sequence, and
	    so forth
	Monitoring
	  Asking questions
	  Clarifying
	    confusions
		Theme
		  Authors'
		    purposes
		  Connections to
		    life
		Point of view
		  Characters' POV
		  Authors' POV
		Structure
		  Story structure
		  Expository
		    structures
		  Types of
		    genres
		  Tension
		Character
		Place
		Time
		Authors' craft
		  Style
		  Text features
		  Symbolic
		    language
			Personal response
			Impressionistic response
			to literature, one's own
			writing, or the writing
			of peers
			  Shares experiences
			  Shares personal
			    feelings
			  Places self in
			    situation
			  Compares self to
			    characters
			Creative response
			  "Play" in response to
			  literature
			    "What if?" [change
			    event in story plot
			    and explore impact]
			  Dramatizing events,
			    characters' attitudes
			    or actions
			  Illustrations of events,
			    characters
			Critical response
			  Analytic response to the
			  "effectiveness,"
			  "purpose," or
			  "coherence";
			  intertextual connections
			    Explain changes in
			    beliefs or feelings
			    Evidence from text to
			    support ideas
			    Critique texts using
			    specific examples
			    Discuss author's
			    purpose
			    Identify author's craft
			    Discuss author's
			    purpose
			    Uses text as mirror of
			    one's own life and
			    as window into the
			    lives of others

suggest that an "increase in awareness of how various authors use literary elements within particular stories enables readers to enter even further into a story world and greatly enrich their reading experiences." By focusing on literary elements—theme, point of view, structure, character, place, time, and author's craft—readers' perspectives may be changed, and taken-for-granted ideas and prevailing social practices can be examined critically.

The fourth curricular area is *response to literature*—personal, creative, and critical. Personal response is the readers' aesthetic response, or "lived-through experience," that Rosenblatt (1991, 1985) has detailed in her transactional theory of reader response. In other words, it is the readers' impressionistic response to the text, often one that occurs during the first reading. Creative response is characterized by the readers' "play" with the literature, as readers place themselves in the situations of the text and relive the experiences, change events in the story in a mental, "what if?" sort of play, creating illustrations of imagined events, and so forth. Critical response is the more analytical examination of readers' response in light of specific literary elements, their lived experiences, and those of others.

Understanding these four aspects of the curriculum provides readers and writers with the language and literacy tools and knowledge base to draw upon during classroom talk about text. This "common knowledge" provides the fuel for them to be able to share their response in coherent and meaningful ways and to raise important questions—whether of author's intent or for clarifying confusions. Dialogue with others about the literature read can "help put events and relationships into a new light, and the interpretations of others can change our own ideas of what we think a story is really about" (Eeds & Peterson, 1995, p. 13). Thus, these four areas can guide teachers in working with students to help them become literate.

OPPORTUNITIES FOR EDUCATIVE CLASSROOM TALK ABOUT TEXT

According to the theoretical perspective outlined above, language-mediated social interactions are the means by which learners develop knowledge and skills, in general. This principle applies directly to literacy learning in today's classrooms, for it is through classroom talk—about language conventions, comprehension, literary elements, and response to literature—that literacy learning occurs. In this section, I describe general features of classroom talk and an instructional model, Book Club, for creating meaningful contexts for talk about text. I use specific examples drawn from a Book Club classroom to illustrate how talk is used to promote students' literacy and subject matter learning.

Features of Classroom Talk

Classrooms have a variety of public/social spaces (Q_I of the Vygotsky Space) that lend themselves to conversations about literacy. This talk can be described in terms of both *content* and *turn-taking patterns* as well as who *controls* the topics and turns (see Erickson & Schultz, 1982; Raphael & Hiebert, 1996). Topics to promote literacy learning may be determined by the curriculum framework, the teacher's in-the-moment decision-making, the students' suggestions during lessons and activities, or some combination of these. Similarly, turns can be teacher-controlled, student-controlled, or shared by both. These different ways in which turns and topics are controlled in classrooms is often dependent on the teachers' role during classroom literacy events (Cazden, 1988).

Raphael and Hiebert (1996) define four different roles teachers employ: (1) explicit instructor, (2) scaffolder, (3) facilitator, and (4) participant. These roles represent, in decreasing order, the degree to which the teacher is "in charge." Teacher as explicit instructor has long been the teachers' primary role. Cazden (1988) describes one of the most common participation structures that characterizes classroom talk when the teacher assumes this role. This pattern is the initiation–response–evaluation (I–R–E), or as Wells (1993) has called it, the initiation–response–feedback (I–R–F) structure. The teacher initiates the question, selects a student to respond from among those who have their hands raised, then evaluates or provides some other form of feedback to the response and begins the process again. This participation structure has been criticized for its highly prescribed and limiting format; for emphasizing comprehension, conventions, and plot but missing opportunities to feature literature as the object of analysis; and for being artificial–unlike any form of authentic discourse in which people asking questions usually do so because they seek answers they do not already have in mind. However, as Raphael and Hiebert (1996) and Wells (1993) suggest, under some circumstances, and if used judiciously, it can be an effective talk structure.

If classrooms are not to be dominated by the teacher in a single role and a single participation structure, other ways of encouraging classroom discourse need to be identified. In literacy instruction, specifically, these participation structures should promote students' learning about the literature and their reflection on the content of the literature as both a mirror of prevailing practices in our society and cultures and a window into distant people, places, and times (Cullinan & Galda, 1994). Further, teachers should be able to instruct through modeling and scaffolding, not merely through "telling," and they should be able to participate in ongoing classroom conversations about books, sometimes as facilitators of these conversations to maintain a fluid discussion among 25 or more participants, sometimes as a participating member with no leadership responsibilities.

The Book Club Project, which began in fall 1989, and ended in spring 1996, was a collaborative public school–university effort designed to create an alternative context for literacy instruction. It was grounded in sociocultural principles that emphasize the importance of language and social interaction in learning. The focus of the project was both curricular–expanding the curriculum focus to include literary elements and response to literature— as well as on emphasizing classroom talk that did not rely on traditional I–R–E participation structures. Instead, the program was designed to encourage talk in large and small groups, with shared teacher and student responsibility for the control of topics and turns and with teachers assuming multiple roles as members of the conversational community.

As such, Book Club classrooms provide a rich source of information about the possibilities for classroom talk about literacy and literature and about ways to encourage and support student talk about text. I begin by briefly describing the program components. Then I present examples of conversations about text that occurred in spring 1995, as members of Laura Pardo's fifth-grade classroom explored the broad issue of human rights as they studied the Civil War, then read historical fiction set during that era.

The Book Club Program

The Book Club Program has, as its central component, small student-led discussion groups called "book clubs." Students' participation in their book clubs is supported by three additional components: *reading*, *writing*, and a whole-class setting called *community share* (see Figure 7.2). The instructional curriculum is designed to teach students the knowledge, skills, strategies, and dispositions they would need to engage successfully in these four components. Talk about text—text created by the students themselves as well as published texts—is emphasized through the book club and community share components.

Community share serves a dual purpose: (1) as a site for whole-class instruction and (2) as a site for whole-class discussions. During community share, teachers can explicitly instruct students in new strategies, literary elements, reading log formats, discussion strategies, and so forth. The content of these lessons is generally driven by the Book Club curriculum, depicted in Table 7.1, or by specific needs that teachers identify through their observations of students' oral and written language participation. Teachers can also use community share as a time to read aloud to their students, providing an opportunity to model and think aloud about the invisible processes that underlie fluent reading. It can be a site to summarize earlier chapters as students move through their book club book, to clarify

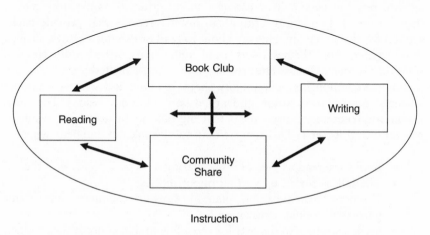

FIGURE 7.2. The Book Club Program.

confusions, and to make predictions about upcoming story events. And, of course, community share is an important context for students and their teacher to share ideas that have emerged through their book club discussions as well as their individual reading and reflection. As such, community share is an important public space within the classroom.

A second component that supports students' book clubs is *reading*. Students in each book club always read the same book. Sometimes, this means that multiple thematically related titles are read and discussed within the classroom; at other times, students across all book clubs read the same title from a whole-class set. Students primarily read silently, though sometimes they elect (or are permitted) to read with a buddy or in small groups, or follow along as the teacher reads to them. Some genres, such as poetry or short stories, lend themselves to choral reading or readers' theater. Students sometimes take books home for reading with and to family members. Finally, students' reading is often supplemented by the teacher reading aloud, sometimes from a theme-related novel (particularly important when each book club is reading a separate book); sometimes from a chapter in the book the students are reading (when, as a class, they all read the same book). In addition to their book club book, for sustained silent reading, students can select thematically related texts displayed in the classroom, or from the broader classroom, school, home, or city libraries. Instruction in reading-related strategies occurs during community share, and the strategies are then practiced during silent reading or as students respond to their texts in their reading logs, part of the writing component of the program.

The writing component consists of short- and long-term writing activities. Short-term writing, such as daily reading log entries, can be teacher-directed (e.g., How to you think Park and Thanh will interact with each other, now that the secret is out?). However, most of the time, students are encouraged to respond personally, creatively, and/or critically as the story moves them to do so. Long-term writing can involve reports that provide background for the novels students are about to read or extended essays, such as those written about themes, intertextual connections, or text-to-life connections that students discuss after reading one or more related texts.

These components—community share, reading, and writing—support students' participation in the student-led book club discussions. They also instantiate recommendations for enhancing talk about texts. For example, Martinez and Roser (1995) suggest that good book talk happens when:

- Books are read as part of units sharing a focus, a topic, or a theme;
- The talk is fueled by writing opportunities;
- Teachers have a flexible plan for how to encourage talk about particular content or themes;
- Students return to the text for rereading and to support their points;
- Students have experienced models who offer genuine responses to the story.

Community share provides the critical site for adult models as well as adult-guided modeling on the part of peers, whereas book club groups provide sites for peer modeling. Students' writing log entries help fuel these conversations. The reading component *during* the Book Club period, and the expectations that students bring both their book and their log entry to each book club discussion, underscores the importance of returning to the text. Finally, Book Club units are framed in terms of a broad theme (e.g., human rights, facing challenges). The activities range from public to private, and students have the chance to use what they have experienced socially as well as to transform these experiences individually.

Classroom Talk to Promote Literacy Learning

We now turn to Laura Pardo's fifth-grade classroom, spring 1995, as she and her students engage in a thematically organized interdisciplinary unit connecting literacy and social studies instruction. Students participate in a 2-week research unit where they work in a variety of grouping arrangements—whole class, small groups, pairs, individually—to study events, people, and contributing causes of the Civil War. They then engage in a 3-week book club unit where they read one historical novel chosen from among four titles: *Shades of Gray* (Reeder, 1989), *Turn Homeward Hannalee* (Beatty, 1984), *Who Comes with Cannons?* (Beatty, 1992), and *Behind Rebel Lines* (Reit, 1988). Throughout the unit, the students listen as Laura reads aloud from Hunt's (1964) *Across Five Aprils*, also set during the Civil War.

The unit provides multiple opportunities for educative talk—between teacher and students in the public/social spaces of the classroom (Q_I), and among students (Q_{IV})—talk that highlights both the four literacy curricular areas and the social studies curriculum and that involves the teacher in roles from explicitly instructing to participating as a member of the conversational group. Patterns of interaction vary across these groups, from primarily teacher- to primarily student-controlled. Table 7.2 lays out a taxonomy of classroom talk in terms of the location of control over content and turn-taking with illustrations of literacy events that characteristically reflect the different patterns.

I examine talk organized around the roles Laura plays within various settings and purposes for classroom talk. I begin with teacher-led talk. First, I discuss a transcript of Laura explicitly instructing students about criteria for creating good inquiry questions. Then, I present three examples in which the teacher-led talk involves scaffolding and modeling, rather than explicit teaching. The first example is teacher modeling during a read-aloud; the second, scaffolding during a comprehension lesson within the context of an activity to activate and build background knowledge related to the Civil War; the third, scaffolding during a mini-lesson on question-asking in reading logs and during Book Club discussions, which builds upon students' experiences with inquiry questions. I then turn to student-led talk, drawing

TABLE 7.2. Overview of Classroom Talk during Literacy Instruction

Control	Context	"Event" or "teacher role"
Teacher control of topic and turn	Whole-class context: community share	• Teacher read-aloud • Teacher as explicit instructor

Shared responsibility: turns and/or topics	Whole-class context: community share
	Small-group context: book clubs
		• Teacher as scaffolder
		  • Teacher revoices students' earlier contributions to give additional visibility or emphasis
		  • Students raise questions
		  • Teacher rewords and extends students' comments
		  • Teacher questioning
		• Teacher as facilitator
		  • Support turn-taking
		  • Repeat students' comments
		  • Redirect students' question to peers
		• Teacher-control of initial topic through reading log prompt
		• Teacher intervenes during small-group discussion

Student control of topic and turn	Whole-class context: community share Small-group context: book clubs	• Teacher as participant • Student-led discussions

extensively from one Book Club group's discussion of *Turn Homeward Hannalee.*

Talk during Explicit Instruction: Evaluating Inquiry Questions

The first example of classroom talk features Laura in the role as explicit instructor as she introduces students to the idea of distinguishing between higher- and lower-quality inquiry questions. Occurring within the first quadrant of the Vygotsky space, this lesson illustrates a classic way in which discourse within this quadrant occurs. This is the second day of their study of the Civil War. Students are going to generate what they *wonder* about, creating questions that will later be used to guide their reading, small group inquiry, and individual research projects. Thus, being able to generate workable inquiry questions is important to the overall success of the 2-week research unit. Laura opens the lesson by reminding them of their work the previous day, recorded in the first column of a wall chart and of their prior experience in similar activities (lines 1–3).[1]

1   Laura: Okay, we talked about the things that we *know*. . . . We have
2   quite a few things up there, but there's a lot of stuff that we *don't*

3   know. There's probably some stuff as I read the story [reference
4   to *Across Five Aprils*, the read-aloud book] that is coming to
5   your mind about what you might *want* to know. Before we put
6   some questions on our chart, though, I want to look at what
7   some good questions might be and what some bad questions
8   might be. (*overhead projector displays examples of questions*)

9   LAURA: We've [done similar activities] before, and we just kind of
10   brainstormed all of our questions. This time because we want to
11   use them for our inquiry, I want us to think about really good
12   questions. So, I'm going to give you an example of some
13   questions that aren't very good questions, and let's talk about
14   why they *aren't* very good inquiry questions. What does that
15   question say? (*points to first question on overhead*)

16   Ss: (*several respond orally*) How many people died in the war?

17   LAURA: Why is that not a good question for inquiry?

Three students respond to the question. Arturo suggests you can simply
look it up in a book, Thea offers that it's hard to pin down an exact answer,
and Derek responds that it could be answered right away. Laura nods, then
reinforces the idea that it is not worthy of a full-inquiry project. She asks,
"How many sentences would it take you to tell the answer to that
question?" Several students call out responses to the effect that it would
be really short, not take much time, and so forth. Laura encourages this
commentary, highlighting that although a question might be "interesting,"
it may not be a good inquiry question (lines 27–28).

18   MEG: Not even a *sentence!*

19   LAURA: Maybe not even a sentence (*nodding toward Meg*), maybe just
20   a number? So could you write a whole report on just that
21   question?

22   Ss: (*in unison*) Nooo.

23   LAURA: Could you write a paragraph even?

24   Ss: Nooo.

25   . . . .

26   LAURA: There's not enough there to do any inquiry. It might be
27   interesting, and we might come across that information when
28   we're studying. . . . That's interesting, but it's not a good question
29   to do our inquiry around.

Julianne then offers what she thinks may be a good inquiry question,
and Laura uses her question as an opportunity to reinforce the notion that
one criterion for a good inquiry question is that it would take "a lot of
sentences" (line 37) to answer.

30 JULIANNE: What about the question, like, uh, "Where were some of
31   the battles at?"

32 LAURA: (to class) What do you think about that, "Where were some
33   of the battles at?" . . . What do you think about that, is it a good
34   question?

35 JULIANNE: (inaudible) list of battles.

36 LAURA: All right, Julianne says, you'd have to list a bunch of battles,
37   and it would take a lot of sentences to do that. . . . Do you think,
38   "Where were some of the battles?" is a better question than,
39   "How many people died?"

The next criterion Laura introduces is the degree to which the question
will help students generate new knowledge.

40 LAURA: Definitely. Let's look at another one.

41 KAMI: (can hear some others as well as read from chart) "Which side
42   won the war?"

43 LAURA: Good question?

44 Ss: Nooo.

45 MEG: Bad!

46 LAURA: Meg?

47 MEG: Because we already know!

48 CHARLES: The North won the war.

49 LAURA: So we don't want to write questions down that we know the
50   answers to; then it doesn't help us to learn new information. If
51   my goal is to have you learn about the Civil War, I want you to
52   learn new stuff. If you already know who won the war, that
53   wouldn't be a good use of our question.

To reiterate the importance of inquiry for generating new knowledge,
Laura turns to the next question, asking Arturo to read, "Did the North
fight the South?" Many students start to laugh and comment, and Bruce
says, "We already know that!" Laura points to the first column on the wall
chart and reads a line that shows that students already knew that the North
won. She then asks Muhammad to read the next question, "When did the
war start?" Laura uses this question to illustrate that although, like the first
question they had discussed, it may be important to know, it does not lead
to inquiry. She then asks Derek to read the next question, "What was an
average soldier's life like in the Civil War?" Several students say that this
is a good inquiry question. Julianne notes that this is a question that you
could write a lot about. Other voices are heard as well, saying things such
as "like a diary" and "lots of information." Laura repeats "like a diary"

and then elaborates with related wonderings: "What did he do during the day?" "How did he fight?" "What was his uniform like?" "What kinds of weapons did he have?" "What did he eat?" She then summarizes, "Good questions make you think of more questions."

In her role as explicit instructor, Laura uses classroom talk to develop a particular area of knowledge—in this case, creating inquiry questions. She is responsive to students' comments, engages them as contributors to the classroom talk, but does not permit the talk to move away from the central focus. Through this talk, she establishes three criteria that will guide her students throughout the inquiry unit as they develop and then conduct research to answer their questions. By the end of the lesson, she will have taught students to judge the quality of their questions by considering the degree to which (1) they require depth of response, (2) they lead to new knowledge generation, and (3) they raise other questions. The degree to which they learned what was taught will be reflected in the quality of questions they generate.

"Modeling" Talk during Teacher Read-Aloud

Reading aloud to students is an important public and social space within the classroom during which teachers can model the invisible processes that underlie successful reading through thinking aloud as they read and inviting students' comments about the text. Similar to the case within explicit instruction, teachers reading aloud to their students generally control turn-taking, though the topic of the discussion may stem from either teachers' or students' responses. However, it is still generally within the teachers' control to determine which topics students raise get the floor. The following segments of classroom talk occurred as Laura read aloud from *Across Five Aprils*. I draw on segments that illustrate Laura's talk (1) to highlight colloquial expression and dialect, (2) to clarify potentially confusing sections of text, (3) to highlight clues to characterization, and (4) to elicit predictions. Her choice of this book as the read-aloud stemmed from its relevance to the unit theme and from her awareness that the text would be somewhat challenging for most of her students to read on their own.

Highlighting Colloquial Expressions. The text of *Across Five Aprils* is rich in colloquial expressions and dialect, an author's craft that Laura has emphasized in various ways. In the following short segment (italicized text indicates words read aloud from the book), notice how she picks up on a student's comment (line 7), using this as an opportunity to highlight a colloquial expression. This illustrates how a topic can be introduced by one of the students, yet still remain under the teacher's control. At this point in the story, Jethro has found Eb, a close friend who has deserted the army. Eb is hiding on Jethro's family's property, which creates suspense for the reader. Will Jethro help his friend? Will he obey the law and report him? Eb, himself, does not know what to do.

1   LAURA: So he's saying, what if I go back? *Jethro sat for a while trying*
2   *to think of some way out of the situation. It appeared more*
3   *hopeless the more he thought. He was frightened. . . . I think*
4   *you'd best eat all you can and rest for a spell. We'll think of*
5   *what's to be done when once you get a little stronger.*
6   S: (*whispering*) Rest a spell?
7   LAURA: "Rest a spell"? What do you think that means?
8   Ss: Rest for a little bit, a little while.
9   LAURA: Rest for a little while, for a little time. *You all but fooled me*
10   *into believing something could be done. . . . Jethro turned away.*
11   I'll bring you a quilt from Nancy's before I go in for the night.
12   . . . Does Jethro sound like he has any indication of turning him
13   in?

Highlighting Potential Confusions. As Laura continues reading, she inserts a brief question to make sure that students understand Jethro's dilemma and the clues the author is providing about the direction his decision is likely to take (lines 12–15). After reading a few more minutes about Eb and why he had deserted, Laura pauses to make a connection from this segment of the text to an earlier discussion they had had during community share. The students had identified the treatment of deserters as one of the issues important to the Civil War. Their treatment was one example of the human rights issue that framed the unit and thus something that Laura and the students discussed frequently.

14   Ss: No
15   LAURA: Not at all. He's bringing him food and blankets. *He walked*
16   *back to his waiting team. . . . But in his 11 years, he had never*
17   *been faced with the responsibility of making a fearful decision*
18   *like the one confronting him. The authority of the law loomed*
19   *big in his mind. . . .* Now he's beginning, Jethro, to look at this
20   issue of desertion. Jethro before always thought desertion was
21   wrong. You signed up, you should go, but now when he sees Eb,
22   he's not so sure. *How do I know what I'd be like if I were sick,*
23   *scared. . . . Eb has been in battle for 2 years . . . a war that has*
24   *no end in sight. . . .* He's doing all this talking inside his head,
25   isn't he? He's thinking about, do you think he's trying to decide
26   whether he should turn in Eb?
27   Ss: Yep, yes.
28   LAURA: He's thinking about this whole *issue.*

Highlighting Literary Elements: Characterization. Laura also uses the read-aloud as a time to highlight literary elements, from point of view (e.g., implicit in her comment in lines 24–26) to characterization. Notice her side comment in line 33 as she pauses to highlight how the author conveys something about Jethro's personality, his sarcasm.

29	LAURA: *What was it that man said the day of the barn raising? It's*
30	*good that you're a boy and don't have to worry yourself about*
31	*this war. Well yes, no doubt about it. Eleven-year-old boys ain't*
32	*got a thing to worry about; this year of 1863s a fine, carefree*
33	*time for an eleven-year-old boy.* . . . He's gotten pretty sarcastic,
34	isn't he? He's not carefree. He's got lots of things to worry about.

Highlighting Prediction Strategy. The fourth segment I present simply sets the stage for a common teacher-invited conversation during read-alouds: engaging students through predictions. Because a key event for Jethro involves his writing to President Lincoln about his dilemma and receiving a reply, Laura sets the stage for students to attend to the event through a simple question (lines 42–43).

35	LAURA: *Mr. Lincoln was a man that looked at problems from all sides.*
36	*Mr. Lincoln was not a far-away man like General McClellan or*
37	*Senator Sumner or Secretary of State Seward.* You met Secretary
38	of State Seward in *The Blue and the Gray.* He was the man who
39	did a lot of talking whenever they met with the President. *Mr.*
40	*Lincoln had plowed fields in Illinois. He had thought of the*
41	*problems.* . . . *But would one dare? A nobody? A boy on a*
42	*southern Illinois farm? Would he dare?* Dare what? What's he
43	thinking of doing?

Many students' voices are then heard, conveying their belief that Jethro will be writing to President Lincoln. They then debate whether or not Lincoln will reply, and Laura prompts this discussion by asking them if they wrote to the President today, would they receive a reply. The discussion continues as Laura closes the book for the day, and students ask her to continue reading. Enthusiasm for the next day's reading has been established, potential confusions in the challenging text have been averted, and some of the author's craft in characterization (e.g., Jethro's sarcasm), point of view (e.g., Jethro's changing thoughts on desertion), and colloquial expression (e.g., "rest a spell") have been highlighted.

Both the explicit lesson on inquiry questions and the read-aloud illustrate the importance of teacher-controlled talk within the class. The inquiry question example illustrates how, through teachers' explicit talk, students can be introduced to conventions that support their learning. The example illustrates how, through teacher talk, students can be provided with a window into otherwise invisible cognitive and social processes. In the next two examples, I present teacher talk in which, although the teacher still does much of the talking, there is more interactive talk and co-construction of knowledge among teacher and students. The teacher's role is one of scaffolder.

"Scaffolding" Talk: Building Background Knowledge

During the March 30th community share, on one of the first days of the thematic unit related to the Civil War, Laura has begun an activity designed to help activate and build students' background knowledge about the Civil War. Each student or pair of students has written down what they know about the Civil War and is now sharing this knowledge with peers during community share, as Laura takes notes in the first column of a four-column wall chart. Thus, this example reflects how students' private activities and thinking can become public. Laura's role is that of scaffolder. Notice in the following segment how she starts with the students' knowledge base about reasons the war was fought, beginning to build their understanding that multiple reasons contributed to the war's beginning. Students' ideas about the reasons for fighting are the focus of conversation throughout the unit.

1   LAURA: Ali, you have something else.

2   ALI: (*inaudible*)

3   LAURA: Okay, Ali said they were fighting over land. Wh-, Wh-, there
4   was something to do with the land. Does anyone know anything
5   more about that?

6   JOSEPH: The land was over the slaves.

7   LAURA: The land was over the slaves? I'm not sure what you mean.
8   (*pause*) They did fight over slavery. But they also, slavery wasn't the
9   only reason. . . . Does anyone know anything else about the land?

Laura accepts Ali's contribution, turning the question back to the students (lines 3–5). Joseph connects the idea of land to the idea of owning slaves, and Laura uses that as an opportunity to suggest that slavery, although an important reason, was not the only one (lines 7–9). Notice also that at this point in the activity and the unit, finding an answer is not as important a goal as getting ideas out for consideration and later inquiry. Bruce then offers another possible reason for fighting over the land, having to do with factories (lines 12–15, 19). Laura builds from Bruce's comment to introduce the term *economy* in line 17.

10   BRUCE: I know something.

11   LAURA: What do you know?

12 BRUCE: Um, I think it was like, the, um, South wanted, like, facto—,
13   factories or something. (*inaudible*) like the cars and stuff, and the
14   South wanted factories. The North wanted all the, uh, like the
15   land and stuff?

16 LAURA: (*turning to the wall chart and writing as she talks*) All right,
17   it had something to do with the *economy*, something to do with
18   factories—

19 BRUCE: —and like, land.

20 LAURA: and something to do with land. We're not sure exactly; I'll
21   put a question mark there too. (*Laura has written under the first
22   column of chart: economy–factory–land*) We know there are
23   some other reasons for the war; we're not sure exactly what they
24   were. But we have a little bit of an idea.

At this point in the conversation, Thea suggests that the reason they
fought over land related to trying to "take over the country." This created
an opportunity to clarify the difference between the Civil War, fought
within our borders, and the Revolutionary War that the students had
studied earlier in the year. Notice that in the following segment, Laura is
able to turn to one of Thea's peers, Meg, to help clear up the confusion
(lines 33–35).

25 THEA: They were fighting . . . so they could take over the country.

26 LAURA: Well, what country did this war take place in?

27 MEG: (*softly*) The United States.

28 LAURA: In where, Meg?

29 MEG: The United States.

30 LAURA: The United States. They were all the same country.

31 STUDENT: (*inaudible*)

32 LAURA: No, this was *just* the United States. Meg, it might be helpful
33   if you tell us, Meg looked up the word *civil*. She asked me if I
34   knew what *civil* meant, and I asked her to please look that up.

35 MEG: The events happening within a community or country.

36 LAURA: Okay, when something happens within the same community
37   or country. It is *not* a war when one country fights another. It is
38   a fight *within* the same country. This is an important thing to
39   know. We were not fighting anyone other than ourselves. (*writes
40   on chart: war within the same country*) And the person that I
41   went to first (*referring to the first comment in the first column*),
42   said, it was the North and the South were the two sides. The North
43   was fighting the South. Look on that map up there, above

44   Katrina's head. Tell me what color it looks like the North is up
45   there.

The conversation continues as Laura asks Katrina to indicate the blue part on the map that represents the North. She then asks the class to look at the yellow that indicates plains states where the pioneers were crossing (a reference to their previous unit of study in social studies) and the war was not yet being fought. She ends by asking Katrina to point to the gray area of the map, representing the southern states. Laura ends this segment by saying, "So, this is the same (*pause*) same country. Civil means same country. North was fighting South."

Through her scaffolding, Laura helps students begin to think about the fact that the reasons underlying the Civil War were many and possibly complex and that the war itself was fought within our own borders. These two important concepts are revisited frequently in other settings such as students' reading log entries and their Book Club discussions, and they are returned to in community share discussions of their reports, novels, and the teachers' read-aloud book. Students initiate many of the topics that were discussed during the lesson, but Laura provides a great deal of support in the discussion.

"Scaffolding" Talk: Questioning, Revisited

Question-asking is an important comprehension, monitoring, and interaction strategy that Laura emphasizes in many ways. We have seen one such illustration in her explicit instruction on criteria for evaluating inquiry questions. In this example, Laura conducts a mini-lesson during an opening community share on question-asking in reading logs and Book Club discussions. In contrast to the lesson on inquiry questions I have described, Laura draws more on students' existing knowledge about questioning, building upon their comments, and, at one point, permitting the students to shift the topic of the conversation entirely.

Laura opens the mini-lesson by telling students that she has noticed in their logs and sometimes in their conversations that some of their questions do not seem to be effective. She then asks students to identify reasons for asking questions within book club, recording their responses on a large chart paper. As she elicits ideas from students, Laura relies on the initiation–response–feedback (I–R–F) participation structure common in instructional settings. In the following segment, Ron (line 3) and Julianne (line 15) each offer a reason for asking questions in their logs or in their book clubs, reasons that Laura builds upon her talk.

1   LAURA: What's the role of questioning in Book Club? Why do we do
2   this? Ron?
3   RON: To help understand the book.

4   LAURA: That's one good reason. To understand or to clarify the book.
5   I'm going to use both words. To *clarify*, *understand* the story.
6   Okay, so some of the questions that you write and some of the
7   questions that you ask have that purpose in mind. (*Laura writes*
8   *on chart paper "to clarify/understand the book"*) There's some-
9   thing confusing in the story that I don't understand. I want some
10   clarification; I want some help. It's not a test. We're not trying
11   to see if the other members in our group read the story. We're
12   trying to get some clarification; one good purpose, What's an-
13   other role of questioning? What's another role, Julianne?
14   (*Julianne and Katrina have hands raised as Laura talks*)

15 JULIANNE: To promote talk.

16 LAURA: To promote talk (*Laura writes on chart as she continues*). Any
17   old kind of talk, Julianne?

18 JULIANNE: No, talk about the book and that you understand it.

Notice that whereas Laura provided elaboration for the first reason, she
turns to the students to suggest ideas for questions that promote talk (lines
15–19, 21–22, 34–35, 42). Still using an I–R–F pattern, Laura sometimes
asks students to elaborate on their point (e.g., lines 21–22), and at other
times she uses her turn to elaborate on what the student has said.

19 LAURA: Good, to promote talk about the book. What kinds of
20   questions do you think promote talk about the book? Can you
21   give me some examples? What kind of questions would promote
22   talk about the book? What kinds of questions would help your
23   group talk about the book? Charles?

24 CHARLES: Opinions, or "Whys."

25 LAURA: Okay, can you give me an example of a question that would
26   be an opinion?

27 CHARLES: Like, uh, well, um, "How would you feel when you heard
28   that your brother might be dead?" (an event that has happened
29   in the movie they watched, in books others had been reading in
30   their book clubs, as well as a possibility that his group had raised
31   about Davy in the book they were reading)

32 LAURA: Okay, this is a common thing that we found happened in the
33   war. Brothers, or husbands were found, were dead. And Charles
34   says an opinion question might be, "How would you feel?" And
35   that's an opinion because everybody's answer might be different.
36   And a "Why?" I like that Charles added, "Why?" If you add a
37   "why" to questions, that often makes a person have to explain
38   a little further and that promotes talk about the book. Julianne,
39   you have another example?

40   JULIANNE: Like, what you think; like, "Do you *think* Davy's really
41   dead or do you think he's alive?"

42   LAURA: Okay, What do you *think* about the story? Do you think
43   Davy's really dead or do you think he's going to be alive? Because
44   they didn't get confirmation in *Hannalee*, did they? Hannalee is
45   in that same point, in maybe thinking that her brother is dead,
46   but not knowing. What are some other examples, Katrina?

47   KATRINA: (*shrugs and smiles*)

48   LAURA: Oh, you want to add something else about questioning?

49   KATRINA: Yeah.

50   LAURA: Okay, go ahead.

51   KATRINA: Something, you could ask a question to see how others feel
52   about the story.

53   LAURA: Okay, feeling-type questions, she says, promote talk about the
54   story. [as seen in Meg's question to Julianne, on May 12th] How
55   did you feel when a certain part of the story happened? (*turns
56   to Katrina*) Is that what you're saying? (*to class*) "How did you
57   feel when you found out Truth met President Lincoln or that
58   Robert was in prison?" Okay. What kinds of questions, Roger,
59   are *NOT* good questions?

   Having established that questions are asked to promote story understanding and talk about text, Laura then asks students to consider questions
that do not achieve these purposes (lines 58–59). Roger offers, "Do you
like the book? Yes or no"; Julianne suggests, "Questions that test a person";
and Brett says, "Number questions." These three "bad examples" can be
traced to the earlier lesson on inquiry questions, suggesting that students
have appropriated and transformed their understanding of criteria for
judging an inquiry question to evaluating questions for their logs and
discussions.

Facilitating Talk within Large-Group Settings

Within community share, it is not unusual for the talk to shift from a formal
teacher-led instructional event to a discussion in response to issues raised
by the students. The community share about good Book Club questions
illustrates this well. After discussing the three "bad examples," Laura called
on Derek, assuming he had a fourth example. However, Derek had a
different agenda in mind, as seen in his response to Laura. Notice that
despite Laura's initial surprise (reflected in her request that he repeat his
question), she shifts her role to one of facilitator as she turns the question
back to his classroom peers (lines 13–14).

 1   DEREK: No, I have something else. I just thought of it. It's not a
 2   question, but it's something like in *The Blue and The Gray*. When
 3   the, when the South hung [*sic*] the people who were helping
 4   sla—, helping get slaves free or whatever? Why didn't the North
 5   do something about it?

 6   LAURA: Say that again.

 7   DEREK: If the South was hel-, I mean, somebody in the South was
 8   helping with slavery or whatever, and they got hung, why didn't
 9   the North do anything about that?

10   LAURA: So, when people in the South were caught helping slaves
11   escape, and some of them were hung, like the man—

12   DEREK: Why didn't the North do anything—

13   LAURA: Why didn't the North do that? Does anybody have any
14   thoughts about that?

15   BRETT:(?) Maybe because they didn't want to get (*inaudible*)

16   LAURA: Any of you guys have any thoughts about that? Some of those
17   southern abolitionists were caught and if they were black they
18   were hung. And even John Brown was hung (*highlighting Ali's
19   earlier report of the pre-Civil War abolitionist's role and his
20   ultimate fate*).

Laura's facilitates the conversation using several strategies. At the
simplest level, she repeats what the students have said, both for emphasis
as well as to ensure that contributions made in soft voices are heard by all
students. She helps students get the floor when many voices are competing
and no one person can be heard. She sometimes "revoices" what students
have said, to make sure that important ideas area not only literally, but
metaphorically, "heard," as occurs in lines 33–36, or lines 18–20 when she
brings in a child's report from the research phase of the unit. In fact,
revoicing Ali's contributions from a few weeks earlier gives her the
opportunity to surface some of the students' confusions about his role.
Although Laura does not address them in the current conversation, through
the students' talk, she is able to identify an area within social studies that
will need revisiting in future lessons (e.g., that John Brown's trial was in
the North, when actually it occurred in Virginia (line 21); and Charles's
confusion about what John Brown had actually done, expressed in lines
41–43 and 59–60).

21   JULIANNE: His [referring to John Brown] trial was in the North.

22   LAURA: His trial was in the North, Julianne says. [Note: West Virginia
23   had changed hands several times throughout the war.] (*Several
24   students begin talking at once and speak over each others' voices,*

25   *all focusing on either trials or the comment about the hangings.*
26   *Laura then calls on Deanna)*

27 S1: [Then how come,

28 S2: [Was that during the war or after the war?

29 S3: [Trials

30 LAURA: (*to Deanna*) I'm sorry, say it again.

31 DEANNA: Like, if black people get caught, they just get hung [*sic*],
32   they don't get a trial or nothing [*sic*].

33 LAURA: A lot of people didn't get a trial, she says, which is exactly
34   right, so they were just hung, kind of on the spot. But Julianne
35   says John Brown DID get a trial. It was in the North. It was the
36   North that sentenced him to be hung.

37 DEREK: Why did they?

38 LAURA: Why? Derek's question is. Why did they do that?

39 JULIANNE: He killed some people

40 LAURA: He killed some people in his raid.

41 CHARLES: No! Because the black people killed some people and they
42   accused him of killing his black people (*inaudible phrase*) at
43   whatever cost. [Note: One of Brown's men had killed a free black
44   railroad worker, a baggage man; John Brown was hanged for the
45   crime of treason against the federal government because he
46   attacked the federal arsenal, starting what he hoped would be a
47   slave insurrection.]

At this point, Laura's role shifts from simply facilitating their discussion to scaffolding their understanding of one of the key issues of the Civil War. Notice the change in both tone (e.g., in line 49, inserting Thea's name to get her attention; the unison response invited by her question in lines 50–51, and the direct statement of information in lines 53–58 and 61–64). She then brings the conversation back to Derek's original question (lines 71–73), indirectly praising him for having raised the important question and later linking the discussion to the broad issue of human rights that has been a theme threading throughout the entire unit as well as the original point of the mini-lesson (lines 81–88). Notice, as well, that she subtly questions students' responses to Julianne's understanding's of the events at Harpers Ferry (lines 34–36), and Charles' understanding (line 61). However, she maintains a focus on Brett's original question—why the North did not intervene in the treatment of abolitionists in the South and the relationship of his point to the broader issue within the unit, human rights.

48 LAURA: I think there's something here we have not talked about yet
49   or maybe we have, and I've forgotten. Even though, Thea, the

50   North didn't believe in slavery, did the North believe black and
51   whites were equal?

52   Ss: No.

53   LAURA: (*softly and sadly*) No. I don't, I don't think so. I think that
54   even though they said they don't believe in slavery, they still
55   thought whites were better than blacks, and so that if black
56   people were involved in attacking white people, that was not
57   good, at all. And that may be *part* of what was involved in John
58   Brown.

59   CHARLES: It's the slave that *he* was helping killed somebody, and they
60   accused *him* of killing the slave—

61   LAURA: Oh, of setting the slaves up to do that? That's my only thought
62   right now is that even though the North didn't believe in slavery,
63   they thought that was not right, they still didn't think they were
64   *equal*; they still didn't think the two groups of people were equal.

65   DEREK: That doesn't seem fair.

66   LAURA: I agree with Derek. That does not seem fair. That's one of the
67   big *issues*.

68   DEREK?: Yeah, remember John? (*Describes an event from the movie
69   but is hard to hear and follow on tape. Speaks for about four
70   sentences*)

71   LAURA: I think that Derek's hit on one of the biggest issues in the
72   whole Civil War, and that is that people weren't treated fairly,
73   and it's not right.

74   JULIANNE: White people didn't treat other white people right.

75   LAURA: (*gesturing to Julianne*) A lot of white people didn't treat other
76   white people fairly. Look at how they treated people in the prison
77   camp.

78   CHARLES: Yeah, but that was because they were on the other side.

79   LAURA: Exactly, but that's still unfair.

80   CHARLES: Yeah.

81   LAURA: It's still not the right way humans should treat other humans.
82   So we've come back to revisit a lot of those same issues again.
83   But, the point here of the mini-lesson, Roger, is I want you guys
84   to consider and continue thinking about questioning; when you
85   write questions in your log, please keep in mind that there are
86   two purposes: to clarify the story or to help you promote talk about
87   the story, and those are the reasons we write or ask questions.

These examples of teacher-led classroom talk reflect the variety such
talk can take, in terms of focus as well as the way in which teachers and

students interact. Such talk provides an important vehicle for students' literacy and content area learning, learning that serves as the foundation for their ability to participate with their peers in meaningful talk about text. In the next example, I turn to a book club discussion among the five students who are reading *Turn Homeward Hannalee*.

Student-Led Classroom Talk: A Book Club Discussion

The student-led book club is an important discourse space where students go public with their thinking about the book and their responses to the book. The book club discussions provide teachers with a window into students' comprehension and interpretation of story content, their strategy use, their knowledge of literary elements and response, and their use of interaction conventions. The five book club members—Charles, Meg, Derek, Julianne, and Brett—have been together as a group for this book, which they began reading on April 25th. The talk that occurs within the May 12 book club is rich in content the students discuss and rich in evidence of their appropriation and transformation of their experiences under Laura's guidance in community share.

Table 7.3 provides an overview of the primary topics the students discuss and how the topics were introduced. This overview illustrates the variety of topics that can occur within a single book club discussion, the way in which both log entries and general comments can spark discussion of a particular topic, and the variance in length of each discussion. I have selected three segments to illustrate these variations. Two segments are sparked by students' questions, although the questions differ in important ways. The question prompting the first illustration was read by Charles from his reading log and represents one designed to promote talk about text—asking for peers' opinions. The question prompting the second illustration was one inviting general comments ("Do you like the book so far?"), a question that in the earlier mini-lesson had been regarded as reasonable but not one that would be worth recording in a reading log. The third segment grew out of the students' debate about what the point of the story was. Further, the three segments reflect different lengths of exchanges, ranging from 16 to 134 lines of dialogue. Finally, the segments illustrate how leadership within a single book club moves among the members, as topics are initiated by three different participants. The three segments are (1) Should Jem Take Off the Bonnet?, (2) The Point of the Book, and (3) Causes of the Civil War.

Should Jem Take Off the Bonnet? Recall that during the mini-lesson described above, Charles had stated that questions that promote talk ask for others' opinions. In this segment, Charles applies that notion in his reading log entry and then within book club and asks his peers for their opinion (lines 2–3) about the situation of one of the main characters'—

TABLE 7.3. May 12th Book Club Discussion Overview: Meg, Derek, Julianne, Brett, and Charles

Primary topic	Initiating event
Throwing the bonnet	Charles's picture in reading log
Should Jem take off the bonnet?	Charles's question: If you were Jem, would you take off your bonnet in front of a soldier?
Consequences of hitting the soldier	Charles's question: Would you hit the soldier that felt your head if you were Hannalee?
Story event sequence	Brett reading his log entry
Transition	
Soldier going up to Jem	Brett's picture description
Turn shift	
The train picture	Derek's picture
Would you escape?	Meg's question: If you were Rosellen, would you rather work for Yankees or try to escape?
Hannalee and the couple	Meg's picture in reading log
Escaping from the couple	Beginning line 130, Meg's reads aloud from log her own response to the question she raised about escaping
Hannalee is taken away	
Feelings/authors craft	Julianne reads her log entries to group
Will they be nice to her?	Meg's question: Do you think that the people that bought Hannalee will be nice to her?
Point of the book	Meg's question: Do you like the book so far?
Causes of the war	Julianne's point to Charles that the kids being captured IS the point to the story

Jem had to wear a bonnet with braids attached to disguise himself as a girl so he would not be separated from his sister, Hannalee, and his brother's fiancée, Rosellen. The children were southerners who had been captured by the Yankees and sent North on a train, to be hired out for work. In this segment, his four peers respond to Charles's question taking different positions. Julianne initially argues that she would never do so ("No way!!"), though she later (line 21) modifies that in response to Brett's position. Brett thinks Jem should remove the bonnet because he "Wouldn't a' liked being called no *girrrl!*" (lines 18–20). Meg suggests that it didn't really matter because "He would've gotten tooken away anyway" (line 10).

```
1   CHARLES:  I also have questions (reading from log, which says "1. If
2             you were Jem would you take of [sic] the bonnet?). If you were
3             Jem, would you take off your bonnet in front of a soldier?
```

4   JULIANNE: *(loudly)* No way!!

5   MEG: They didn't do anything to him, and plus—

6   CHARLES: They took him away from his sister!

7   BRETT: [They took him *home* so he could

8   MEG: [But he was

9   CHARLES: [They took him to some other guys

10 MEG: He would've gotten tooken away anyway 'cause that *lady* was
11   gonna take him.

12 BRETT: And then, um . . .

13 JULIANNE: Yeah, but he took a chance because what if they *did* do
14   something to him?

15 CHARLES: Yeah, I guess he just didn't wanna be *(pause)* *(mouths*
16   *"oops" silently as Brett begins to talk)*

17 BRETT: [I woulda done it, I
18   wouldn't a' liked
19   being called no
20   *girrrl*!

21 JULIANNE: Well, I would admit, if I had to dress like a boy,

22 CHARLES: [Yeah, but stilllll,
23   you might have a
24   chance of being with
25   your sister.

26 BRETT: No, because other people were picking you.

27 CHARLES: But, you could've gone to the same person as, it depends,
28   it's fate!

29 JULIANNE: And besides, I wouldn't do it because *(pause)* what *if* they
30   punish you? I wouldn't want to take that chance.

31 MEG: Uh-huh.

Charles's question promotes students' talk about a significant event in the book, for it is Jem's removal of the bonnet that leads to the characters' separation. The students respect each others' positions and govern themselves in terms of allowing peers to speak. For example, in lines 15–16, Charles appears to interrupt Brett, but then abruptly stops, saying "oops" under his breath. However, he is not reluctant to challenge a peer if he disagrees, as seen in lines 22–25 and lines 27–28, challenging first Julianne, then Brett. In short, this segment illustrates how a particular type of question, talked about and valued during the mini-lessons on good Book Club questions, was appropriated by students for use within their small-group discussions.

The Point of the Book. The next illustration reflects a much briefer conversation that serves an important purpose as a turning point or bridge in the discussion. It is prompted by a question from Meg that she did not have written in her log. The question, in line 32, follows a 9-second pause in their conversation, a pause that I characterize as a "break-down," where students were muttering under their breath or arguing whether Hannalee was 11 or 12 years old, but clearly, they did not care enough about it to look in the book. In the mini-lesson on questions, a question Laura and the students discussed as being reasonable to ask, but not one that needed to be recorded in a log was, "How do you like the book?" Meg asks a form of this question, possibly in an attempt to rescue the conversation. Her question does, in fact, raise an interesting debate about the point of the book, with Charles and Julianne serving as the leaders in the conversation, but it is not without some false starts. Notice that in contrast to the first segment describing their response to Charles's question about the bonnet, this segment initially feels stilted and lacks substantive engagement with the content of the book.

32   MEG: So you like the book so far, Julianne?

33   JULIANNE: Yes, I do. I (*inaudible*) back the pages. (*Charles and Brett*
34   *continue to draw; Derek stands up and looks at Brett's log*
35   *drawings*) I knew it would be exciting.

36   MEG: Why do you like it?

37   JULIANNE: It's got a lot of action in it, and it's very good description.

38   CHARLES: It's, slow.

39   JULIANNE: SLOW???

40   CHARLES: Like, when I play (*computer?*) games, if games are *stupid*,
41   to get caught up in things, and everything takes too long, I call
42   it slow. Everything goes by too slow [*sic*].

43   JULIANNE: This isn't as slow as some of those other—

44   CHARLES: There's no *plot* in it.

45   JULIANNE: I think there is—

46   CHARLES: There's no *point* in it.

47   JULIANNE: There IS a point in this! They're *captured*; that IS the point.

Meg's attempt to rescue the conversation is successful. This brief exchange between Charles and Julianne captures the interest of their peers, and the conversation becomes energized around the idea of the capture.

Causes of the War. The third segment I present is the longest of the three and shares the substantive focus that we saw in the first segment. It is initiated by Julianne's comment to Charles that getting captured is the point of the story. The students' discussion within this segment weaves among events in the book, the students' prior knowledge from studying the Civil War, and their personal response to the texts. Charles opens the segment by taking issue with Julianne's use of the term, "captured." His use of the metaphor "slaves" in line 48 elicits Meg's comment about the North acting as if slavery were wrong, but then hiring slave labor. The students' talk then moves among three key ideas: (1) the possible hypocrisy of the North's stance toward slavery, (2) the human rights issues at the root of the war, and (3) the cause(s) of the Civil War.

48   CHARLES: They're not *captured*. They're being taken as slaves to a,
49   northern place.

50   JULIANNE: [Yeah, that's like

51   MEG: [I don't, I think like, they're um, the North is saying how
52   it's wrong to have slaves and all that, but they're

53   BRETT: Immigrants, that's what they are, immigrants.

54   MEG: Uh, huh, and they're taking the people from the South and
55   making *them* work.

56   JULIANNE: I don't—

57   BRETT: (*pounding desk*) As in the immigrants!

58   JULIANNE: [So what are these people fighting for?

59   BRETT: [As in the immigrants, not a slave!

60   MEG: (*to Brett*) An immigrant is where [*sic*] you come from another
61   *country*.

62   BRETT: Yeah!

Recall that on March 30 Meg had been the student who had looked up the meaning of civil war and shared that it meant a war fought within a single community or country. Here, she notes that the immigrants were not part of the issues between North and South because they were not from this country.

63   JULIANNE: So they're just like the black people.

64   CHARLES: But the white people,
65   the white people from the North
66   didn't have slaves.

67   JULIANNE: That's exactly what they're doing with these people.
68   (They're using them like slaves.

69   MEG: [It's, except for they're white. . . .

70   JULIANNE: If, if, if *they* keep slaves, and the North, the South keeps
71   slaves—

72 CHARLES: But, they're fighting for slaves. Part of the reason they're
73   fighting for slaves, right?

74 JULIANNE: Right. But they're having slaves themselves.

At this point, Charles begins to build an elaborate argument explaining why northerners would gladly take in the southerners to work almost as slaves. He believes it is because the northerners see these people as traitors, and thus not deserving of any better treatment, and that this, in fact, is not the same as owning slaves. He further complicates the argument with his reminder that the North had believed in slavery prior to the Emancipation Proclamation.

75 CHARLES: Yeah, think. If you were the North, would you take a slave
76   from the South? You wouldn't take a slave from the North, but
77   you'd take a slave from the South, right?

78 MEG: No, I—

79 CHARLES: You hated the South. They're traitors.

80 JULIANNE: Yeah. (*Meg nods*)

81 CHARLES: This person is a traitor. You take 'em as a slave, wouldn't
82   you? You gotta think like that woman.

83 JULIANNE: Like that woman, yeah, she's a traitor, I'd take her (*she*
84   *shrugs*).

85 MEG: (*frowning expression on her face*) But (*pause*)

86 CHARLES: That's my point. I don't think she'll treat her nice.

87 MEG: Think about it. That lady, she um, er that couple would be a
88   traitor too because the North was *against* slaves and then they
89   just went and bought—

90 DEREK: [And they, and they—

91 CHARLES: But think! This is a slave, this is a slave of the SOUTH!

92 MEG: [got a lady to do work!

93 CHARLES: The South's a traitor!

94 JULIANNE: I know, and, but it's still like, I mean, I'm just saying that
95   it's similar, so what are they fighting for, anyway?

Julianne now segues into the third main topic of this segment, the reasons the Civil War was being fought. On the table are two reasons—slavery and secession—and the students begin to weigh the relative contribution of each.

96 CHARLES: Yeah.

97 MEG: I know.

98   CHARLES: Well, it was, because the South wanted to secede.

99   JULIANNE: Yeah.

100 CHARLES: And the North didn't want 'em to.

101 DEREK: Yeah, they, yeah.

102 CHARLES: That was the whole main reason, practically.

103 DEREK: They had slaves.

104 JULIANNE: But the other reason was slaves.

105 DEREK: Yeah.

106 JULIANNE: People in the North didn't like slaves, but they're taking
107   them. It doesn't make any sense.

108 DEREK: And they also they set them free.

109 CHARLES: But they could have been before the Emancipation Procu-
110   lation [sic].

111 JULIANNE: Yeah, I think so.

112 CHARLES: That's another thing. That's what I was saying before. They
113   had slaves. They had slaves. Even Lincoln had slaves. They had
114   slaves before.

115 JULIANNE: I know.

None of the students challenge Charles's assertion, and Julianne, in fact, agrees with him. Yet Lincoln was poor, so it is unlikely that he had slaves, and there is no historical evidence that this was the case. Thus by creating opportunity within the public/individual quadrant for students to make public their individual thoughts, teachers can identify areas that need additional guidance or instruction.

Students were sources of support for each other's learning, as witnessed in the short exchange below between Charles, Brett, and their peers.

116 CHARLES: Emancipation proculation [sic]. After he wrote that, all the
117   slaves were free.

118 BRETT: (sort of moving a finger for emphasis) Emancipation *Procla-*
119   *mation.*

The students debate the pronunciation of "proclamation," then continue with their discussion of the ethics of slavery and the position of the North on this issue. Lincoln's role comes in (lines 138–140). What is impressive about their discussion is the knowledge base on which they are drawing, the sources of information they name (e.g., reading a book, line 129; talking with their teacher, line 128), their ability to interact with each other, without adult leadership, around complex issues, and their intensity within the discussion.

120 JULIANNE: But *part* of the reason why the South wanted to secede is
121   if they didn't, they wouldn't be able to have slaves anymore.
122   That's why they wanted to secede so they could still have their
123   slaves.

124 CHARLES: How do you know that?

125 MEG: Yeah.

126 JULIANNE: Because, um, I read a book—

127 BRETT: It's so obvious!

128 JULIANNE: I figured it out. Ms. Pardo told us about it too. That was
129   one of the reasons they wanted to secede. Yeah, the North was
130   saying, "You guys can't have slaves." And they wanted slaves.

131 DEREK: *(points to chart on wall) (inaudible)* There are certain slave
132   states that are in the union, so when . . .

133 CHARLES: *(looking at Derek)* Yeah, we had slaves in the union. During
134   the war, they had slaves.

135 JULIANNE: Yeah.

136 MEG: Then, why are they saying—

137 CHARLES: Basically, I'm thinking the whole thing, the whole thing in
138   the North is about the South seceding. They didn't really care
139   about the slaves that much until Lincoln wrote the Emancipation
140   Proculation [*sic*].

Interestingly, the next day, students would read in the text itself, that "They [northerners] treated us Georgia folks like we were slaves—like they owned us and we had no say over anything at all" and later, describes Hannalee as "slaving away" (p. 79). Further, a few pages later, a character says to Hannalee, "Do you think I relish having a dirty little traitor in my house?" (p. 81). This conversation shows that they not only have targeted some of the author's points, but that they engaged in these ideas in ways that they found interesting and meaningful.

The dual purposes of the students' discussions are pedagogically crucial. One purpose has to do with students engaging in critical thinking and problem solving. We want students to interact with text in personally interesting and meaningful ways, and to think critically about what they are reading. Too often, the ways in which we have asked students to engage with text were primarily to restate text information that their teacher or the text publishers had in mind when they presented students with comprehension questions. Too often, these ways of text engagement encouraged a "fill in the blank" mentality rather than one of critical reasoning. As seen in the examples presented, students in Laura's classroom are engaged in constructing meaning about very sophisticated ideas for which there may not be consensus even among mature readers. Thus, the second pedagogical purpose of student talk leads directly to the reason underlying the need for balance between student and teacher talk. This purpose is of providing a window into students' thinking, a window that brings insights to inform teachers' lesson planning.

In this classroom, Laura conducted mini-lessons in the days following these conversations to address students' misunderstandings and confusions. Some of the mini-lessons were simple lessons on vocabulary (e.g., the correct pronunciation of the word "proclamation"), while others were more substantive (e.g., the meaning of border and free states in terms of presence or absence of slavery. Lincoln's stance on slavery, the distinctions between economic and social slavery). What is crucial is that multiple purposes are served by balancing student and teacher talk—neither stands alone as a primary means to ensure student learning.

CONCLUDING COMMENTS

This chapter has focused on the role of classroom talk in the debate about instruction. I have argued that classroom talk is a significant topic of concern as we consider the issue of *balancing instruction*. A key question with regard to classroom talk is, "What do we wish to balance?" Areas of balance occur within the curriculum, among participants, and in multiple-grouping arrangements. In terms of curriculum, classroom talk should not be simply about skills. Nor should it be simply about literature. Nor should it be focused solely on reader response. Students' personal response to their reading was critical for their sustained engagement in literacy practices. The talk about literature—literary elements as well as ways of responding—provided them with a foundation for engaging with the texts in multiple ways. However, the talk about skills and strategies was equally important for their increasing sophisticated engagement in literacy events.

In terms of talk among participants, the conversations highlighted in this chapter reveal the importance of the teachers' roles both in explicitly as well as indirectly scaffolding students' learning. Classroom talk should not be dominated either by teacher or students. Many studies have shown repeatedly that classroom talk is dominated by the teacher's control over topics and turns, most often using (or overusing) the I–R–E/F pattern of interaction. This pattern has been criticized as being too limiting, and arguments have been offered in favor of more student, and more student-led, talk. Yet the examples above suggest that there is an important place for teacher talk and that there are ways of interacting—even within the I–R–E/F patterns—that engage the students in important ways and provide a firm basis for their peer-led interactions in pairs, small groups, and even whole-class settings. However, talk among and by students contributes greatly to their ability to work through such complex issues as why the

U.S. Civil War was fought—debating issues that are as complex to historians as to these young students. Further, the students' talk provides an important window into their degree of understanding, leading to spontaneous instruction within "teachable moments," as well as planned instruction at other points in time.

Finally, classroom talk should occur in different group settings. Students' talk differs when students are working with a single peer, in a small group, or in a large class. It differs when the teacher is present and when the students talk among themselves. As teacher educators prepare teachers to work with their students in diverse settings, they must rethink the contexts in which they themselves are taught. Our teacher education programs must broaden the focus to include not only the content that historically has been their focus but also include (1) different contexts and related purposes for classroom talk, (2) means for teaching students to engage in meaningful talk, and (3) experiences on which they can draw in their teaching. That is, current and future teachers need opportunities to experience educative talk in a variety of settings.

With a strong basis in their own backgrounds and in what they teach students, teachers can have high expectations for their students when they are given consistent opportunities to engage in talk with peers. Meg, Charles, and their peers had been in book clubs almost daily since the start of the academic year. Their earliest conversations were not as engaging, not as rich, and certainly not as sustained as the one described above. Laura Pardo used the public and social spaces of her classroom effectively to teach, model, and scaffold her students' literacy and content area learning. She provided multiple contexts for them to appropriate and transform these experiences, from individual work in various writing activities to paired projects and small-group inquiry activities to book clubs. She also created many activities that led to students' publication of their thinking—through visible recordings in their reading logs to tape recordings of their book club sessions. By doing so, Laura created specific formal and mini-lessons in areas of need.

Balance is critical. Our field has seen too many pendulum swings over the years. Although we may now question the long-accepted maxim that "a quiet classroom is a learning classroom," there is always the danger that if classroom talk is not meaningful, the pendulum will swing back. As our field has come to understand the important relationship among language, thought, and literacy learning, we must guard against underestimating the value of talk in today's classrooms.

ACKNOWLEDGMENTS

My thanks to Laura Pardo and her fifth-grade students for their participation in the study; to Cindy Brock for her comments on the chapter; and to John Works, Jr., for sharing his knowledge of the Civil War.

NOTE

1. The following conventions are used within the dialogue presentations: / = one second pause; [= point of overlapping speech; S = unidentified student speaker; . . . = omitted text; *italics* = text read aloud. Note that all dialogue is presented as spoken, not edited for grammar, content, or pronunciation.

REFERENCES

Almasi, J. F. (1995). The nature of fourth graders' sociocognitive conflicts in peer-led and teacher-led discussions of literature. *Reading Research Quarterly, 30*(3), 314–351.

Beatty, P. (1984). *Turn homeward, Hannalee.* New York: Troll.

Beatty, P. (1992). *Who comes with cannons?* New York: Scholastic.

Cazden, C. (1988). *Classroom discourse: The language of teaching and learning.* Portsmouth, NH: Heinemann.

Cullinan, B. E., & Galda, L. (1994). *Literature and the child* (3rd ed.). Fort Worth, TX: Harcourt Brace.

Dole, J. A., Duffy, G. G., Roehler, L. R., & Pearson, P. D. (1991). Moving from the old to the new: Research on reading comprehension instruction. *Review of Educational Research, 61*(2), 239–264.

Eeds, M., & Peterson, R. L. (1995). What teachers need to know about the literary craft. In N. L. Roser & M. G. Martinez (Eds.), *Book talk and beyond* (pp. 10–23). Newark, DE: International Reading Association.

Erickson, F., & Schultz, J. (1982). *Counselor as gate keeper: Social interaction in interviews.* New York: Academic Press.

Gavelek, J. R., & Raphael, T. E. (1996). Changing talk about text: New roles for teachers and students. *Language Arts, 73,* 182–192.

Gambrell, L. B., & Almasi, J. F. (Eds.). (1996). *Lively discussions: Fostering engaged reading.* Newark, DE: International Reading Association.

Harré, R. (1984). *Personal being: A theory for individual psychology.* Cambridge, MA: Harvard University Press.

Hunt, I. (1964). *Across five Aprils.* New York: Berkeley Books.

Martinez, M. G., & Roser, N. L. (1995). The books make a difference in story talk. In N. L. Roser & M. G. Martinez (Eds.), *Book talk and beyond* (pp. 32–41). Newark, DE: International Reading Association.

McMahon, S. I., & Raphael, T. E., with Goatley, V. J., & Pardo, L. S. (1997). *Book Club.* New York: Teachers College Press.

Paratore, J. R., & McCormack, R. L. (Eds.). (1997). *Peer talk in the classroom.* Newark, DE: International Reading Association.

Pearson, P. D. (1986). Twenty years of research in reading comprehension. In T. E. Raphael (Ed.), *The contexts of school-based literacy* (pp. 43–62). New York: Random House.

Pearson, P. D., & Stephens, D. (1993). Learning about literacy: A 30-year journey. In C. Gordon & G. Labercane (Eds.), *Foundations and conceptualizations of the reading process* (pp. 4–18). Boston: Ginn Press.

Raphael, T. E., & Goatley, V. J. (1994). The teacher as "more knowledgeable other": Changing roles for teaching in alternative reading instruction programs. In C. Kinzer & D. Leu (Eds.), *Multidimensional aspects of literacy research, theory and practice* (pp. 527–536). Chicago: National Reading Conference.

Raphael, T. E., Goatley, V. J., McMahon, S. I., & Woodman, D. A. (1995). Promoting meaningful conversations in student book clubs. In N. Roser & M. Martinez (Eds.), *Book talk and beyond* (pp. 71–83). Newark, DE: International Reading Association.

Raphael, T. E., & Hiebert, E. H. (1996). *Creating an integrated approach to literacy instruction.* Ft. Worth, TX: Harcourt Brace.

Raphael, T. E., & McMahon, S. I. (1994). "Book Club": An alternative framework for reading instruction. *The Reading Teacher, 48,* 102–116.

Reeder, C. (1989). *Shades of gray.* New York: Avon Books.

Reit, S. (1988). *Behind rebel lines.* Orlando, FL: Harcourt Brace.

Rosenblatt, L. M. (1985). The transactional theory of the literary work: Implications for research. In C. Cooper (Ed.), *Researching response to literature and the teaching of literature: Points of departure.* (pp. 33–53). Norwood, NJ: Ablex.

Rosenblatt, L. M. (1991). Literature S.O.S.! *Language Arts, 68,* 444–448.

Short, K. G., & Pierce, K. M. (1990). *Talking about books: Creating literate communities.* Portsmouth, NH: Heinemann.

Tierney, R. J., & Cunningham, J. W. (1984). Research on teaching comprehension. In P. D. Pearson, R. Barr, M. L. Kamil, & P. Mosenthal (Eds.), *Handbook of reading research* (pp. 609–655). New York: Longman.

Vygotsky, L. S. (1978). *Mind in society: The development of higher psychological processes* (M. Cole, V. John-Steiner, S. Scribner, & E. Souberman, Trans.). Cambridge, MA: Harvard University Press.

Wells, G. (1993). Reevaluating the IRF sequence: A proposal for the articulation of theories of activity and discourse for the analysis of teaching and learning in the classroom. *Linguistics and Education, 5*(1), 1–38.

Wertsch, J. V. (1985). *Vygotsky and the social formation of mind.* Cambridge, MA: Harvard University Press.

Wertsch, J. V. (1991). *Voices of the mind.* New York: Oxford University Press.

CHAPTER EIGHT

Intellectually Stimulating Story Discussions

RICHARD C. ANDERSON
University of Illinois at Urbana–Champaign

CLARK CHINN
Rutgers University

MARTHA WAGGONER
Teacher, Danville, IL

KIM NGUYEN
University of Illinois at Urbana–Champaign

Recently, there has been renewed appreciation that talking with others is a powerful factor in children's intellectual growth. Regrettably, at the same time, there has been the growing realization that the patterns of talk that predominate in American classrooms provide little intellectual stimulation. In her book *Classroom Discourse*, Cazden (1988, p. 134) wrote:

> In school lessons, teachers give directions and the children nonverbally carry them out; teachers ask questions and children answer them, frequently with only a word or a phrase. Most important . . . the roles are not reversible. Children never give directions to teachers, and rarely even ask them questions except to request permission. The only context in which children can reverse interactional roles with the same intellectual content, giving directions as well as following them, is with their peers.

Prime time for serious talk among peers is during the story discussions that are a fixture of the reading and language arts lesson. Virtually every elementary school student in the United States engages in a story discussion for 15–25 minutes on most school days. In the typical classroom, these are teacher-led, small-group discussions, although variations such as whole-class discussions or student-led, small-group discussions are also prevalent. Whatever the format, the story discussion is one of the major opportunities afforded in the school day for language development and intellectual growth. Even a modest innovation in techniques for conducting story discussions could have an enormous cumulative impact, if it were adopted widely.

In this chapter, we describe *recitation*, the conventional approach to story discussion, and *collaborative reasoning*, a new approach to story discussion designed to be more intellectually stimulating. In addition, we summarize results from classroom studies comparing recitation and collaborative reasoning.

Altogether we have been participant observers in several hundred collaborative reasoning discussions, as well as a number of recitations, in 19 fourth- and fifth-grade classrooms in east central Illinois. The classrooms are in schools situated in socioeconomically diverse rural communities and middle- and low-income areas of small cities. We have videotaped about 150 of the discussions and transcribed about 100 of the videotapes. The results we report in this chapter are based primarily on analysis of discussion transcripts.

RECITATION: THE CONVENTIONAL APPROACH TO STORY DISCUSSION

Recitation is an entrenched classroom practice in which the teacher controls most aspects of communication. The teacher maintains continuous control of the topic by asking a seldom-broken string of *assessment* questions. An assessment question quizzes students about something already known to the teacher. The assessment question is to be distinguished from a *genuine request* for information; here the questioner does not already know the answer. The teacher's assessment questions are the means for leading a discussion group in a point-by-point review of the day's story. In addition to quizzing students about story facts, during the recitations we have observed, teachers always ask a few questions, usually near the end of the discussion, designed to illicit students' feelings about the character's predicament and to allow them to express whether they liked the story.

Recitations have the predictable, repeated initiation–response–evaluation (IRE) pattern: teacher *initiation*, student *response*, followed by teacher *evaluation* (Mehan, 1972; Sinclair & Coulthard, 1975). The teacher controls turn taking. Following a teacher question, students bid for turns by raising their hands. The teacher chooses the student who will respond. This student has the floor until the teacher takes control again, evaluating the response of the student and then initiating the next IRE cycle. Research suggests that most of the talk during recitations is teacher talk; students collectively express from a third to a half of the words (Cazden, 1988).

The manifest purpose of a discussion that takes the form of a recitation is to assure that the students know the story. This does not necessarily mean that they are to lift answers verbatim from the text. Skillful practitioners encourage students to express points in their own words and search to determine whether students can make the inferences necessary to bridge events in the story. Presumably, in addition to assuring that students know today's story, recitations are employed in the service of such longer-term goals as inculcating a disposition to read carefully for detail and cultivating a sense of the plot line in different kinds of stories.

COLLABORATIVE REASONING: AN ALTERNATIVE APPROACH TO STORY DISCUSSION

Collaborative reasoning is one of a number of approaches to story discussion which, in one or more of several ways, allow students greater expressive latitude than a recitation (Commeyras, 1994; Eeds & Wells, 1989; Raphael & McMahon, 1994; Short & Pierce, 1990). Collaborative reasoning is intended to stimulate critical reading and critical thinking and to be personally engaging (see Waggoner, Chinn, Yi, & Anderson, 1995).

The goal of collaborative reasoning goes beyond simply introducing children to the forms of language required to be a successful discussion participant. The ultimate goal includes inculcating the values and habits of mind to use reasoned discourse as a means for choosing among competing ideas. Gee (1992, p. 20) has defined a *discourse* as a "characteristic way of talking, acting, interacting, thinking, believing, and valuing, and sometimes characteristic way[s] of writing, reading, and/or interpreting." The discourse of reasoned argumentation is spoken in congressional chambers, courts of law, scientific research groups, humanities seminars, executive suites, and union halls, wherever rational decision making and orderly resolution of disputes are prized. Collaborative reasoning is intended to provide one of the otherwise rare opportunities for elementary school children to begin to acquire the discourse of reasoned argumentation.

Prior to a collaborative reasoning discussion, the students read a story silently at their seats. When they gather as a group, the teacher initiates the discussion with a single *central question* about a significant issue faced by the story characters. For example, *My Name Is Different* (Prasad, 1987) is a story about a young Chinese American boy who changes his name because he is anxious to fit into his new, mostly Anglo school. The question is, "Should Chang Li have changed his name?" *Stone Fox* (Gardiner & Sewall, 1980) is a story about Willie, a boy whose grandfather has been ill and unable to pay the taxes on the farm. Willie enters a dogsled race intending to use the prize money to pay the taxes. His chief competitor is Stone Fox, a Native American man, who uses winnings from dogsled races to buy back tribal lands. Willie is leading in the race, because he has taken a short-cut across a frozen lake, when his dog drops dead from exhaustion 10 feet from the finish line. The question is, "Should Stone Fox (who is running second) win the race himself or let Willie win?"

In a collaborative reasoning discussion, the students are asked to take public positions on the central question and then offer reasons and supporting evidence for their positions. They are expected to listen carefully and evaluate each others' arguments. When they disagree, they are encouraged to challenge with counterarguments. As the discussion proceeds, the students are supposed to weigh the reasons and evidence offered and decide whether to maintain or change their original positions.

Open participation is encouraged in collaborative reasoning. That is, students speak without raising their hands and without being chosen by the teacher. They are urged to speak one at a time and to avoid interrupting each other, as in an adult conversation about a serious subject. The rationale for open participation was termed the "balance of rights" hypothesis in a seminal paper by Au and Mason (1981, p. 150), who argued "that higher levels of productive student behavior are probable if there is a balance between the interactional rights of the teacher and children."

The teacher's role during collaborative reasoning is to promote independent thinking and student management of turn taking (see Waggoner et al., 1995). Specific teacher moves hinge on the degree of control students currently have over thinking strategies, the dynamic of a particular group, and the course that the discussion has taken. Depending upon the situation, the teacher may decide to challenge a reason, ask for clarification, offer a counterargument or prompt for evidence to support a position.

The teachers attended a half-day workshop to learn about the role of facilitator during collaborative reasoning discussions (see Waggoner et al., 1995). During this session, we presented the goals and fundamental principles of the collaborative reasoning approach. Then the teachers learned about strategies for promoting reflective thinking and collaboration among their students. These strategies include (1) prompting students for their positions and reasoning; (2) demonstrating reasoning processes by thinking out loud; (3) challenging students with countering ideas that they have not thought of; (4) acknowledging good reasoning; (5) summing up what the students have said; and (6) using the vocabulary of critical and reflective thinking.

Teachers saw video clips of exemplary discussions conducted by other teachers. We gave the teachers suggestions on specific types of moves that would challenge students to think deeply about the stories and reflect on their positions. Finally, the teachers engaged in role playing to practice being a facilitator of collaborative reasoning discussions.

Back in their classrooms, the teachers received one-on-one guidance from a research team member on how to apply the collaborative reasoning strategies. Each teacher extended the approach to fit her or his personal and classroom situation. For instance, one teacher felt it was important that the students be able to keep track of one another's position on the issues. She created a set of "position cards" that students displayed to let others know their current opinion. The same teacher added a debriefing period at the end of each discussion to give students feedback on their reasoning and their contribution to the group. These elements since have been incorporated into the collaborative reasoning format.

ASPECTS OF TALK DURING STORY DISCUSSIONS

In this section, we summarize data that bear on the hypothesis that collaborative reasoning leads to enhanced student participation during discussions (see Chinn, Anderson, & Waggoner, in preparation). The data are based on an analysis of 16 discussions, including a collaborative reasoning discussion and a recitation with a high-ability group and a low-ability group in each of four classrooms. The recitations were videotaped during a baseline period prior to the introduction of collaborative reasoning. The collaborative reasoning discussions were videotaped later, after the classes had had about 3 months of experience with collaborative reasoning. The story was counterbalanced: Eight of the groups discussed *Stone Fox* during the recitation and discussed *My Name Is Different* during collaborative reasoning. The assignment was reversed for the other eight groups.

Among the differences we expected to see during collaborative reasoning as compared to recitation were (1) more student talk and less teacher talk, as indexed by length of utterances, turns for speaking per minute, words spoken per minute, and proportion of all words uttered by students in comparison to the teacher; (2) more student–student turn sequences without an intervening teacher turn; (3) more interjections by both students and the teacher; (4) more back-channeling comments such as "Uh huh," "Right"; and (5) fewer teacher questions overall and a shift from assessment questions to open-ended questions.

All of the foregoing predictions were confirmed. The rate of student talk increased dramatically, from 66 words per minute during recitation to 111 words per minute during collaborative reasoning. There was a small decrease in amount of teacher talk, from 75 words to 57 words per minute. The percentage of total talk by the teacher declined from 53% during recitation to 34% during collaborative reasoning, and this decline appeared in both high and low groups in every classroom.

As anticipated, runs of consecutive student turns accounted for 45% of full-student turns during collaborative reasoning, as compared to only 6% during recitation. Interjections increased during collaborative reasoning, because participants had to compete for the floor, and back-channeling comments also increased, because the discussion became more conversational.

Total teacher questions declined from a rate of 4.2 per minute during recitation to 2.2 per minute during collaborative reasoning. Whereas 53% of teachers' questions were assessment questions during recitation, only 9% were assessment questions during collaborative reasoning. There was a corresponding increase in teachers' open-ended questions, from 30% during recitation to 56% during collaborative reasoning.

Several of the features of participation during collaborative reasoning are illustrated in the following excerpt from a discussion of *Stone Fox*. Here is the beginning of the discussion:

TEACHER: Okay, what are some of your reasons for whatever position you have taken?

[Many students talk at once.]

TEACHER: Remember, one person at a time.

NATE: Well, I think Stone Fox should just go ahead and win the race because, um well I mean, Willie's dog is dead. And I mean, I mean, he can't like bring the dog back to life and have the dog go ahead and win, but and so I think that Stone Fox should just go ahead and win.

MARLA: Nate, Nate, just—this story made me think of my dog because we had to get rid of my dog because of my little sister and I didn't think it was fair, because my little sister, did something. Wouldn't you, pretend you are little Willie, and you are almost ready to win a race and save your grandfather's land and then you're 10 feet away, just 10 feet, and then your dog dies. Wouldn't you be very upset? I mean, I would've, I would've just sat there. I mean I wouldn't have done anything. I think they, I think that um they should just let them make it a tie and they can split it and Willie's grandfather can try and pay the rest of it, since he got better all of a sudden.

Both Nate and Marla made longer contributions than would be seen during a recitation. The two students spoke one after another without an intervening teacher turn. In fact, Nate's utterance initiated a run of 20 student utterances before the teacher spoke again. Marla addressed Nate by name and responded directly to his argument. During collaborative reasoning, students typically look at each other when they speak, often address each other by name, and often pick up on and respond to each others' remarks. During recitation, students typically look at the teacher when they speak, seldom refer to each other by name, and seldom pick up on each others' remarks.

The content of Marla's utterance is interesting in several respects. She began with an intensely personal reflection that shows she was deeply engaged in the story world. In the middle of her utterance is a use of a question that we call a "rhetorical challenge." There is a recurrent pattern to rhetorical challenges:

- Address a classmate by name.
- Describe a story situation or hypothetical situation similar to a story situation.
- Ask what the classmate would do or how he or she would feel in this situation.

Rhetorical challenges begin with pat phrases such "Pretend you were" or "Say you were" to introduce the hypothetical situation. The question about what the classmate would do or feel is not a genuine request for information. Instead, it is a rhetorical question intended to get the classmate to agree with the questioner's position. In a set of 20 collaborative reasoning transcripts, we discovered 28 rhetorical challenges involving 17 different children. Marla was one of four children who issued two or more rhetorical challenges.

Several indicators suggest that children were more engaged, responsive, and interested during collaborative reasoning than during recitation. The rate at which children spoke almost doubled, and rate of talking can be considered to reflect emotional involvement. Competition to get the floor was often intense, as is reflected, for instance, in the increased rate of interjections. Collaborative reasoning discussions were significantly longer than recitations, even though, as far as we know, teachers were under the same constraints to make time for arithmetic, get the children out to recess, and finish before lunch. Probably the teachers let the collaborative reasoning discussions run longer because they realized the discussions were productive and saw that the children were highly engaged. The content and form of children's utterances during collaborative reasoning often revealed engagement, as illustrated in Marla's reflection about her dog.

THE LOGIC OF CHILDREN'S ARGUMENTS

In this section, we examine the logic of children's arguments during collaborative reasoning. A comparison with the logic of arguments during recitation is impossible for the simple reason that few, if any, of children's utterances during recitation can be construed as arguments.

One's first impression is that children's arguments during these discussions are extremely vague and elliptical. An analysis of 40 arguments from 20 collaborative reasoning discussions revealed that all 40 contained loosely constrained pronouns and other vague expressions that had to be resolved for the meaning to be clear, and that 36 were missing premises required by recognized patterns of valid inference, such as *modus ponens* and *modus tollens* (see Anderson et al., 1997).

Upon closer examination, however, the vagueness in children's arguments proves to be more apparent than real. Generally children are as informative as they need to be, because the unstated or vaguely identified information usually is *given* in the sense that it is readily inferable by other active participants in the discussion. That is to say, the information is explicitly stated in the story everyone had read, explicitly stated earlier in the discussion, or is a matter of common knowledge and belief. We have concluded that children almost certainly understand each other most of the time and almost certainly appreciate the force of each other's arguments (Anderson et al., 1997).

Consider, for example, the following utterance from a discussion of *Stone Fox*. Here understanding depends upon disambiguating several vague expressions. The argument itself is also mildly elliptical. We supply what perhaps may be regarded as unstated premises[1]:

MARCUS: I think *that*$_1$'s cheating because *it*$_1$'s the same thing as taking drugs and running. I mean, *it*$_2$ will make you a little stronger, and you will speed up. And so, *that*$_2$ will be the same thing as going *right through the path* because *that*$_1$ will give you a head start just like the drugs will.

RANDY: It does not say at the beginning that there's no short cuts.

[Several lines omitted]

MARCUS: Well, *he* did cheat, and so I think Stone Fox should win.

The interpretation of the vague pronouns *that* and *it* is very easy in the context of the discussion. The immediately preceding speaker mentions Willie's taking a short-cut, so the intended referent of *that*$_1$ is clear. Once *that*$_1$ has been pinned down, the other occurrences of *that* and *it* fall readily into place. The presumption that *going right through the path* means the same as taking a short-cut is not justifiable on strictly linguistic grounds. This is one of those communication problems that has to be solved using one's representation of the whole episode and with a heavy reliance on the principle that, whatever the surface form of their utterances, speakers intend to express ideas that make sense. Evidently, Marcus was understood because no one asked him what he meant. Indeed, Randy, the next speaker, responds to Marcus under the assumption that he meant taking a short cut. The *he* in Marcus's second utterance refers to Willie, because Willie is the last male mentioned in the preceding discussion and, also, because Willie is the only character mentioned in the story who might be considered to have been cheating. Thus, the seemingly vague terms in Marcus's utterance were undoubtedly understood by the other participants.

Turning now to the structure of the argument, Marcus is displaying analogical reasoning, reasoning from a clear case to the case being debated.

Explicit premise: Taking drugs before a race to speed you up or give you a head start is cheating.
Explicit premise: Taking a short cut is equivalent to taking drugs.
Explicit premise: Willie took a short cut.

Explicit conclusion: Willie cheated.
Implicit premise: Cheaters should not win.
Implicit conclusion: Willie should not win.
Implicit premise: Either Willie or Stone Fox should win.
Finally, therefore: Stone Fox should win.

The premise, *Cheaters should not win,* is a truism that Marcus can assume all of the other participants in the discussion believe. Likewise, the intermediate conclusion, *Willie should not win,* seems patently obvious. The premise, *Either Willie or Stone Fox should win,* can be considered to be a given, even though there were several other teams in the race, because it was framed by the question the children were discussing, namely whether Stone Fox should let Little Willie win the race.

Reasoning founded on general principles is commonly assumed to be the highest form of moral argumentation (Berkowitz, Oser, & Althof, 1987; Kohlberg, 1984). When we looked at children's arguments to determine whether they were, in fact, reasoning from general principles, in most cases there was insufficient evidence to make a determination. In just three of the 40 arguments subjected to detailed scrutiny did it seem apparent that the speaker was using a general principle to back an argument.

The children seem to regard general principles as truisms that can be taken for granted, as in the case of Marcus who did not bother to mention as part of his argument the principle that *Cheaters should not win.* If this is the right interpretation, it follows that a principle is more likely to be articulated when it *cannot* be taken for granted. This is exactly what we found when we again searched through all of the collaborative reasoning discussion transcripts. General principles were more often made explicit when the principle was paradoxical or surprising in some way, which might make it difficult to understand, or the principle was implicated in a dispute.

An example of a surprising principle that was expressly stated appeared in a discussion of *My Name Is Different* (Prasad & Pileggi, 1987), the story about the Chinese boy who changes his name because he is eager to fit in at his new school.[2]

SAM: Well, I still think he shoulda kept his real name.

TEACHER: Why do you think he should keep his real name?

SAM: Well, 'cause it's the only one at school, and . . .

TEACHER: So it's : (???)

MORGAN: *(hard to hear)* : It's different from :: everybody else.

GRETCHEN: :: I think it's good being different.

Ss: Mh hmm. Yeah.

GRETCHEN: It's kinda neat, because people just

JIMMY: I don't agree.

GRETCHEN: No, 'cause then (*laughs*) ::: I think it's neat to be different because, dif—, 'cause different people do different things, and everybody has different personalities and different w—, ways of thinking.

When Sam argues that Chang Li should keep his real name because *it's the only one at the school,* the teacher is confused. Perhaps to clear up the teacher's confusion, Morgan offers a paraphrase of Sam's point. Gretchen evidently discerns that the teacher's real problem is that she has failed to grasp the unstated principle that lies behind Sam's argument, so Gretchen extends the argument with *I think it's good being different.* People conventionally assume the opposite—that it's good to be like others; indeed, this was the position maintained up to this point in this discussion and throughout an earlier discussion of the same story by another group of children in this class. Because the principle is surprising, it cannot be assumed to be a given and must be expressly stated, an obligation that Gretchen fulfills.

EXPLICIT REFERENCES TO STORY INFORMATION

During any story discussion, the majority of student and teacher contributions of more than a few words contain information that has some basis in the story. In a smaller number of instances, the information is *explicitly labeled* as coming from the story. That is, it is marked with a phrase such as, "The story said," "In the beginning it said," "On page 18 it says," and most commonly just, "It said."

In this section, we examine the discourse functions served by explicitly marking information as from the text and how explicit marking is influenced by the interplay between teachers and students and between students and other students. The analysis is based on eight collaborative reasoning discussions, two from each of four classrooms, and eight recitations, two from each of the same four classrooms. Most attention is given to explicit references to story information during collaborative reasoning, with a briefer treatment of recitation and a comparison of the two forms of discussion.

Students made an average of 8.8 explicit references to story information during a collaborative reasoning discussion but only 1.3 explicit references during a recitation. Teachers' references to story information were the mirror image of student references. There were 3.6 teacher explicit teacher references to story information per collaborative reasoning discussion but 21.8 references per recitation.

Why did students explicitly identify some story information as coming from the story? During collaborative reasoning, in the majority of cases the answer seems to be that the student was claiming the authority of the text to establish a proposition as a fact that could be used as evidence, as in the following exchange during a discussion of *Stone Fox*:

TEACHER: Or is it? Would you agree with Lisa that he [Stone Fox] doesn't have any reason to win the race, but Willie does?

MICHAEL: I think he doesn't have any reason//

DENNIS: He doesn't have//

MICHAEL: because it said in the story that he won about all the races, a lot of them. I think he should at least you know tr— not win one and let Willie anyway because his grandfather's really sick. So, I think he should let Willie win.

In his last contribution quoted above, Michael clearly intends his citation of the text as backing for his position that Stone Fox does not have a compelling reason to win the race.

Teachers prompted for story information twice on average during collaborative reasoning discussions. The prompt usually took the form of asking students if they could find support for their positions in the text. In every case that we analyzed, a student succeeded in finding support in the text. This must mean that the teachers did not issue these prompts unless they were aware that the text contained information that could be used to support the student's position. Students sometimes advanced arguments for which there was little apparent text support, but we did not see teachers prompt for text information in support of these arguments.

In 11 of the 16 instances in which teachers prompted for story information during a collaborative reasoning discussion, the purpose was more than simply checking story memory. The following excerpt from a discussion of *My Name Is Different* illustrates the typical role these prompts played:

TEACHER: Um, Jake, can you find anything in the story that sh—, that, uh, is evidence that he, in fact, does like the new name Charley? [no response from Jake] Or can anyone find some evidence that would indicate that?

ANNA: Um, it says when he was talking to Dan at luncheon, he says, "it's Chang-Li, Chang-Li at home and Charley at school. And that's the way I want it."

TEACHER: Very good. Can anyone find any other evidence that would support that?

The manifest immediate purpose of this exchange was to elicit whether there was textual evidence to support a position. The larger pedagogical purpose was to instill the disposition to support positions with evidence.

During collaborative reasoning, students often quoted the text following teacher prompts for text support; that is, they read aloud relevant sentences directly from the text. This happened, especially, when the teacher asked if students could "find" any evidence in the text; when the teacher simply asked if there "was" any evidence in the text, students would identify information but were less likely to read it aloud or cite the place in the text where it could be found.

The next to the last turn in the episode below illustrates a teacher prompt for supporting story information during a collaborative reasoning discussion of *My Name Is Different.*

JENNIE: But that, but he wants to be called Charley. Because, so he can fit in. He should explain that. And then, maybe more people would want him to keep his name because they don't have any hard feelings or anything like them, and they like that name, some people might like it.

A STUDENT: Japan.

TEACHER: Do you think people would be interested in learning more about him?

JENNIE: Mm hmm.

A STUDENT: Yeah. (*Todd shakes his head.*)

TEACHER: Is there any evidence of that, in the story?

JENNIE: Yeah, kind of, like um Dan and his friends, when they were watching him, and they kept asking him why they had to jump over the fire and stuff.

Usually, as in the example above, a student responding to a teacher prompt for text evidence did *not* mark the information he or she provided as from the text. There was no need to; that it was to be information from the text was a constraint the teacher had already furnished. Thus when students did mark information as from the text during collaborative reasoning discussions, they did so because of influences beyond teacher prompting.

The principal influence that we were able to discover was whether a point was disputed. Here is an excerpt from a discussion of *Making Room for Uncle Joe* that illustrates the role of dispute in calling forth explicit text references. *Making Room for Uncle Joe* (Litchfield & Owens, 1984) describes a family that has an uncle with Down syndrome who must find a new place to live. The question is, "Should Uncle Joe be invited to live with the family?"

JAMES: Well, now, I'm in between, because it is his [Uncle Joe's] choice, and we don't know what he said, I mean . . .

Ss: He said he would. He said that he wanted to.

ALVIN: Yeah, he said . . .

STEPHAN: He wanted to stay, because . . .

ALVIN: : Right here . . .

CRYSTAL: : He helps Beth with her :: piano lessons, and he teaches himself at the piano.

ALVIN: ::: It says, and it says . . .

ALVIN: He said, "I wanna stay here (???) so I can work hard, and pay for my food," and it's there all the time. (???)

The teachers cited the story on 1.1 occasions per collaborative reasoning discussion. Most of the occasions arose when the teacher assumed the role of Devil's Advocate, as illustrated in the episode below from a discussion of *Making Room for Uncle Joe*. The students were all defending the position that Uncle Joe should live with the family, so the teacher entered the discussion to present an argument on the other side and supported it by citing text evidence:

TEACHER: Okay, at the beginning of the story Uncle Joe came to live with the family when his home closed. Um, at the end of the story he had a chance to go and live with some other people, and he liked the idea that maybe he was going to be independent, [and] he would live on his own and earn his own money. What do you think about that idea? He wants to go out and earn his own money and live on his own. Bryan?

Teachers seldom praised the use of story information in collaborative reasoning discussions. On the few occasions where praise was seen, the function was to reinforce use of evidence to support reasoning, as in the episode below from a discussion of *Making Room for Uncle Joe*:

BRIAN: It says here that, on the last page it says, [reading] "Yuppee shouted Amy. She climbed into Uncle Joe's lap and gave him a big hug." And then it said, "And Uncle Joe, he looked so happy, nobody cared that he had forgotten to comb his hair or [he left a mess of] of crumbs around his plate on the floor. (???) on the floor. We all knew in many ways Uncle Joe is a neat guy."

TEACHER: Okay, [Jared?: good] good use of story evidence, Brian. You shot down my challenge. Okay. What about the fact that they're gonna have to drive in to work every day. Will dad get tired of doing that [Bryan: No!] if he's living with them all the time?

Claims based on what was not in the text served interesting rhetorical purposes in collaborative reasoning discussions. One purpose was to attack the credibility of an opposing position as in Jerry's remark in the following episode from a discussion of *Amy's Goose* (Holmes & Tudor, 1977). This is a story about a farm girl who is starting to nurse an injured goose back to health. The question is should she let the goose fly south with the rest of the flock.

LAURA: Well, it could die in the cage //

JERRY: How do you know? There's not any evidence.

LAURA: He could get his neck stuck in it or anything.

Inferences based on what was *not* said in the story were also used as backing for arguments. The episode below is from a discussion of *Stone Fox*. The issue is whether it was legitimate for Willie to take a shortcut across a frozen lake. Nate argues that it was legitimate because the story does not mention rules prohibiting this maneuver.

TODD: It's on page 238, I think.

SS: (*reading together*) "Instead of following the turn, Willie took a short cut across the lake."

NATE: But it doesn't say in the beginning of the story that there's no shortcuts.

TEACHER: Some people would say that if somebody takes a shortcut and gets off the race path, that's cheating//

KATHERINE: But//

TEACHER: —and so, you don't deserve to win.

[Shouting]

TEACHER: Excuse me, one person at a time. Let's let Katherine have a chance.

KATHERINE: But it does not matter, bec— well I don't know, but it said no one else *dared* to go across the lake, so it does *not* actually, I mean, it says that on the page, so I don't really know if he cheated or not, because it just says nobody else dared to go across the lake.

[Shouting]

TONY: It doesn't say in the story, er it didn't really say the rules of the race, but . . .

Turning now to recitations, students cited the story an average of 1.1 times per discussion, a much lower rate than the same students exhibited during collaborative reasoning. Furthermore, a close analysis shows that most of the apparent citations of the story during recitations ought to be discounted. Six of the total of nine instances were references to letters described in the story, *Making Room for Uncle Joe,* as in the following excerpt.

TEACHER: Good. So things were comfortable. They were finding good things about having Uncle Joe there. And then another letter came. And what did it say? Jody?

JODY: It said that the social worker found an apartment for him to live in and then everybody didn't want him to go.

The student, Jody, is referring to a text described within a text. Referring to the letter mentioned in the story is not equivalent to citing the story, as we have defined it. Thus the frequency of citations of the story, indeed, of all explicit student references to the story, was vanishingly small during recitations.

In contrast, teachers prompted for story information an average of 16.6 times per recitation. This high rate is the defining characteristic of a recitation. In virtually every instance, the teachers appeared to be quizzing students to check for complete and accurate story memory, manifest in such phrases as "Does anyone remember . . . ?"

Teachers cited the story 5.1 times per recitation. The immediate function of citing the story usually seemed to be to locate a question in relation to the stream of events described in the story and thus constrain the answer to the question, as in the following recitation.

TEACHER: Okay, yesterday we read the story, *My Name Is Different.* Can anyone tell me at the beginning of the story why Chang Li had to go to a different school, Warren?

WARREN: Yes, because the other school was too crowded.

We did not complete a quantitative analysis of teacher praise for use of story information during recitations. However, almost every student response that contained accurate information was at least acknowledged ("Okay," "Mm hmm") and many were praised ("Right," "Very good"). The teacher's purpose seemed to be to reinforce displays of knowledge.

SUMMARY

Comparison of two different approaches to story discussion, recitation and collaborative reasoning, reveals remarkable differences not only in group interactions but also at the level of discussion content. At the level of group interactions, we see a one-way I–R–E pattern of interactions between students and their teacher during recitations. Here, the teacher typically controls all aspects of the conversation, from topic selection to assigning speaking rights to students. Rather than talking with one another, students talk mostly to the teacher. In contrast, a collaborative reasoning discussion contains a more complex pattern of interactions among students and their teacher. More transactional in nature, there is a "balance of rights" (Au & Mason, 1981) in the interactions between students and teacher. Students negotiate for speaking turns and the topic of conversation with one another. As a consequence, there are more interjections and student-to-student sequences of turns during the collaborative reasoning discussions. Probably because of increased engagement, and release from the conventional rigamarole of turn-taking, student words per minute almost double. Corresponding changes in the teacher's role appear. They express slightly fewer words per minute, ask many fewer assessment questions, and ask somewhat more open-ended questions.

At the level of the content of the discussions, a recitation consists of a review of the main points of a story. Teachers pose questions that are directly tied to the events in the stories to assess students' knowledge. Mostly directed at the teacher, students' responses usually express specific information contained in stories, and less frequently express inferences bridging story events or affective responses to story circumstances, and almost never express arguments about an issue raised in the story.

During collaborative reasoning discussions, most utterances express arguments, challenge the arguments of other participants, or respond to challenges with elaboration and supporting information. These arguments frequently seem vague and elliptical. However, close analysis suggests that generally participants are as informative as they need to be, because the unstated or vaguely identified information usually is *given* in the sense that it is readily inferable by other active participants in the discussion (Anderson et al., 1997). Utterances during collaborative reasoning often reflect a personal affective response to circumstances facing story characters and are usually directed toward other students, rather than toward the teacher.

During recitations, students seldom ever make explicit references to the story, whereas teachers frequently do. Teachers refer to the story to prompt students to remember information and to frame questions in a manner that constrains the answers. During recitations, teachers nearly always acknowledge or praise accurate student displays of story information.

Collaborative reasoning presents a quite different picture. Students make frequent explicit references to story information, chiefly to bolster arguments with evidence. Teachers make sparing use of explicit story references. When they do use them, the purpose is to back up their own arguments, elicit supporting evidence from students, or to reinforce students' spontaneous use of evidence.

NOTES

1. "that$_1$, it$_1$" = taking a short-cut across the lake; "that$_2$, it$_2$" = taking drugs; "going right through the path = taking a short-cut across the lake; "he" = Willie.

2. ". . ." indicates a pause of about 3 seconds; "//" indicates that a speaker was interrupted; "(???)" indicates the transcriber couldn't make out the speech; and ": : :" indicates overlapping speech.

REFERENCES

Anderson, R., Chinn, C., Chang, J., Waggoner, M., & Yi, H. (1997). On the logical integrity of children's arguments. *Cognition and Instruction, 15*(2), 135–167.

Au, K. H., & Mason, J. M. (1981). Social organizational factors in learning to read: The balance of rights hypothesis. *Reading Research Quarterly, 17,* 115–152.

Berkowitz, M. B., Oser, F., & Althof, W. (1987). The development of sociomoral discourse. In W. Kurtines & J. Gewirtz (Eds.), *Moral development through social interaction* (pp. 301–321). New York: Wiley.

Cazden, C. B. (1988). *Classroom discourse: The language of teaching and learning* (p. 134). Portsmouth, NH: Heinemann.

Chinn, C., Anderson, R., & Waggoner, M. (in preparation). Patterns of participation during different kinds of story discussion.

Commeyras, M. (1994). Promoting critical thinking through dialogical thinking reading lessons. *Reading Teacher, 46,* 486–494.

Eeds, M., & Wells, D. (1989). Grand conversations: An explanation of meaning construction in literature study groups. *Research in the Teaching of English, 23*(1), 4–29.

Gardiner, J. R. (M. Sewall, illus.). (1980). *Stone fox.* New York: Crowell.

Gee, J. P. (1992). *The social mind: Language, ideology, and social practice.* New York: Bergin & Garvey.

Holmes, E. T., & Tudor, T. (1977). *Amy's goose.* New York: Crowell.

Kohlberg, L. (1984). *The psychology of moral development: The nature and validity of moral stages.* San Francisco: Harper & Row.

Litchfield, A. B. (G. Owens, illus.). (1984). *Making room for Uncle Joe.* Niles, IL: A. Whitman.

Mehan, H. (1972). "What time is it, Denise?": Asking known information questions classroom discourse. *Theory into Practice, 18*(4), 285–294.

Prasad, N. (S. Pileggi, illus.). (1987). *What it means to be proud: My name is different.* Toronto: Grolier.

Raphael, T. E., & McMahon, S. I. (1994). Book club: An alternative framework for reading instruction. *Reading Teacher, 48,* 102–116.

Short, K. G., & Pierce, K. M. (1990). *Talking about books: Creating literate communities.* Portsmouth, NH: Heinemann.

Sinclair, J. M., & Coulthard, R. M. (1975). *Towards an analysis of discourse: The English used by teachers and pupils.* London: Oxford University Press.

Waggoner, M., Chinn, C., Yi, H., & Anderson, R. (1995). Collaborative reasoning about stories. *Language Arts, 72,* 582–589.

PART THREE

WRITING AND LEARNING TO WRITE

CHAPTER NINE

Some Things We Know about Learning to Write

SARAH WARSHAUER FREEDMAN

University of California, Berkeley

In this chapter, I focus on learning to write during the secondary school years, especially for those students who are behind in their reading and writing skills and who are not succeeding in school. These students may enter high school never having read a whole book or written any extended prose; they may have spent their time in school in the lowest academic tracks, and they may be in danger of dropping out of school. Using findings from recent research, I offer a vision of how classrooms and schools can form and reform themselves to help these students increase their literacy skills and become participants in the academic conversation.

I focus on a low-tracked, multiethnic, inner-city, grade-9 classroom in the United States, in which formerly low-achieving adolescents, under the tutelage of master teacher Bridget Franklin, begin to reach high literacy standards.[1] Bridget's class was one of 20 that collaborated on a research project comparing learning to write in schools in Britain and the United States. As part of the research, about 500 inner-city students in grades six to nine exchanged their writing and served as audiences for one another for an entire school year. Half of the classes were in London and half were in the San Francisco Bay area. For the writing exchanges, each U.S. class was paired with an age-appropriate partner class in England. For example, Bridget's grade-9 class was paired with Philippa Furlong's Form 4 (grade-9) group. Alex McLeod at the University of London Institute of Education, along with teacher Ellie O'Sullivan, coordinated the British end of the exchanges, while I coordinated the United States end as well as the entire project. The goal of the research was to look at teaching writing in the two countries, from the points of view of research teams, teachers, and students on both sides of the Atlantic to get some new ideas about how best to meet the needs of all of our students. The complete results of the research are published in *Exchanging Writing, Exchanging Cultures* (Freedman, 1994).

In the San Francisco area we worked with varied kinds of classes, but we decided intentionally to work with some of the lowest tracks and to try to design activities to help students move out of these tracks. The majority of students in Bridget's group, 68%, were African American, and 80% were members of some minority group; they also were mostly male, 79%—a mismatch with the demographics of the school, which was 50–50 male/female and 50% minority—not atypical for low-tracked U.S. inner-city classrooms. Bridget was acutely aware of the injustices of the tracking system and has worked tirelessly to convince administrators in her school and her school district to abolish it. She has been somewhat successful and has written a great deal about her work with "detracking."

In Britain, mixed-ability classes are more common, and Philippa, Bridget's partner for the writing exchange, taught a mixed-ability group. The demographics of Philippa's class matched those of her school. Both her class and her school were composed of about 50% Afro-Caribbean students and 25% white students. The remaining 25% were bilingual children of families from the Indian subcontinent, Africa, and the Mediterranean. At the time of this research, Philippa was in her fourth year of teaching the same group of students; she began teaching them when they entered her school in Form 1 (U.S. grade 6).

As was the case for Bridget's and Philippa's classes, students in all of the paired classes in the study exchanged writing across the academic year, with the paired teachers and often their students working together to make their writing programs for the year center on the exchange activities. For a year-long curriculum, it was critical to move beyond pen-pal letters and to center the exchanges on a variety of types of writing. The idea was to exchange substantive pieces of work that would be of interest to students in another country. Although personal writing was encouraged and even facilitated, the main academic business of the exchanges was to provide an occasion for students in the two countries to write substantial pieces for a distant, but real, whole-class audience. The writing included, for example, autobiographies, books about the schools and communities, fiction and poetry, essays about books students had read, and opinion pieces about important and often controversial issues. The paired classes frequently decided to engage in parallel topics for writing.

The writing exchanges provided a theoretically sound curricular framework, including meaningful and varied types of writing for a peer audience. They were designed to support the cross-national study and also to engage the student writers. However, like all activities, they are insufficient to stimulate writing growth. Theoretically sound activities are necessary but provide no panacea. Rather, deeper principles guide the implementation of theoretically sound activities, and it is the adherence to the deeper principles that leads to academically successful classrooms. In the next section, I offer a brief description of the strategies that I found key to a successful writing exchange and that I hypothesize underlie effective practice in the teaching of writing. This section is followed by an illustration of how Bridget puts each strategy into practice.

STRATEGIES FOR TEACHING WRITING

The first strategy for Bridget (as well as for other exchange teachers) was to integrate the students' social worlds and their academic worlds. The exchange was designed purposefully to break into the peer network and to make literacy something that would be respected and valued, something "cool" to do. Ogbu and others (Fordham, 1988; Fordham & Ogbu, 1986; Ogbu, 1974, 1985, 1990) have identified social forces that work against disaffected students. Most problematic is the fact that the peer group disdains school success and rejects students who do their school work, making them social outcasts. Given the adolescent desire to be accepted, it is crucial to reverse this dynamic. As part of the writing exchanges, we encouraged sharing student culture, including rap music and graffiti tags (secret names the students use with one another and in the graffiti writing they do, often in public places). We also gave students a role that we hoped ultimately would have status in the peer group; the students were enlisted as fellow researchers, as partners with the university team and their teachers in finding out how schooling in England was similar to and different from what they experienced in the United States. As researchers, the students' opinions were valued because they could contribute important information to the study itself. Finally and perhaps most importantly, the exchange enlarged the social world of the students, in the case of Bridget's group, to include a mixed-ability class from another country with many students who were deeply engaged in school and in literacy activities. This enlarged peer group weakened the deleterious effects of the tracking system that is so pervasive in U.S. schools. The result was that Bridget's students were curious about the students in England, and they wanted to be recognized and valued by them. But interactions occurred only through writing. In the end, Bridget engaged students academically by intermingling their academic and social worlds.

A second strategy Bridget used to support her students' emerging interests in literacy was to structure her classroom both to create a whole-class literacy community and to attend to the needs of each developing individual. She allowed different students to write in different ways, depending on their needs. At the same time she provided a space that was welcoming for groups of friends, to the point where her students and their friends in other classes often "hung out" in her classroom during lunch. She also had a number of successful strategies for involving usually noninteracting parents and bringing them and their voices into the classroom.

Bridget's third strategy was to maintain high expectations for her students and to provide a kind of instruction that would help students to meet high standards. To move the exchange from activities in which students just practiced writing to activities in which they improved their skills, Bridget used the writing that came from England to help her students analyze, talk about, and then practice what makes a piece successful and what appeals to a distant audience. She then helped her students incorporate features that were missing or that were not effective in their own pieces. It is important to note that Bridget and the other teachers at her school were working with University of California, Berkeley Professor Rhona Weinstein on a project in which they studied their expectations and the effects of those expectations on their students' performance (Weinstein et al., 1991).

Bridget's fourth strategy was to involve her students in activities that they cared about by working together with them to craft the literacy curriculum. She neither turned over curricular decision making to the students nor left them out; rather she and her students decided jointly what projects to do to send to England. As part of this process of joint decision making, Bridget watched to be sure her students were taking on increasingly challenging tasks, both in substance and scope, as the year went on.

SCENES FROM BRIDGET FRANKLIN'S CLASSROOM

Integrating the Social and Academic

How did Bridget merge the students' social and academic lives? Although it was not a letter-writing, pen-pal exchange, the program began with letters, many of which were more social than academic. Through these letters, the students began to develop social connections within their own class and with the British class, that both allowed them to get to know the needs of their audience, to trust the audience, and to feel safe communicating with it. It was these social relationships that formed the base for future, more traditional academic work.

When the U.S. students wrote their letters, they had not yet received letters from England. Bridget recalls that, "They wrote a very safe, kind of formal letters. . . . That's just how they felt that they were supposed to write" (Interview, December 13, 1988). As Easy E., a student in Bridget's class, confirmed, "I mean people were, we were at first, um, we were like, tightened—tightened up, you know" (Interview, March 21, 1988). Indeed, Easy E.'s letter seems tight:

Dear Girls and Boys in England,

My name is Easy E. and I am 14 years old and I love to play sports like football, basketball, and track.

I've played football and run track for a team but I've never played basketball for a team.

(*He concludes*)

I would like to know if any of you girls or guys have any plans to come to America and visited.

I would like to know something you think that makes your school special. Here at El Cerrito High School we have our own radiostation.

Your friend . . .

Easy E.

Slightly more adventurous, another student, Geya, writes:

Hi, My name is Geya Anderson but mostly everyone at home and school calls me Gey. I am a black afro American and I am 5 ft. 2 in. I have black hair that goes down to my neck. When I was small I had very long hair but as I grew up it kind of broke off. Most of the time I still wish I had long hair but I know that if I keep it up my wish just might come true.

(*Then after describing her family, she writes*)

You know I would like to ask you something now if I am kind of making you angry then I apologize but I would like to know if you have any black people out there. The reason I am asking is because I only see the other color on T.V. and I was just curious.

Geya's question about whether there are blacks in England and her comment about the absence of black people on English television provoked a profound discussion in Philippa's class about the representation of blacks on English television, one that continued all year.

Cool J. sums up the U.S. students' initial sense of the English audience at this point: "They're so far away, I was thinking of them like aliens" (Interview, March 10, 1988).

Then the English letters arrived, and the students "over there" were suddenly no longer aliens. Most important in opening the social connections was the following letter from Titch:

Hi to all you funky def people, in 9th grade, it's Titch.

I will start by telling you a bit about my self, I am 14 years old and will be 15 years on January 2nd. . . .

I go to an school called Hampden Jones, I am in the 4th year [which just started].

I suppose its quite good fun, doing our project and finding things out for your self.

At the moment we are doing course work for are New exam, GCSE.

In England our years are different from the ones in America, we have years and you have grades.

Well enough about school, ill talke about the things I do!!!

I love going out with friends espeacially travlling.

I Also Love raving at Jams [parties].

That brings me on to another point. I am one person who canot do with out music.

Especially, Hip Hop, Soul, Reggaie. I hate heavey metal and all of that pop.

You must write me, who ever I am speaking to?!?

I have been to America, New Jearsy It was beautiful. When I grow up I would love to come over and live. [Hopefully] England is not bad, I suppose most of the time its pretty cold, Apart from that its okay

oh before I forget I am also an freaky person, well me and my couson Louise she is in the same class and is also writing a letter to you all. We wear really freaky outfits. As for the hair, our hair, well that's freaky too.

I do suppose your freaky too who ever you are?

I have got an Tag, it is Pride

thats what I am know as

Anyway I will hope
ill here from you.
[address] Here my address
again.
Love ya
Titch
xx

Although from Philippa's point of view Titch was not the most eloquent writer, she spoke to her audience quite well. Philippa reported that Titch was the only student in the class who had needed special help with her skills. Titch was masterful, though, at establishing common ground with Bridget's students—through her use of language, her musical tastes, her love of parties, and even her love of the United States. Titch made herself so likable and real that many of the grade-9 boys in Bridget's class fell in love with her, quite literally, and several of the U.S. girls became jealous. No teacher could have given the academic plans for the exchange as effective an endorsement as Titch did when she wrote, "I suppose it's quite good fun, doing our project and finding things out for your self"; or when she pleaded, "You must write me, who ever I am speaking to?!?"

Easy E. stressed the importance of Titch's letter as well as several other British letters to his class's attitudes and to their immediate comfort and identification with this new audience:

At first . . . I wasn't really interested . . . I guess everybody, you know, we just took it like an assignment . . . you know, we gotta do this for a grade

... She [Bridget] explained it, but I guess, we didn't really catch on until after, you know, we got letters from England, and everybody was like wow! ... So we really like got into it, and we started telling them about like what we do out here, and it was really fun. But like in the first beginning, I guess we were just like, you know, we were just, you know, we'll do what she says 'cause that's what she wants.

The way they wrote their letters, it was really like I mean they were our friends, and we didn't even really meet them. I mean it was you know they was talking to us and I was like, I mean, you know, I never . . . expected nothing like it.

They did basically what we did, but it was just, you know, they were in a different country and stuff. And it was just like it was another me over there. (Interview, March 21, 1988)

So all of a sudden the British audience went from being "like aliens" to being "like another me over there." Quite a transformation. Ice T. devoted a special section of his autobiography to Titch. He drew a picture of a rose on the computer which he surrounded with small hearts and on which he wrote, "FRESH YOU ARE LIKE A ROSE." Also in the middle of his autobiography, he wrote a quite protective note to her:

I hope to get a letter from Titch because she is freaky. My friend Easy E. and all the boys in the class really like Titch but someone should tell her that freak means a whole different meaning in America than it does in England. It does not mean what you think it means—out here it means that you like to have sex a lot. I hope you are not mad at me for telling you this.

The students were playing with multiple meanings of the word *freak* that were then common in the popular culture, including those in the then popular song, *Superfreak,* by Rick James.

Like Ice T., his friends Cool J. and Easy E. also discussed feeling an immediate closeness to the students in England once these letters arrived. Cool J. went a step further to emphasize the positive effects on his writing: "Now I . . . feel like I know some of the people over there—you just open up and write to them" (Interview, March 10, 1988).

Bridget used the exchange to draw her students in socially. This kind of writing was fun for them. They were motivated to write, and they saw a function for writing in their lives. They were comfortable bringing in aspects of their youth culture and telling about their homes, and they were definitely enlarging their social networks. The next challenge was to transfer their enthusiasm to more traditionally academic pieces of work.

Meeting Individual Needs and Creating Community

To attend to her students' individual needs, Bridget allowed students to be drawn into the exchange in different ways. Although she worked hard to create a safe community, she also accepted and made room for students' different ways of learning. It certainly would have been easy to let the social, vocal, and enthusiastic large group of black male students take over, but Bridget saw other students who were responding differently, who did not feel an immediate closeness. These students were allowed a slower route to getting to know the British students. Geya, who was open at first, became more cautious in her responses than the boys. A loner in her own class, she took time to warm up to the students from abroad. Although less "tight" than Easy E. in her first letter, Geya began the year feeling much more comfortable with Bridget as an audience than with her peers in her own class or with the students in England. Bridget built on this:

> From the very first she [Geya] wrote really long things. Now that's not true of her papers for them [the British students]. But when she writes stories for me, or she writes summaries or something, she really takes her time.

> She's just terrifically shy, and that's very inhibiting with her writing when she's writing for somebody else, but when she's writing for me, I think she really, she wants to please me a lot. (Interview, February 24, 1988)

Given the diverse ways the students were responding to the British audience, how did Bridget allow for the differences? How the students composed their autobiographies provides an example. First, they worked in class on computers and the computers offered the students an opportunity to collaborate if they wanted to. Easy E. describes how they helped each other:

> She [Bridget] wanted, uh it [the autobiography] to be perfect I guess. And so everybody was okay okay, I'll change this and you know so it was, I mean everybody helped each other out and stuff. And so then we got on the computers, and you know we were thinking about, oh I think I should change this and you know we were asking each other for help and everybody was helping each other. . . . We were having fun I mean, cause I get—I—no— think I can speak for everybody when I say um, most of—most of the kids in the class we never did nothing like that. It just—we just got into it and it was exciting and we wanted to keep it going, keep going. (Interview, March 21, 1988)

Cool J. confirms this collaborative spirit:

> In my class, Run helped me. You know me and him we'd—we would always work next to each other 'cause we both sports fans, so we talk

about the hoop game or—and you know I'd ask him—you know we'd—
we'd just helped each other out. I'd ask him how you spell this and how
should I put this and it went the same for him. We helped each other a
lot. (Interview, March 10, 1988)

It would be easy to let Easy E. "speak for everybody," as he says he
can do, to hear only his positive message. But Rose, for example, when
asked if she worked with anyone at the computer, replies, "No. Um I do
better by myself" (Interview, March 2, 1988). Geya, too, in keeping with
her caution about a peer audience, describes her difficulties composing
publicly at the computer:

> Every time I get ready to write, or to type or something, everybody would
> try to come over my shoulder and look and I don't like that. . . . They
> just come and watch and try to peek at my stuff. Say "Don't look, get
> away!" And I'll be hiding with my hands. They just trying to steal my
> stuff. . . . They nosy. They want to know what I do. 'Cause I'm a loner,
> and you know, I like to—I like being by myself. And they just want to
> know what my business is, "Yeah that's my business, get away!" (Inter-
> view, March 21, 1988)

In the same interview, when she was asked, "Is there anybody that—
that you—you let share it with?" Geya replied quickly, "Ms. Franklin."

Bridget took care to allow students with academic needs as different
as Geya's and Easy E.'s to find their own ways into writing in her classroom.

High Standards and High Expectations

Bridget's third strategy involved maintaining high expectations by providing
time for explicit talk about what makes good writing and by encouraging
the students to become conscious of their decisions as writers. She quite
deliberately used the British writing to help her students analyze and
articulate for themselves what makes writing effective—to help them
develop metacognitive awareness, to know that they know general principles behind effective writing. Then they began to imitate the effective styles.
As they talked about the British work, the U.S. students discussed the
qualities that made the British autobiographies interesting and made the U.
S. students as readers feel that they actually knew the British writers.
Bridget writes in her journal:

> I noticed that as I went along it was easy to point out things about
> effective writing to the kids. The British kids who write the most
> interesting autobiographies were those who *showed* not *told* and who
> gave enough background information to make themselves clear. Those
> whose stories were mere lists of places and events received the poorest

ratings by my students. We talked a lot about the students that we liked best from what they wrote and the students we felt we knew best (usually one and the same), and we discussed why we had those feelings. The kids clearly got the point that they need to "jump off the page" in order to engage their reader.

Bridget helped her students anticipate and meet the needs of the British students, encouraging their attempts through their writing to gain entry into the social lives of the distant class while at the same time working with her class to take the academic steps necessary to write to a general rather than an individual audience.

Finally, Bridget worked with her students to make curricular decisions. This negotiation of activities is something that was less common among the U.S. teachers than among the English ones. It was also a fully articulated theory in England. In the United States, we tend to talk about student-centered curriculum in which we individualize instruction. Teachers in England tend to reject the term "student centered" because to them it does not take into account notions of community. Although Bridget did negotiate with her students, it is not something she or any of the U.S. teachers talked about, nor were their negotiations part of a well-developed theory. The teachers in England explained clearly what is involved in their kind of negotiation. They also showed how their notions of negotiation differ from what most U.S. educators think about when they conceptualize a negotiated curriculum:

> It's not like ... within that negotiation there's complete anarchy ... There's a certain level of negotiation which is between them and myself about choosing something which, yes, is interesting, but also sometimes it's choosing something which will stretch them as learners. And so you're working together to develop and push them to higher standards and to produce better material and, and more interesting work. (Interview, British teacher, Fiona Rodgers, August 20, 1992)

There are clear roles for both the teacher and the students. There is no giving up of power; rather, both teacher and student gain power. The teachers in England stressed the importance of their students' assuming responsibility, but they agreed that their students had to be taught to assume responsibility gradually across years of time. Since British teachers usually keep the same group of students for 2 years or more, this gradual exchanging of responsibility was supported in England in ways that it is not in the United States.

The British teachers also agreed that students learn to write by practicing a variety of types of writing—but only when they are motivated to do so. They saw it as their job to set contexts to motivate their students. The most motivating contexts, these teachers believed, spring from the community of learners in the classroom. For this reason community building is valued over individualization. The teachers in England explained that each child does not have a different program of study because that approach devalues the role of the classroom culture and in particular the way discussions, activities, and frequently writing are motivated by the interaction of students with each other and with their teacher.

If a student is not motivated to practice and master certain types of writing, teachers in England consider it their failure in setting motivating contexts. Unmotivated students are never expected to write on a topic just because it is assigned; rather, they are expected to do a different activity that *is* motivating. For example, in a grade-8 equivalent class taught by another of the teachers in England, Peter Ross, his very able student Dickens (a pseudonym he chose) only wanted to write stories. Peter saw it as his job to try to interest Dickens in doing other kinds of writing. In his interviews early in the year, Dickens commented about what he called "factual writing": "In my opinion that's pretty boring. . . . I prefer being inventive." As the year went on, he spoke about his teacher's role in motivating him to want to do other sorts of writing. The class wrote books about London for U.S. readers, and Peter, who had formerly led walking tours for tourists, took his students on some local trips to help them gather material for this "factual" writing.

> I like what I'm doing now, about writing about London because I think the way Mr. Ross planned that was to make it interesting to start with, like taking us all round London to see, you're taking in all the sights . . . I think we treated that day out not as a school trip but sort of more of a leisure trip. I think that might be the way Mr. Ross planned it. So that we'd be more interested in it when we came back.

Peter used the force of the classroom community, in particular the community adventure of touring London, to motivate Dickens as well as his other students. By the end of the year Dickens had reached the point of believing that "factual writing" was okay, depending on what type of writing it is:

> I think it depends for me on the type of information writing it is. Cause what I don't like doing, what I hate, really hate, about English, is when you have to read a book and then write about five pages on it. I can't stand that. That's awful.

We left Peter with the challenge of getting Dickens excited about writing about books.

Across the varied exchanges, those classrooms that followed this philosophy of negotiation of the curriculum were most successful with this underachieving population of students. This kind of negotiation both honors Delpit's (1988) call for explicit instruction and the call of those who talk about empowering students. But it is a different kind of "empowering" than we talk about here in the United States. Basically, teacher and students work as a team, with each having important decision-making roles and with the assumption that students have to be taught to assume these roles.

SAMPLING WHAT THE STUDENTS ACCOMPLISHED

As the social writing continued, Bridget helped her students to produce a number of serious academic pieces. For his holiday paper in January, Cool J. wrote about the birthday of Dr. Martin Luther King Jr. In an interview, Cool J. expressed his strong motivation for writing on this topic. First of all, he was frustrated with some of his fellow students' attitudes about their heritage, "Most of the blacks in the class and in that school, you know, they just walk around like it ain't no big trip, you know." Cool J. believes strongly that it is important to recognize those who have come before us and the contributions that they made to our present society. He writes the following heartfelt words about his thoughts on the occasion of Dr. King's birthday:

> I celebrate Dr. King's birthday by just thinking about what he did for me. Dr. King didn't want to be remembered for all the awards he won and his education, but for what he did for his people. Times aren't as bad as they used to be, but in some parts of Southern America blacks are still treated like # * @ %. Last year in Georgia blacks got together to march (led by Reverend Jesse Jackson) in an all-white county in honor of Dr. King. The whites didn't want the blacks to march. The whites threw rocks and sang "go home nigger's." But blacks kept on keeping on.
>
> Dr. King won a lot of awards. One of the most famous was the Nobel Peace Prize. Dr. King touched a lot of people's lives. Because of Dr. King Reverend Jesse Jackson is running for the democratic spot for the up coming presidential election. Rev. Jesse Jackson isn't the first black person to run but, the first to have a national campaign. In Arizona which is a state in the U. S. their govenor didn't want to honor Dr. King's birthday. I'm kind of upset that it took from 1968 to 1983 to honor Dr. King's birthday.
>
> I hope you like what I wrote to you. And I would like to hear from a black student and hear what he or she knows or has to say.

In an interview, Cool J. says that this piece of writing "came from the heart . . . I thought about all he did, not just for blacks, but for everyone, you know. He was a good man." When asked if he had to choose just one piece of his writing to go to England, which would it be, Cool J. replied that he would send the Martin Luther King Jr. piece rather than his own autobiography because "Little Cool J. you know they can wait to know about

Cool J." Dr. King is already famous, and "because it is a different country maybe they should know about him."

The English research team reported that Cool J.'s essay had a great impact on the students in Philippa's class. When the holiday papers arrived, the students in England sat in groups of three or four reading, and Philippa invited each student to choose one to read aloud to the class. Tootsie, after reading Cool J.'s piece, announced to the class that she was going to read this one aloud and that she was going to write to Cool J. about it. Tootsie's need to respond to Cool J. was so urgent that, encouraged by Philippa, she wrote on the back of a letter Philippa was preparing to send to Bridget:

> To Cool J., I'm just writing a short message to say that I thought your essay on the national holiday of Martin Luther King was very interesting and that I agreed with your point that it took them from 1968 up to 1983 before they decided to honour the many great things that he did. Not only for black Americans but for people all over the world.

Cool J. proudly volunteered, "I received a note from Tootsie. She said she liked it and appreciated how I wrote it, and she agreed with my point that it took from 1968 to 1983 just to honor his birthday" (Interview, March 10, 1988).

In her February letter, Philippa reported an enthusiastic response of the English students to the U.S. holiday essays, crediting the exchange audience—and by implication its cross-cultural aspect—with dramatically heightening motivation for writing in her class. Cool J.'s friend, Easy E., informed the U.S. researchers that the English kids especially liked Cool J.'s piece because "he wrote about Martin Luther King, and you know, they don't have that holiday so, they were interested in that" (Interview, June 10, 1988).

When the holiday papers arrived from England, Ice T. recalled that "Miss Franklin lined us up in like a circle, and she passed one out to everybody, we all read it, we read it out loud." It is important to note here that the students needed support reading; otherwise they would not have been able to take advantage of the metacognitive opportunity or to make the social connections. It is not easy to read and appreciate students' writing that comes from another country, and students need help on multiple levels.

As the year went on, Geya began to write to the English students with the kind of trust she had placed earlier only in Bridget even though she remained too shy to open up to her U.S. peers. We see here the "pay-off" Bridget got for allowing Geya her own way into the exchange. For the Shakespeare assignment—to help students connect to the motivations of Romeo and Juliet—Bridget asked each member of the class to write about a rash deed of his or her own. Geya told about a truly rash deed of her own, cutting school when she was 12 to go off with a 21-year-old man. Geya hoped the English students would learn from her mistake even though she emphasized that she did not actually do anything really bad.

Easy E. who wrote about his father's rash deed explains how he differentiates between audiences now:

> Like if I was talking to um Ice T. or Rex or you know, just one of my friends I be with everyday, just you know, writing a letter to them, you know and you know we be together everyday, so I would say, man wasn't that crazy what my father did, you know and have it you know where they you know, man that was, man I would never do that, you know and have em so you know they would probably laugh, and say you know just you know, something really different because you know, I be with them all the time. This is just some of like a way you know you can make em laugh, so you can just write something. (Interview, April 28, 1988)

Finally, some of Bridget's students wrote moving responses to controversial issues papers from their English correspondents. For example, Geya, now fully engaged, wrote a response to a piece arguing against abortion. In her response, which was longer than the original piece, Geya concurred that abortion is basically wrong, but after a brief paragraph in which she states this point and qualifies it, she quickly moves on to discuss her feelings about teenage pregnancy. She marks this shift in concern: "Now on the mother of the child that is having a child is a different matter, not the murder part but the taking care of the child part." She later reveals:

> . . . all the girls that I know are pregant and are 13–17 yrs. old it seems to me that they are just saying I don't care anymore so getting pregant is the first answer to their supposibly problem and I just don't think it is fair It just hurts my heart to see all the young people getting pregant and don't have a red cent to take care of it.

She concludes that the parents of such pregnant girls must take some blame for their daughters' predicaments and goes on to write about how thankful she is that her mother watched, warned, and looked out for her:

> I am so lucky without even knowing it and as soon as I go home today I'm going to thank my mom so much and tell her much I love her and that I'm so glad she taught me the strings and glad that she shows me that she loves me. I believe that if the parents was there when the child needs them then this can prevent alot of pregancies. Don't You Think So!!!!!!!!!!!!!

This writing ends with 13 exclamation points.

In his goodbye letter, Easy E. reviewed his writing across the year and explains how his views about the exchange shifted:

> I've been looking over some of the papers that I have wrote at the first part of the year and I wound out that I like most of them but some parts

I feel different about like when I said wrighting to you would be just another assignment for me.

When I first made this statement I didn't know how much fun it would be to write to you guys. . . . once I new my way around the school and started to meet more and more new people I started to feel good about myself and I really got into writeing to you guys.

Fittingly, Geya, whose needs might have remained invisible in many classrooms, included a tribute to Bridget, an important last word that provides an essential insight into why Bridget's students seemed, across the board, to get so much from their exchange:

You know what I like about going and being school is my teachers I never knew of a teacher being so understanding and noticable as I noticed with my English teacher Mrs. Franklin I mean I noticed when she is really concerned what happens to most of her students that tries to help themselves.

Geya, the loner, was allowed social entry into the academic life of this very social exchange just as the more sociable Cool J., Easy E., and Ice T. were.

At the end of the term, Easy E. talked about how he would transfer what he learned in the exchange to his future efforts at writing. When asked whether he could apply what he learned about writing for the exchange to writing for school next year, Easy E. reflects:

I was writing to some friends, and so then I cared, about what I was writing, and . . . then you know that slowed it down, and you know I took my time, and you know I got it all. Finished and, that would be, a way I would write to a teacher, I would make sure everything's, you know . . . best as it could be.

CONCLUSION

Implicit in this chapter are four recommendations for reforming classrooms to meet the needs of low-achieving students. The recommendations center on the following four basic strategies that Bridget Franklin and other exchange teachers illustrated through their practice:

1. Attend to the students' sociocultural worlds as well as to their cognitive processes; intertwine the social and the academic.
2. Look carefully at ways to reorganize classrooms to allow students flexibility as they write while at the same time provide them with the supportive structures they need. This involves creating a safe, community-centered classroom that binds a group of students together but that also

meets individual needs. Such community-focused classrooms attend to individual needs but move beyond student-centeredness.

3. Uphold high standards by challenging students to tackle increasingly complex tasks and by providing them with the explicit support they need to meet these challenges. Attend to both process and product, to fluency and accuracy.

4. Share curricular decision making with students; both teachers and students should have strong voices and substantial input into what happens inside the classroom.

ACKNOWLEDGMENT

Portions of this chapter have been published previously in Freedman (1994) and Freedman (1995). Copyright 1994 by Sarah Warshauer Freedman; copyright 1995 by the National Council of Teachers of English. Reprinted by permission.

NOTE

1. All teachers, schools, and students are identified by pseudonyms.

REFERENCES

Delpit, L. (1988). The silenced dialogue: Power and pedagogy in educating other people's children. *Harvard Education Review, 58,* 280–298.

Fordham, S. (1988). Racelessness as a factor in black students' school success: Pragmatic strategy or Pyrrhic victory? *Harvard Educational Review, 58,* 54–84.

Fordham, S., & Ogbu, J. (1986). Black students' school success: Coping with the burden of "acting white." *The Urban Review, 18,* 176–206.

Freedman, S. W. (1994). *Exchanging writing, exchanging cultures: Lessons in school reform from the United States and Great Britain.* Cambridge, MA: Harvard University Press; Urbana, IL: National Council of Teachers of English.

Freedman, S. W. (1995). What's involved?: Setting up a writing exchange. *Language Arts, 72,* 54–64.

Ogbu, J. (1974). *The next generation: An ethnography of education in an urban neighborhood.* New York: Academic Press.

Ogbu, J. (1985). Research currents: Cultural–ecological influences on minority school learning. *Language Arts, 62,* 860–869.

Ogbu, J. (1990). Minority status and literacy in comparative perspective. *Daedalus, 119*(2), 141–168.

Weinstein, R. S., Soulé, C., Collins, F., Cone, J. K., Melhorn, M., & Simontacchi, K. (1991). Expectations and high school change: Teacher–researcher collaboration to prevent school failure. *American Journal of Community Psychology, 19*(3), 333–403.

CHAPTER TEN

Young Writers: The People and Purposes That Influence Their Literacy

JANE HANSEN
University of New Hampshire

From their communities, to their families, to their classrooms, several factors influence young writers. At the center of children's forward movement, however, is their own desire to learn. Their teachers, friends, and parents strive to keep their children's passion for learning alive. As young writers become increasingly able to evaluate their own surroundings, and the role writing plays, their ability to write, talk, read, and think expands.

I begin this chapter with two pieces written by young writers, one by a very young writer and one by a child who is more accomplished. Then I fill in the difference between these two writers with several examples of children's writing and show what teachers, families, and friends have done to help the children grow as learners.

TWO YOUNG WRITERS

Jessica

At the age of 3, Jessica decided to write a book, stimulated by the many books her parents had read to her. She tore the only piece of paper she could find into small sheets so her book would have pages, and created a title page (see Figure 10.1).

FIGURE 10.1. The Cat and the Mouse.

She then wrote her three-page story, ended it, and read it to her dad (see Figures 10.2–10.5).

Jessica knew that writers create books with plots and begin their books with titles. She knew they present some content in illustrations and some in print. She has figured out some important information about what writers do. Jessica is a writer; she can write—and read.

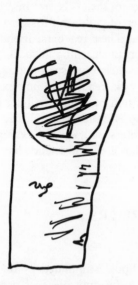

FIGURE 10.2. The cat is chasing the mouse.

FIGURE 10.3. The cat is almost catching the mouse!

FIGURE 10.4. The cat finally caught the mouse!

FIGURE 10.5. The end.

Daniel

At the other end of my continuum about young writers is Daniel and his book about whales (see Figures 10.6–10.16).

Daniel's first-grade class studied whales during the spring. His teacher not only read picture books to the children, she shared information from books with chapters. Daniel's class had time every day to write about topics of their choice, in forms of their choice. Daniel decided, on his own, to write a chapter book about whales. He wrote, "Whales are brave and smart," in "New Hampshirese." In that dialect, he does not pronounce the

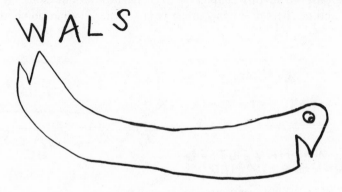

FIGURE 10.6. (Whales.)

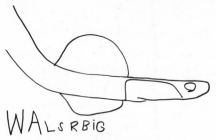

WALSRBIG

FIGURE 10.7. (Whales are big.)

WAS R B RAV A N B D SMO+

ƛAR I 0 0 FEE+

FIGURE 10.8. (Whales are brave and smart. They are 100 feet [long].)

PE©O P L E R HN+iNOYL

FIGURE 10.9. (People are hunting oil.)

PhOTOQ

KiLU WAL S

FIGURE 10.10. (Part Two Killer Whales.)

letter *r*, so it does not appear in his writing. His writing shows how carefully he listens to sounds.

Part two of Daniel's book is about killer whales. In this section, he gives the salient information that killer whales are dangerous and big.

Part three of the book is about blue whales. Notice how Daniel devotes a chapter to each kind of whale. He not only has figured out that chapters are a way to organize information, he follows a similar format for the first sentences within his second and third parts. As a writer, Daniel knows a great deal about what writers do.

My purpose in this chapter is to answer three questions: What do parents and teachers do to encourage young writers? What do children do

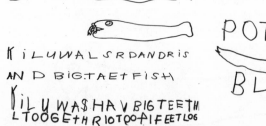

Ҝ iLUWAL S R DANDR iS

AN Ɒ BiG.TAE+FiS+

Ⱶ iL U WA$ HA V BiG TEE+Ħ
L TOOGE+Ħ R IOTQO-ƒi FEET L0G

FIGURE 10.11. (Killer whales are dangerous and big. They eat fish. Killer whales have big teeth, all together 10 to 41 feet long.)

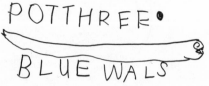

POTTHREE●

BLUE WALS

FIGURE 10.12. (Part Three Blue Whales.)

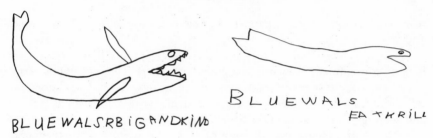

FIGURE 10.13. (Blue whales are big and kind.)

FIGURE 10.14. (Blue whales eat kill.)

FIGURE 10.15. (Blue whales are having a baby.)

FIGURE 10.16. (Baby whales [are] big.)

to spur their own learning? For what purposes do children write? These are relatively new questions. Writing, and particularly the writing of young children, became a discipline only about 25 years ago. The "Three R's" have been around for a long time, but the "Writing R" had seldom been researched, since previously we thought that young children could not compose. We equated writing with handwriting, correct spelling, and neat papers, tasks young children often cannot achieve. Once we realized that young children can write, gave them opportunities to do so, studied them, helped them, and taught them to evaluate themselves, we became increasingly aware of the differences among these young writers.

THE EVOLUTION OF RESEARCH ON WRITING

Young writers are as different from each other as are adult writers. Research on writing began with studies of older writers, then moved to younger ones. Finally research moved to the teaching of writing. Now, there are many articles, book chapters, technical reports, and books on writing instruction and writers of all ages. From this research we know a great deal about the writing processes of professional writers, nonprofessional adult writers, and students. We know about writing in school and in the real world. We know, for example, that in their daily lives, adults write for purposes. They write telephone messages, create banners and signs, compose memos and songs, and write letters.

When professional writers give us advice, they tell us about their lifelong commitment to their development as writers. They constantly write, read, and seek responsive evaluation from others. Thus, in schools, we strive to create environments in which students write daily, read as writers, and seek responsive evaluation from others.

The central factor in evaluation of a piece of writing is whether other persons understand it. However, it is often difficult for teachers to maintain this focus within their daily responses to students' writing. Prior to the surge of writing research, evaluations of writing focused on punctuation, spelling, and other important conventions—but perfect punctuation does not a good piece of writing make. From research, we have learned to put mechanics, content, and effectiveness in their respective places.

A central force that propels writers is their desire to tell someone something. Writing comes from within the writer. He or she wants to make a mark on the world. Look, for example, at the first message written by Paul at the age of four:

SSHiDCA

Paul wrote these letters on a 4-foot banner to greet his mother on her return home after several nights away. He told her it said "Welcome Home."

In her detailed study of a young writer, which was her Harvard dissertation, Paul's mother, Glenda Bissex (1980) explains that Paul's banner was his first attempt to put letters together to form a message. He knew that writers present their messages in horizontal fashion and that their messages have a purpose. They are not just random marks on paper.

Paul's mother was tremendously impressed. She did not criticize his efforts for their lack of correctness. Her responsive evaluation showed her appreciation of his major accomplishment as a writer, an important stance for parents and teachers to take. More than reading, writing is affected by self-confidence and willingness to try. Writers must know that their efforts will be met with respect and interest.

Graves (1983), one of the pioneers in the research on writing instruction in primary classrooms, studied children in classrooms in which their teachers respected the children's early writing efforts. The teachers conferred with their young writers to find out what the children's intentions were in their writing, and they used these conferences as the primary settings in which not only the teachers evaluated the children but they listened to the children's own evaluations of their efforts. The children and teachers talked about what the children did in the process of learning to write, the information they tried to convey, and the conventions they used to express their messages effectively. Graves researched these conferences in classrooms in which teacher–child interactions are supportive and children view themselves as capable persons.

Similarly, positive parent–child interactions influence writing. Parents, for example, who make such comments as, "I'd offer you some punch but I can't guarantee it because Lisa made it," undermine their children's self-confidence. Such negative comments can interfere with children's growth as writers (Snow, Barnes, Chandler, Goodman, & Hemphill, 1991).

To honor children's efforts is in accordance with another line of research that has come into being alongside the research on writing, emergent literacy (Sulzby, 1992). Within this body of work, we have learned to question an earlier theory of literacy development based on a notion of *readiness*. Readiness quickly became "not ready." Children were declared "not ready" to read because they did not know the letter names, could not draw people with a certain degree of sophistication, or could not perform skills that appeared on various long lists.

The research on emergent literacy has helped us to see young children as competent, accomplished individuals. They are always ready for a next step, and there is no ultimate step against which we can evaluate them. We view them as learners who live and learn among siblings, classmates, and adults who include them in lots of experiences, talk with them, listen to them, read to them, and write with them.

The situations in which children experience writing, reading, uses of print, and talk vary tremendously (Heath, 1983). In some homes and communities, children hear stories regularly but seldom become involved in reading; in other homes, children seldom hear stories but take part in the reading of labels on soup cans and cereal boxes. Some children and their families read books, newspapers, and magazines. Writing is an extremely rare act in some homes, but letter-writing is common in others. In some communities, print opens doors; in others, it restricts thinking. As educators, we have only recently started to use information about literacy in our students' communities and families to inform our creation of classroom environments in which children feel the need to write.

Rasinski (1988) studied his son Mikey's kindergarten class, in which Mikey loved to write and read, and Mikey's more traditional first-grade class, in which Mikey lost confidence in his ability to write. When Rasinski asked his son what he thought was the major difference between kinder-garten and first grade, Mikey said that he had more say in his assignments in kindergarten. He enjoyed being able to determine where he could do his work, how he might do it, and with whom he could collaborate. In first grade, the opportunities for him to make his own choices were rare. Research has made clear the need for classrooms to remain places in which young writers determine who they write for and for what purposes. It has also provided the impetus for us to strive, against odds, to establish classrooms in which writers are likely to flourish.

FIGURE 10.17

YOUNG WRITERS STRIVE TO MAKE
THEIR FIRST WRITTEN STATEMENTS

When we study their efforts, we find that all children, as they become writers, make essentially the same discoveries in essentially the same order, with a great deal of variation across and within writers. As the marks they make on paper begin to resemble print, children place these letter-like shapes in rows, and they assume the letters have meaning. Kibi produced the text shown in Figure 10.17 and asked, "What did I write?" (Harste, Woodward, & Burke, 1984, p. 108).

Kibi knows that print carries meaning. She has yet to learn, however, that she has to inscribe that meaning.

FIGURE 10.18

Soon, beginning writers convey their intentions. Megan (Harste et al., 1984, p. 109) wrote the letter shown in Figure 10.18 and read, "Dear Mary, I hope you bring me here every day. The end, Megan."

Megan is a writer with a statement to make and the means to convey her intentions.

Eventually children purposefully start to copy letters and want to write their names, the ultimate in meaningful statements. Adam (Schickedanz, 1990) tried several times within a 2-month period, and finally learned to write his name (see Figures 10.19–10.22).

In his first effort, Adam sees the necessity to draw himself to show who he is. By the time he tries again (Figure 10.20), he relies solely on print and practices the letter *A*, albeit on its side (many children spend a brief period of time writing letters with abandon in regard to directionality. Just

FIGURE 10.19   FIGURE 10.20

FIGURE 10.21   FIGURE 10.22

as a chair is a chair, regardless of its direction, so it seems to be with letters). Shortly, thereafter, however, Adam writes his name in left–right order, with vertical letters (Figure 10.21). Finally (Figure 10.22), he writes *Adam*.

Whereas all children want to write their names, they do not all follow Adam's exact process. Within an overall continuum of growth that shows much similarity across children, variation for individual children is the hallmark of writing development (Avery, 1993). This variation makes the teaching of writing difficult. We cannot create a scheme to pace all children through, but their growth does respond to what we do.

Adults plan experiences with the children in mind, include the children in their daily lives, engage in reflective talk with them, read to them, engage in explorative talk with them, and give children time to experiment with crayons, paper, and pencils. Through play, purposeful trial-and-error, and responsive evaluation, children figure out how to communicate. Adam (Schickedanz, 1990) frequently saw his mother write. One day as she was writing notes, he wrote this one to her:

AAA
OOO

He read:

"Dear Mom,
I love you."

Adam had a message in mind, wrote it in an appropriate form, and wrote it to a particular person. Writers write in formats that satisfy their purposes. Adam used different letters for the two lines of his message. He knew there was some purpose for the existence of different letters and some kind of an order for print. Most significant, he had an important message and a feeling that this message would be especially powerful if presented in written form, so he forced himself to figure out how to say what was on his mind.

When Taylor and Dorsey-Gaines (1988) studied literacy in inner-city families, they found many similar examples of love notes and cards written by the children to family members. Newkirk (1989) also found many examples of letters, lists, and other nonnarrative writing in young children's efforts. The need to use print drives young children's writing, as it does their oral language.

RESEARCH ON LANGUAGE DEVELOPMENT EXPLAINS BOTH ORAL AND WRITTEN LANGUAGE

The need for an audience is inherent in children's acquisition and development of oral language. They learn to talk amid others, know that words serve them, and struggle to get others to understand their messages. Exactly how children do this is unknown, but Schickedanz (1990) notes that major theories have emerged as explanations for child development: the behaviorist, nativist, and cognitive-developmentalist theories. Each theory offers a different explanation for changes in behavior. The behaviorists believe that external motivators bring about learning. They break down learning into parts and sequence it from simple to complex to eliminate errors. They believe that knowledge is built piece by piece.

To nativists, development is explained by genetic maturation. Nativists believe in the concept of readiness. Adults wait until children are ready before attempting to teach them. Children move through stages and change according to developmental milestones that emerge with neurological development that is controlled by genes.

Cognitive-developmentalists believe that growth occurs when children try to resolve contradictions or problems in their lives and that they prefer to spend some of their time working on moderately difficult tasks as different from always focusing on very easy or extremely difficult dilemmas. They learn new things when they are in the "zone of proximal development," (Vygotsky, 1978), which is the zone in which children can understand something with responsive help from another. It is cognitive-developmentalist theory that underlies what we know about children's growth in written and spoken language.

Toddlers work very hard to try to say what is on their minds, and adults bend down to child level to try to understand the oftentimes unclear sounds and messages children try to convey. Young children say what is on their minds as best they can, and they improve at this task of learning to talk when the people to whom they talk respond supportively to their efforts. Toddlers ask for a cookie when they think there is a chance they might get one. Children learn language in meaningful situations. They do not say, "I want a cookie now!" just for the exercise of it. They do not learn primarily by imitation, or by repetition, or by practicing phrases or words in isolation.

Children usually admire the adults around them and love to tell the big people about their little, very important experiences, dreams, and fears. Adults listen and children talk more. They will talk and talk and talk and talk. Children adjust their talk; they talk differently to their peers and to smaller children, and they even vary their talk to different adults. Children consider their audience. They learn to talk because they have something to say, and they say it in the appropriate situation to the proper person—or, at least, as with us, they try.

The environment in which children learn to talk, write, and read is key to their development (Morrow & Strickland, 1988). Classrooms in which teachers support oral language development are classrooms in which children's writing can also be fostered. Power (1989) writes about the numerous benefits to three young boys in a classroom in which they had the freedom to talk with each other every day during writing. The boys learned about content from each others' topics, skills, and social skills. Young writers grow when they do not always rely on the teacher and when their natural desire to communicate is recognized and valued.

Young Writers Want to Learn
Sound–Symbol Correspondences

Paul (Bissex, 1980) became extremely frustrated with his mother one day. He wanted her attention, but she was reading. When he talked to her, she mumbled, "Hmmmmm." Paul walked away, penned these four letters and shoved them between her eyes and her book:

RUDF

She read, "Are you deaf?", closed her book, and looked in amazement at her young, victorious son. Both of them knew he had accomplished a major feat: This was his first piece of writing that his mother could read.

Similar to learning to talk, children develop as writers among people who understand and pay attention to what they have to say. Interested people look up, assess the situation, and marvel at the young writers. When their writing brings results and attention, children feel its power.

To his fundamental, necessary understanding that writing carries messages, Paul brought phonemic awareness (Adams, 1990) and the tool of phonics. Over the following months, his own desire to write motivated him to sharpen this tool as he found more and more situations in which he had something to say. As he wrote, he asked his mother what letter he needed to represent various sounds. Because of the different letters we use to represent any one sound, his mother usually asked him what word he was writing, and then gave him the letter.

Other children follow paths that are different from Paul's. Some do not write at home at early ages. Daniel came to first grade, along with seven of his classmates, unable to write his name. He had not attended school of any kind, and he responded, as did all the other children who could not write their names, with "Yes," when asked the question, "Can you write?" on their first-ever day of school. His teacher responded, "I put several kinds of paper over there. You may choose some and write." This young writer produced the drawing shown in Figure 10.23, but without three letters.

He wrote at a table with other young writers. Some drew as he did. Some drew pictures that represented stories, others wrote sentences, words, and letters, and some children produced both print and drawings. Every morning, each child wrote in a "book" of 9- by 12-inch sheets of blank newsprint, and in the afternoons, the entire class met on the carpet in one corner of the classroom for a phonics lesson during which the teacher

FIGURE 10.23

taught specific sounds to the children with actions and picture cards kept as references on the tables throughout their classroom.

Daniel's teacher divided the class into five mixed-ability groups and met with one group each morning while the other groups wrote and chatted at various tables. The children and teacher all brought their writing books to the teacher's table where they wrote and talked. The teacher entered into their conversations as they wrote. During these weekly sessions, each child also read to the teacher everything he or she had written during the week since the last meeting with the teacher. During the second week of school, as Daniel told the teacher about his first piece of writing, she said, "I think you can write some letters on your picture. What sound do you hear when you say *person?*" Daniel said /p/. They continued with *sun* and *lollipop,* and Daniel wrote his first-ever letters. They were not random letters—they made sense in the context of the composition he had initiated.

Daniel wrote his first message, as different from his labeled drawing, on the Monday of the third week of school. He had spent the weekend with his father, hiking in the mountains. He came into the classroom excited, chose a fat, black marker, drew some mountains, and wrote the text shown in Figure 10.24.

To his teacher, he read, "I climbed mountains" and told her about his

FIGURE 10.24

weekend. For children in classrooms in which they write and share, writing gives them an opportunity to share news with the teacher, with nearby children, and with the entire class, if the child shares on that day. A particular child will not necessarily have the entire class as an audience, but each child can always count on the children he or she writes and talks with at whichever table he or she chooses to work. This choice of audience is crucial to children's growth as writers and readers.

Whereas Daniel spurted forward from labeled drawings to a complete story with both a picture and text, some children move into their stories in slightly different ways, such as the child who wrote the story shown in Figure 10.25. The child had jumped in leaves, then drew a picture and labeled it with a verb to show the action. This piece of writing gave the child entry into a conversation about her after-school play. In time, she will write sentences, even though Daniel wrote sentences without ever writing verbs to explain the actions in pictures of his experiences. Daniel moved directly from labels of objects to stories of events, complete with both a picture and a sentence.

Children typically learn vowel sounds after they learn initial and final

FIGURE 10.25. Up.

consonant sounds. Ellen Blackburn Karelitz (1993, p. 42) shares this example of a day she helped Robert insert an *i* in *fish*:

EBK: What did you write here? One ... ?

ROBERT: "One fish died."

EBK: "One fish died." So, you have to say ... one fish—/f/ /i/ /sh/.

ROBERT: /f/ /i/ /sh/. (*Doesn't know what to write for /i/.*)

EBK: How did you write fish on your other page?

ROBERT: (*turning back*) Let's see ... (*looking at word*) ... /f/ /sh/.

EBK: Yes, you didn't know about the /i/ sound yet.

ROBERT: /i/.

EBK: You know a new letter sound [from a class lesson], /i/ so the /i/ would come in the middle of the /f/ and the /sh/. Now you learned this sound, so why don't you put it in.

ROBERT: (*Writes the i.*)

With his teacher's help, and from interactions with the other children who write and talk around the table as he writes, Robert consistently includes more and more vowels in his words. He sounds out his words with increasing adeptness throughout his first-grade year.

Young Writers Try to Segment Language into Words

Young writers' efforts take a great deal of energy. Paul Bissex, as I mentioned earlier, asked his mother for letters to match the sounds he heard when he first started to write. After a few months of this, he stopped asking for help. He wrote on his own. When children's writing first takes off, they frequently connect their ideas into strings of words, as different from Daniel who wrote "I C M," with spaces between his "words." The piece of writing shown in Figure 10.26, from a first-grade child's science notebook of observations on a jack-o-lantern's demise, shows a string of letters.

"I especially liked Jack" portrays this boy's ability to write a complete sentence with interesting words. "Especially" is a word he would not use if he were in a classroom in which correct spelling received more emphasis than did phonics. When children write with the words they speak, they use complicated words, as different from what they might write if they were expected to write with correct spelling.

Writing about Jack, the young boy sounded out to his heart's delight. Young writers work impressively hard to figure out how to represent words like "especially." They laboriously sound out every bit of everything they write, as they write letters one at a time. It takes them a great deal of time

FIGURE 10.26

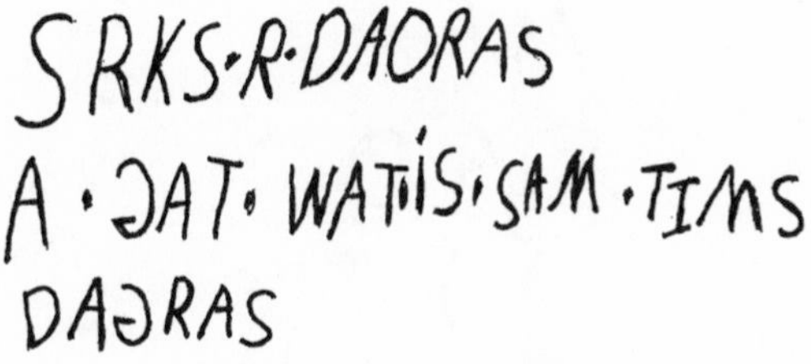

$S RKS \cdot R \cdot DAORAS$

$A \cdot \partial AT \cdot WATiS \cdot SAM \cdot TI \Lambda S$

$DA \partial RAS$

FIGURE 10.27. (Sharks are dangerous. A great white is sometimes dangerous.)

to write their thoughts, and they struggle day after day to write more thoughts, for as long as they have a sense of the worth of their efforts.

Talk is an important part of a writing and reading classroom. We do not expect children to write what they can say, but their talk moves them forward. If we expect them to write as much as they say, we frustrate them. This is one reason why the dictation we sometimes take from children can be problematic. They often cannot read all the words we take down when they tell us a story, but a child can usually read what she writes when she puts it down herself.

As the strings of words become longer, children become frustrated when they try to read them. They vow to do something about this. Sometimes the impetus to use spaces comes from the child's own observations of the spacing in books or in friends' writing. Sometimes the impetus for change comes from the teacher and sometimes from other children. Regardless, children always begin to use spaces. In so doing, they sometimes put dots as dividers between every word, such as Chad did (Figure 10.27; Avery, 1993, p. 94).

Other children write in vertical form to keep their words separate, as did the first-grade child whose writing is shown in Figure 10.28.

Some children simply put a finger between each word, which can raise interesting problems in this computer age. For example, one computer-resource teacher wondered why the children pressed the space bar several times between each word. "Because there has to be room for a finger," the children told her!

Young Writers Document Their Growth

An increasingly larger number of teachers ask their young writers to document their growth and to write explanations of their landmark entries. When Delicia learned to leave spaces between her words, she placed a piece of writing in her portfolio in which she used spaces, and wrote her explanation of why she had placed a new entry in her portfolio (see Figure 10.29).

FIGURE 10.28

FIGURE 10.29

Children who keep their own records of their growth, and are articulate about their changes, begin purposely to plan what they will do when they write (Hansen, 1998). Delicia created goals for herself. She considered, for example, whether to write her first two-page piece of writing, or whether to experiment with the placement of her pictures around her text as she has seen professional writers do in children's literature. When the classroom milieu is one of experimentation, children listen to the accomplishments of their classmates and the suggestions of their teachers. They study the techniques of professionals in the books they read and in those read to them, weigh their options, and choose which challenges they think they can handle, given the support they feel.

Heather, a first-grader, produced the drawing shown in Figure 10.30, complete with her evaluation of her growth, affixed to her original on a post-it note.

Heather has learned to use periods (in her text, but not in her note of explanation!), and she writes, "I can put a word." Heather wrote this reflection in April and had looked back over her earliest pieces of writing from the beginning of the year when she had written no words. Now, she "can put a word" on paper. She can see her own development and knows she will move forward.

An important beginning point for each child is to know what she can

FIGURE 10.30

do as a writer. Children make lists of "Things I Can Do as a Writer." This baseline of competence gives them the confidence they need to take the initiative writers need. Teachers help their students find their leading edges. When children share their writing, teachers ask them what they feel good about in their drafts. They learn what a child has tried that is new. They celebrate the child's efforts and find out what the child wants to try next.

Sometimes children need help when asked what they want to do next. They do not know what to write about, or what they want to try that is new, or what they want to learn to read. Teachers can encourage children to ask others for ideas. Teachers can help children realize they have something to say and can help them figure out whom to write to and in what form. Teachers can help children analyze their own work as they are writing, regularly show children various strategies, and help them develop an awareness of when to use various processes. With guidance, each child can continuously set goals to lead her- or himself onward, keep the records of what she or he is learning and write notes to explain her or his accomplishments.

Young Writers Want to Write More Complete Messages

Young children feel the release of fluency when they can write the sounds they hear, segment language into words, and think about themselves as writers. A great deal of a message may still remain off the page, to be learned when the child reads her writing to her friends and they ask questions, but more information appears on the page, and a page it often is.

Children Write More Complete Messages— On One Sheet of Paper

As they try to put more complete accounts of their adventures on one page, children break the convention of drawing a picture on the top of a sheet of paper and of writing a complete story in one sentence. A first-grade boy wrote the two parts of his text on each side of his illustration (see Figure 10.31).

He read, "My brother took me to *Wet and Wild* [an amusement park], and I went down the water slide."

In the fall of first grade, Amanda appeared at her classroom door, distraught. She drew and wrote: *My teddy bear got lost. My father found it by his bed. The end.* (See Figure 10.32.)

She read her writing to her teacher, and as the two of them talked about this sad experience, the teacher asked, "How did you feel when he found it?"

"Happy," answered Amanda, and crossed out "The end." She added: *When he found it I was happy. The end.* (See Figure 10.33.)

FIGURE 10.31

FIGURE 10.32   **FIGURE 10.33**

FIGURE 10.34   FIGURE 10.35

On another day when Amanda read this message to the children at the table, they wanted to know what she did when she realized her teddy was lost.

"I cried," she said.

Her teacher asked, "If you decide to add that, where would you put it?"

After some searching, Amanda pointed to the space after the word *lost.*

Her teacher penciled an arrow in that space and said, "Now you can remember where to write *I cried* if you decide to add that."

Later, Amanda added a short sentence (see Figure 10.34).

In the afternoon, Amanda wanted to share her writing with the entire class. After she read, they asked her what she did with her teddy, and she said, "I like to sleep with him," which she later added to her now complete story (see Figure 10.35).

She added and added, with assistance from her teacher and friends. In an atmosphere in which children want to share their news and others are interested enough to ask questions, children's fluency grows.

Amanda's example serves in contrast to a second-grade boy who said to his teacher, "I'm not gong to work on my Nintendo draft anymore. I'm going to start something new."

"Why?" she asked.

"I almost threw it away," he added, as he looked away from her.

"Why?"

"Because no one commented on it. Only about three people did. Most people get about five comments when they share. Well, I only got about two, and those two don't count. They asked things I'd said. Nobody cares about Nintendo in here. If people gave me different ideas I might have changed it, but no one in here likes Nintendo except Zach. They don't know anything about Nintendo. Someone asked where the characters were before they left. I had said that! Someone else wanted to know the name of the third character. I'd said that, too."

Receiving no response prompts the writer to evaluate his work negatively. It is the teacher's responsibility not only to evaluate the students' work in a way that gives them the energy writers need to continue, but to teach the students to evaluate each other in a similar way. Teachers teach, model, demonstrate, and reteach these skills throughout the year.

Teachers encourage children's fluency in other ways, as did one kindergarten teacher. As a class, the teacher and students reviewed the sequence they had followed to carve their jack-o-lantern for Halloween, and then each child thought of something he or she did in everyday life that he or she performed in a certain order. The children folded sheets of paper in quarters and drew–wrote their sequences. One boy created this step-by-step process (see Figures 10.36–10.39):

FIGURE 10.36. (1. Out of my bed,)   **FIGURE 10.37.** (2. onto the floor,)

FIGURE 10.38. (3. down the stairs,)   **FIGURE 10.39.** (4. to feed my cat.)

Some children's writing suddenly fills a page when a moment becomes significant. One spring day, a first-grade boy came into his classroom ready to write. He had news (see Figure 10.40).

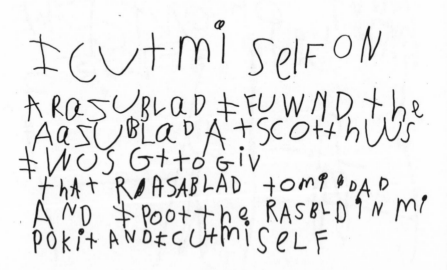

FIGURE 10.40. (I cut myself on a razor blade. I found the razor blade at Scott's house. I was going to give that razor blade to my dad, and I put the razor blade in my pocket and I cut myself.)

The boy's fluency spurted with the sense of urgency he felt about the experience he wanted to share with his class. Notice, however, his interesting sequence. He uses a flashback! In his excitement, he tells his punch line first, and then explains the details, ending where he began: *I cut myself.* A well-crafted little piece of writing, all on one page.

Children Write Even Longer Messages— On Several Sheets of Paper

The confines of a page appear to offer security for some children and anxiety for others. To go beyond the page is a breakthrough for many, a liberation. A first-grade boy, while his teacher was reading a novel (as distinct from a picture book) to his class, noticed something new and decided to try it (see Figures 10.41, 10.42, and 10.43).

The boy excitedly shared the writing with an adult who tried to find out from him why he was so pleased with this piece of writing. Unable to explain the child said, "Wait! I'll be right back!" He returned with the book his teacher was reading to the class, opened it, pointed to the last word on one page, and said, "Look," as he turned to the top of the next page, "it just goes on up here."

This child had discovered that a thought need not fit on one page. If need be, you could continue a thought on to the next page. He was the first writer in his class to do this, shared his discovery with them when they all met to share, and soon a few other children, sensing the potential of

FIGURE 10.41. ("What are we baking, mommy?" "We are baking)

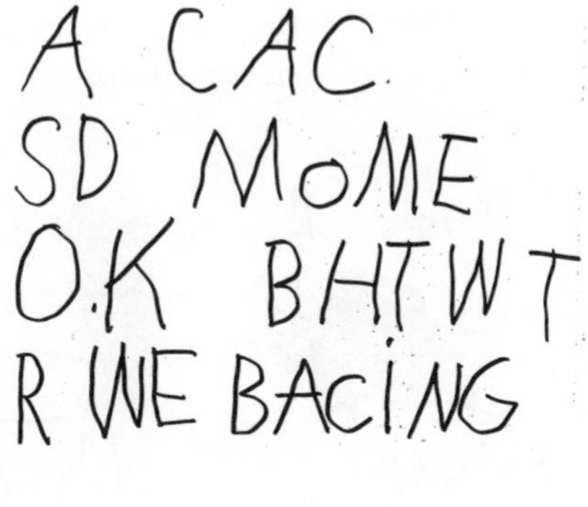

FIGURE 10.42. (a cake," said Mommy. "O.K., but what are we baking?")

A ESTR
CAC WoW
i LiC IT

FIGURE 10.43. ("An Easter cake." "Wow! I like it!")

this child's endeavor, started to continue their written thoughts on to following pages. The culture of the classroom honors the risks children take. An intense desire to do something pushed this young writer on to the next page.

Kelly, another first grader, used three pages, with both print and illustrations to show the passage of time in her work (Figure 10.44; Hubbard, 1989, p. 34).

In explaining her work to Hubbard, who always sought the children's interpretations of their work, Kelly said, "You see, the steamboat here (in the second drawing) is *in* the storm. This is the water coming down here. On the page before, you can see, the storm is just coming. (Notice the black on the left margin.) I'll make the black on the other side now, going away to show the storm is going away."

Children's desire to make sure their meaning is clear can lead them to novel strategies that we would never think to introduce to them. They set

FIGURE 10.44

their own purposes, and resolve them, when they write daily for their own intents and on topics and in genres that will most effectively suit their intentions.

Katrina's decision to create a long piece of writing grew from her excitement about some new information she acquired. A second grader, her study of vultures fascinated her. She knew she had learned a lot from her own reading and a field trip and decided to write her first information book in which she displayed her knowledge on four pages, plus a title page (see Figure 10.45).

Katrina shared her book with a big, quiet smile, and answered questions. She knew baby vultures are fuzzy because she held one on a field trip, and she knew the word *swoops* because her friend uses it. Her precise vocabulary reflects her desire to present her information in the most accurate, interesting way possible.

Katrina's teacher has taught the children to respond when they share with the class. They tell Katrina what they learned from her and ask questions to learn even more from this expert seated before them. They not

FIGURE 10.45

A ivre mason book about Vulturs

(An information book about Vultures)

(page 1) When the volcr is born they are Fosy.

(When the vulture is born they are fuzzy.)

(page 2) The volcr ests met a lot.

(The vulture eats meat a lot.)

(page 3) The Volcr sw suawps down and pics up a mos.

(The vulture swoops down and picks up a mouse)

(page 4) The Volcr has a sarp beek To ripe The met.

(The vulture has a sharp beak to rip the meat.)

only want to know about vultures, they want to know how she learned what she knows. She tells them, and the learning extends beyond the words on Katrina's pages to what the children learn from books and each other.

TEACHERS PROMOTE THE GROWTH OF YOUNG WRITERS AND READERS

Writing and reading for young children are to be joyful, and children learn best in an atmosphere in which they feel at home. Primary classrooms are quiet but not silent. The children talk. They cooperate. The room is not competitive. They help each other learn as much as possible. This represents a huge change from the not-too-distant past when children sat in rows, in desks isolated from each other. They could not talk because the teacher feared that if they did talk, their work, handed in at the end of the day, would not be their own. Children, in turn, feared making errors.

We now foster experimentation, and children surprise us with their creations, as one young boy did one day in the spring after his class had observed an older class at his school. He wrote *How to Make Maple Syrup* (Figures 10.46–10.47).

The boy who wrote this story was excited when he read to his class. He read with great drama, knowing he had a winner. No one else in the class had ever written anything like this! He not only included sounds, but

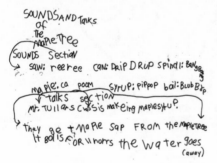

FIGURE 10.46   FIGURE 10.47

Sounds and Talks of the Maple Tree

Sounds Section
       saw: ree ree   can: drip drup spindle: bang bang
       maple: ca poom   syrup: pip pop boil: blub blop
Talks Section
       Mr. Tullar's class is making maple syrup. They get maple sap from the maple tree. It boils for 11 hours. The water goes [away].
       It evaporates. Then it's syrup. The end

he used new punctuation, the colon, in an appropriate way, and a period after the abbreviation for Mr. He used one period correctly at the end of a sentence, evidence that he knew this skill, but did not take the time to use it consistently. As writing teachers, it is our challenge, when we look at particulars, to keep the voice in this writer alive. We want him to continue to write.

Sometimes we have to work very hard to create the environment a child needs to write. When Chris Gaudet (Fueyo, 1991), a first-grade teacher, asked Stephen, "How do you plan to write your story?" Stephen answered, "I'm gonna be a plane," and proceeded to fly around the classroom, arms outstretched, improvising his story, complete with sound effects. His teacher learned the importance of drama, blocks, and other forms of play to her students' compositions.

Many teachers use literature to expand their children's writing. Stephens (1989) read leads from several of her first-graders' favorite children's books and challenged the children to write more interesting leads for their writing. Joe wrote: *Splash! I slipped on a rock and fell into a tide pool at Grace Oliver's Beach. The water was like the coldest ice cube in the world!*

Teachers strive to find whatever works to help their children feel the excitement of writing. There are no routines that work for all children in a classroom of diverse learners. Dave, a second-grader in Ostrow's first- to third-grade classroom (Ostrow, 1995), often wrote about the Civil War, a long-standing interest. One day Jill suggested that he use his information to create a poem instead of a story, and he wrote:

> Black men in chains
> Rebel masters yelling
> and whipping
> Rebel women watching
> in terror
> screaming, yelling
> All horrible.
> Horse stamping
> Sun rising
> Heart broken rebels
> Tattered flag being
> rolled up
> War over
> Peace. (Ostrow, 1995, p. 55)

Teachers of young children take both students' writing and their own seriously. They not only write for themselves, they often use their own writing to demonstrate a skill or strategy. For example, a teacher shares a short, simple, lively piece of her own writing, and the children respond. They ask her questions about an apple pie contest she entered. She answers their questions and shows them the title of her narrative, with which she is dissatisfied. She asks them to suggest alternative titles for her, and they do so. The group response and group lessons help keep the writers energized.

The teaching of writing and reading remains complex, sometimes daunting (Allen, Michalove, & Shockley, 1993; Purcell-Gates, 1995). As a profession, we are beginning to see the larger picture of learning to write and read. Teachers evaluate themselves constantly in their efforts to become better able to create classrooms in which writers and readers grow. The following list, adapted from Temple, Nathan, Burris, and Temple (1988), shows what teachers gradually learn to do as they create classrooms in which they can credibly expect their young children to flourish as writers:

1. Use interactions with parents as opportunities to learn from them.
2. Provide time every day for children to write on topics and in genres of their choice and to learn to read from books of their choice.
3. Supply materials, such as charts and accessible books, that help children write and read.
4. Encourage children to interact and help each other as they write and read.
5. Evaluate children with sensitivity to their development as well as to their intentions.
6. Help children keep track of their progress in a systematic way.
7. Read to the children more than once a day from children's literature, your own writing, and the children's writing.
8. Teach children to read to the class each day from children's literature, your writing, and their own writing.
9. Teach children to respond after someone reads to them.
10. Publish children's writing in a variety of forms for a variety of audiences.

The value of various forms and functions to a writer's growth has been purported for years (see, e.g., Britton, Burgess, Martin, McLeod, & Rosen, 1975), but it still tends to be quite common to organize classrooms in which students do not write with their own purposes to real audience. Nor do students necessarily learn to read from books and other materials that they feel compelled to figure out. As our profession gradually begins to appreciate the processes young children use when they learn to talk to various people in different settings, for a variety of purposes, in supportive situations, we more fully understand the environments that foster writing. We strive to create those contexts in our classrooms. One principle of writing that research over the last two decades strongly shows is: Writing is a social activity.

And it is not. I end this chapter with the importance of the individual from deVilliers and deVilliers (1982, p. 143). They write about oral language and the fascination on our part when toddlers try, in unexpected ways, to express themselves, but I use their insights to inform what we know about writing. Teachers of young children find it exciting to watch unique individuals emerge, on paper, before their eyes.

REFERENCES

Adams, M. J. (1990). *Beginning to read: Thinking and learning about print,* Cambridge, MA: MIT Press.

Allen, J., Michalove, B., & Shockley, B. (1993). *Engaging children: Community and chaos in the lives of young literacy learners.* Portsmouth, NH: Heinemann.

Avery, C.(1993). *. . . And with a light touch: Learning about reading, writing, and teaching with first graders.* Portsmouth, NH: Heinemann.

Bissex, G. (1980). *GNYS AT WRK: A child learns to write and read.* Cambridge, MA: Harvard University Press.

Britton, J., Burgess, T., Martin, N., McLeod, A., & Rosen, H. (1975). *The development of writing abilities 11–18.* London: Macmillan.

deVilliers, P., & deVilliers, J. (1982). *Early language.* Cambridge, MA: Harvard University Press.

Fueyo, J. (1991). Reading "Literate sensibilities": Resisting a verbocentric writing classroom. *Language Arts, 68,* 641–648.

Graves, D. (1983). *Writing: Teachers and children at work.* Portsmouth, NH: Heinemann.

Hansen, J. (1998). *When learners evaluate.* Portsmouth, NH: Heinemann.

Harste, J., Woodward, V., & Burke, C. (1984). *Language stories and literacy lessons.* Portsmouth, NH: Heinemann.

Heath, S. B. (1983). *Ways with words: Language, life, and work in communities and classrooms.* Cambridge, MA: Cambridge University Press.

Hubbard, R. (1989). *Authors of pictures, draughtsmen of words.* Portsmouth, NH: Heinemann.

Karelitz, E. B. (1993). *The author' chair and beyond: Language and literacy in a primary classroom.* Portsmouth, NH: Heinemann.

Morrow, L. M., & Strickland, D. (1988). Reading, writing, and oral language. *The Reading Teacher, 41,* 240–241.

Newkirk, T. (1989). *More than stories: The range of children's writing.* Portsmouth, NH: Heinemann.

Ostrow, J. (1995). *A room with a different view: First through third graders build community and create curriculum.* York, ME: Stenhouse.

Power, B. M. (1989). Beyond "Geddinagrupe": A case study of three first-grade collaborators. *Language Arts, 66,* 767–774.

Purcell-Gates, V. (1995). *Other people's words: The cycle of low literacy.* Cambridge, MA: Harvard University Press.

Rasinski, T. (1988). The role of interest, purpose, and choice in early literacy. *The Reading Teacher, 41,* 396–400.

Schickedanz, J. (1990). *Adam's righting revolutions: One child's literacy development from infancy through grade one.* Portsmouth, NH: Heinemann.

Snow, C., Barnes, W., Chandler, J., Goodman, I., & Hemphill, L. (1991). *Unfulfilled expectations: Home and school influences on literacy.* Cambridge, MA: Harvard University Press.

Stephens, D. (1989). First graders taking the lead: Building bridges between literature and writing. *The New Advocate, 2*(4), 249–258.

Sulzby, E. (1992). Transitions from emergent to conventional writing. *Language Arts, 69,* 290–297.

Taylor, D., & Dorsey-Gaines, C. (1988). *Growing up literate: Learning from inner-city families.* Portsmouth, NH: Heinemann.

Temple, C., Nathan, R., Burris, N., & Temple, F. (1988). *The beginnings of writing* (2nd ed.). Boston: Allyn & Bacon.

Vygotsky, L. S. (1978). *Mind in society.* Cambridge, MA: Harvard University Press.

PART FOUR

STANDARDS AND ASSESSMENT

CHAPTER ELEVEN

Reading Assessment and Learning to Read

PETER AFFLERBACH
University of Maryland at College Park

Reading assessment must play a central role in our efforts to help every child learn to read. Effective assessment is critical for children's early and ongoing reading development: It provides information that informs educational practice and helps create opportunities for students' reading achievement. To meet standards of validity and reliability, assessment must be aligned with current understandings of learning to read (Messick, 1989). As important, early-reading assessment must describe to all the stakeholders who are interested in young children's reading development the accomplishments of students and teachers (Airasian, 1993) and their achievement in relation to learning-to-read benchmarks (Afflerbach, 1996).

In this chapter, I examine the assessment of learning to read and the development of reading-assessment programs. First, I focus on the evolving understanding of the nature of early reading. Second, I examine efforts to develop assessments that align with this understanding. Next, I examine the alignment of reading-assessment programs with the needs of school community members, paying particular attention to issues of inclusion and consequential validity. I then consider the related issues of the coordination of reading-assessment programs and communication within these programs. In the final section, I examine the central role that teachers and students can take in the assessment of learning to read. This broad view of the challenge of creating useful assessments of learning to read reflects my belief that good assessment is more than a matter of designing valid instruments and procedures. Good assessment results from systemic and

239

inclusive development efforts that focus on the validity, reliability, and utility of assessment information.

A recent dictionary of literacy terms gives the following definition of assessment:

> the act or process of gathering data in order to better understand the strengths and weaknesses of student learning, as by observation, testing, interviews, etc. Note: Some writers use the term assessment to refer to the judgments or evaluations made after data are gathered. (Harris & Hodges, 1995, p. 12)

I add to this definition that assessment is administered, taken, evaluated, reported, and interpreted by people who have a variety of values, beliefs, and instructional practices.

FOUR CHARACTERISTICS THAT INFLUENCE LEARNING TO READ

It is important to align current understandings of how children learn to be successful readers with the assessment materials and procedures we use to measure and describe this learning. Evolution in the understanding of the nature of reading development (Adams, 1990; Pressley & Afflerbach, 1995; Verhoeven, 1994) contributes to a complex picture of the young reader, and this creates numerous assessment challenges. Evolving knowledge of how and what children learn as beginning readers must provide guidance for the development of useful reading assessments. It is beyond the scope of this chapter to describe in detail all the possible ways and means of assessing learning to read in accordance with all competing models of what reading is and of how children learn to read. Indeed, creating assessments that are inclusive of competing paradigms and beliefs related to learning to read is an enormous challenge to effective assessment.

Because it is a model of reading that is inclusive of an important array of early readers' characteristics, I focus on "engaged reading" (Alvermann & Guthrie, 1992). Engaged reading is a helpful model for setting goals and priorities for learning-to-read assessment programs. The engaged early reader develops in relation to four characteristics: (1) cognitive skills and strategies, (2) motivations for reading, (3) content-domain knowledge, and (4) social knowledge of reading acts. Individual students may possess these four characteristics at different levels of development. Throughout this chapter I discuss engaged reading in relation to Effie, a first grade student who is learning to read. Effie is at a nascent stage of metacognition in reading, and she is working toward independence in word decoding. She possesses a wealth of content-domain knowledge of dogs. She is motivated to read aloud with her parents, but she is limited in her knowledge of other types and purposes for reading.

As we consider the diverse characteristics of developing readers, we must pay attention to the contexts in which students learn to read and to the variability in reader characteristics within these contexts allows for the development of assessments that describe how situational variables influence learning to read (Brown, Collins, & Duguid, 1989; Greeno, Pearson, & Schoenfeld, 1996).

Cognitive Skills and Strategies

Effie possesses particular emergent literacy knowledge and skills, including an understanding of print and word concepts (Sulzby, 1985). She knows that books may be read aloud or silently. Through her experiences in her home, community, and school, she is developing familiarity with the rule-governed nature of print, and she is actively refining her understanding of how print is related to speech. Her decoding skills are evolving (Stanovich, 1991). Effie has considerable phonemic awareness, an evolving understanding of sound–symbol correspondences, and orthographic knowledge of spelling patterns used in English (Goswami & Bryant, 1990). She uses these skills and strategies to decode print into spoken counterparts and to determine words that are in her listening vocabulary, including *cat, step,* and *red.* She has a burgeoning sight-word vocabulary that reflects her experiences and learning in her home and the world around her. This vocabulary, with a heavy loading of canine-related sight words (*dog, bone, dachshund, boxer, kennel*), contributes to flashes of fluency in her otherwise laborious oral reading of short sentences in relatively simple stories.

Effie's accomplishments also include the increasing ability to use cognitive strategies to construct meaning. Effie's sense of story is evolving from a tacit understanding to a growing awareness of how her prior knowledge can be used to make inferences. She is increasingly aware of the role that she can play in creating meaning. Her reading strategies also include the ability to focus on important information, to ignore unimportant information, and to summarize. As she develops further as a young reader, Effie's strategies will include setting goals and monitoring progress toward these goals. Her use of skills and strategies should become increasingly fluent with successful practice, which will lead to frequent automaticity in their use (Pressley & Afflerbach, 1995).

Motivation for Reading

Effie arrives at school with a set of reading-related motivations (Guthrie & Wigfield, 1997). Because her parents have read to her regularly, Effie has built associations of security and love around the act of reading. She is motivated to read about animals because she likes them. She will unfailingly choose a colorfully illustrated book about animals over any other type of book. Her motivation contributes to her attempts to decode the unfamiliar words found within these books. Motivation also leads Effie to request a class visit to the school library so that she can borrow picture books about animals. Although she is not as motivated to read books with a preponderance of print, Effie is motivated to please her teacher, and this provides her with the incentive to try to read content-area books. It helps her choose reading in the face of competing and attractive alternatives.

Motivation steers Effie toward reading. It helps her persevere when the act of reading presents difficulties. Her early and successful encounters with print have contributed to her perceptions of self-efficacy as a language user and reader, and this fuels her further reading attempts. She is beginning to see herself as a reader who is capable of success.

Content-Domain Knowledge

Effie's prior knowledge for text content is strongly related to how and how successfully she constructs meaning. Prior knowledge is represented, in part, by vocabulary that reflects her considerable experience and learning in particular content domains (Chi, Glaser, & Farr, 1988). Effie has a wealth of knowledge about types of dogs, their origins, and their characteristics. Her knowledge of dogs contributes to her high motivation to read about them, to her sight-word vocabulary, and to the occasionally fluent phrase in her oral reading. This prior knowledge also fuels the accuracy and appropriateness of her inferences (Graesser & Bower, 1990). Thus it is not surprising that her reading performance may be optimized when she reads materials about dogs (Anderson & Pearson, 1984).

Social Knowledge about Reading Acts

Effie is learning new information about what reading is and how it is used, which adds to her developing schema for the social nature and uses of reading. Her life prior to schooling included diverse and rich language experiences in the home and community. She is privileged in that her home literacy experiences mesh well with what is expected of her as she progresses through first grade (Heath, 1983). This affirms her prior experiences with reading and language. She is also privileged in that the knowledge she constructs outside school is regularly used inside school (Moll, 1992). Her parents often ask her questions about books that they read aloud to her at bedtime—a routine that is reflected in the questions asked by her first-grade teacher about the books that are read aloud in class. As a result of her home routine, Effie listens to her teacher with a goal of being able to answer her questions. After the teacher reads aloud, Effie participates in discussions with classmates about stories and their characters and settings. She also listens in a manner that demonstrates that she has received encouragement to respond personally to what she reads (Rosenblatt, 1978).

Effie continues to develop social orientations toward the act of reading. As she participates in a question–answer session based on her teacher's read-aloud or discussing interpretations of stories, Effie's thoughts and actions reflect increasingly complex social and cognitive worlds (Vygotsky, 1978). As she masters the decoding of familiar words and constructs understandings of the stories read in class, Effie increasingly anticipates how, when, and why she might use meaning constructed from reading in future social situations. This is an indicator of her evolving familiarity with the culture of reading (Bruner, 1996).

Effie has much work to do to become a successful and independent reader. She is similar, however, to many early readers in that she brings a large array of skills and strategies, motivations, knowledge, and social awareness to each act of reading. If we value developing readers' growth related to these characteristics, we must design reading assessments that measure and describe growth in each of them. This will allow the construction of a comprehensive portrait of the young reader and a description of the individual differences among students in each learning-to-read classroom. This information can shape school and classroom reading experiences in a positive way for children who are learning to read. Moreover, it can help us fully appreciate what schools, teachers, and students accomplish.

ASSESSING THE STUDENT CHARACTERISTICS THAT INFLUENCE LEARNING TO READ

Psychometric theory and classroom practice should coalesce as we conceptualize how to assess students' learning-to-read progress. As the construct of early reading evolves, so must the means of assessing early reading achievement. Historically, much assessment trails evolving understandings of early reading, resulting in assessments that are incomplete and cautious in their accounting of children's diverse characteristics and accomplishments. This gap must be closed with assessment that describes the full range of student development, reading-program worth, and teacher accomplishment. In this section, I refer to specific assessment routines and materials that measure and describe the critical characteristics of engaged students who are learning to read.

Measuring the Precursors of Learning to Read

Early reading assessment serves the critical need of identifying and describing what students possess (or need to develop) as they begin their school reading careers. We are fortunate to have an array of carefully developed, useful early reading assessments. The Concepts About Print (Clay, 1985) routine provides information related to students' understandings of story structure, print awareness, and sound–symbol correspondences.

Students' emergent reading behaviors with storybooks can be classified according to schemes and observation checklists developed by Morrow (1989), Neumann and Roskos (1993), and Sulzby (1985). These schemes and checklists promote observation and examination of young children as they label and comment on pictures in storybooks, create an oral account of pictures, and combine it with printed words to create a story, and use print to read a story.

The varying developmental stages of young readers require that teacher observation and evaluation play a central role in assessment. Formal assessment may be less appropriate. In addition to using the published and commercially produced checklists and observation forms, teachers may use their own constructed checklists and forms to describe how students make cognitive and social sense of their early encounters with print. These tools can tap constructs such as print awareness and provide information about students' knowledge of how books are held, how pages are turned, how print is followed, as well as about student familiarity of concepts such as author, title, letter, sentence, and spaces in-between words (Johnston, 1997). These lists may be informed by (and tailored to) the needs of particular students, teachers, and schools.

Skills, Strategies, and Vocabularies

As a fledgling reader, Effie's information processing may be described through assessments of tasks at the word level and below. These tasks include identifying printed letters and their related sounds, distinguishing phonemes, blending consonants and vowels, and decoding words. Effie must learn word-recognition skills, and she must develop an extensive vocabulary. Such aspects of early reading are the historical focus of many reading assessments, and there are numerous assessments that provide basic, reliable measures of them (e.g., MacGinitie & MacGinitie, 1989). However, these reading assessments reflect the conceptualization of reading as an act of information processing and cognition, with the result that they measure only a critical but limited array of factors that influence learning to read. These factors are assessed with considerable detail, detail we might expect from an assessment enterprise that has benefited from copious resources and concerted refinement efforts over the better part of this century. The piecemeal nature of many large-scale, commercially produced reading assessments is actually best suited to these mechanical aspects of learning to read.

Much work remains to be done to develop valid measures of young students' comprehension processes and products. We are just beginning to see a movement away from the one correct, multiple-choice answer to comprehension questions (Williams, Reese, Campbell, Mazzeo, & Phillips, 1994). For example, alternative assessments of comprehension may ask students to provide written or oral responses to open-ended comprehension questions. Performance assessments may tap comprehension of text. These assessments often assume comprehension (e.g., a student writes a comparison of two fictional characters, with comprehension assumed because it is necessary to have if the student is to accurately craft the written response) and may have limited use for students who are learning to comprehend text. However, they cannot provide detail on how students use what they understand. Think-aloud protocols also offer an opportunity to tap young readers' cognitive and metacognitive strategy use (Pressley & Afflerbach, 1995). This information may be used to describe young readers' strengths and needs. Think-aloud protocols, however, must be interpreted with caution when used with young readers, as verbal ability can influence the nature of the verbal report and the assessment inferences drawn from it.

Student knowledge of sound–symbol correspondences and their consonant blending abilities also can be assessed using reading inventories. Whether commercially published or teacher-made, these reading inventories can provide detailed information about the mechanics of reading, such as knowledge of letters, the ability to recognize and pronounce initial and final consonants, the ability to recognize and pronounce long and short vowels, and the ability to discriminate between the spoken letters, such as m and n. Assessment items may also measure and describe young readers' sight-word vocabulary. Depending on students' development as readers, these tasks may reflect either the conscious application of skills that require reader attention or the automatic application of skills.

Reading inventories also can provide information about the skills and cognitive processes that underlie oral reading. Through analysis of tape recordings of young readers' oral reading, it is often possible to determine a student's strengths and weaknesses in decoding and sight-word vocabulary. Such process measures also help teachers understand the development of a student's reading fluency and its possible influence on comprehension.

Running records (Johnston, 1997) provide similarly detailed information about students' reading skills and strategies. This is done through the on-line examination of students' processes as they read increasingly difficult passages and apply and use cognitive and metacognitive strategies (e.g., Swearingen & Allen, 1997). For example, running records may show that Effie is overreliant on context and less prone to use the graphophonic cueing system to decode new words (i.e., she reads "The dog ate the bone" for "The dog ate the burger"). An episode of Effie's rereading can provide information that permits the inference that metacognition is taking place (i.e., Effie is rereading because she has detected a difficulty). Comprehension is also inferred from products such as responses to multiple-choice questions or short fill-in items.

Motivation and Attitudes

Effie's motivation to read and her achievements in reading have a symbiotic relationship: Success motivates her to read further, and further reading influences her future success. Our understanding of motivation's contribution to successful early reading is increasing; yet the assessment of reading motivation only recently has received the attention that is commensurate with its importance. The Motivation to Read Profile (MRP; Gambrell, Palmer, Codling, & Mazzoni, 1995) contains two instruments, a reading survey and a conversational interview, that describe elementary-school students' motivations. The reading survey focuses on a student's self-concept as a reader and the value that the student places on reading. The conversational interview provides information about the factors that motivate reading, including students' favorite authors, the books and stories they find most interesting, and how and where they locate reading materials of interest to them. The interview includes questions grouped in three sections that measure student motivation related to reading narrative text, reading informational text, and general factors of reading motivation.

A related assessment tool, the Elementary Reading Attitude Survey (ERAS), contains 20 items that examine students' attitudes toward academic and recreational reading (McKenna, Kear, & Ellsworth, 1995). Academic reading items include reading in school, taking a reading test, reading aloud in class, and learning from a book. Recreational reading items gauge how students feel when they read books, when they receive books for gifts, when they read instead of play, and when they go to a bookstore. Information gathered through ERAS can be used to focus efforts so that curriculum and instruction build on Effie's positive attitudes, or help shape them.

MRP and ERAS both describe student growth, and both are promising because they supply formative and summative information about motivation and learning to read. However, both assessment tools require modifications to provide information about the motivations of students who are just learning to read. Along with teacher observations of students and their motivations, the tools can provide diagnostic and descriptive information that can help teachers understand what texts and contexts contribute to students' enthusiastic reading. Descriptive assessment information can be used to help understand how students such as Effie become motivated to learn to read.

Content-Domain Knowledge

Historically, many reading tests have sought to control bias by controlling or removing students' domain knowledge from the reading act. A result is that the tests contain passages about obscure topics that few (if any) students know anything about. There is one correct answer to every test question, and the constructive nature of comprehension and the importance of divergent thinking based on prior knowledge are ruled out of the assessment experience. Such tests yield scores that may be relatively free from prior-domain knowledge bias, however, they create a reading scenario that is divorced from current conceptualizations of reading as a constructive process that is enabled by prior knowledge.

An alternative is to acknowledge the existence and influence of prior knowledge and to observe students as they use prior knowledge to decode, recognize words, and build meaning from texts. This alternative presents the ongoing challenge of developing indices of students' prior knowledge for particular texts (Langer, 1987). Indices of student prior knowledge for text that is used in reading assessment allow for determining both the prior knowledge a student brings to the act of reading and the knowledge that he or she gains from successful reading. Furthermore, such indices may help demonstrate how students use prior knowledge in the construction of meaning, and they may allow for permissible inferences of the influence of prior knowledge on comprehension. We should expect a continuing tension as we examine the fine line between prior knowledge as an enabling resource in the construction of meaning and prior knowledge as a biasing factor in reading assessment.

The existing measures of students' prior knowledge include more formal checklists, interviews, and inventories that teachers may use in the classroom. The widely used K–W–L routine (Ogle, 1986) helps students reflect on their prior knowledge as they begin content area work. The K–W–L form and routine can make transparent much of what students know about a curriculum topic. It can also promote reflection and meta-cognition, as students set goals in relation to their prior knowledge and then monitor these goals.

Knowledge of students' interests and prior knowledge combined with careful observation and questioning can provide teachers with a wealth of information. A benefit of knowing the extent of students' prior knowledge is that this information can help teachers establish reading experiences in familiar content domains. Here, students' established knowledge may allow them to demonstrate optimal reading performances at their current levels of competence. For example, Effie can read a simple text about dogs, and she may be able to decode, recognize sight words, and read with some fluency. Assessments of this best-case scenario (in terms of Effie reading from a position of strength) can provide details about the knowledge that students bring to and take from the act of reading. The assessments also enable Effie to work through zones of her proximal development in which prior knowledge facilitates increased performance. Further development of prior-knowledge measures should focus on reliable tools that help us understand what content-domain knowledge individual students know, and how this figures in their learning to read and learning from text.

Social Knowledge and Action Related to Learning to Read

Effie possesses a growing awareness of the power and uses of reading. She also has a tacit understanding that particular reading situations require that she take particular stances toward the texts she reads. For example, she expects to be entertained by Dr. Seuss books. She knows to listen carefully when her teacher reads to her class about butterflies from a science book. The Measuring Reading Activity Inventory (MRAI; Guthrie, McGough, & Wigfield, 1994) describes the depth and breadth of students' reading in and out of school. The inventory requires students to respond to questions about their reading in school and their reading for enjoyment. MRAI can be used in a pre- and postreading fashion to examine beginning readers' reading habits and experiences across the school year or marking period. It may also be used as a diagnostic tool to help teachers and parents understand what types of reading their children are experiencing and what types may remain unfamiliar.

Despite the importance of young readers' increasing exposure to diverse texts and reading tasks, measures of this aspect of reading growth are few. Teacher observations, portfolios, and students' self-reports all can provide records and descriptions of students' increasing reading activity and knowledge. With this information, students may be afforded an increasingly wide range of reading materials and experiences that contribute to further reading growth.

Assessment must honor a broad view of young children learning to read. A collection of assessment materials and procedures aligned with this conceptualization of the beginning reader would help in accurately measuring, describing, and anticipating students' development. We need to know what emergent literacy abilities students bring to school and what beginning reading skills and strategies they possess. Assessment should tell us how students who are learning to read use their prior knowledge to help construct understanding. We need assessments that describe the relationship of motivation to readers' developing decoding skills and word-recognition strategies. Assessment should provide information that describes students' development as readers in the situated, social contexts of reading and schooling. In addition, we need assessments that accurately measure the interactions of these factors and that describe how they contribute to reading growth and success.

Present initiatives in early-reading assessment should be informed by past experiences with large-scale, high-stakes reading assessments. A first caveat is to avoid assessments (or entire assessment programs) that provide only a partial description of the developing reader. A collection of assessments must capture the complexities of learning to read to provide the information that is critical to fostering young students' growth in all aspects of early reading. A regimen of reading-assessment materials and procedures that is focused narrowly on one aspect of learning to read may lead to instruction and learning that is similarly narrow. Performance on a conso-nant blend checklist will not tell us anything about Effie's developing sense of reading or her fledgling attempts to self-monitor. Similarly, a motivation checklist will not tell us of her needed work with certain sound–symbol correspondences.

Second, as early-reading assessments are aligned with the four charac-teristics of engaged reading, the developmental appropriateness of these assessments of learning to read should be continually monitored. A group-administered, norm-referenced formal assessment of emergent literacy may be well-intentioned but ill-informed. Young children may not understand the concept of a formal test (or any other assessment) or the expectations that are placed on them. The ethics of placing students in such assessment situations should be questioned.

Third, the makers and users of assessments must be vigilant and continually check reading assessments for possible bias. Effie is privileged in that there is a close match between the talk in her home and the talk in her school. Her experiences prior to schooling provided a strong entry point into the school reading program. Across the array of learning-to-read assessment, there must be care in the interpretation of dialect and awareness of how students' prior cultural knowledge and experiences can influence performance on learning-to-read assessments (Farr & Trumbell, 1997).

Aligning Reading-Assessment Programs with the Needs of Stakeholders

Assessment takes place in a context of limited school resources, competing assessment agendas, and numerous constraints on student, teacher, and school time. Thus, it is imperative to develop coherent reading-assessment programs that align learning-to-read assessment with the needs of different school community members. Most schools, classrooms, districts, and states participate in a de facto series of assessments, and, thus, they lack an integrated and comprehensive reading-assessment program. A useful and comprehensive reading-assessment program can be achieved by asking concerned school community members to examine their reading-assessment needs and to inventory the coverage of existing assessments. This determi-nation can contribute to a group of core assessments that provides needed information for different audiences (Afflerbach & Johnston, 1993). Table 11.1 presents different audiences of learning-to-read assessments in Effie's classroom, school, and community, along with their respective needs. These needs are represented by typical questions the audiences might ask of reading assessment.

The many audiences of reading assessment may have different values, beliefs, and practices related to literacy and early reading, and different needs for reading assessment. As a result, they will have different definitions and criteria for determining the usefulness of reading assessment. Useful

TABLE 11.1. Audiences for Reading Assessment and Questions That Are Asked of Reading Assessment

Audience	Representative questions asked by audience
Legislators	Are schools meeting state goals and standards?
	Are particular school districts notable for their levels of performance?
State education department	Are new learning-to-read programs working? Which ones?
Taxpayers	Is our money well spent?
Parents	How is my child doing?
	What can I do to help my child become a better reader?
School administrators	How are the teachers doing?
	Is buildingwide or districtwide initiative working?
Teachers	Is my instructional optimal?
	Are students' learning goals met?
	Is my placement of students accurate?
	What does this student need in terms of remedial or accelerated curriculum?
Students	What's this thing called reading assessment?
	What kind of reader am I?
	How did I do on the assignment?
	How am I doing on the recent task?
	How is reading assessment helpful to me in my development as a reader?
	What have I accomplished, and what do I have to do still?

reading assessment is inclusive of and sensitive to the array of traits and behaviors that students learning to read may exhibit. It is also responsive to the needs of those who use reading-assessment information. Without these features, reading assessment may achieve validity in a vacuum—and little else. That is, reading assessment may meet psychometric criteria for validity but fail the test of providing useful information for particular stakeholders interested in helping children learn to read.

The process of determining the audience and purposes of reading assessment is intertwined with inclusion: What is needed from a comprehensive assessment program cannot be determined without consulting all legitimate stakeholders. Inclusive reading-assessment programs provide for the broad representation of experts (and their conceptions of audiences and purposes) in the development and use of reading assessment. The inclusion should contribute to better communication and understanding of the potential uses and misuses of assessment information and better coordination of the overall program. Inclusion can provide an accurate account of the types of reading-assessment information that parents or that teachers must have. For example, Effie's parents can inform decisions about the types of reading assessment and reading-assessment information that best help them build strong collaborative efforts between home and school. Teachers can inform the selection process so that the final array of assessments provides formative and summative information related to their students' needs. There are numerous professional development opportunities embedded within the assessment development and selection process. Lack of inclusion will result in an assessment program that is incomplete and that leaves legitimate stakeholders lacking the important assessment information they need.

Success stories are most often thoughtful and carefully planned initiatives (Allington & Walmsley, 1995) that include parental participation in Chapter 1 programs (Winfield, 1995), and the Accelerated School Model (Hopfenberger & Levin, 1993). In these programs, stakeholders are expected to take responsibility for particular work and are rewarded with parental empowerment and voice in school governance. With early reading assessment, this voice might contribute to the determination definition of audience needs and the development of assessment contents.

When the high-stakes reading-assessment agenda is determined by a statewide education department, a districtwide committee, or a national campaign—agencies the needs of all stakeholders may not be considered (Stephens et al., 1995). The hegemony of a mandated high-stakes assessment may displace other more locally useful assessments and agendas, including those of teachers, students, and parents.

Consequential Validity and Consequences of Reading-Assessment Practices

It is important to consider fully how reading-assessment information is used. This notion of consequential validity of assessment has received a great deal of attention from the psychometric community (Messick, 1989; Moss, 1995; Tittle, 1989). Use of normative performance data, including test scores, percentile rankings, and grade-level equivalents can have varied and strong consequences on teachers and students in beginning-reading programs. Students may be placed in particular reading groups or classrooms, reading programs may be adopted, sanctioned or discontinued, and teachers' efforts and accomplishments may or may not receive acknowledgment as a consequence of the use of assessment information, most frequently test scores. Each of these actions can impact how and how well students learn to read. For example, Effie's placement in a reading group is based in part on her reading-test scores. Effie's teacher feels pressure regularly to use particular teaching materials and methods that provide a good match with mandated assessments and that improve students' scores on tests.

In addition to the consequences of using assessment scores, it is important to consider the consequences of assessment programs, routines, and cultures. Reading-assessment programs can have deleterious effects on teachers. For example, when the daily routines of districts, schools, and individual classrooms are overly influenced by high-stakes assessments, teachers may narrow the curriculum and teach to goals set by others (Johnston, Afflerbach, & Weiss, 1993; Moss et al., 1992). Those teachers who believe that learning to read is determined by students' ability to use a limited range of basic skills and strategies that may be tested in high-stakes assessments will not find this troublesome. Those teachers who conceptualize learning to read as involving social, motivational, knowledge, and strategic components will not find all they need in limited measures of beginning reading. A consequence of limited assessment of learning to read may be the underestimation of the values of programs that contribute to students' motivation and reading-related social growth. For example, Effie's reading program continually provides her with new reading experiences because a beginning-of-the-year assessment indicated that she had quite narrow (albeit rich) reading experiences.

Further, reading-assessment programs may encroach on instructional time. Reading test preparation may take time from reading and reading instruction. And high-stakes reading assessment may influence the reading curriculum. A consequence is reduced time on task, and the consequence of this is fewer opportunities for teachers to teach and for students to develop the array of characteristics of engaged early readers (Afflerbach, Almasi, Guthrie, & Schafer, 1996).

The research literature related to work in teachers' professional development demonstrates that teacher reflection and personal decision making are key components in effective schools (Ashton & Webb, 1986). When assessment is developed and chosen far from the classroom, teachers may decide not to allow it to commandeer the curriculum. Because they see a lack of alignment between assessment and the reading curriculum, teachers may limit the use of the assessment to inform instruction and learning.

Including or excluding particular audiences in the development of a learning-to-read assessment program may produce troubling results, such as skepticism about tests and assessments, in general, and distrust in the school system that administers and uses them. Lacking inclusive reading assessment, particular stakeholders may come to believe that their needs are not served and that reading-assessment information is not useful even if it is deemed valid by some traditional means (Johnston et al., 1993).

A further consequence of the use of particular reading-assessment materials and practices is that they may create habits that lead teachers and students to believe that they should remain on the side lines of assessment, relegated to the roles of test giver and test taker. Reading assessment that creates dependent students is in direct conflict with research descriptions of accomplished readers who are independent and in control of the reading situation. For example, metacognitive research demonstrates the necessity of building competency in monitoring one's progress as a reader (Baker & Brown, 1984). Students learning to read may also be learning that reading assessment is done *to* them and *for* them, rather than *with* them and *by* them. A consequence is that students may become spectators rather than participants in classroom reading assessment. There is the lost opportunity to help students more towards independence. Unfortunately, the resources of time given to mandated, large-scale reading assessments can have the consequence of discounting and discontinuing other types of reading assessment, including teacher- and student-centered reading assessment.

Large-scale districtwide and statewide reading assessments are often labeled *high stakes* because they are presumed to have potentially serious consequences for students and teachers. In fact, all reading assessment should be high stakes, or it is not worth the time, effort, and money it requires. For the classroom teacher and for students learning to read, there is nothing so "high stakes" as regular, accurate, and useful reading assessment.

We need to anticipate the consequential validity of our assessments and the consequences of assessment programs, materials, and procedures. Too often the consideration of the consequences of assessment is limited to the use of learning-to-read test scores, and these are determined after the facts of development and implementation of reading-assessment programs. More effective and useful learning-to-read assessment materials and procedures will result from a priori consideration of consequences.

Coordination and Communication of Reading Assessment

Successful assessment of learning to read is not only a matter of choosing the appropriate instruments and procedures or of seeking the involvement of all legitimate stakeholders. It is a matter of planning an assessment program that captures the many characteristics of learning to read and provides needed information to diverse audiences about learning to read. Unfortunately, assessment in Effie's school lacks coordination. The learning-to-read assessment program consists of a blend of formative and summative assessment, commercially produced and teacher-made assessments, individual and group assessments, mandated and teacher-selected assessments, and process and product assessments. This mix reflects numerous assessment initiatives and agendas from the classroom, school, district, and state. The information provided by these assessments may be useful or useless, contentious, or well-received. The information provided by each of the assessments may be unique, or redundant.

Reading-assessment initiatives begin inside and outside classrooms, and they compete for class time. Coordination of these assessments (especially as informed by community discussion of needs) may eliminate redundant measures and highlight areas in which assessment is desired but not conducted. For example, across the school year there may be individual, classroom, schoolwide, districtwide, and statewide reading assessments that yield three similar measures of Effie's word recognition ability but no information whatsoever related to her motivations for reading. Coordination of the program could realign the assessments to reflect the valued behaviors and to include measures related to the development of student motivation. The coordination of reading assessment will also provide a means for determining whether particular audiences are getting information that is useful.

Coordination of the reading-assessment system may also help relieve the assessment burden felt by so many teachers, students, and school administrators (Afflerbach et al., 1996). When different audiences are served by a core group of assessments, time, money and effort may be saved for other critical school tasks, and the negative encroachment of assessment on school time can be minimized. An accounting of time devoted to reading assessment may demonstrate that a particular classroom or school is devoting too much or too little time to their learning-to-read assessment program.

The coordination of a comprehensive reading-assessment program across grade levels can provide opportunities for checkpoints that allow for determining students' movement from emergent literacy toward the first benchmark performances and standards of reading. It may also lead to the development of a program that provides diagnostic information to help teachers and students as it informs school board members and legislators and their learning-to-read policy making. When assessments serve more than one audience, there is the realization of a common language among different groups. This can be a powerful tool in establishing trust and efficiency in assessment programs.

Reading-assessment initiatives and programs must be accompanied by effective communication of the nature, purposes, and results of the assessment. Without effective communication, the means and goals of reading assessment may be unknown to or misunderstood by people who might otherwise be enthusiastic supporters, consumers, and users of particular reading-assessment information. For example, if community members do not fully understand the value of the portfolios that all students in Effie's class keep, they may not support teacher efforts related to portfolios. If a reading-assessment program has been successful in building consensus goals among the various consumers of reading-assessment information, the communication task is not as daunting, for important information has already been shared among constituents through the inclusion process. In contrast, a reading-assessment program constructed without consultation of all stakeholders will garner considerable numbers of questions related to unknown aspects of the assessment. In addition, there may be considerable skepticism or mistrust of assessments that are chosen without consensus. A reading-assessment program or procedure that is developed exclusive of particular stakeholders may not be valued for several reasons. School community members may distrust it, they may not understand it, or they may resent it because they were not consulted in the development process.

THE CENTRAL ROLE OF TEACHERS IN ASSESSING LEARNING TO READ

The classroom is the site where assessment agendas and actions converge, and where assessment demands and responsibilities are placed on teachers and students. Teachers are best situated to collect useful assessment information related to students' learning to read. Throughout this chapter, I have implied that teachers must be more involved in reading assessment. How prepared are they to do so?

The results of comprehensive studies of teachers' assessment and evaluation processes reveal often ineffectual teacher-assessment practices in different school settings (Stiggins & Conklin, 1992). Stiggins and Conklin cite the teachers' assessment training (or the distinct lack of this training) as a key factor influencing the usefulness of the assessment. Most teachers receive limited preservice assessment training, and few have ongoing professional development opportunities for learning assessment as they are teaching. Few take more than a single state-mandated assessment course. Although Stiggins and Conklin's (1992) investigations did not focus on early-reading instruction and assessment, their results emphasize the need for professional development opportunities for teachers to develop assessment expertise.

The task of becoming a consistent and insightful assessor of students who are learning to read is difficult for many teachers. The broadened conceptualization of the engaged early reader demands an increased scope and level of efficiency in teachers' assessments. Yet state certification programs typically require only one (or no) course dedicated to assessment. Schafer and Lissitz (1987) found a distinct mismatch between what teachers consider to be the most important assessment information for their classrooms and the content that is offered in educational measurement classes. In the majority of cases, the content of instruction was not programmatically relevant for teachers, nor was it presented in a systematic manner. In many educational measurement courses, for example, teachers learn how to construct multiple-choice tests. If a teacher believes that this is the best means for measuring the complexity of students learning to read, then learning how to construct multiple-choice tests is appropriate. However, multiple-choice tests are only one means of tapping one aspect of reading comprehension. If models of reading suggest that more complex and detailed measures are necessary, then learning to construct multiple-choice tests is not sufficient.

It is ironic that teachers are best situated but often ill prepared to gather and use reading-assessment information. When teachers are given the opportunity to develop reading assessments and use them consistently, they may not be prepared to meet the challenge. Thus teachers' professional development should include work that helps build and conduct assessments of early reading that provide useful information. State certification requirements, college of education degree requirements, and professional development guidelines should provide the incentives to teachers who have worked to become reliable assessors of their students' progress as developing readers.

TEACHER-CENTERED EARLY-READING-ASSESSMENT PROGRAMS

What happens when teachers have professional prerogative and administrative support to design and implement reading assessments? The evidence of useful teacher assessment of young students' reading comes from several sources. Each describes teachers' schoolwide and districtwide efforts to build appropriate reading assessments (Au, 1994; Hoffman et al., 1996; Valencia & Place, 1994). Teachers were central in each of these efforts to gain approval and support for their projects, to develop reading assessment, and to align it with the curriculum. Each of these teacher-initiated assessment projects focused on measuring the complexities of learning to read, and each received support at the district and building levels that was critical for success.

The Primary Assessment of Language Arts and Mathematics (PALM; Hoffman et al., 1996) was developed by classroom teachers, in part as a reaction to the districtwide use of the Iowa Tests of Basic Skills to monitor elementary school quality. A group of teachers questioned the appropriateness of the Iowa Test of Basic Skills as a measure of young students' literacy learning and petitioned the Board of Trustees of the Austin, Texas, Independent School District for a more suitable assessment. Through the teachers' efforts, a waiver from the standardized testing of first graders was granted from the central administration, and a charge to develop a more appropriate early literacy assessment was given to the teachers.

PALM was developed with the goal of providing useful assessment information for teachers, parents, administrators, policy makers, and students. The PALM goals statement was circulated to all first-grade teachers in the district, and their participation was invited. The PALM team created a reading-development profile that describes a range of characteristics and behaviors related to students' emergent reading, early reading, fluent reading, and expanding reading abilities. Emergent reading behaviors include pretending to read, showing linearity and directionality when interacting with print, and deriving meaning from environmental print. Early reading-development measures described students' uses of letter–sound associations to predict and confirm words, students' ability to recognize common words, and students' ability to locate details. Although the PALM descriptors focus in part on skills and strategies, PALM also includes procedures and reports that provide information related to how students choose books based on personal interest, how they persist with text that goes beyond immediate knowledge and linguistic development, how they make judgments about the reliability and worth of the material, and how students make connections between literature and their own lives. Thus, PALM assesses skills and strategies, motivation, domain knowledge, and social uses of reading.

In their descriptions of portfolio-assessment programs Au (1994) and Valencia and Place (1994) point out the positive and central contributions that teachers can make to the growth of student readers. Au (1994) describes a comprehensive early literacy portfolio-assessment program that utilizes running records to determine students' word-reading strategies, and samples of student writing to assess student reading comprehension and vocabulary knowledge. Students' responses to literature that is read aloud by teachers or read by the students themselves are also assessed. Valencia and Place (1994) describe the development of the Bellevue Literacy Assessment Project literacy assessment. Teachers created instructional outcomes that reflected current understanding of reading and literacy. This portfolio project received support from parents and administrators, who charged teachers with developing an assessment program that met their needs for accountability and for providing details of student learning. The assessment project allowed for the development and use of assessments that provided information for improving instruction, increasing student ownership of learning, and reporting accomplishments and challenges to stakeholders outside the classroom. The portfolio in first grade was used to collect information on students' written retellings of stories and their reading logs, free writing, and book reports.

The encouraging picture that emerges from these reading-assessment development projects is that teachers are central to reading-assessment reform programs that provide useful assessment information to diverse audiences. These recent examples of reading-assessment development may inform systemic reading-assessment initiatives with a cautious enthusiasm. They provide details related to gaining support for assessment reform; developing, piloting, and refining the assessment instruments and procedures; and the effective communication of assessment information among stakeholders. These scenarios are in contrast to the teacher assessment described by Stiggins and Conklin (1992), which painted a fairly dismal picture of teachers' ability to assess student learning.

An important lesson from these reading-assessment programs is that positive change in reading assessment takes large amounts of time and effort. Assessment programs are often contemplated, adopted, or created in response to immediate needs. The urgency of these situations contributes to a timeline for development and implementation that is most often too short for the piloting and refinement phases that high-quality, early-reading assessment programs demand. It is helpful to remember that many current large-scale standardized reading tests represent the product of thousands of hours of the development process. These tests have histories of use over decades that allow for regular adjustment and refinement. Innovative learning-to-read assessment initiatives should be given sufficient time and funding to realize their full potential.

THE STUDENT ROLE IN EARLY-READING ASSESSMENT

An ultimate goal of reading instruction is to help all students develop as independent and successful readers. Central to independence and success in reading is the ability to self-assess, and self-assessment should have its beginnings in learning to read. It is common to perceive assessment as a measure of learning and less common to think of assessment as an opportunity for teaching and learning. A shortcoming of many learning-to-read assessment materials, procedures, and programs is their failure to help students initiate movement toward independence in their ability to self-assess.

Considerable evidence points to the centrality of metacognition in successful reading (Baker & Brown, 1984). A reader encountering on-line difficulties must be able to realize that there is a problem, identify the problem, initiate a fix-it strategy, and get back on track. For example, Effie reads the sentence "The boy rode a house" for "The boy rode a horse." She is capable of detecting the problem because she is learning to regularly ask "Does that make sense?" Her teacher's consistent modeling of such questions, as is used in reciprocal teaching (Palincsar & Brown, 1984), provides the foundations for Effie's internalization of assessment routines that can develop into sophisticated metacognition. Across Effie's career as a beginning reader, teacher modeling helps her focus on particular aspects of reading in relation to the reading task at hand. Although it may be difficult to imagine some beginning readers as independent assessors of their own work, it is possible to help them begin building awareness of the importance of assessment.

Reading instruction that fails to help students understand and internalize the ways and means of assessment ultimately will produce readers who are not capable of controlling the act of reading. An important educational outcome of successful learning-to-read instruction and assessment is the student who is increasingly familiar with the culture of assessment and is a contributing member of that culture. Unfortunately, too much assessment relegates the child to the sidelines of assessment. Reading assessment that is done *for* young children will keep them on the sidelines. Efforts must focus on doing assessment *with* students and on making the reading-assessment routines understandable to students.

CONCLUSION

Reading assessment can enhance the teaching and learning of reading. For this to happen, reading assessment must be aligned with what we understand about the nature of learning to read. Concerted efforts to align assessment with current knowledge of learning to read will produce increased construct validity for these assessments. Thus assessment will provide comprehensive portraits of emerging readers and include measures of strategies and skills, motivations, social uses of reading, and content-area knowledge.

Equally as important, assessment must be aligned with the needs of stakeholders, all of whom are concerned with children's growth and achievement in reading. This can be accomplished through a reading-assessment program that is developed in an inclusive manner, so that the needs of all stakeholders are voiced and considered, and the consequences of reading assessment are discussed and fully understood. The assessment must be sensitive to the nature of learning to read as defined by the different stakeholders in the particular classrooms, schools, and communities in which the assessment is conducted. In addition, attention must be paid both to the coordination of learning-to-read assessment efforts and to the effective communication of reading-assessment ways and means.

Involvement of teachers and students in central assessment roles will yield regular and useful assessment information that helps students who are learning to read. Effective programs will introduce students to the importance and necessity of growing familiar with the culture of assessment and will build the foundation for students as independent assessors and evaluators of their own reading.

As we strive to attain an alignment between the complexities of learning to read and how they are measured, and the alignment between stakeholders' needs and learning-to-read assessment information, we need to undertake an additional, critical endeavor: examining the relationship between reading assessment and students' reading achievement. We must better understand the intricacies of how assessment influences students' learning to read. We need to link theories of effective reading assessment with theories of successful reading instruction and exemplary student learning. There is surprisingly limited understanding of the use of teachers' assessments of early reading. Thus, we lack a theory of how reading assessment connects with reading instruction and student learning and achievement.

When children learn to read, we assume that the instructional program is successful and that reading assessment is providing the requisite information for teachers to make good curricular decisions. When children fail to learn to read, instructional methods and materials (or children themselves) are most often blamed. Reading assessment rarely is cited as a contributing cause of reading success or failure, despite the role it may play in teacher decision making and in shaping the learning-to-read curriculum. Student achievement serves as a proxy for valid, useful assessment. Clearly, we need to examine the agency of reading assessment in promoting early reading achievement. Future reading-assessment research must build on recent accomplishments related to the development of authentic assessments of reading (Valencia, Hiebert, & Afflerbach, 1994) and to heightened awareness of the utility and consequences (Moss, 1995; Tittle, 1989) of assessment to focus on this connection between reading assessment and reading achievement.

REFERENCES

Adams, M. (1990). *Beginning to read: Thinking and learning about print.* Cambridge, MA: MIT Press.

Afflerbach, P. (1996). The engaged assessment of engaged reading. In L. Baker, P. Afflerbach, & D. Reinking (Eds.), *Developing engaged readers in home and school communities* (pp. 191–214). Hillsdale, NJ: Erlbaum.

Afflerbach, P., Almasi, J., Guthrie, J., & Schafer, W. (1996). *Barriers to the implementation of a statewide performance assessment program: School personnel perspectives* (Research Report No. 51). Athens, GA: National Reading Research Center.

Afflerbach, P., & Johnston, P. (1993). Writing language arts report cards: Eleven teachers' conflicts of knowing and communicating. *Elementary School Journal, 94,* 73–86.

Airasian, P. (1993). *Classroom assessment* (2nd ed.). New York: McGraw-Hill.

Allington, R., & Walmsley, S. (1995). *No quick fix: Rethinking literacy programs in America's elementary schools.* New York: Teachers College Press.

Alvermann, D., & Guthrie, J. (1992). *Themes and directions of the National Reading Research Center* (Perspectives in Reading Research No. 1). Athens, GA: National Reading Research Center.

Anderson, R., & Pearson, D. (1984). A schema-theoretic view of reading. In P. Pearson, M. Kamil, R. Barr, & P. Mosenthal (Eds.), *Handbook of reading research* (Vol. 1, pp. 255–291). White Plains, NY: Longman.

Ashton, P., & Webb, R. (1986). *Making a difference: Teacher's sense of efficacy and student achievement.* New York: Longman.

Au, K. (1994). Portfolio assessment: Experiences at the Kamehameha elementary education program. In S. Valencia, E. Hiebert, & P. Afflerbach (Eds.), *Authen-*

tic assessment: Practices and possibilities (pp. 103–126). Newark, DE: International Reading Association.

Baker, L., & Brown, A. (1984). Metacognitive skills and reading. In P. Pearson, M. Kamil, R. Barr, & P. Mosenthal (Eds.), *Handbook of reading research* (Vol. 1, pp. 353–394). White Plains, NY: Longman.

Brown, J., Collins, A., & Duguid, P. (1989). Situated cognition and the culture of learning. *Educational Researcher, 18,* 32–42.

Bruner, J. (1996). *The culture of education.* Cambridge, MA: Harvard University Press.

Chi, M., Glaser, R., & Farr, M. (1988). *The nature of expertise.* Hillsdale, NJ: Erlbaum.

Clay, M. (1985). *The early detection of reading difficulties.* Portsmouth, NH: Heinemann.

Farr, B., & Trumbell, E. (1997). *Assessment alternatives for diverse classrooms.* Norwood, MA: Christopher-Gordon.

Gambrell, L., Palmer, B., Codling, R., & Mazzoni, S. (1995). *Assessing motivation to read* (Instructional Resource No. 14). Athens, GA: National Reading Research Center.

Goswami, U., & Bryant, P. (1990). *Phonological skills and learning to read.* Hove, United Kingdom: Erlbaum.

Graesser, A., & Bower, G. (1990). *Inferences and text comprehension.* San Diego, CA: Academic Press.

Greeno, J., Pearson, D., & Schoenfeld, A. (1996). *Implications for NAEP of research on learning and cognition. Report to National Academy of Education.* Washington, DC: National Academy of Education.

Guthrie, J., McGough, K., & Wigfield, A. (1994). *Measuring reading activity: An inventory* (Instructional Resource No. 4). Athens, GA: National Reading Research Center.

Guthrie, J., & Wigfield, A. (1997). *Reading engagement: Motivating readers through integrated instruction.* Newark, DE: International Reading Association.

Harris, T., & Hodges, R. (Eds.). (1995). *The literacy dictionary: The vocabulary of reading and writing.* Newark, DE: International Reading Association.

Heath, S. (1983). *Ways with words: Language, life, and work in communities and classrooms.* Cambridge, MA: Harvard University Press.

Hoffman, J., Worthy, J., Roser, N., McKool, S., Rutherford, W., & Strecker, S. (1996). Performance assessment in first-grade classrooms: The PALM model. In D. Leu, C. Kinzer, & K. Hinchman (Eds.), *Literacies for the 21st century: Research and practice* (pp. 100–112). Chicago: National Reading Conference.

Hopfenberger, W., & Levin, H. (1993). *The accelerated middle schools resource guide.* San Francisco: Jossey-Bass.

Johnston, P. (1997). *Knowing literacy: Constructive literacy assessment.* York, ME: Stenhouse.

Johnston, P., Afflerbach, P., & Weiss, P. (1993). Teachers' evaluation of teaching and learning of literacy. *Educational Assessment, 1,* 91–117.

Langer, J. (1987). The construction of meaning and the assessment of comprehension: An analysis of reader performance on standardized test items. In R. Freedle & R. Duran (Eds.), *Cognitive and linguistic analyses of test performance* (pp. 103–124). Norwood, NJ: Ablex.

MacGinitie, W., & MacGinitie, R. (1989). *Gates-MacGinitie reading tests* (3rd ed.). Chicago: Riverside.

McKenna, M., Kear, D., & Ellsworth, R. (1995). Children's attitudes toward reading: A national survey. *Reading Research Quarterly, 30,* 934–956.

Messick, S. (1989). Validity. In R. Linn (Ed.), *Educational measurement* (3rd ed., pp. 13–103). New York: Macmillan.

Moll, L. (1992). Literacy research in community and classrooms: A sociocultural approach. In R. Beach, J. Green, & M. Kamil (Eds.), *Multidisciplinary perspectives on literacy research* (pp. 211–244). Urbana, IL: National Conference on Research in English.

Morrow, L. (1989). *Literacy development in the early years.* Englewood Cliffs, NJ: Prentice-Hall.

Moss, P. (1995). Themes and variations in validity theory. *Educational Measurement: Issues and Practice, 14,* 5–13.

Moss, P., Beck, J., Ebbs, C., Matson, B., Muchmore, J., Steele, D., Taylor, C., & Herter, R. (1992). Portfolios, accountability, and an interpretive approach to validity. *Educational Measurement: Issues and Practice, 11,* 12–21.

Neumann, S., & Roskos, K. (1993). *Language and literacy learning in the early years.* Fort Worth, TX: Harcourt Brace Jovanovich.

Ogle, D. (1986). K-W-L: A teaching model that develops active reading of expository text. *The Reading Teacher, 39,* 564–570.

Palincsar, A., & Brown, A. (1984). Reciprocal teaching of comprehension-fostering and monitoring activities. *Cognition and Instruction, 1,* 117–175.

Pressley, M., & Afflerbach, P. (1995). *Verbal protocols of reading: The nature of constructively responsive reading.* Hillsdale, NJ: Erlbaum.

Rosenblatt, L. (1978). *The reader, the text, the poem: The transactional theory of the literary work.* Carbondale: Southern Illinois Press.

Schafer, W., & Lissitz, R. (1987). Measurement training for school personnel: Recommendations and reality. *Journal of Teacher Education, 38,* 57–63.

Stanovich, K. (1991). Word recognition: Changing perspectives. In R. Barr, M. Kamil, P. Mosenthal, & P. Pearson (Eds.), *Handbook of reading research* (Vol. 2, pp. 418–452). New York: Longman.

Stephens, D., Pearson, P., Gilrane, C., Roe, M., Stallman, A., Shelton, J., Weinzierl, J., Rodriguez, A., & Commeyras, M. (1995). Assessment and decision-making in schools: A cross-site analysis. *Reading Research Quarterly, 30,* 478–499.

Stiggins, R., & Conklin, N. (1992). *In teachers' hands: Investigating the practices of classroom assessment.* Albany, NY: State University of New York Press.

Sulzby, E. (1985). Children's emergent reading of favorite storybooks: A developmental study. *Reading Research Quarterly, 20,* 458–481.

Swearingen, R., & Allen, D. (1997). *Classroom reading assessment of reading processes.* Boston: Houghton Mifflin.

Tittle, C. (1989). Validity: Whose construction is it in the teaching and learning context? *Educational Measurement: Issues and Practice, 8,* 5–13.

Valencia, F., Hiebert, E., & Afflerbach, P. (1994). *Authentic assessment: Practices and possibilities.* Newark, DE: International Reading Association.

Valencia, F., & Place, N. (1994). Literacy portfolios for teaching, learning, and accountability: The Bellevue literacy assessment project. In F. Valencia, E. Hiebert, & P. Afflerbach (Eds.), *Authentic assessment: Practices and possibilities* (pp. 134–156). Newark, DE: International Reading Association.

Verhoeven, L. (1994). *Functional literacy: Theoretical issues and educational implications*. Amsterdam: Benjamins.

Vygotsky, L. (1978). *Mind in society: The development of higher psychological processes*. Cambridge, MA: Harvard University Press.

Williams, P., Reese, C., Campbell, J., Mazzeo, J., & Phillips, G. (1994). *1994 NAEP: A first look*. Washington, DC: National Center for Educational Statistics.

Winfield, L. (1995). Change in urban schools with high concentrations of low-income children: Chapter 1 schoolwide projects. In R. Allington & S. Walmsley (Eds.), *No quick fix: Rethinking literacy programs in America's elementary schools* (pp. 214–235). New York: Teachers College Press.

CHAPTER TWELVE

Standards and Assessments: Tools for Crafting Effective Instruction?

P. DAVID PEARSON
Michigan State University

My thesis in this chapter is that reading researchers and practitioners need to pay more attention to the related questions of what should be taught (the standards) and what should count as evidence of growth and accomplishment in the early stages of reading (the assessment tools). To support this thesis, I examine the current state of knowledge about the role and efficacy of standards and assessments in the teaching and learning of reading, especially early reading. This examination includes three parts:

1. An overview of the policy terrain to determine how reading standards and assessments are regarded in the larger reform efforts sweeping the country and how they are used, intentionally or unintentionally, to influence the teaching and learning of reading.
2. A deliberate analysis of the conceptual and technical issues surrounding assessment, with special emphasis on two aspects of assessment—the new performance assessments that have arisen in the last decade and the assessment of early reading development in kindergarten through grade 2.
3. A set of suggestions for a program of research studies that might improve the capacity to assess growth and accomplishment of reading and writing from kindergarten through grade 3.

STANDARDS AND ASSESSMENTS AS POLICY TOOLS

National Standards

The professional and public rhetoric about standards and assessment reveals contradictions, paradoxes, and dilemmas. Policymakers, public figures, parents, and others outside the educational community call for higher standards to help guide the way to better schools and more challenging curricula. They also call for more rigorous assessment to hold schools, teachers, and students accountable to those standards. Standards and assessments are viewed, by some at least, as an important part of the "solution," as key components of any attempt to reform public education (see O'Day & Smith, 1993; Simmons & Resnick, 1993; Smith & O'Day, 1991).

Standards have not been universally admired and accepted. To the contrary, they have gathered a small but vocal army of critics (see Ravitch, 1995). With the possible exception of the standards for teaching history, no set of curriculum standards has been as roundly criticized as the standards for English language arts developed by the International Reading Association and the National Council of Teachers of English (IRA/NCTE, 1996). Those who think that specificity is required to achieve reform attack the English standards for being so vague as to be unmeasurable (Diegmueller, 1996; Riechmann, 1996; Shanker, 1996). Many political conservatives attack them for what they view as an underlying epistemological commitment to constructivism (each individual has to construct knowledge out of experience), which these groups view as a thinly veiled conspiracy to support moral relativism (Jacobs, 1996; *Wisconsin State Journal*, 1996). Educational liberals and radicals view all standards as organized attempts to centralize curriculum and assessment, and, in the process, to marginalize the role that teachers and, most of all, students can play in determining curriculum at the school and classroom level (Grassroots, 1995; Shannon, 1996). In my view (see Pearson, 1996; Pearson, in press), the Standards for English Language Arts (IRA/NCTE, 1996) are, more or less, what national standards ought to be—very general (and therefore vague) guidelines that leave lots of room for others (states, districts, schools, teachers, and communities) to interpret them in more specific ways and, hence, to attach greater consequences to their implementation.

Although vagueness and values have attracted the greatest public and professional attention, I am more concerned about the issues and questions that the standards do not include—namely questions of early literacy, particularly reading instruction. The reluctance of the national standards, as well as the standards developed in most states (e.g., Michigan State Board of Education, 1995), to address the difficult and controversial issues of early reading means that we, as a profession, have failed to provide guidance to those who need it most: teachers, especially novice teachers, of young children. As a result, novice teachers are vulnerable to the vagaries of both the ideological and commercial marketplaces.

Assessment

Like standards, assessments have received mixed reviews. In many circles, they are touted as a linchpin of reform (Resnick & Resnick, 1992). For example, the New Standards Project (Simmons & Resnick, 1993), the National Board for Professional Teaching Standards (1989), the Coalition of Essential Schools (Sizer, 1992), several states in the United States (Valencia, Hiebert, & Afflerbach, 1994; Valencia, Pearson, Peters, & Wixson, 1989), and several countries throughout the world have all created new and different assessments as a leading component in their reform initiatives. In the first term of the Clinton presidency, the United States federal government entered the scene; Goals 2000 and the reauthorization of the Elementary and Secondary Education Act, the major U.S. program for compensatory education, explicitly privileged content and performance standards and accompanying assessments by requiring that states develop and hold themselves accountable to both in return for the receipt of federal dollars (Smith, Cianci, & Levine, 1996). In his second term, even as this chapter is being written, President Clinton is pressing vigorously for a national, voluntary test to ensure that every child in America is reading "on grade level" by the end of third grade (Clinton Administration, 1997).

Yet assessments of all stripes—from the most conventional multiple-choice variety (see García & Pearson, 1994; Shepard, 1989; Valencia & Pearson, 1987) to newer alternative assessments (Mehrens, 1992; Pearson, DeStefano, & García, in press)—have attracted both champions and critics. Conventional (standardized, multiple-choice) assessments attract two sorts of criticisms. First, opponents accuse them of failing to measure what really counts, especially in an era in which critical thinking, problem solving, and collaboration are regarded as such important attributes in society, the workplace, and the schools (Wiggins, 1993). Second, in situations in which there are consequences, for individuals (e.g., the SAT or the ACT), for teachers, or for schools (e.g., comparative state assessment results), standardized tests are criticized for exerting an undesirable, almost insidious, influence on curriculum and teaching (Haladyna, Nolan, & Haas, 1991; Smith & Shepard, 1988). Because teachers feel compelled to have their students perform well on these tests, they engage in preparation behaviors that, in the long run, are counterproductive. This compulsive preparation behavior results in a phenomenon labeled *test-score pollution*—an increase in a test score that is not accompanied by a parallel increase in the underlying cognitive phenomenon being measured (Haladyna et al., 1991).

Alternative assessments have been criticized for their failure to meet conventional standards for testing, such as reliability and concurrent validity (see Linn, 1993; Linn, DeStefano, Burton, & Hanson, 1995;

Pearson et al., in press). These concerns notwithstanding, even as critics decry the narrowing effects of conventional tests and the denial of services that result when they are used to determine program entry or exit, our society and our educational system continue to devote substantial time, energy, and money to assessments of all sorts. As a society, we seem to be able to live neither with nor without them.

EXAMINING THE TECHNICAL
BASES OF ASSESSMENTS
Standardized Assessments

The deleterious effects of formal, standardized assessments on teaching and learning are well documented (García & Pearson, 1994; Shepard, 1989; Smith, 1991), especially when they assume such high stakes that they become implicit blueprints for curriculum development. Because they are built on principles of decomposition (breaking down a complex task such as reading into its subcomponents) and decontextualization (removing reading from the demands of natural situations so that judges can draw more definitive conclusions about how students are performing), they encourage comparable decomposition and decontextualization strategies during instruction (see Pearson & Stallman, 1990). Although this is not a new concern (see Pearson & Johnson, 1975) and although it is not unique to early literacy, more recent documentation of the extraordinary influence of standardized tests on the curriculum and on the instruction provided to students in compensatory programs (Dorre-Bremme & Herman, 1983; Herman & Golan, 1991) suggests that little has changed in 30 years.

The persistence and ubiquity of conventional standardized assessments, especially in the face of such criticism, often are attributed to their utility. Proponents of standardized tests claim these instruments provide teachers, parents, administrators, and the public with useful information. But this claim of utility is open to question. First, it is difficult to determine who finds tests useful, at least within school communities (Valencia, 1990): administrators say that teachers like the data; teachers say that the administrators need them. The work that my colleagues and I have completed (Brenner, Pearson, Boyd, & Prico, 1996; Pearson, Brenner, & Packard, in press), as well as the work of Hoffman and his colleagues (Hoffman et al., 1996) reveal virtually no support among teachers for the use of standardized tests. Parents, however, do support their use, claiming that standardized tests serve as valuable external "checks" on the accuracy of the evaluations of their children provided by report cards, portfolios, and other school-based assessments (Bisesi, 1997; Pearson et al., in press). Policymakers (Pearson et al., in press) regard standardized tests as useful for program evaluation-accountability purposes; however, they see little or no use for them in tracking the progress of individual students. Even when parents or policy makers cite the specific, limited utility of standardized tests, they rarely (in our own work, never; Pearson et al., in press) cite any positive impact of the tests on curriculum, instructional practices, or learning plans for individual students.

The criticisms of decontextualization, decomposition, and lack of utility, although applicable at all levels, are especially salient in the primary grades where our formal assessments are particularly influential and pernicious. Compared to assessments for older students, formal (standardized, multiple-choice) assessments of early-literacy have attracted even more pointed criticism for their potential to corrupt early literacy curricula and teachers' instructional practices (Smith & Shepard, 1988; Stallman & Pearson, 1990). Stallman and I (1990) reviewed virtually all of the assessments available for kindergarten and grade 1, either as free-standing commercial products or as parts of commercial basal-reading programs. We found consistent disregard of the idea that skills, strategies, and knowledge are best evaluated in contexts in which they are used. It is small wonder that primary-grade teachers are seldom surprised when critics of conventional assessments point out the obvious—that these tests can tell teachers very little about the real literacy of young readers and writers and that at best they reveal whether students have learned the skills within instructional programs geared to the tests that accompany them.

Performance Assessment in Reading

The essence of performance assessment, and the central feature that most clearly distinguishes it from conventional assessment, is its emphasis on engaging students in the cognitive process about which the examiner wishes to draw inferences. A rough synonym might be "direct assessment," or, as it is more commonly expressed, "authentic assessment." As their use has expanded, performance assessments have acquired a number of synonyms—portfolio assessment, authentic assessment, on-demand performance tasks, assessment by exhibition, curriculum-embedded assessment, or situated assessment—all of which capture some aspect of this central feature.

After a 5- or 6-year honeymoon during which all but the most ardent supporters of conventional assessments gave the alternative assessment movement time to work out its problems, many observers, even those who would like these alternatives to succeed, are beginning to doubt their benefit (e.g., Mehrens, 1992; Pearson et al., in press). Observers are requesting evidence that alternative assessments are valid, reliable, useful, feasible, and maybe even empowering to teachers and students. Some psychometricians have even developed standards by which these new assessments ought to be evaluated (Linn, Baker, & Dunbar, 1991).

With few exceptions, the data on performance assessments are not encouraging, at least when they are used for high-stakes judgments about groups (accountability reporting) or gatekeeping decisions for individuals (entry into or exit from special programs).

Reliability Issues

Performance assessments have been plagued by concerns about the unreliability of judgments made by those who evaluate student work. For example, in Vermont, which is now in the fifth year of using performance assessments, it has proven difficult to obtain interjudge consistency on the scores given to student writing portfolios with the rubrics being used (Koretz, Klein, McCaffrey, & Stecher, 1994; Koretz, Stecher, & Diebert, 1993). On the other hand, those who have used on-demand writing assessments for many years (for a review and analysis, see Dunbar, Koretz, & Hoover, 1991) have been able, given rigorous standards for training judges, to establish interjudge reliability coefficients as high as .80, (but with an overall range between .30 and .85).

Generalizability

A far more daunting hurdle for performance assessments is that it has proven difficult to demonstrate stability from one performance task to the next (Shavelson, Baxter, & Pine, 1992). This lack of generalizability between tasks seems to extend across a number of domains—writing, reading, math, and science. When educators began using alternative assessment, some argued that assessments should be crafted in a way that makes them optimally suited to the situations in which they were given. The generalizability data certainly document the situated character of these assessments! The question now is: What sorts of decisions can be made about individuals, classes, or schools, with such task-specific information? It is very hard to make general statements about a student's reading ability or achievement or about a school's performance when the validity of the conclusions that can be drawn depends upon the material read, the manner of assessment, the amount of teacher or peer scaffolding provided, and the format of the assessment.

As a point of contrast, conventional multiple-choice assessments demonstrate high levels of interitem generalizability; reliability coefficients in the range of .85 to .95 are not uncommon on standardized tests. Having documented this serious generalizability problem for performance assessments, I must acknowledge that the remarkable reliability and generalizability of conventional assessments are achieved at great cost to their validity and utility. The outward illusion of trustworthiness conveyed by reliability coefficients that approach unity is not very satisfying when these tests fail even the most superficial of validity criteria—"Does this activity look like what we mean by reading and writing?" Their overall value is eroded even more when more sophisticated validity questions are asked, such as those dealing with construct validity (see Snow, 1993) or consequential validity (see Messick, 1989). Thus important questions about what the tests are about ("What do scores on standardized reading tests have to do with the underlying psychological construct of reading?") and how the tests impact upon the lives of individuals and groups ("What are the instructional consequences of their use to individual children?") are not asked. Instead, test developers are content to demonstrate content validity (showing that the objectives measured by the items map onto one or more curricular frameworks) or concurrent validity (showing high correlations with other, usually well-established, reading assessments).

Interpretive Dilemmas

One of the unique characteristics of performance assessments, indeed one of the characteristics that earns them the authenticity label, is their provision for student collaboration during the assessment process. Students are often encouraged to work together to produce a final product, or at least to assist (in activities such as brainstorming) and to critique, through peer review of draft documents, one another along the way to independently developed final products. The social character of these assessments raises a problem in test interpretation, aptly captured in the title of a paper by Meryl Gearhart and her colleagues: *Whose Work Is It?* (Gearhart, Herman, Baker, & Wittaker, 1993). The professional quest for authenticity, which would encourage social interactions, runs headlong against the societal need to make important gatekeeping decisions, which are almost always about individual students. Although there is no ultimate resolution to this dilemma, some suggestions have been made (Pearson et al., in press) for coping with the dilemma by making sure that the contextual conditions of performance (e.g., what sort of help did the students receive? by whom?) are well-documented.

The Elusive Nature of Reading Assessment

The most vexing goal of reading assessment is finding a way to assess reading directly. The elusive character of this goal is by no means a new discovery; it has puzzled reading researchers for the better part of this century (see Harrison, Bailey, & Dewar, in press). Years ago (e.g., Thorndike, 1917), when educators first realized that understanding what is read was a legitimate index of reading accomplishment, they found that they had to resort to indirect indices, such as open-ended and multiple-choice questions. Frustrated that they could not observe comprehension directly as it was taking place (*on-line*, so to speak) during the process of reading, they began a search that has occupied successive generations of researchers for almost a century. That search has been an attempt to answer the question: What are the best possible artifacts or products from which we can draw inferences about what is (or must have been) going on during the act of comprehension? We never see either the clicks or the clunks of comprehension directly; we only infer them from distant indices. This elusiveness is not limited to any particular format of reading assessment. It applies equally to conventional and performance assessments.

Ironically, by moving to performance assessments, we may, in fact, be moving even further away from the process of comprehension itself. Clearly performance assessments employ formats that involve other cognitive and linguistic skills and competencies, such as writing. And the question is whether the engagement of other skills, and in some cases, media other than print, complicates and compromises the capacity of an assessment to provide information about reading, particularly reading comprehension. When a performance assessment is employed—with multiple opportunities for discussions, the inclusion of multiple texts (even video/audio texts), and a heavy burden on writing—it is hard to argue that we are very close to observing and documenting the process of comprehension itself.

A sample taken from work with New Standards (1993) illustrates this dilemma quite forcefully. In a grade-8 pilot task (which is no longer a part of the New Standards repertoire) entitled *The Man and His Message,* students read, view, listen to, and write a wide range of texts related to the theme of response to social injustice. The texts and tasks require students to wrestle with the tension between Dr. Martin Luther King, Jr.'s, message of nonviolent protest as a means of social change and the response of violence that was prevalent in Los Angeles during the riots that followed the verdict in the Rodney King case. The culminating task requires students to write a letter to another teenager in which they present their views on the tension between violent and nonviolent reactions to social injustice. Over the course of five to eight class periods, the students encounter the "texts" in Figure 12.1 and the tasks in Figure 12.2.

Data from all of the activities (except the peer response) were examined by raters to create a holistic reading score. The dilemma is evident: On one hand, the tasks reflect authentic literacy activities and goals—the kind of integrated, challenging activities students ought to be engaged in if they are to demonstrate their ability to apply reading and writing to everyday

- A video about the Civil Rights Movement entitled *A Time for Justice*
- An article about the Civil Rights Movement entitled "Confrontations"
- An article about Ghandi from Scholastic's SEARCH magazine
- An oral rendition of King's "Letter from a Birmingham Jail"
- Printed versions of other King speeches
- An excerpt from a *Time* magazine account of the Rodney King riots in Los Angeles
- Two CNN video accounts of the riots: *Rage of Despair* and *Roots of the Problem*

FIGURE 12.1. The Man and His Message "texts."

- Collaboratively complete separate cognitive webs on key concepts from the reading (Dr. Martin Luther King, Jr., Civil Rights Movement, Nonviolent Resistance)
- Keep an ongoing log/chart of emerging learnings from all the different texts
- Answer straightforward "assignment-like" questions
- Display the similarities and differences of King and Ghandi in a modified Venn diagram
- Write a letter to a fellow teenager expressing your views on the ethical and political consequences of violent versus nonviolent responses to social injustice

FIGURE 12.2. The Man and His Message tasks.

problems. On the other hand, do these tasks really constitute a measure of reading? Or are they simply an index of the uses to which reading (or perhaps more accurately, the residue or outcomes of reading) can be put when it is complemented by a host of other media and activities? For purposes of planning instruction, does it matter? How close do we need to be to the phenomenological act of comprehension to decide what a student needs to do next? Perhaps assessing the cognitive and performance consequences of comprehension (what you can do with ideas once you have understood them) is all teachers need to do for classroom assessment purposes. Perhaps only theorists and psychologists need to distinguish between the bits that came from the reading and those that came from other informational sources.

Tasks such as these, which are exactly the sort of tasks that are championed in the name of challenging assessments and integrated curricula, create a paradox for those concerned with reading assessment. Because we cannot get inside the head to see comprehension as it occurs, we must always rely on indirect evidence of its nature and quality. In the quest to create assessment tasks that support integrated curriculum and challenging assessment, however, we may be moving even further away from the phenomenological act of reading. The choice that must be made is not appealing. It appears to pit psychometrically elegant assessments that tell us nothing about real reading and writing against psychometrically suspect assessments that "feel right." Even though I am doubtful that we will ever resolve this paradox, I believe that we can present our data more honestly by providing careful descriptions of our tasks, our scoring procedures, and the contexts in which they are completed. We can, for example, document the evidence we are actually using to draw inferences about student achievement. We can scale response to reading tasks along a dimension that we might label "distance from reading as a phenomenological act." We can examine the relationships among scores obtained in response to different combinations of media (print, audio, and video) and in different response formats.

Such an approach is consistent with Lipson and Wixson's (1986) admonition to regard assessment as an interactive phenomenon, one in which the assessment of a student's competence is couched in terms of the types of texts, tasks, and conditions at work when the assessment was completed. Frankly, we know much too little about the impact of media and response format on the quality and validity of judgments we make about individual students. Intuition suggests that the requirement of writing responses creates a stumbling block that yields a gross underestimate of reading comprehension for many students. Even when task writers try to escape the boundaries of conventional writing by encouraging students to use semantic webs or visual displays, they do not fully achieve their goals. These formats place great emphasis on written expression, albeit of a different sort.

Some have advocated resorting to oral-response formats precisely to avoid the contaminating (and typically limiting) influence of writing on the assessment of comprehension. The major problem introduced by oral-response formats is, of course, feasibility—how can teachers find time to "interview" individual students about their responses to text? A second concern about oral-response formats, at least for students who write well, is that because they are more spontaneous, oral responses may not provide students with the opportunity to demonstrate deliberation and thoughtfulness. The matter of response format is all the more problematic in the case of second-language learners, for whom not only writing but also language dominance comes into play (García & Pearson, 1994). For example, when Spanish bilingual students respond to English texts in Spanish rather than in English, they receive higher scores on a range of tests.

These difficulties notwithstanding, a substantial commitment of effort and energy to this agenda, which involves the feasibility of assessing the impact of variety in text and response formats, is likely to yield substantial dividends for understanding how best to cope with the frustration at not being able to "get at" reading directly when we try to assess it.

PROGRESS ON EARLY LITERACY ASSESSMENT

Earlier I asserted that the development of standards and assessments for early reading and writing has been slighted. The vast majority of state assessment systems begin at grade 4, as does our one nationally sponsored assessment, the National Assessment of Educational Progress. Although the publishers of standardized tests make achievement tests available for use as early as grade 1, many districts follow the logic of state assessments and delay their use until grades 3 or 4. Even the recent flurry of work on performance assessments (e.g., California Learning Assessment System, 1994; New Standards, 1997) and portfolio assessment (e.g., Murphy & Smith, 1991; Tierney, Carter, & Desai, 1991) has been focused on developing these tools for older students.

The question is: Why has so much effort been directed toward the assessment of older students? The benevolent answer is that as a profession and as a society, we have made an implicit decision to offer teachers of early literacy as much latitude as possible in meeting the instructional and assessment needs of their students. The logic is something like this: If assessment for accountability begins at the point at which we are more concerned about outcomes, such as reading comprehension scores, than about the processes that led to those outcomes, primary teachers will have considerable instructional latitude in assisting young readers, some of whom may be experiencing developmental lags in their progress toward comprehension. Primary teachers indicate that they are grateful for this hands-off attitude, with their gratitude often expressed as allusions to the plight of teachers in grades 4 and above who have to spend so much time getting students ready for district and state exams (see Pearson, Brenner, et al., in press). The cynical answer is that we avoid assessment issues to avoid the most controversial issues in teaching reading: The phonics–whole language or skills–whole language debate, for example, is sharper and meaner in the primary than in the intermediate grades.

Whatever the motivations, with a few notable exceptions (Barrs, Ellis, Tester, & Thomas, 1988; Chittenden & Spicer 1993; Clay, 1985), we have largely avoided the question of establishing benchmarks that might mark progress along the way from grade 1 to grade 4. Perhaps if the politics of early literacy had not changed so dramatically in the last few years, the need for more elaborate and more fully validated assessments of early progress might not seem so acute. But the politics have changed, and more and more attention is now focused on early literacy. In several states (e.g., California Reading Program Advisory, 1996; California Reading Task Force, 1995; Colorado Legislature, 1996), legislators have called for earlier indicators of student accomplishment, usually clothed in the rhetoric of helpfulness (i.e., we need to learn whether early intervention is needed). Personally, I wish that this press for increased accountability were not responsible for focusing attention on early literacy. I would rather that we had undertaken the task because we realized that monitoring the progress of early literacy is an important professional responsibility in its own right, one that needs no external prodding. Nonetheless, it is important that we undertake research studies that will provide us high-quality information about the efficacy, validity, and utility of assessment programs for early literacy.

SOME EXEMPLARY STUDIES

To say that there is little information about the efficacy and validity of early-reading assessments is not to say that there is no information. Some scholars have completed exemplary validation studies of assessment tools and systems for young readers and writers. Because they have overcome the difficulties and dilemmas outlined in my earlier remarks, these successful efforts should give hope that an all-out effort in early literacy assessment will provide the profession with the intellectual energy and assessment tools needed to make sense out of our debates and conflicts.

South Brunswick

Several teachers and administrators in South Brunswick, New Jersey, have collaborated to build a districtwide, primary-grade developmental portfolio to replace standardized tests in grades K–2. The portfolio is used as the primary vehicle for reporting to key constituencies (Chittenden & Spicer, 1993; Salinger & Chittenden, 1994). First, it is used by teachers and students to make day-to-day instructional decisions about the work to be completed by individuals and groups. Second, it is the main tool for parent communication. Toward the end of each reporting period, teachers examine the work in student portfolios and use a developmental rubric to place each student somewhere along a continuum that moves through a successive set of levels, ranging from emergent through beginning to independent reader. Within each level, there is an early and an advanced phase. These teacher judgments, along with the student work and rubric undergirding it, are shared with parents in conferences. Third, the developmental portfolio is the basis of program-accountability reporting to administrators and the community. Annually, the frequency of students falling in each level of the continuum are aggregated by classroom and school and, eventually, for the district, to create trendline reports that can be used by administrators and policymakers to monitor program effectiveness.

Teachers collect a variety of artifacts, including writing samples, running records, sight-word reading lists, spelling inventories, responses to literature, retellings, and notes on interviews with students. The efficacy, validity, and utility of the system has been evaluated in a series of studies by Chittenden and his colleagues at the Educational Testing Service (ETS) (Bridgeman, Chittenden, & Cline, 1995; Jones & Chittenden, 1995; Salinger & Chittenden, 1994). Essentially, these researchers found that they can achieve high (.85–.90) levels of interrater reliability, reasonable correlations with other indices of literacy achievement, and very high levels of user satisfaction among the "clients" of the system almost a decade after its initial introduction into the district. Although the portfolio system has become the main tool for measuring and reporting progress in the primary grades, I must acknowledge that both state tests and standardized tests are used in the higher grades in the schools in South Brunswick.

Primary Language Record

At P.S. 261 in New York City (Farr & Darling-Hammond, 1993), teachers have started to use the Primary Language Record (PLR) (Barrs et al., 1988) to improve the quality of information available to themselves and to students, parents, and administrators for making decisions about individual student progress and instructional needs as well as teaching emphases. Over several years, many teachers at P.S. 261 have participated in increasingly widespread staff development efforts to increase the use and impact of the PLR within the school community.

PLR includes some very familiar informal diagnostic tools: running records, writing samples, systematic observations, and interviews with students and parents. Like the South Brunswick rubric, PLR places students on descriptive continua with underlying dimensions such as fluency and experience. (This similarity should not be surprising in light of the fact that the South Brunswick group acknowledges the use of PLR scales in creating their own; Jones & Chittenden, 1995.)

The teachers and principals at P.S. 261 report high degrees of satisfaction with PLR. Specifically they note the impact of PLR on teacher knowledge of individual students, the quality of everyday curricular decisions, and communication with parents about student progress. As with the South Brunswick teachers, the teachers at P.S. 261 obtain what they regard as very useful specific information to share with parents, and they are able to place each student on one or more continua of growth toward a standard of expertise. Unlike the South Brunswick experience, however, at P.S. 261, PLR has not displaced standardized tests in the primary grades, which continue to be given, according to the teachers at the school, at an ever-alarming rate.

PLR has been used widely in London, England, where it was initially developed, with reports of considerable success (Barrs et al., 1988; Feeney & Hahn, 1991; O'Sullivan, 1995). But perhaps the most ambitious experiment is taking place in California, where a group of teachers (Barr, 1995) have adapted it considerably to their own needs and uses, even changing the title to the California Learning Record (CLR). For the California adaptation (Barr, 1995), Barr and her colleagues have studied both the reliability of the scoring procedures and its perceived usefulness and impact on teaching (Barr & Hallam, 1995, 1996). Five levels of achievement were established; the scale ranges from literal reader at the bottom through four successive levels of accomplishment (less accomplished, moderately accomplished, accomplished, and exceptionally accomplished). In both 1995 and 1996 moderation processes, scorers agreed with one another on student placement into one of the levels up to 85% of the time at school sites and 70–80% of the time across sites within a region. To date, only anecdotal evidence regarding the utility and impact of CLR on instruction has been analyzed; those data indicate that the battery is useful in designing appropriate instruction for students across a wide range of achievement levels.

Diagnostic Survey

No account of early literacy assessment should omit the battery of tests developed by Clay and her colleagues in New Zealand (Clay, 1985). The

Diagnostic Survey battery includes concepts about print, running records, and other reading and writing tests. As a whole, the battery provides information about

1. The level of difficulty of material at which students can read successfully;
2. The strategies, both positive and negative, that students have developed to cope with text reading;
3. Their emerging control over key concepts about print (how text works, directionality, position, etc.);
4. Control over basic reading and writing vocabulary; and
5. Spelling development.

Although I was unable to locate any direct evaluations of the validity, reliability, or utility of the Diagnostic Survey, its central role as a system for monitoring the development of students enrolled in Reading Recovery programs provides a great deal of indirect evidence about its characteristics. To observe Reading Recovery teachers for a week or two is to discover that they use these tools religiously for monitoring both daily and long-term progress. They know not only the letter–sound correspondences and conventions that students control in reading and writing but also the level of text challenge that students can handle, the words they can read and write as sight words, and the stage of spelling conventionality that they are working toward. Perhaps the best evidence for the construct validity of the tests in the battery is that students who do well on them experience much higher success in transferring their skills to classroom reading curricula than do students who perform poorly on them during their Reading Recovery training.

Although to my knowledge no one has conducted either complex path analysis or factor analysis, or even simpler correlational analyses of these relationships, these correlations are implicit in the evaluations of the efficacy of Reading Recovery as an intervention program (for several early studies of Reading Recovery's effectiveness, see Clay, 1985; for more recent work, see Pinnell, Lyons, Deford, Bryk, & Seltzer, 1994): Success in Reading Recovery (which is indexed by these measures) translates into success in school (which is usually indexed by a variety of converging measures, including standardized test scores, the difficulty of materials that children handle in classroom learning situations, and teacher judgments of success). Its convergence on multiple indices of school reading success is powerful evidence of its construct validity. I was unable to locate any studies in which the reliability of judgments made by teachers employing the Diagnostic Survey had been examined. Nor was I able to locate any studies evaluating its utility in settings other than one-on-one tutoring. This instrument is a perfect example of the sort of assessment tool that cries out for more careful study and evaluation. It could prove to be a highly reliable and useful classroom assessment tool, but there is no evidence to determine whether it is.

Primary Assessment of Language Arts and Mathematics

In Austin, Texas, teachers from the Austin schools and researchers from the University of Texas at Austin have collaborated to create a primary-grade assessment system designed to provide constituents with high-quality, high-integrity information about progress in early literacy and math (Hoffman, Worthy, Roser, & Rutherford, Chapter 13, this volume; Hoffman et al., 1996). Teachers initiated the system because they were tired of being held accountable to standardized tests that they knew did not measure what they were teaching or what students needed to learn. Instead they wanted to be held accountable to a set of indices that better represented their instructional goals and students' learning needs.

Dubbed PALM, for Primary Assessment of Language Arts and Mathematics, the system has three complementary components: (1) curriculum-embedded assessments, (2) taking-a-closer-look assessments, and (3) on-demand assessments. The curriculum-embedded assessments consist, as they do in many classrooms, of collections of ordinary work samples, observational notes, and anecdotal records. This is the stuff of everyday, ongoing assessment that leads to impressions and judgments of student progress within the classroom curriculum. The taking-a-closer-look assessments are designed to be used selectively by teachers when they are puzzled or unsure about the progress of individual students. Again, they rely on tools that are familiar to skilled practitioners: informal reading inventories, running records of oral reading fluency and accuracy, miscue analyses, think-alouds, and problem-solving scenarios. The on-demand assessments move more in the direction of performance tasks of the sort that have been used in districtwide and even statewide efforts to implement alternative assessments (see Valencia et al., 1994). The PALM team has developed and evaluated several on-demand tasks in what is best described as a sweeps week. For a given week, several artifacts are systematically collected and scored. The artifacts include:

- A personal journal in which students write whatever they wish.
- A response journal for a book read aloud by the teacher.
- A response journal for a free-choice book read independently by the student.
- An adaptation of the K–W–L (Ogle, 1986) for expository texts.
- An oral reading task (two passages, one familiar and one unfamiliar) scored for accuracy, rate, and self-correction.
- An inventory of reading habits, attitudes, and self-concept.

In their validation work, Hoffman and his colleagues (Hoffman et al., 1996) collected data for all of these indices and used them to place each student on a developmental profile (a scale remarkably similar to those used by South Brunswick and PLR); information about overall performance as well as performance on specific artifacts was used for reporting student progress to parents.

In studying the efficacy and validity of PALM, Hoffman and his colleagues (Hoffman et al., 1996) have tried to answer three questions: (1) Can it be successfully implemented? (2) Does it contribute to more informed teaching and testing? (3) Does it provide data that are comparable to or better than that provided by the district-administered standardized test? They were able to answer all three questions to some degree. First, PALM can be implemented. Teachers can find the time to collect the data and to score them with reasonable levels of interjudge reliability. Second, from interviews with teachers on its use, it is possible to conclude that PALM does lead to more informed decision making. In contrast to reports that they found no instructional utility for standardized measures, teachers reported that they actually used the data to make instructional decisions for individuals and groups. Third, PALM does provide data that are statistically comparable to and, by the standards of the participating teachers, qualitatively superior to those provided by the Iowa Tests of Basic Skills (ITBS), the district-administered standardized test. Through a combination of measures from all three components of PALM (curriculum-embedded, taking-a-closer-look, and on-demand) Hoffman and his colleagues were able to explain 73% of the variance on the ITBS.

Whether high levels of variance in common with standardized measures are good or bad depends on one's perspective. Because students are ranked in substantially the same order by either the ITBS or the PALM battery, one could argue, in the name of efficiency and cost, for ITBS. On the other hand, because teachers hold PALM data in much higher esteem and use it more extensively, it can be argued that PALM is more cost-effective than ITBS because it provides the same ranking information as does the standardized test (assuming that someone actually wants or needs that information) and, without additional cost, a great deal of pedagogically useful information.

The evidence for the qualitative superiority of PALM assessments comes from interviews with teachers and students: As one student put it, "on the ITBS they only know if you got the right answer, but on the journal, they knew what you were thinking."

The Work Sampling System

Meisels and his colleagues have spent several years developing and documenting the efficacy of an individually oriented performance assessment system for children, K–5 (Meisels, 1996; Meisels, Jablong, Marsden, Dichtelmiller, & Dorfman, 1994; Meisels, Liaw, Dorfman, & Fails-Nelson, 1995). The Work Sampling System (WSS) consists of three components: (1) developmental guidelines and checklists covering eight early-childhood curricular areas, one of which is language and literacy; (2) portfolio–

systematic collections of student work that "illustrate their efforts, progress, and achievements" (Meisels et al., 1995, p. 280); and (3) summary reports, which are tied to the portfolios and the observations that undergird the checklists.

Most impressive in the development of WSS is the extensive evaluation of its psychometric characteristics. Meisels and his colleagues (Meisels et al., 1995) have evaluated the reliability and validity of the system and its components in an extensive tryout. As for reliability, they found that the internal consistency of the individual scales on the checklist (e.g., language and literacy, concept and number, or personal/social development) ranged from .87–.94, and the reliability between occasions (fall, winter, and spring) varied from .69–.89. For the summary report, which entailed use of the information in the portfolios, the interjudge reliability ranged from .68–.88. Validity (criterion validity) was evaluated by examining the correlations between components of the WSS and conventional indices of student progress, such as the Woodcock–Johnson Reading Test (Woodcock & Johnson, 1989) and McCarthy Scales of Children's Abilities (McCarthy, 1972). Correlations validated expected relationships: The language and literacy scale correlated to a high degree with the Woodcock–Johnson test but to a low degree with the McCarthy scales.

Projects such as PLR, the Diagnostic Survey, the South Brunswick Developmental Portfolio, PALM, and WSS provide hope that assessments that are at once useful and trustworthy for the primary grades are within our reach. But much work remains to be done. Compared to the incredible investment of resources for the assessment of more advanced readers, for both conventional and alternative forms of assessment, primary-level assessment has barely scratched the technical and conceptual surface. If one sums all the dollars spent by states and districts on alternative assessments at grade 4 and higher, then it is clear that primary-level assessment has a lot of catching up to do.

CONCLUSION

I conclude with three points, one about systems of assessment (to be contrasted with individual tests), a second about professional development, and a third about the importance of supporting an all-out effort to examine and improve early literacy assessment.

Assessment Systems

In introducing this idea, I extend a theme introduced by Afflerbach in Chapter 11. By an assessment system, I mean a deliberately organized set of assessment tools that provides all of the clients of the assessment system with the best information possible to make the sorts of judgments and decisions each client group needs to make.

Assessment systems will not work unless certain assumptions about their use are met. In my view, they will not work unless all concerned parties are willing to overcome their current paranoia about testing. Participants must be willing to think of external tests as broad-gauge, indirect indicators of school and program accomplishment rather than as blueprints for the curriculum. They must be willing to give tests, even high-stakes tests, that they do not explicitly prepare students to take. Unless participants are willing to forego such explicit preparation, tests will continue to have their pernicious, curriculum-narrowing effect.

Examined from the relationship of assessment to curriculum, another way of making the same point is the argument that it is as important for our system to have some *curriculum-free* assessments as it is to have *curriculum-embedded* assessments; that is, there must be some standards that are so fundamental to our construct of literacy that they are an important and legitimate outcome of any literacy curriculum. Perhaps the term curriculum-free is less appropriate than another, such as "common-core." The point is that we need consensus on such measures, and we have to agree that we do not need to do anything special to prepare our students to respond to them. I wish I were more optimistic about our capacity to overcome the impulse to "teach to each and every test" and to find the ground that is common to all literacy curricula.

The essence of an assessment system is matching tools to audience and purpose. In the following table, I lay out my reading of the information needs (expressed as decisions to be made and/or questions to be answered) of the various clients of the assessment system. For each type of decision, I suggest the types of assessment data that would be most appropriate. I believe that we should quit speculating about which approach is *the* definitive or most valid approach and remember to add the qualifiers, "for whom" and "for what purposes," when evaluating the efficacy of any approach to assessment.

If validity is the ultimate criterion for judging the worth of a test, it must also be the ultimate criterion for judging the worth of a system of assessments. If so, then we must ask the questions: How can we ever know whether an assessment system was actually working as it was intended? What counts as evidence of the validity of the system? How does it differ from the evidence we use to gauge the validity of a test?

When we judge the validity of a test, we try to answer several important questions:

1. Does it measure the intended trait? (construct validity)
2. Is it consistent with the curriculum? (content validity)
3. Does it behave like other measures of this domain? (concurrent validity)
4. Does it result in appropriate decisions for users? Do they get what they need? (consequential validity)
5. How much effort is required to obtain the information? (feasibility)

TABLE 12.1. The Assessment Needs of Different Clients of the Assessment System

Client	Decisions to be made; questions to be answered	Assessment tools
Students	How am I doing? What shall I do next?	Portfolio entries (self-evaluated) and/or feedback from benchmark tasks
Teachers	Have the kids met my learning goals? How did my teaching go? How can I help Amy? Should Amy enter X?	Portfolio entries and benchmark tasks • Curriculum-embedded tests • Informal diagnostic tools • An array of converging evidence
Parents	How is my child doing? Compared to the average student?	• Portfolios/work samples • Normed reference test of some sort
Administrators	How effective is our program? How are our teachers doing?	Aggregated data of some sort (portfolios, norm-referenced tests
Policymakers	How well are schools meeting public expectations?	Trends, over time, on some aggregated data • Norm-referenced test would do just fine
Taxpayers	How well is our money being spent?	Trends, over time, on some aggregated data • Norm-referenced test would do just fine

6. How do users judge the quality and appropriateness of the information they receive? (utility)

For *system* validity, we surely want all of the assessments in the system to meet these criteria, but we also want to evaluate the validity of the system as a whole. I am unaware of any endeavor in which a school or an institution or a state has undertaken the evaluation of a system. But as I think about how one might undertake such an evaluation, it occurs to me that above and beyond knowing the validity of the individual pieces, we will want answers to at least three other questions:

1. Are all of the important dimensions of the domain assessed? This question speaks to the issue of domain or content validity. Just because the items are from the appropriate domain is not enough to establish their system validity. For the system to be valid, the entire domain must be adequately represented.

2. Are the clients of the system getting the information they need to answer the questions they want answered? This question speaks to the criterion of utility, and emphasizes the "tailoring" of information to the audience who will use it.

3. Are clients making the right decisions? This question addresses issues of consequential validity. It must be answered by examining the impact of such assessments on the lives of individuals and groups who are affected by the results of the assessments. The ultimate test is whether appropriate placements and instructional decisions are made. Particularly important to examine are egregious misapplications of the system; other things being equal, we want assessments that do no harm.

Professional Development

The question of professional development is central to any attempt to reform or improve assessment practice. All assessments require underlying knowledge for effective use. But the knowledge requirements of portfolio and performance assessments are even greater than those of conventional assessment, and the knowledge requirements for situated assessments of early literacy may be greater still.

A cynical reading of the popularity of standardized testing is that these tests have been explicitly engineered to remove judgment from the hands of teachers. Because standardized tests automate judgments about student achievement and competence, little, if any professional knowledge is required of teachers to make "fair and accurate" decisions. By contrast, when teachers evaluate or describe carefully, performances and student work—just as when judges score performances in the artistic or athletic domains—they must embrace human judgment, with all its fallibility and attendant problems of bias and subjectivity. When scores are referenced to standards rather than norms, judgment becomes an inherent part of the assessment process.

Assessments that place a premium upon teacher judgment make sense only under the assumption that high levels of professional knowledge—about subject matter, language, culture, and assessment—are widely distributed in the profession. The implications for professional development are very serious: When the assumption of professional knowledge is suspect, substantial investments in staff development will be necessary. Our educational system (and the society that pays its bills) has to decide to whether to make this investment or to resort to tests that require little or no interpretation. If we make the latter decision, then we sentence our students to yet another era of learning for tests unworthy of emulation, and we place our teachers in a situation that calls into question their professionalism.

My own work with teachers trying to build new assessment schemes underscores the importance of teacher knowledge and the construct of a community of professional judgment (see Myers & Pearson, 1996). In the scoring of both complex performance tasks and portfolios, the key element in whatever success we experienced was bringing teachers together in remote conference settings to wrestle with, both collaboratively and dialectically, the question of what counts as evidence of quality in student work. This was obvious to the teachers in their evaluations of the conferences, and it was equally as apparent to those of us who organized the events. When asked why such experiences have proven valuable, language arts teachers told us that in the process of judging the quality of student work, they are forced to consider a range of important professional concerns and bodies of knowledge—the language arts curriculum (and the opportunities it provides or ignores), the language and cultural perspectives that students bring to their learning, and issues in assessment itself. Our experience is typical within the performance assessment movement. Others (e.g., Jones & Chittenden, 1995) have found similar unintentional results for scoring conferences.

Coping with the professional challenge is at once the simplest and most complex agenda—simple because the only real answer is a program of professional development that ensures the requisite knowledge base is put into place in the profession, and complex because the will of our society to make such a commitment to the professional development of teachers is questionable.

The Importance of This Effort

The time is right for an all-out effort to build better assessments for early literacy. To accomplish this goal, we must work on three fronts simultaneously: (1) we have to build better assessment tools; (2) we have to examine how sets of tools operate as systems, how they can be transformed into synergistic rather than competitive entities; and (3) we have to figure out how to ensure that our teachers gain the knowledge they need to guarantee that the information provided by such a system will be used for the benefit of all students. Having admitted my cynicism for society's commitment to teachers and students, let me close by suggesting that even this Sysiphean task should not discourage us from an all-out effort to build and validate a compelling array of tools for early literacy assessment. Few enterprises will have as much positive impact on the lives of children, parents, and teachers, not to mention the positive impact on the consciences of policy makers.

REFERENCES

Barr, M. A. (Ed.). (1995). *California Learning Record: Handbook for teachers*. San Diego: Center for Language in Learning.

Barr, M. A., & Hallam, P. J. (1995). *Findings from the 1995 California Learning Record regional moderations*. San Diego: Center for Language in Learning.

Barr, M. A., & Hallam, P. J. (1996). *California Learning Record, 1996 moderation report*. San Diego: Center for Language in Learning.

Barrs, M., Ellis, S., Tester, H., & Thomas, A. (1988). *The Primary Language Record: Handbook for teachers*. Portsmouth, NJ: Heinemann.

Bisesi, T. (1997). *The potential value of a performance-based assessment for filling the information gaps in an assessment system: A social validity study of the assessment information needs and uses of school administrator, classroom teacher, students, and parents*. Unpublished dissertation, Michigan State University, East Lansing, MI.

Brenner, D., Pearson, P. D., Boyd, J., & Prico, P. (1996, December). *Glendale's new assessment: The archival portfolio*. Charleston, SC: National Reading Conference.

Bridgeman, B., Chittenden, E., & Cline, F. (1995). *Characteristics of a portfolio scale for rating early literacy* (Center for Performance Assessment Report No. MS95-01). Princeton, NJ: Educational Testing Service.

California Learning Assessment System. (1994). *Elementary performance assessments: Integrated English-language arts illustrative material*. Sacramento: California Department of Education.

California Reading Task Force. (1995). *Every child a reader*. Sacramento: California Department of Education.

Chittenden, E., & Spicer, W. (1993). *The South Brunswick literacy portfolio project*. Paper presented at the New Standards Project: English Language Arts Portfolio Meeting, Minneapolis, MN.

Clay, M. M. (1985). *The early detection of reading difficulties* (3rd ed.). Portsmouth, NH: Heinemann.

Clinton Administration. (1997, February). *A call to action for American education*. Press release in advance of the State of the Union Address.

Colorado House Bill 96-1139. (1996). *An act concerning the literacy skills of pupils in kindergarten through the third grade*.

Diegmueller, K. (March 20, 1996). Standards for language arts are unveiled. *Education Week, 15*(26), 1, 13.

Dorre-Bremme, D., & Herman, J. (1983). *Assessing student achievement: A profile of classroom practices*. Los Angeles: UCLA, Center for the Study of Evaluation.

Dunbar, S. B., Koretz, D., & Hoover, H. D. (1991). Quality control in the development and use of performance assessments. *Applied Measurement in Education, 4*, 289–304.

Farr, B., & Darling-Hammond, L. (1993). *The Primary Language Record at P.S. 261: How assessment transforms teaching and learning*. New York: National Center for Restructuring Education Schools and Teaching.

Feeney, K., & Hahn, P. (1991). *Survey of reading performance in year 2: Summer 1991*. Lewisham, England: Lewisham Education.

García, G. E., & Pearson, P. D. (1994). Assessment and diversity. In L. Darling-Hammond (Ed.), *Review of research in education* (Vol. 20, pp. 337–391). Washington, DC: American Educational Research Association.

Gearhart, M., Herman, J., Baker, E., & Whittaker, A. K. (1993). *Whose work is it? A question for the validity of large-scale portfolio assessment* (CSE Technical Report No. 363). Los Angeles: UCLA, National Center for Research on Evaluation, Standards, and Student Testing.

Grassroots. (1995, March). *Grassroots working party on standards for democratic classrooms.* Paper distributed at NCTE Spring conference, Minneapolis, MI.

Haladyna, T. M., Nolan, S. B., & Haas, N. S. (1991). Raising standardized achievement test scores and the origins of test score pollution. *Educational Researcher, 20,* 2–7.

Harrison, C., Bailey, M., & Dewar, A. (in press). Responsive reading assessment: Is postmodern assessment of reading possible? In C. Harrison & T. Salinger (Eds.), *Assessing reading 1: Theory and practice.* London: Routledge.

Herman, J., & Golan, S. (1991). *Effects of standardized testing on teachers and learning: Another look* (CSE Technical Report No. 334). Los Angeles: UCLA, Center for the Study of Evaluation.

Hoffman, J., Worthy, J., Roser, N., McKool, S., Rutherford, W., & Strecker, S. (1996). Performance assessment in first-grade classrooms: The PALM model. In D. Leu, C. Kinzer, & K. Hinchman (Eds.), *Literacies for the 21st century* (pp. 100–112). Chicago: National Reading Conference.

International Reading Association/National Council of Teachers of English. (1996). *Standards for the English language arts.* Newark, DE: International Reading Association.

Jacobs, J. (1996, April 6). Learning the language in plain gibberish. *San Jose Mercury News,* 5.

Johnson, D. D., & Pearson, P. D. (1975). Skills management systems: A critique. *The Reading Teacher, 28,* 757–764.

Jones, J., & Chittenden, E. (1995). *Teacher's perceptions of rating an early literacy portfolio* (Center for Performance Assessment Report No. MS95-01). Princeton, NJ: Educational Testing Service.

Koretz, D., Klein, S., McCaffrey, D., & Stecher, B. (1994). *The reliability of the Vermont portfolio scores in the 1992-93 school year.* Burlington: Vermont Department of Education.

Koretz, D., Stecher, B., & Deibert, E. (1993). *The reliability of scores from the 1992 Vermont portfolio assessment program* (Technical Report No. 355). Los Angeles: UCLA, Center for the Study of Evaluation.

Linn, R. L. (1993). Educational assessment: Expanded expectations and challenges. *Educational Evaluation and Policy Analysis, 15,* 1–16.

Linn, R. L., Baker, E. L., & Dunbar, S. B. (1991). Complex, performance-based assessment: Expectations and validation criteria. *Educational Researcher, 20,* 15–21.

Linn, R., DeStefano, L., Burton, E., & Hanson, M. (1995). Generalizability of New Standards Project 1993 pilot study tasks in mathematics. *Applied Measurement in Education, 9*(2), 33–45.

Lipson, M. Y., & Wixson, K. K. (1986). Reading disability research: An interactionist perspective. *Review of Educational Research, 56,* 11–136.

McCarthy, D. (1972). *McCarthy scales of children's abilities.* New York: Psychological Corporation.

Mehrens, W. A. (1992). Using performance assessment for accountability purposes. *Educational Measurement: Issues and Practices, 11*(1), 3–9, 20.

Meisels, S. J. (1996). Using work sampling in authentic assessments. *Educational Leadership, 54*(4), 60–66.

Meisels, S. J., Jablon, J., Marsden, D. B., Dichtelmiller, M. L., & Dorman, A. B. (1994). *The work sampling system: An overview* (3rd ed.). Ann Arbor, MI: Rebus Planning Associates.

Meisels, S. J., Liaw, F., Dorfman, A., & Fails-Nelson, R. (1995). The work sampling system: Reliability and validity of a performance assessment for young children. *Early Childhood Research Quarterly, 10,* 277–296.

Messick, S. (1989). Validity. In R. L. Linn (Ed.), *Educational measurement* (3rd ed., pp. 13–103). New York: American Council on Education, Macmillan.

Michigan State Board of Education. (1995). *English language arts: Model content standards for curriculum.* Lansing: Michigan State Board of Education.

Murphy, S., & Smith, M. A. (1991). *Writing portfolios: A bridge from teaching to assessment.* Markham, Ontario: Pippin.

Myers, M., & Pearson, P. D. (1996). Performance assessment and the literacy unit of the New Standards Project. *Assessing Writing, 3*(1), 5–29.

National Board for Professional Teaching Standards (1989). *What teachers should know and be able to do.* Detroit: Author.

New Standards. (1993). *The man and his message.* Pittsburgh, PA: Author.

New Standards. (1997). *Performance standards.* Rochester, NY: Author.

O'Day, J. A., & Smith, M. S. (1993). Systematic reform and educational opportunity. In S. Fuhrman (Ed.), *Designing coherent policy: Improving the system* (pp. 250–312). San Francisco: Jossey-Bass.

Ogle, D. M. (1986). K–W–L: A teaching model that develops active reading of expository text. *The Reading Teacher, 39,* 564–570.

O'Sullivan, O. (1995). *The Primary Language Record in use.* London: Centre for Language in Primary Education.

Pearson, P. D. (in press). Standards in the English language arts. In J. Squire & J. Flood, (Eds.), *Encyclopedia of language arts practice.*

Pearson, P. D. (1996). Response to the Standards for the English language arts. *Reading Today, 13*(5), 8.

Pearson, P. D., Brenner, D., & Packard, B. (in preparation). *A districtwide view of early reading instruction and assessment.* Forest Hills, MI: Forest Hills School Board.

Pearson, P. D., DeStefano, L., & García, G. E. (in press). Dilemmas in reading assessment. In C. Harrison & T. Salinger (Eds.), *Assessing reading 1: Theory and practice.* London: Routledge.

Pinnell, G. S., Lyons, C. A., Deford, D. E., Bryk, A., & Seltzer, M. (1994). Comparing instructional models of the literacy education of high-risk first graders. *Reading Research Quarterly, 29,* 8–39.

Ravitch, D. (1995). *National standards in American education: A citizen's guide.* Washington, DC: Brookings.

Reading Program Advisory. (1996). *A balanced, comprehensive approach to teaching reading in Prekindergarten through grade three.* Sacramento: California Department of Education.

Resnick, L. B., & Resnick, D. P. (1992). *Assessing the thinking curriculum: New tools for educational reform.* In B. R. Gifford & M. C. O'Connor (Eds.), *Changing assessments: Alternative views of aptitude, achievement, and instruction* (pp. 37–75). Boston: Kluwer Academic Publishers.

Riechmann, D. (1996, March 16). Teachers' language standards called vague. *Pittsburgh Post-Gazette,* p. 6.

Salinger, T., & Chittenden, E. (1994). Focus on research analysis of an early literacy portfolio: Consequences for instruction. *Language Arts, 71,* 446–453.

Shanker, A. (1996, April 7). What standards? *New York Times,* p. 7.

Shannon, P. (1996). Mad as hell. *Language Arts, 73,* 14–19.

Shavelson, R. J., Baxter, G. P., & Pine, J. (1992). Performance assessments: Political rhetoric and measurement reality. *Educational Researcher, 21,* 22–27.

Shepard, L. (1989). Why we need better tests. *Educational Leadership, 46*(7), 4–9.

Simmons, W., & Resnick, L. (1993). Assessment as the catalyst of school reform. *Educational Leadership, 50*(5), 11–15.

Sizer, T. (1992). *Horace's school: Redesigning the American high school.* Boston: Houghton-Mifflin.

Smith, M. L. (1991). Put to the test: The effects of external testing on teachers. *Educational Researcher, 20,* 8–11.

Smith, M. L., & Shepard, L. (1988). Kindergarten readiness and retention: A qualitative study of teachers' beliefs and practices. *American Educational Research Journal, 25,* 307–333.

Smith, M. S., Cianci, J. E., & Levin, J. Perspectives on literacy: A response. *Journal of Literacy Research, 28*(4), 604–609.

Smith, M. S., & O'Day, J. (1991). Systemic school reform. In S. H. Fuhrman & B. Malen (Eds.), *The politics of curriculum and testing* (pp. 233–267). Briston, PA: Falmer Press.

Snow, R. (1993). Construct validity and constructed-response tests. In R. Bennett & W. Ward (Eds.), *Construction versus choice in cognitive measurement* (pp. 45–60). Hillsdale, NJ: Erlbaum.

Stallman, A. C., & Pearson, P. D. (1990). Formal measures of early literacy. In L. M. Morrow & J. K. Smith (Eds.), *Assessment for instruction in early literacy* (pp. 7–44). Englewood Cliffs, NJ: Prentice Hall.

Thorndike, E. L. (1917). Reading as reasoning: A study of mistakes in paragraph reading. *Journal of Educational Psychology, 8,* 323–332.

Tierney, R. J., Carter, M. A., & Desai, L. E. (1991). *Portfolio assessment in the reading-writing classroom.* Norwood, MA: Christopher-Gordon.

Valencia, S. W. (1990). National survey of the use of test data for educational decision making. In P. Afflerbach (Ed.), *Issues in statewide reading assessment* (pp. 75–100). Washington, DC: American Institutes for Research Association.

Valencia, S. W., Hiebert, E. H., & Afflerbach, P. (1994). *Authentic reading assessment: Practices and possibilities.* Newark, DE: International Reading.

Valencia, S. W., & Pearson, P. D. (1987). Reading assessment: Time for a change. *The Reading Teacher, 40,* 726–733.

Valencia, S. W., Pearson, P. D., Peters, C. W., & Wixson, K. K. (1989). Theory and practice in statewide reading assessment: Closing the gap. *Educational Leadership, 47*(7), 57–63.

Valencia, S. W., & Sulzby, E. (1991). Assessment of emergent literacy: Storybook reading. *The Reading Teacher 44,* 498–501.

Weiss, B. (1994). California's new English-language arts assessment. In S. W. Valencia, E. H. Hiebert, & P. Afflerbach (Eds.), *Authentic reading assessment: Practices and possibilities.* Newark, DE: International Reading Association.

Wiggins, G. (1993). *Assessing student performance: Exploring the purpose and limits of testing.* San Francisco: Jossey-Bass.

Wisconsin State Journal. (1996, March 29). Our opinion: Language arts standards are worthless, p. 4.

Woodcock, R. W., & Johnson, M. B. (1989). *Woodcock–Johnson psychoeducational battery—Revised.* Allen, TX: DLM Teaching Resources.

CHAPTER THIRTEEN

Performance Assessment in Reading: Implications for Teacher Education

JAMES V. HOFFMAN
with JO WORTHY, NANCY L. ROSER,
and WILLIAM RUTHERFORD
University of Texas–Austin

Some years ago I accompanied my daughter Jessica to her first "painting" class in a summer program offered through a local art institute. After some brief introductory remarks, the instructor stated her goals for the program. I remember her words distinctly: "I will not teach you to draw or paint better than you do now, as much as I will help you see the world around you differently. This is ultimately what will help you improve your painting the most." Whether these words were lost on the audience of 9-year-old children anxious to dip into the splendid colors surrounding them, I don't know, but her words were not lost on me.

My work with novice teachers has taught me that just giving them formulas, or packaged plans for lessons, or labels for methods can produce some short-term satisfaction and sometimes even the illusion of expertise. But such strategies will produce neither good teaching for the moment nor good teachers for a lifetime. I have experienced the greatest moments of success as a teacher educator when I have been able to help those I work with see deeper into the world with which they interact on a daily basis. When I help others see a developing reader's performance as evidence of creativity and not deficit, I have made a contribution that may lead eventually to more effective teaching. When I help others see the complexity of reading as a social act, where before they saw only simple behavioral responses to a print stimulus, then I have made a contribution that may lead eventually to more effective teaching.

What we see in teaching and learning is shaped in large measure by the tools we use to examine their interaction. Our assessment tools and strategies always represent the learner in a particular light; no assessment is neutral in its perspective (Johnston, 1992). A norm-referenced achievement test that requires the student to read passages and answer comprehension questions is rooted in a particular set of assumptions about the learner, the curriculum, the social context for learning, and teaching (Stallman & Pearson, 1990). A surprisingly different image of the learner may emerge if we use tools that are based on different (and even nontraditional) assumptions. Whether it is because they are more familiar to us, because they are so easily reduced to numerical interpretations, or because they give us answers to the questions we feel capable of addressing, traditional forms of reading assessment have continued to dominate in education.

But today many are challenging traditional forms of assessment as too limited in their perspective and too empty in their potential to inform (Winograd, Paris, & Bridge, 1993). Some are advancing performance assessment, with its emphasis on insights gained through ongoing inquiry, as a worthy alternative to traditional assessment (Guthrie, Van Meter, Mitchell, & Reed, 1994). "Performance assessment" makes assumptions about the learner that are fundamentally different from those made by traditional assessments and that, therefore, have the potential to reveal a different view of the learner. Perhaps when this different perspective is revealed, a higher quality of instruction is free to emerge. If this is the case, then a different perspective on the place of assessment in teacher education emerges as well.

In this chapter, I illustrate th:s principle in a concrete way. First, I elaborate on a recent experience I had working with a small group of teaching colleagues in the Austin Independent School District. I then attempt to connect this experience to a broader understanding of performance assessment and its potential for teacher education.

THE PALM PROJECT

In the fall of 1993, a small group of first-grade teachers in Austin, Texas, raised questions at their local campuses regarding the value of the Iowa Tests of Basic Skills (ITBS) as a measure of their students' literacy. The teachers expressed concerns about ITBS's validity ("The test does not really measure what we are teaching or what the students are learning") as well as its utility ("The results are not helpful in making instructional decisions"). The teachers decided to approach the district's central administration with a request for a waiver from standardized testing for first-graders.

They presented their proposal to the associate superintendent for curriculum. New to the district, the associate superintendent expressed support for the initiative and recommended that the group prepare a plan for an alternative assessment to replace ITBS. Toward that end, the teachers first adapted a developmental checklist from another district, making minor modifications to suit local needs. The associate superintendent arranged for the group to meet with the district's Board of Trustees to present their request for a waiver. Over 100 first-grade teachers appeared at the Board meeting in support of the request for the waiver. The presentation to the Board was effective, and a waiver was granted. In fact, the waiver was extended to all first-grade teachers in the district not just the group making the request. As a result of concerns expressed by some Board members, however, an evaluation study was mandated for the 1994–1995 school year.

The alternative assessment system developed by the group was informally piloted during the spring semester, 1994. Planning for a full-scale evaluation study for the upcoming school year was also initiated. A planning team consisting of six first-grade teachers and two university-based teacher educators (Jo Worthy and I) worked to refine the original checklist into a comprehensive assessment plan. The overarching goal was to develop an assessment plan to address the needs of teachers, as well as parents, administrators, policymakers, and students. Over the course of several months the Primary Assessment of Language Arts and Mathematics model (PALM) emerged.

PALM is a performance-based assessment model that incorporates features of informal assessment with portfolios. The model consists of three basic types of assessment strategies: *curriculum-embedded* (or ongoing assessments), *taking-a-closer-look* assessments, and *on-demand* assessments.

Curriculum-Embedded Assessments

Curriculum-embedded assessment refers to the data gathering teachers may do in conjunction with their ongoing instruction. For example, effective teachers are constantly observing their students as they engage in learning activities. They monitor students for the quality of their work. They continuously adapt instruction in response to these observations. In addition, they make long-term instructional decisions based on their students' performances. The PALM model affirms the common-sense practice of skillful observation as a worthwhile, trustworthy, and significant part of a comprehensive assessment plan. The PALM model also requires that teachers take time periodically to document their observations in some way. Documentation may take the form of collecting samples of student work along with notes from the teacher (or the student) explaining why this work is important evidence for learning. Documentation may also take the form of anecdotal notes of student engagement in various learning activities. The

PALM model requires that teachers collect their observations of all students on a regular basis.

Taking-a-Closer-Look Assessments

The second type of performance assessment in the PALM model refers to the data that teachers gather as part of their in-depth study of individual learners. Again, close-up inspection of particular skills is and has been a part of the practice of most effective teachers. From time to time, individual students present their teachers with a challenge. Teachers must learn to ask and gather data that help them decide: Where is *this* student in his or her development? What does he or she need? Why is she or he performing in the way(s) I have observed? The toughest challenges do not all arise at the same time, and they do not always involve the same students. Nevertheless, the puzzles are there because all students are different and respond in different ways. Good teaching (and good assessment) demands adjustment for those individual differences. Within the PALM model, the taking-a-closer-look assessments provide all teachers with the tools and methodologies for systematic observation that the most effective teachers already use. For example, close-up assessments provide for collecting anecdotal records, conducting interest inventories, and setting learning goals. Strategies useful in this type of assessment are quite familiar to most teachers, and the list of strategies is always expanding.

- *Interviews/conversations*: Talking and listening with students about what they are thinking, learning, questioning, understanding.
- *Informal assessments*: Administering and interpreting informal reading inventories, opportunities for problem solving, miscue analysis procedures, running records, think-alouds, etc.
- *Dynamic assessments*: Varying instruction conditions to determine how students respond to different kinds and levels of support.

These are just a few of the many ways in which teachers can "take a closer look." They are not typically done with all students at the same time; rather, they are seen as strategies to be applied selectively on an as-needed basis. The PALM model suggests teachers incorporate these strategies to record and interpret performance as a supplement/complement to their ongoing, curriculum-embedded assessment strategies.

On-Demand Assessments

On-demand assessments involve data gathering within a particular time frame and under prescribed conditions. Typically, demand assessments are focused on documenting and interpreting student performance on specific learning tasks. These tasks are designed to be authentic in the sense that they reflect the kinds of learning activities with which the students are familiar in their classroom instruction. The tasks are controlled in terms of certain key variables (e.g., materials) to permit comparisons over time (for an individual child) as well as comparisons of an individual child with his or her peers. The specifics of the demand assessments may vary from time to time. To explain the demand tasks, it is useful to look at the demand tasks that were actually used as part of the 1994–1995 PALM evaluation study. The teachers themselves developed a schedule to be followed and the tasks to be used. The tasks were designed to mirror the kinds of classroom activities that were part of the "typical" instructional routines. The assessments were designed to occur over 1 week and scheduled for the first week in May. To insure commonality and comparability across sites, a guide for teachers described how the demand assessment tasks were to be conducted.

The demand assessments tasks in the area of language arts included the following:

1. *A Personal Journal.* All students participating in the project worked in specially designed response journals for the week of the demand assessments. Students were given a time each day to write in their journals. The teacher discussed and modeled entries. Sharing (reading from and talking about the journal entry) was a part of the classroom routine.

2. *Literature Response Journal: Read Aloud* (responding in writing to a story read aloud by the teacher). Students daily wrote their thoughts and responses to a chapter book read aloud by the teacher. In spring 1995, the chapter book was *Did You Carry the Flag Today Charley?* After each chapter was read aloud, the students wrote in their response journals. Again, sharing of journal entries was encouraged.

3. *Literature Response Journal: Free Choice* (writing in response to self-selected books). A reading library was set up in each classroom. The libraries were similar across all classroom sites in terms of the number of books and the types of selections available. The students were given time each day to do free-choice reading as well as to respond to reading in their journals.

4. *Learning from Text Experience.* Students wrote what they already knew about a topic, what they wanted to learn, and, eventually, what they had learned. An informational trade book, *Snakes* by Seymour Simon, was the focus for this assessment. Before reading the book aloud to the class, teachers directed the students to write in their journals everything they knew about snakes. After the read-aloud, the students were given an opportunity to write about what they had learned that was new to them from the book. Discussion followed the writing.

5. *Oral Reading/Shared Reading Exercise.* The teacher reviewed with the class a book (*The Chick and the Duckling*) that had been read during the year as a part of the regular reading program. Following a review of the book, the students individually read the book aloud to the teacher. In

addition, the students read a second book of comparable difficulty that they had not seen before. Teachers rated the fluency of both read-aloud performances. Student performance was analyzed using quantitative and qualitative techniques.

6. *An Interview/Inventory*. Each student met individually with his or her teacher to discuss reading habits, attitudes, and sense of self as a reader/writer. The discussion was organized around a series of probes requiring scaled responses.

In an ideal world, students engaged in the demand tasks would not notice any major disruptions to normal activity.

The three types of performance assessment work together to provide a rich data base on student progress. Interpretations of student performance are recorded in the student developmental indicator profile (a checklist) and further documented in their portfolios. These data are used by multiple audiences (e.g., teachers, administrators, parents) for decision-making purposes.

In late summer, during the district's inservice for first-grade teachers, an information session was offered explaining the PALM initiative. A total of 22 teachers from 13 different schools, including several of those from the original group of teachers, volunteered to participate in the evaluation study.

The volunteer teachers and university-based teacher educators met four times over the academic year in all-day, inservice sessions and in a number of small-group committee meetings. These working sessions were focused on refining the PALM model and on coordinating data collection for the evaluation study. The district's research and evaluation division identified a group of comparison teachers to be included in the study (matched to PALM teachers based on years teaching experience and school contexts). The comparison teachers, along with PALM teachers, participated in extensive interviews regarding their perspectives on and experiences with assessment strategies. We made a decision at this time to focus our attention on the area of language arts. Attention to the mathematics component of the PALM model was deferred.

The evaluation study of the PALM model was designed to address the following questions:

1. Can the PALM alternative assessment model be implemented successfully in first-grade classrooms that serve a wide variety of student populations and with teachers representing a wide variety of instructional philosophies and experience?
2. Does the PALM model contribute to more informed teaching and testing in a way that standardized testing does not?
3. Will the PALM model yield data for other audiences (e.g., administrators) that are comparable to or more informing than the data generated though the standardized tests?

We collected data over the course of one academic year using both quantitative and qualitative methodologies. Because of the design of the evaluation study, the participating teachers were required to administer ITBS in the spring of the year. Ironically, as fate would have it, the only first-grade teachers who actually administered the ITBS test to their students this year were the teachers who had launched the protest.

In terms of the participants' perspectives on PALM, all of those participating described their teaching as more effective as a result of using the new assessment plan. They commented that the model helped focus their attention more sharply on indicators of development, and that as a result, their instructional decisions were enhanced.

- "I didn't assess as often until I used the Developmental Indicator Profile. I'm more focused now."
- "The kids enjoyed it; we actually spent more than a week so it gave a better assessment of student performance."
- "This helps me rethink what I am doing."

They described the model as an improvement in terms of helping them to organize information on students in a meaningful way. They commented on the value of the model in communicating with parents regarding individual student progress. They reported positive feelings about what they would be able to pass on to the students' future teachers that would assure continuous progress. Finally, they felt affirmed in the fact that the assessment strategies associated with PALM reflected their teaching efforts.

- "This is my own philosophy. This is what ought to be done."

No teacher in either the PALM group or in the comparison group viewed ITBS testing (or the results) as a positive influence on their teaching ("I learn nothing from ITBS. I hope I never see it again"). In fact, the vast majority of the teachers in both groups viewed ITBS as worse than a waste of time. Many teachers saw the test experience itself as defeating to children ("I only had two cry today") and inappropriate as a measure of the teaching and learning tied to the district's language arts curriculum. The interviews with the comparison teachers (i.e., those not participating in the PALM training or implementation) revealed a combination of confusion and concern over assessment in the district. When the comparison teachers were asked about the district's policy in regard to assessment of children's basic understandings, nearly all responded that they were uncertain. Most were operating under the assumption that there were no expectations/requirements for assessment at first grade, and thus teachers were free to do whatever they wanted to do (including nothing). Most of the teachers reported relying on informal measures of student progress.

We also addressed the effectiveness of PALM from a more quantitative perspective. The teachers were asked to rank their students (from highest to lowest in terms of reading- and writing-skill levels) the week prior to ITBS testing. We then computed the correlations of teachers' rankings of students (i.e., on perceived skill level in reading) with the students' performance on the ITBS reading subtest. The overall correlation between the teacher's rankings and the ITBS total reading score was strong and positive ($r = .58$). Separating out the correlations for the PALM teachers and the comparison teachers, we found the PALM teachers rankings to be correlated with ITBS performance at a higher level ($r = .62$) than was the case with the comparison teachers ($r = .38$ level). When we ran correlations *within* classes relating rankings to ITBS scores, the average correlation across all teachers was even higher ($r =.75$). Twelve of the 17 teachers in the PALM group had correlations higher than the mean of .75. Only 6 of the 14 teachers in the comparison group had correlations higher than the mean. We interpreted these patterns as indicating that the PALM teachers, based on their intensive involvement in performance assessment over an entire year, were more sensitized to differences and strengths. This interpretation is consistent with Wolf's (1993) notion that participation in performance assessment leads to more informed instruction. We have no direct evidence that their instructional decision making was better as a result, but clearly the awareness of performance levels was higher.

No one doubted going into the evaluation study that we would be able to demonstrate positive effects at the classroom level; we were cautious though regarding our ability to demonstrate to the other stakeholders (specifically, administrators) that the PALM model could provide them with useful information. To make a convincing argument, we compiled the data from several sources: the developmental indicator profile, ITBS, teacher ratings (e.g., of students' oral reading fluency), teacher rankings of student performance, and the results of demand assessments (e.g., writing in response to a story read aloud). A quantitative score from the developmental profile was derived by summing the number of indicators. A scoring rubric was developed for the student journals completed as part of the demand assessments. The journals were scored on a holistic scale for overall quality, as well as on analytic scales for accessibility, spelling, other writing conventions, sentence fluency, word choice, voice, and response/comprehension. The journals completed during the demand assessment were scored by trained raters, with two raters scoring each journal independently. Student performance was scored in terms of: accuracy of word recognition, number of self-corrections, and a teacher rating of student fluency. Three scores were also derived from the inventory of beliefs, attitudes, and habits. These scores represented the average rating of students on the questions that probed their viewpoints regarding reading.

A regression analysis was computed using variables representing the key elements of the PALM model to predict the reading students' reading scores on ITBS. Based on the conceptual structure of the PALM model and the findings from the intercorrelational analysis, the following variables were included: (1) the total score from the third and final developmental indicator profile rating; (2) the holistic rating score of the journal used in the demand assessment; and (3) the fluency rating for the oral reading of the unfamiliar text. The results of this multiple regression analysis yielded an R value of .86 suggesting a strong concurrent validity with the results of ITBS for reading. All three of the variables included in the PALM model contribute significantly to the prediction. This finding suggests that the properties of the PALM model to gauge the development of reading abilities and skills in a normative sense are quite strong. These data provide comparable performance rankings to ITBS. This analysis also suggests that all aspects of the PALM model (curriculum-embedded assessments, taking-a-closer-look assessments, and on-demand assessments) are essential to its success.

We concluded that the PALM model, when implemented fully, provides teachers with information they view as informative to instructional decision making. The PALM model yields data on students from a performance-assessment perspective that are consistent and converging. In addition, we demonstrated that the psychometric properties of the PALM model are at least as strong as those of the standardized test, and we provided data that are equally informative and trustworthy to a wide variety of external audiences. (For a complete report on the findings from the evaluation study see Hoffman et al., 1995.)

Based on the findings from the evaluation study, the school district has made a commitment to expand the use of PALM to all first-grade classrooms. Further, the district has made a commitment to expanding the program from first grade to include all of the primary grades and from language arts to mathematics.

IMPLICATIONS FOR TEACHER EDUCATION

Performance assessment, as exemplified in the development and application of the PALM model, offers great promise for the field of reading education. A well-conceived performance assessment model can help us bridge the gap between data that are informative to teachers and students as the "internal" audience for assessment and data that are informative to the external audiences such as administrators and policymakers (Wixson, Valencia, & Lipson, 1994). We can find the answers to the different questions we might have in the same reality. We do not need to develop parallel lines of assessment that may disrupt our common goal to educate. We can grow to understand what it means to build trust into an assessment plan and come to some common ground on "what counts." Should we succeed in developing performance assessment models along these lines, the implications for fundamental changes in education are far reaching and fundamental.

But I want to take the implications of this experience with PALM in a different direction. I want to focus on the implications of a well-conceived plan for performance assessment on teacher education. Although I write from the perspective of a university-based teacher educator who works with preservice and inservice teachers, this is not the only point of reference to be implicated. Supervisors, administrators, and curriculum directors often assume the role of teacher educator in their interactions with their colleagues. Reading specialists and classroom teachers sharing with their colleagues in professional development settings are teacher educators. Our interactions with parents in building home–school connections involve teacher education. Our interactions with tutors and classroom volunteers who work directly with our students involve teacher education.

We have a tendency (I hesitate to call it "natural") to engage in a *telling* mode when we assume our teacher educator role. We prescribe our routines, our strategies, our "tricks of the trade," our style as the model to be followed. Why is this? Is it because we think we have a corner on the truth? Is it because we know only one way? Is this imposition a way of establishing control or authority over others? Is it out of expediency (e.g., "I have parents coming in tomorrow to help with reading, and I have to give them something to do")? I suspect there is some truth in each of these explanations—at least I can confess to having used all of the above. If I regard those I work with simply as tools to achieve my goals for my *real* clients (i.e., the students assigned to me), then this highly directive pattern of use might be rationalized. But as soon as I regard all those with whom I work as *real* students or, better still, co-learners, then the prescriptive approach is doomed to fail.

The alternative is to help those we work with see the complexity we see. Sharing a perspective on literacy acquisition, introducing strategies for taking a closer look at the reading process, reflecting on individual differences, etc., are some of the ways in which we help reveal the complexity of learning to read. The problem solving and instructional decision making that follow do not guarantee success, but at least, the foundation is well-laid, and the mechanisms for judging success are in place.

I would like to point the reader of this chapter to all of the research evidence that supports this perspective for teacher education, but there is little in the way of empirical evidence for such a view. Certainly, this perspective is in opposition to the dominant trend toward teacher education in reading that leans heavily on packaged programs that train teachers to perform in specific ways. The findings from the PALM study suggest that teachers who engage in performance assessment are more aware of their students' abilities than are those who have not been encouraged in this direction. But there is no evidence that this knowledge directly informs teacher decision making let alone student achievement. The relationship of teacher knowledge to teaching practices to student achievement is axiomatic to our field, and it is startling that so little evidence has been accumulated to reflect this relationship. Perhaps future studies that focus on documenting teacher knowledge of their students' abilities and its relationship to teaching practices and achievement will take us further than the early studies that failed to document relationships between teacher knowledge of reading and effectiveness.

Although I look forward to research along this line, I suspect that such studies will reveal that teacher knowledge of student abilities contributes to but does not guarantee effective teaching. Jessica's art teacher may have succeeded in helping her students see the world differently, but this was no certain path to an art career. Performance assessments and the insights they provide are not an end. Certainly we have all known those who assess so much they never get to the point of teaching anything. Performance assessments are a constant reference point for all of us who strive to teach. They create puzzles for us to reflect on and problems for us to solve that traditional forms of assessment may never reveal. The struggle anthropologists refer to as "making the familiar strange" in a good ethnography is a worthy corollary for teachers and assessment. If our tools for assessment simply serve up answers for the questions we already have, then no surprises await us. If our tools push us beyond the obvious and into the unknown, then all sorts of possibilities emerge.

All of the teachers involved in the PALM project assessed in similar ways, but the same singularity of purpose could not be said for their teaching. The teaching was diverse in terms of curriculum, classroom organization, and instructional strategies. The teaching differences reflected differences in philosophical orientations and beliefs, but just as important, the teaching differences reflected differences in student needs. To require or even suggest that a single teaching plan is the ideal would be in error. I share with Duffy (1997) the belief that we must "authorize [teachers] to adapt instructional models to the situation, and to invent learning situations which captivate students." Through the successful application of performance assessment we can create accountability systems that are meaningful to teachers. We can create a context for the development of new knowledge about practice that teachers can embrace with professionalism and dignity.

REFERENCES

Duffy, G. (1997). Powerful models or powerful teachers? An argument for teacher-as-entrepreneur. In S. Stahl & D. Hayes (Eds.), *Instructional models in reading* (p. 356). Hillsdale, NJ: Erlbaum.

Guthrie, J., Van Meter, P., Mitchell, A., & Reed, C. (1994). Performance assessments in reading and language arts. *The Reading Teacher, 48,* 266–271.

Hoffman, J. V., Worthy, J., Roser, N., McKool, S., Rutherford, W., & Strecker, S. (1995). Performance assessment in first-grade classrooms: The PALM model.

Forty-fifth yearbook of the National Reading Conference (pp. 100–112). Chicago: National Reading Conference.

Johnston, P. H. (1992). *Constructive evaluation of literate activity.* New York: Longman.

Stallman, A., & Pearson, P. D. (1990). Formal measures of early literacy. In L. Morrow & J. Smith (Eds.), *Assessment for instruction in early literacy* (pp. 7–44). Englewood Cliffs, NJ: Prentice Hall.

Winograd, P., Paris, S., & Bridge, C. (1993). Improving the assessment of literacy. *The Reading Teacher, 45,* 108–116.

Wixson, K. K., Valencia, S. W., & Lipson, M. Y. (1994). Issues in literacy assessment: Facing the realities of internal and external assessment. *Journal of Reading Behavior, 26,* 315–337.

Wolf, K. P. (1993). From informal to informed assessment: Recognizing the role of the classroom teacher. *Journal of Reading, 36,* 518–523.

PART FIVE

TEACHING AND
TEACHER EDUCATION

CHAPTER FOURTEEN

Professional Development in the Instruction of Reading

VIRGINIA RICHARDSON
University of Michigan

Following a 5-year study of teacher change in reading instruction under-taken with Patricia Anders, I found myself describing a "new" form of staff development that seemed particularly useful in change processes that required fundamental alterations in beliefs about reading, learning to read, teaching reading, and/or the nature of knowledge. This new form of staff development contrasts with a more traditional, or training, approach that has and continues to be the dominant form of staff development in schools in the United States. The major conceptual difference between the two forms is that the anticipated change outcomes—that is, what the teachers are supposed to do in their classrooms at the end of the process—is prespecified in the latter form, but not in the former. The new form is variously called inquiry-approach, collaborative, mutual adaptation, and in the case of Anders and my own (Richardson & Anders, 1994) formally called the Practical Argument Staff Development Process. It is voluntary and individualized with respect to the nature of the change toward which the teacher and staff developer works. This form was found to be effective in fostering deep reflection, belief change, change in practice, the development of a change orientation, and a strong sense of individual autonomy (Richardson, 1994a). Further, the study that examined this process provided some indication of positive change in student achievement (Bos & Anders, 1994).

As I spoke about this new form of staff development to various groups, I was met with similar reactions by state and federal policy makers (here and in other countries): "Very interesting, but how does this help me?"

"What should we be doing about this?" "We can't really frame a policy around it" "I don't think this helps me very much." They pointed out that this form is labor intensive and lengthy. Further they said that they did not know what to do with the voluntary nature of this "new" form. Can a staff development program that is based on notions of voluntary change and change in directions determined by the individual teacher be mandated? Even at the school-district level, this new form of staff development is difficult to contemplate and support. These reactions led me to rethink the nature of this form of staff development, not from the standpoint that "It simply can't be done in this policy context," but from the standpoint of whether the new form works for the benefit of students. In particular, I began to reexamine the sense of individual autonomy that is enhanced by the new form of staff development.

I begin this chapter with a brief description of the two forms of staff development. I then describe my experiences in working on staff development issues at a school-district level as I asked the question: "Why don't school districts implement staff development in a way that takes advantage of the relatively clear-cut, research-based findings about effective staff development?" I then address the question of whether the new form of staff development actually does meet the needs of students, and I conclude by suggesting that the new form of staff development may need some alterations.

TWO APPROACHES TO STAFF DEVELOPMENT

The more traditional form of staff development begins with someone outside the school determining that a process, method, or system should be implemented in classrooms. The conception of teacher education represented in this form is that of the training model that has, at its core, a clearly stated set of objectives and learner outcomes. For Cruickshank and Metcalf (1990), these outcomes are teaching skills. Showers, Joyce, and Bennett (1987) have added thinking processes to the list of outcomes. Sparks and Loucks-Horsley (1990, p. 241) have identified a number of important assumptions inherent in the training model, including the following:

- There are behaviors and techniques worthy of replication by teachers in the classroom.
- Teacher-education students and teachers can learn or change their behaviors to replicate behaviors in their classroom.

Many of the staff development programs in this category are relatively short-term, involve teachers in several hours or several days of workshops, and have limited follow-up activities (Goldenberg & Gallimore, 1991).

Such programs have a chance of succeeding only with those teachers whose beliefs match the assumptions inherent in the innovation; and even then, these teachers might not try the new innovation. In fact, Joyce (1981, cited in Meyer, 1988) estimates that such practices garner an implementation level of 15%.

More recently, however, an understanding of the qualities needed in staff development processes has entered the consciousness of staff developers and school district officials. These qualities have been summarized by many, including Fullan (1990), Griffin (1986), Loucks-Horsley et al. (1987), McLaughlin (1991), and Ward (1985). These qualities include the following:

- The program should be schoolwide and context-specific.
- School principals should be supportive of the process and encouraging of change.
- The program should be long-term, with adequate support and follow-up.
- The process should encourage collegiality.
- The program content should incorporate current knowledge obtained through well-designed research.
- The program should include adequate funds for materials, outside speakers, and substitute teachers to allow teachers to observe each other.

The question of whether the teachers have a choice of attending (or not) the staff development is included as an important quality by some but not by others.

Recent staff development processes of this sort focus on ways of thinking and teacher action rather than on behaviors. They employ as many of the qualities mentioned as possible. Gallagher, Goudvis, and Pearson (1988) call this form "directed development," and Meyer (1988) provides a strong argument for such an approach to staff development. Shachar (1996) and Rich (1990) have gained insight into the staff development process through their attempts to help teachers implement cooperative learning in their classrooms. In this country, Lester and Onore (1990) had considerable success in developing in teachers the process approach to writing using an inquiry approach. There have been staff development programs in constructivist approaches to the teaching of math (e.g., Acquarelli & Mumme, 1996; Wood, Cobb, & Yakel, 1991) and project approaches to teaching science (Blumenfeld, Kracjik, Marx, & Soloway, 1994).

Context appears to play a particularly important part in the success of these programs. Anyon (1994) describes vividly an urban school in which she was attempting to work with teachers in developing cooperative learning techniques. She watched a parent whipping a student in the face with a belt in the hall of the school, and then listened to the teachers' frustrated stories of the day and their negative descriptions of students. Anyon reported that she wondered what she was doing in the school and why anyone thought cooperative learning would help. A number of the teachers did begin to use cooperative learning; however, Anyon concluded that changes in the social, economic, and political context outside the school and classroom would have to be made to help this school significantly (see also Berliner & Biddle, 1995).

Even if the project is successful, as determined by the percentage of teacher participants who immediately implement the process in their classrooms, the longer-term effects are questionable. For example, in a 4-year study of a Hunter staff development process, Stallings and Krasavage (1986) found that in the third year, teachers implemented the desired behaviors much less often than they had in the first 2 years. Further, the opposite effects may be created—that is, teachers clinging to a way of teaching they learned in a staff development program that is no longer deemed appropriate (see also, McLaughlin, 1991).

Several hypotheses are used to explain the disappointing long-term effects of the Hunter model: Stallings and Krasavage (1986) suggest that the model could not sustain teachers' interest:

> We believe that the innovative practices teachers learn will not be maintained unless teachers and students remain interested and excited about their own learning. . . . A good staff development program will create an excitement about learning to learn. The question is how to keep the momentum, not merely maintain previously learned behaviors. (p. 137)

This leads us to the question of the long-term goals of these programs. Do we want teachers to continue using a process, method, or approach into the distant future? Probably not. Many of us assume that something new and better will come along that will be more appropriate for teachers to use. This discussion of long-term goals leads to the second form of staff development, called the Practical Argument Staff Development (PASD) process (Richardson & Hamilton, 1994).

The second form of staff development attempts to develop in teachers a more systematic and reflective approach to their own change process. This form has its roots in what Chin and Benne (1969) describe as the "normative reeducative" approach to change. This approach is based on concepts of personal growth and development, as well as on collaboration within the organization that leads to collective change. Staff development within this approach includes programs that took place in the teacher center movement (Devaney, 1977). Such programs were also described by Rubin (1978) and by Katz (1979), in what she called the Advisory Model of Professional Development. Gallagher et al. (1988) call the approach "mutual adaptation," which, they suggest, is the best form for dramatic change such as shifts in orientations and beliefs.

The PASD process that Anders and I developed (Anders & Richardson, 1991) is based on the conception that teachers actually change all the time. These changes, while often minor program adjustments, can also be quite dramatic (Richardson, 1994a). The norms of the workplace and the systemics of the context also affect teachers' considerations of change in practice (Placier & Hamilton, 1994). When teachers try new activities, they assess them on the basis of whether they *work*; that is, whether they fit within the teacher's set of beliefs about teaching and learning, engage the students, and allow the teacher the degree of classroom control she or he feels necessary. If the activity does not work, it is quickly dropped or radically altered.

The decision as to whether a new activity works, however, is often not conscious, is highly personal, and may be based on experiences and understandings that are not relevant to the particular setting in which instruction is taking place. Teachers make decisions on the basis of a personal sense of what works: But without examining the beliefs underlying a sense of working, teachers may perpetuate practices based on question-able assumptions and beliefs. In response to this new understanding of change, a normative conception of teacher as inquirer has evolved that provides a vision of a teacher who questions her or his assumptions and is consciously thoughtful about her or his goals, practices, students, and contexts.

The PASD process was designed to help teachers, both in groups and individually, inquire into their beliefs and practices in relation to current research on reading and practices described by other teachers, and to support their attempts at change. It was a voluntary and collaborative process. This form is similar to the one described by Tierney, Tucker, Gallagher, Crismore, and Pearson (1988) as the Metcalf Project. The characteristics of the PASD process were summarized in Richardson and Anders (1994) in this way:

- The collaborative process is not based on a deficit model of change. Rather than beginning with the premise that teachers are doing something wrong and/or not doing something correctly, the collaborative process assumes that reflection and change are ongoing processes of assessing beliefs, goals, and results. Experimental changes in practice may, in fact, lead to less than desirable effects. The important element, therefore, is the development of a change and reflection orientation to allow the teacher to continue to question both new and old practices.
- The desired outcomes are not particular behaviors and skills, but an awareness on the part of teachers of their ways of thinking and instructional practices, and of the moral, empirical, and situational grounds for them. The purpose is procedural—to create an ecology of thinking and deliberation. Therefore, it is not possible to state, at the

beginning of the process, the behavioral objectives of the process. The objectives can only be stated in general terms related to reflection and change.

• Change is not considered to be static. That is, there is no reason to suggest that a change in practice that follows the staff development will still be in place several years later. In fact, it is hoped that teachers will continue to change after completing the staff development.

• It is not expected that the group of teachers will decide on a direction for change upon which all of the teachers will agree. Each teacher is free to follow his or her own lines of inquiry and change. Thus, a research design that relies on aggregated data will probably not be appropriate except for very large and encompassing questions such as "Did the teachers change practices?"

• We are not interested, solely, in changes in behaviors and actions, but also in the rationale and justifications that accompany the new practices. We want to be able to examine whether teachers are taking control of the justifications for their practices, rather than suggesting a rationale based on external influences such as a school board policy. We are also interested in the degree to which teachers take responsibility for their action and assume ownership of their practices. (pp. 163–164)

We found that over the 3-year period, teachers changed their beliefs and practices in directions that related to the various dialogues that we had with them, either in their school groups or individually in the practical argument sessions.[1] Bos and Anders (1994) conducted a substudy and found that the students of the teachers who participated in the staff development process achieved more in certain aspects of reading comprehension than did the students in a contrast school. In a follow-up done 2 years later, it was found that the teachers had continued to change (Valdez, 1992). It would appear that the teachers had developed a change orientation that led them to reflect continually on their teaching and classrooms and to experiment thoughtfully with new practices. The teachers had become confident in their decision-making abilities and took responsibility for what was happening in their classrooms. Thus they had developed a strong sense of individual autonomy and felt empowered to make deliberate and thoughtful changes in their classrooms.

An examination of the characteristics of the more effective traditional form and the new form of staff development indicates some commonalities. For example, both forms suggest that the staff development process be context-specific, conducted over an extended period of time, and provide support and follow-up to the teachers in the learning process. The differences concern the content of the process—prespecified in the traditional form, and determined by individual teachers in the newer form. In addition, the voluntary nature of the program is suggested in only some of the research on the traditional form but is required of the newer form. Is it these latter characteristics of the newer form that make it difficult for policy makers and school districts to implement? The next section explores this possibility.

SCHOOL DISTRICT INTERESTS
IN STAFF DEVELOPMENT

Two staff development projects in which I was involved in a school district in the Southwest helped me begin to answer the questions concerning the administration of staff development programs in school districts. The first project involved my meeting a number of times with the administrative Outcomes Objectives Task Force responsible for implementing a set of exit objectives that had been developed in the community and were being realized at all grade levels (Richardson, 1994b). The second project involved developing and implementing a staff development process within one of the elementary schools in the district.

A major element of the outcomes project was the implementation of a staff development process. The administrators were also concerned with how they were going to measure some of the objectives such as *work ethic*. During our meetings, I kept thorough notes on the discourse of the administrators. I found that test scores were continually referred to in the meetings. Although the administrators exhibited sophisticated under-standings of standardized testing issues and were well acquainted with newer, more authentic assessment techniques, they continually came back to the low reading scores in the schools—scores that were continuing to go down. Although the administrators also questioned the validity of the measures, they were interested in raising the test scores.

The administrators expressed little trust in the teachers, although they often described individual teachers as "wonderful." They also described individual teachers as "problems." However, their generalizations about the teaching force were made from the negative examples not the positive ones. Their concept of change in teaching behavior was always one of changing to a program introduced by someone outside the classroom. The adminis-trators never explored individual change and development as a concept. In accord with the literature, they viewed major change as something that happened at the school level not at the individual teacher level. When I interjected a comment about voluntary change, there might or might not be a pause in the conversation, but it would move on as before. Individual teacher autonomy was not a consideration, although the administrators expressed some acceptance of the importance (but not the necessity) of making sure that a majority of teachers in a school wanted the change. Although the administrators planned and provided many short staff devel-opment activities for the district teachers, these were not perceived as major change efforts. For these administrators, major reform took place at the school level, involved all teachers in a school, and got them all to use the same instructional system. Interest focused almost solely on the nature of the reform rather than on the change process.

In the meantime, the school district had targeted four schools to receive staff development that would help them increase students' reading scores. The school staffs were given some choice in this process. Two schools dropped their *Reading Recovery* programs and adopted *Success for All* (Slavin et al., 1994), one decided on a self-esteem program, and one selected a modified inquiry approach after the staff had listened to Anders and me describe it. The administrators were very positive about *Success for All.* The rationale for adopting the program that seemed important to them was that every teacher in school would be involved in doing the same thing at the same time and that all students would be targeted.

I found this rationale to be interesting and compelling, particularly as we began to work in the inquiry school. We found that the teachers were deeply divided between those who used the whole-language approach and those who used approaches that were more structured with some phonics instruction, but never completely phonics. In some classrooms, the nature of the reading program was hard to describe, either by us or by the teachers. At one grade level, the teachers felt that they had been told to teach only to the whole group and that basal reading programs were not good. They had, therefore, developed elaborate worksheet exercises for their students that were used by all teachers at a given grade level. Students in this school could start out in a whole-language classroom in kindergarten, move to a highly structured, "semiphonics" program in grade 1, experience a workbook approach to reading instruction in grade 2, and shift into a literature-based whole-language program in grade 3. We were concerned that this dramatic lack of coherence was not very effective and perhaps detrimental for the low-achieving students in this school.

The questions that I continued to pursue after this experience are the following: (1) Is lack of coherence in approach to reading instruction across grade levels detrimental for the students? Or was the real problem that a number of the teachers had not developed an adequate program of reading instruction, whatever their approach? (2) If coherence is called for, what does this say about individual teacher autonomy? (3) To achieve coherence, do we need to import highly structured models of reading instruction such as *Success for All* and use the "directed development" model of staff development (Meyer, 1988)? To approach these questions, I looked into the literature on autonomy and empowerment.

INDIVIDUAL AUTONOMY AND EMPOWERMENT

The *new* form of staff development increases teachers' sense of individual autonomy and empowerment. Teachers in our study seemed to gain control over their teaching. This helped them adopt a reflective change orientation in which they were willing to continue to question what they do and the results of their practices, and experiment with new processes. These mental processes are thought of as good for teachers (Barksdale-Ladd & Thomas, 1996). Autonomy and empowerment are thought to produce thoughtful, confident teachers who are able to empower their students (Ayers, 1992; Fagan, 1989).

There are two approaches to the definitions of autonomy and empowerment. One focuses on organizational structural conditions that allow teachers freedom to do what they think is best (or "what they want to do," as described by many administrators). The second focuses on the nature of the experience for the individual and on mental activities. In much of the organizational literature, autonomy is defined as *freedom* or *liberty* (Johnson, 1991) of the individual, acting as a single entity. Conditions favoring this definition of autonomy are particularly prevalent in secondary schools. Pellegrin (1976) describes secondary teaching as "idiosyncratic specialization," and Cusick (1983) as "entrepreneurial teaching." There is little evidence of collective decision making in secondary schools (Little, 1991), and, as Corcoran (1991) suggests, without a collective approach, attempts at reform in secondary schools will probably not succeed.

The definition of autonomy that suggests freedom comes close to the concept of empowerment that is found in much of the literature on reform in the 1980s (Bachrach & Shedd, 1988; Lightfoot, 1986; Maeroff, 1988). Teachers were empowered by allowing them to participate in some of the decision-making processes of the school.

The sense of autonomy that Anders and I encountered in the reading instruction study, however, was not just one of *freedom*. It was closer to Deardon's (1975) conception that ties autonomy to activities of the mind.

> A person is autonomous . . . to the degree that what he thinks and does in important areas of his life cannot be explained without reference to his own activity of mind. That is to say, the explanation of why he thinks and acts as he does in these areas must include a reference to his own choices, deliberations, decisions, reflections, judgments, plannings or reasonings. (p. 63)

This more individual and mental definition of autonomy may also be seen in recent concepts of empowerment that include: confidence in the ability to make decisions (Barksdale-Ladd & Thomas, 1996) gained through knowledge of the teaching profession (Lichtenstein, McLaughlin, & Knudsen, 1992).

Autonomy and empowerment in teachers does not guarantee that teachers will make the most appropriate decisions. Deardon (1975) also points out that at least with the development of autonomy in children we cannot avoid risk and error. And, of course, this is probably the greatest fear about the development of autonomy in teachers. A conscious choice that an autonomous teacher makes may be ineffective or worse for her students. Autonomy and sense of control does not guarantee the *right* or a common approach—which is one of the ambiguous elements of an inquiry approach to staff development. Giving teachers control over the direction of change may lead teachers in many different and uncontrollable directions. This possibility may frighten school district administrators, just as sharing curriculum control with students is unacceptable to some teachers.

Perhaps autonomy with accountability is the answer to this dilemma. But should that be individual or collective accountability, or both? The school district administrators with whom I worked were looking beyond the accountability of the individual teacher to that of the school. This relates, in part, to how the newspapers and other policy levels look at test scores. However, there is a sound educational rationale for such an approach. After all, a student travels though many classrooms in a schooling career, and the nature of that longitudinal experience is important. Thus, although accountability attached to individual autonomy may be useful, it is perhaps more important to consider accountability at the student level over time. One way to do this is to look at cross-sectional school-level data, although this is not completely congruent with longitudinal student data. But does an increase in accountability affect individual autonomy; and does the combination affect student achievement?

Smylie, Lazarus, and Brownlee-Conyer's (1996) longitudinal study of the relationship between teacher participation in school-level decision making and instructional outcomes has shed some light on the teacher autonomy and accountability tradeoff. They found that in schools that implemented a well-managed, participative decision-making process, the teachers' sense of individual autonomy (defined as *freedom*) decreased, whereas their perception of being held accountable increased. Further, student achievement increased in these schools.

Does this mean that we should move to directed staff development programs that decrease the potential for individual autonomy and increase accountability? I feel compelled to resist, primarily because of the long-term goals of staff development programs. Is there no approach to staff development that brings teachers in a school together to provide some consistency for the students, yet preserves and encourages the sense of reflection, an orientation to change, and a feeling of autonomy?

COLLECTIVE AUTONOMY:
A COMMUNITY OF PRACTICE

The literature that may help us out focuses on community. For one can think of the school as a community of practice (or learning), particularly if practice is defined in MacIntyre's (1981) terms. He suggests that practice is "any coherent and complex form of socially established cooperative human activity," which aims at achieving the standards defined by the activity (p. 175). The concept of *practice,* then, can only be thought of within a community. As Pendlebury (1990) points out, MacIntyre is a strong proponent of the position that considers communities of practice as genuine communities. Further, he stresses the social nature of the individual: "We are never more (and sometimes less) than the co-authors of our own narratives (p. 213)."

Pendlebury then considers what these approaches mean for the teachers in a school and suggests that the pursuit of individual "liberty as license" (i.e., "I have the right to do what I feel I should in this class") can be detrimental to students and the profession. On the other hand, a concept of independence may be beneficial to the community. However, independence, in the sense suggested by Pendlebury, suggests that members of a community are granted equal respect and concern. And this requires that there is an agreed-upon conception of the good life. Thus the consideration of autonomy should be thought of within a community of practice in which there is "ongoing critical discussions of the goods, standards and procedures which is [sic] necessary for a thriving practice" (Pendlebury, 1990, p. 274).[2]

The important concept, here, is that of critical discussions. We do not want to eliminate autonomy and the sense of control. At the same time, we want a group of teachers to understand the nature of the schooling experience from the standpoint of a student traveling through the school, not just a student in an individual teacher's classroom. And we want them to talk with each other about this journey, as well as about goals for the students and the teaching practices in use. There should be some degree of understanding of the various ways in which one's fellow teachers define the goals for the students, and although it may not be necessary to establish one program of reading within the school, teachers should be aware of and hopefully respect other approaches and help students in the transition from one approach to another.

Thus what we are looking for is a staff development program that permits the development of individual autonomy but also fosters a community of learners within the school. It is possible that such a program would lead to somewhat more eclectic approaches to the teaching of reading. As Throne (1994) suggests, focusing on the needs of individual children in her classrooms has led her to a process in which she employs practices from several approaches. She is not suggesting that the theories are useless in practice; but rather that one theory alone does not reflect the realities of a classroom. She states:

> In over twenty-five years of teaching, I have yet to find one single approach that meets all children's needs. What I have learned, however, is that whatever method or approach I use, its problems must be

examined along with its advantages. . . . Examining both the advantages and the problems of different approaches helps teachers to critique and evaluate how the programs they create and those they are required to implement affect children's learning. Searching for the single, correct answer that has no problems or limitations takes classroom teachers from one curriculum reform to another and back again. A dialogue between teachers and theorists that reflects the advantages, problems, and limitations of different approaches and theories would benefit teachers more than a dialogue that pushes the pendulum from one opposing viewpoint to another. (pp. 204–205)

One would expect that teachers who are working together in a school to focus their programs on the longitudinal experiences of their students may develop quite eclectic approaches in their reading programs.

Perhaps this practitioner's sense of the ways of bringing theory into the dialogical conversations that constitute the newer forms of staff development is one means of helping teachers achieve an individual sense of autonomy with a feeling of accountability to the child's learning that extends beyond the grade level that she or he teaches to the schooling received by the child by the teacher in conjunction with her or his colleagues.

CONCLUSION

Staff development is often viewed as the most important element in a reform process. Ultimately, it is the teachers who must change if a reform is to take effect. Two forms of staff development were described in this chapter, each with a research base that suggests effective characteristics of the processes. One form works with individual teachers on problems identified by the teacher and staff developer, and the other sets content and outcome goals prior to the commencement of the staff development.

What form should a school district adopt if it wishes to increase the reading achievement of its students? In the case described in this chapter, the school district chose a staff development program that attempted to standardize the behaviors of the teachers as they were teaching reading. The program was voluntary but at the school level. All teachers in a given school underwent the reform process. Questions related to this process concern the possible loss of feelings of autonomy and empowerment on the part of the teachers and the length of time the changes will last.

At the same time, this analysis questioned the newer form of staff development that is individualistic and may be effective for students in a given classroom but may not provide the necessary coherence for students as they pass from one grade level to the next. This coherence may be particularly important in the development of reading ability and for students who have particular difficulty in developing these abilities. The analysis then addressed whether it is possible to generate a staff development approach that avoids the externally mandated standardization of a teaching approach while it provides students with grade-to-grade coherence in program.

The suggestion arrived at is that the individualistic and empowering form of staff development be extended to the group level that involves all teachers in a given school. This form of staff development would allow for individual autonomy, but autonomy as thought of within a community of learners. In such a community, individual members are granted equal respect and concern, but the focus is on developing and agreeing upon the longitudinal goals and concerns for students as they pass through the grade levels within the school.

It is also acknowledged that such a program may lead to a more eclectic approach to the teaching of reading. As Thorn (1994) points out, in meeting the needs of all students in the class, she requires a variety of approaches that stem from different theoretical frames. It may also be the case that in bringing teachers together to focus on the longitudinal nature, expectations and standards of their students' experiences may lead to what may be viewed as a theoretically eclectic program. But the program that evolves from such a process, if it remains reflectively fluid, may be the best program for the particular student body within the specific context.

NOTES

1. Practical reasoning has been described by Fenstermacher (1979) as reasoning that leads to an action. Practical arguments are constructed and reconstructed on the basis of the reasoning used in an action. In practice, this involves the use of videotapes of teachers in their classroom that are viewed and discussed by the teacher and staff developer. See Fenstermacher (1994) for a thorough description of the process.

2. Deep concerns have been expressed about a communitarian approach. Anyone who has grown up in an extended family understands the plusses and minuses with respect to issues of power and control. Noddings (1996) points to the potential problems of building communities in school and elsewhere, including the type of coercion that comes about without violence: "Often in the name of equality, it presses for uniformity, common aspirations, a white-collar identity, and the suppression of difference" (p. 267).

REFERENCES

Acquarelli, K., & Mumme, J. (1996). A renaissance in mathematics educational reform. *Phi Delta Kappan, 77*(7), 478–484.

Anders, P., & Richardson, V. (1991). Research directions: Staff development that empowers teachers' reflection and enhances instruction. *Language Arts, 68,* 316–321

Anyon, J. (1994). Teacher development and reform in an inner-city school. *Teachers College Record, 96,* 14–31.

Ayers, W. (1992). Work that is real: Why teachers should be empowered. In G. Hess, Jr. (Ed.), *Empowering teachers and parents. School restructuring through the eyes of anthropologists* (pp. 13–28). Westport, CT: Bergin & Garvey.

Bachrach, S. B., & Shedd, J. B. (1988). Power and empowerment: The constraining myth and emerging structures of teacher unionism in an age of reform. In J. Hannaway & R. Crowson (Eds.), *The politics of reforming school administration* (1988 Yearbook of the Politics of Education Association, pp. 139–160). New York: Falmer.

Barksdale-Ladd, M. A., & Thomas, K. F. (1996). The development of empowerment in reading instruction in eight elementary teachers. *Teaching and Teacher Education, 12*(2), 161–178.

Berliner, D., & Biddle, B. (1995). *The manufactured crisis.* New York: Addison-Wesley.

Blumenfeld, P. C., Kracjik, J. S., Marx, R. W., & Soloway, E. (1994). Lessons learned: How collaboration helped middle-grade science teachers learn project-based instruction. *Elementary School Journal, 95*(5), 539–551.

Bos, C., & Anders, P. (1994). The study of student change. In V. Richardson (Ed.), *Teacher change and the staff development process: A case in reading instruction* (pp. 181–198). New York: Teachers College Press.

Chin, R., & Benne, K. D. (1969). General strategies for effecting changes in human systems. In W. G. Bennis, K. D. Benne, & R. Chin (Eds.), *The planning of change* (2nd ed.). New York: Holt, Rinehart & Winston.

Corcoran, T. (1991). Schoolwork: Perspectives on workplace reform in public schools. In M. McLaughlin, J. Talbert, & N. Bascia (Eds.), *The contexts of teaching in secondary schools* (pp. 142–166). New York: Teachers College Press.

Cruickshank, D., & Metcalf, K. K. (1990). Training within teacher preparation. In W. Houston (Ed.), *Handbook of research on teacher education* (pp. 469–497). New York: Macmillan.

Cusick, P. A. (1983). *The egalitarian ideal and the American high school: Studies of three schools.* New York: Longman.

Deardon, R. (1975). Autonomy and education. In R. Deardon, P. Hirst, & R. Peters (Eds.), *Education and reason* (pp. 58–75). London: Routledge & Kegan Paul.

Devaney, K. (1977). *Essays on teachers' centers.* San Francisco: Far West Laboratory for Educational Research and Development.

Fagan, W. (1989). Empowered students: Empowered teachers. *The Reading Teacher, 42,* 572–578.

Fenstermacher, G. D. (1979). A philosophical consideration of recent research on teacher effectiveness. In L. S. Shulman (Ed.), *Review of research in education* (Vol. 6, pp. 157–185). Itasca, IL: Peacock.

Fenstermacher, G. D. (1994). The place of practical arguments in the education of teachers. In V. Richardson (Ed.), *Teacher change and the staff development process: A case in reading instruction* (pp. 23–42). New York: Teachers College Press.

Fullan, M. (1990). Staff development, innovation and institutional development. In B. Joyce (Ed.), *Changing school culture through staff development* (pp. 3–25). Alexandria, VA: Association for Supervision and Curriculum Development.

Gallagher, M., Goudvis, A., & Pearson, P. D. (1988). Principles of organizational change. In S. J. Samuels & P. D. Pearson (Eds.), *Changing school reading programs* (pp. 11–39). Newark, DE: International Reading Association.

Goldenberg, C., & Gallimore, R. (1991). Changing teaching takes more than a one-shot workshop. *Educational Leadership, 49*(3), 69–72.

Griffin, G. (1986). Clinical teacher education. In J. Hoffman & S. Edwards (Eds.), *Reality and reform in clinical teacher education* (pp. 1–24). New York: Random House.

Johnson, S. M. (1991). The primacy and potential of high school departments. In M. McLaughlin, J. Talbert, & N. Bascia (Eds.), *The contexts of teaching in secondary schools* (pp. 167–186). New York: Teachers College Press.

Joyce, B. (1981). *Guaranteeing carryover from workshops to classrooms.* Invited address, University of Oregon, Eugene, OR.

Katz, L. (1979). *Helping others learn to teach: Some principles and techniques for inservice educators.* Urbana, IL: ERIC Clearinghouse on Early Childhood Education.

Lester, N., & Onore, C. (1990). *Learning change.* Portsmouth, NH: Boynton/Cook.

Lichtenstein, G., McLaughlin, M., & Knudsen, J. (1992). Teacher empowerment and professional knowledge. In A. Lieberman (Ed.), *The changing contexts of teaching. 91st yearbook of the National Society for the Study of Education* (pp. 37–58). Chicago: University of Chicago Press.

Lightfoot, S. L. (1986). On goodness in schools: Themes of empowerment. *Peabody Journal of Education, 63,* 9.

Little, J. W. (1991). Conditions of professional development in secondary schools. In M. McLaughlin, J. Talbert, & N. Bascia (Eds.), *The contexts of teaching in secondary schools* (pp. 187–223). New York: Teachers College Press.

Loucks-Horsley, S., Harding, C., Arbuckle, M., Murray, L., Dubea, C., & Williams, M. (1987). *Continuing to learn: A guidebook for teacher development.* Andover, ME: Regional Laboratory for Educational Improvement of the Northeast and Islands/National Staff Development Council.

MacIntyre, A. (1981). *After virtue. A study in moral theory.* London: Duckworth.

McLaughlin, M. W. (1991). Enabling professional development: What have we learned. In A. Lieberman & L. Miller (Eds.), *Staff development for education in the 90's* (pp. 61–82). New York: Teachers College Press.

Mearoff, G. I. (1988). *The empowerment of teachers: Overcoming the crisis of confidence.* New York: Teachers College Press.

Meyer, L. (1988). Research on implementation: What seems to work. In S. J. Samuels & P. D. Pearson (Eds.), *Changing school reading programs* (pp. 41–57). Newark, DE: International Reading Association.

Noddings, N. (1996). On community. *Educational Theory, 46,* 245–267.

Pellegrin, R. (1976). Schools as work settings. In R. Dubin (Ed.), *Handbook of work, organizations, and society* (pp. 343–373). Chicago: Rand McNally.

Pendlebury, S. (1990). Community, liberty and the practice of teaching. *Studies in Philosophy and Education, 10,* 257–263.

Placier, P., & Hamilton, M. L. (1994). Schools as contexts: A complex relationship. In V. Richardson (Ed.), *Teacher change and the staff development process: A case in reading instruction* (pp. 135–159). New York: Teachers College Press.

Rich, Y. (1990). Ideological impediments to instructional innovation: The case of cooperative learning. *Teaching and Teacher Education, 6*(1), 81–91.

Richardson, V. (1994a). Conducting research on practice. *Educational Researcher, 23*(5), 5–10.

Richardson, V. (1994b). Standards and assessments: What are their educative potential? In M. Dietz, V. Richardson, & P. D. Pearson (Eds.), *Setting standards and educating teachers* (pp. 15–36). Washington, DC: American Association of Colleges of Teacher Education.

Richardson, V., & Anders, P. (1994). A theory of change. In V. Richardson (Ed.), *Teacher change and the staff development process: A case of reading instruction* (pp. 199–216). New York: Teachers College Press.

Richardson, V., & Hamilton, M. L. (1994). The practical argument staff development process. In V. Richardson (Ed.), *Teacher change and the staff development process: A case in reading instruction* (pp. 109–134). New York: Teachers College Press.

Rubin, L. (1978). *Inservice education of teachers: Trends, processes, and prescriptions.* Boston: Allyn and Bacon.

Shachar, H. (1996). Developing new traditions in secondary schools: A working model for organizational and instructional change. *Teachers College Record, 97,* 549–568.

Showers, B., Joyce, B., & Bennett, B. (1987). Synthesis of research on staff development: A framework for future study and state-of-art analysis. *Educational Leadership, 45*(3), 77–87.

Slavin, R. E., Madden, N. A., Dolan, L. J., Wasik, B., Ross, S. M., & Smith, L. (1994). "Whenever and wherever we choose": The replication of "Success for All." *Phi Delta Kappan, 75,* 639–647.

Smylie, M., Lazarus, V., & Brownlee-Conyers, J. (1996). Instructional outcomes of school-based participative decision-making. *Educational Evaluation and Policy Analysis, 18,* 181–198.

Sparks, D., & Loucks-Horsley, S. (1990). Models of staff development. In W. R. Houston (Ed.), *Handbook of research on teacher education* (pp. 234–250). New York: Macmillan.

Stallings, J., & Krasavage, E. (1986). Program implementation and student achievement in a four-year Madeline Hunter follow-through project. *Elementary School Journal, 87,* 117–138.

Throne, J. (1994). Living with the pendulum: The complex world of teaching. *Harvard Educational Review, 64,* 195–208.

Tierney, R., Tucker, D., Gallagher, M., Crismore, A., & Pearson, P. D. (1988). The Metcalf Project: A teacher-researcher collaboration. In S. J. Samuels & P. D. Pearson (Eds.), *Changing school reading programs* (pp. 207–226). Newark, DE: International Reading Association.

Valdez, A. (1992). *Changes in teachers' beliefs, understandings, and practices concerning reading comprehension through the use of practical arguments: A follow-up study.* Unpublished dissertation, University of Arizona, Tucson, AZ.

Ward, B. (1985). Teacher development: The challenge of the future. In S. Hord, S. O'Neal, & M. Smith (Eds.), *Beyond the looking glass* (pp. 283–312). Austin: Research and Development Center for Teacher Education, University of Texas.

Wood, T., Cobb, P., & Yakel, E. (1991). Change in teaching mathematics: A case study. *American Educational Research Journal, 28,* 587–616.

CHAPTER FIFTEEN

The Rhetoric of All, the Reality of Some, and the Unmistakable Smell of Mortality

EDWARD J. KAMEENUI
University of Oregon

The Wingspread Conference was about learning to read, and as such, it was about reading and understanding words. Although Voltaire once remarked that "Language is very difficult to put into words," words are all we have. In the last 10 years, many people have exchanged "words," even harsh, sometimes rancorous ones on the topic of learning to read. Such disagreements are expected, because as G. K. Chesterton pointed out, "What is the good of words if they aren't important enough to quarrel over? Why do we choose one word more than another if there isn't any difference between them?" As one who majored in English as an undergraduate and who has had serious midnight skirmishes with Euripides, Shakespeare, Keats, Dickinson, and others, I find it difficult to get at the meaning of things without first grappling with the words. After all, the words come first.

For the purposes of this chapter, I pick on just one word, a small one at that, but its size is enormously deceptive. The word is *all*. *All* is a popular word these days for many people, including educators, politicians, policy makers, stakeholders in the public and private sectors, and professional organizations seeking to give guidance to their membership on standards of student and teacher performance.

Why focus on *all*? Focusing on the word *all* is etymologically dangerous because it is a word that has acquired penumbral first amendment rights. It is a word imbued with the right to enlarge itself to fit the context of its linguistic neighborhood and to enhance its lexical associates, which include words such as *freedom, equality,* and *liberty,* or strings of words such as "All men are created equal" and phrases such as "The readiness is all." The truth is that when we use *all,* we don't really mean *all,* and we don't expect *all* to take *all* seriously, but if some or even a few are listening carefully and are serious about *all,* then *all* could really come to mean *all.*

So, why pick on *all?* The goal of the Wingspread Conference according to the letter of invitation, was "a national agenda for the language arts" and an agenda that offers a "scholarly treatment" of the issues and speaks "clearly to policymakers and practical educators." I commend the conference's organizers, Dick Anderson, Jean Osborn, David Pearson, and Blouke Carus, for striking the right focus, one that is long overdue. A national agenda, I assume, is an agenda for *all* children, *all* teachers, *all* schools, and *all* states to use as a framework for making, as the letter of invitation indicated, "reasoned decisions about reading and writing instruction." Ah yes, *instruction.* There is a word that has been "missing in action" in the last few years. I will come back and grapple with that word later.

Well, *all* is not well in schools these days, at least not for *all* children, and many if not *all* politicians, parents, and educators, are calling for not only a better education, but a better education for *all* children. As I see it, schools are faced with at least three immediate and alarming challenges: (1) To teach students who are more diverse in their learning characteristics and literacy needs than ever before (Hodgkinson, 1991, 1992); (2) to respond meaningfully to the popular and persistent call by people in professional, political, and educational realms to educate *all* children; (3) to demonstrate to the public that the education of all children is not merely a "vision" but is warranted and attainable; that is, we have the means to do it; we simply need the will and the right contingencies.

In the remainder of this chapter, I explore, however briefly, these alarming challenges: (1) the learning and literacy diversity of *all*; (2) the call for educating *all*—or more narrowly for our purposes ensuring high levels of reading achievement for *all* children by the end of third grade; and finally, (3) the challenge of designing an educational system that meets the first two challenges head on and with reasonable success. To address these challenges, I explore two critical principles that are essential to the design of an education for *all* children.

First, we need to gain reasonable agreement on the professional knowledge base that determines how best to teach all children. How do we best teach beginning reading? Such agreement requires that we grapple with the criteria for determining what comprises that professional knowledge base. What model of evidence is required before we determine that a practice is effective, cost-efficient, sustainable, and practical for teachers to use with all children? Without this knowledge base and the scientific evidence to support it, we will have no basis for improving the profession (Carnine, 1996).

Second, we need to embrace and insist upon a proactive accountability system (Carnine, 1996). Too often research-based practice is readily supplanted by what is popular and fashionable but unwarranted by the scientific evidence (Kameenui, 1993). Moreover, in the absence of proactive accountability that is the hallmark of most professions, we place in enormous jeopardy the public trust that is public education and the lives of all children who, every day of the week, desperately count on its effectiveness.

THE LEARNING AND LITERACY DIVERSITY OF *ALL*

The conditions facing schools are changing dramatically, and the educational and instructional challenges implied by these conditions are potentially paralyzing. Over the past 20 years, the proportion of diverse learners in America's schools—children of poverty, students with disabilities, students for whom English is not the first language (Hodgkinson, 1991, 1992)—has grown dramatically. The states whose populations are growing most rapidly are states with a high percentage of minorities, especially minority youth (Hodgkinson, 1992). These changing societal trends are summarized in Table 15.1.

A review of these demographics suggests that the playing field is not level for many of the children we educate today. These children (1) live in greater levels of poverty than any time in modern history; (2) enter school with extraordinary experiential differences; (3) have school performances that grow more negatively discrepant from their average-achieving peers over time; and (4) require higher levels of education to compete in a global, information-driven society (Hodgkinson, 1992).

The importance of how a child's early family experience translates into vocabulary knowledge, motivation, and intellectual confidence is revealed in a book entitled, _Meaningful Differences in the Everyday Experience of Young American Children_ (1995) by Hart and Risley of the University of Kansas. The researchers' goal was to document what happens in children's early experience that could account for the intractable differences in the rates of vocabulary growth among 4-year-olds. These researchers observed 42 families for 1 hour each month for almost 2½ years to learn about what went on in homes with 1- and 2-year-old children learning to talk. They found that the vocabulary differences among children from professional families, working-class families, and welfare families at the time of school entry were bigger, more intractable, and more important than they had originally predicted. In simple terms, they found that the children from welfare families did not hear as many words as children from professional and working-class families and that the words they did hear were not very encouraging or supportive of their learning. For example, the average child in a welfare family heard half as many words (616 words per hour) as the

TABLE 15.1. Demographics and Societal Trends

Schools are facing a period of rising enrollments after a long period of decline (Indicator 38, *The Condition of Education 1995*).

Many more students speak a language other than English at home and have difficulty speaking English, a likely indication that even more students may have difficulty reading and writing English (Hodgkinson, 1992).

Many children live in poverty (21% or 15.3 million), and these children typically live in neighborhoods and attend school together (Indicator 44, *The Condition of Education 1995*).

In 1970, there were 6.7 million single parents; in 1992, there were 15 million. Conversely, the " 'Norman Rockwell' family—a working father, housewife mother, and two children of public school age—was SIX percent of all households for most of the decade" (Hodgkinson, 1992, p. 3).

During the 1980s, the poverty rate for children increased 11%, reaching 17.9% of all children by 1989. By 1993, the level had increased to 23%, "one of the highest youth poverty rates in the 'developed' world and has shown little inclination to decline" (Hodgkinson, 1993, p. 620).

Two of seven children come from homes in which English is not the first language (Hodgkinson, 1992).

The fastest growing demographic group in the country from 1980 to 1990 was the prison population, which increased 139% with recent rates estimated at 300%. The United States has the highest prison population in the world (Hodgkinson, 1992).

Eighty-two percent of America's prisoners are high school dropouts. At about $40,000 per prisoner per year, taxpayers spend roughly five times as much money to house a prisoner as they do to educate a child (Hodgkinson, 1992).

Every 59 seconds, a baby is born to a teen mother. Every 30 seconds, a baby is born into poverty. Every 5 seconds of the school day, a student drops out of public school (Children's Defense Fund, 1992).

---

average child in a working-class family (1,251 words per hour) and one third the words of the average child in a professional family (2,153 words per hour). Hart and Risley concluded that "Just to provide an average welfare child with an amount of weekly language experience equal to that of an average working-class child would require 41 hours per week of out-of-home experience as rich in words addressed to the child as that in an average professional home" (p. 201).

THE CALL TO EDUCATE *ALL*

There appears to be strong consensus that the bottom 35% of America's students have serious educational problems, which will mean serious economic problems for their generation. Their performance, according to the educational demographer Hodgkinson (1992), is "truly awful" (p. 8). Because of the increasing importance of education to the U.S. economy, national leaders are demanding more not only from the highest-performing students, but from all students, including students with diverse learning needs and disabilities. Moreover, higher-order thinking and mastery of content-area subjects are expected of all students. As Resnick (1987) has stated, "Although it is not new to include thinking, problem solving, and reasoning in someone's school curriculum, it is new to include it in *everyone's curriculum*" (author's emphasis, p. 7). The increased expectations for diverse learners are manifested in national curriculum outcome standards and are found in Table 15.2.

The reality about standards is that they are absolutely meaningless in the absence of contingencies or, in the current terminology, accountability. They are also meaningless in the absence of effective means for achieving them. Standards inspire vision but do not require that schools, teachers, and publishers deliver the kind of curriculum and instruction required for all students to meet the standards (Porter, 1993).

The demands to raise expectations for all students, including those with diverse learning needs and disabilities are coming from advocates, educators, and the federal law (e.g., the Individuals with Disabilities Education Act, or IDEA) reauthorization mandates access to the general education curriculum. When individuals with disabilities are included in the equation of educational change and reform, however, the challenge of increasing the performance levels of *all* children is absolutely chilling. The U.S. Department of Education's Report to Congress (1995) on the educa-

---

TABLE 15.2. Increased Expectations for Diverse Learners

- *National Council of Teachers of Mathematics*: "We believe that *all* students can benefit from an opportunity to study the core curriculum specified in the Standards" (Commission on Standards for School Mathematics, 1989, p. 259).

- *The National Center for History in the Schools:* "A reformed social studies curriculum should be required of *all* students in common, regardless of their 'track' or further vocational and educational plans" (National Center for History in the Schools, 1992, p. 9).

- *The National Science Education Standards:* "The commitment to science for *all* implies inclusion not only of those who traditionally have received encouragement and opportunity to pursue science but of women and girls, all racial and ethnic groups, students with disabilities, and those with limited proficiency in English" (National Science Education Standards, 1993, p. 1).

- *The Standards Projects for English Language Arts*: "promote equality of educational opportunity and higher academic achievement for *all* students" (The Standards Projects for English Language Arts, 1993, p. 2).

- *Goals 2000*: "Challenging national performance standards that define what *all* students should know and be able to do in core subject areas such as science, math, history, geography, language, and the arts, and support local reform efforts to make those standards a reality in every classroom" (Goals 2000, p. 2).

tion of the country's children with disabilities reveals the magnitude of this challenge (see Table 15.3).

If we narrow the goal to obtaining high levels of reading achievement for *all* children (not *some* or *many*, but all) by the end of third grade, the challenge is within reach but no less demanding. As Adams (1990) points out, "If low-achieving students can be brought up to grade level within the first 3 years of school, their reading performance tends not to revert but to stay at grade level thenceforth." The downside is that "If we fail to bring students' reading to grade level within those first few years, the likelihood of their ever catching up is slim, even with extra funding and special programs" (pp. 27–28). For example, in a longitudinal study of students with poor word identification skills in the third grade, Felton and Wood (1992) found that most students failed to significantly improve their basic reading skills by the end of eighth grade.

ATTAINING AN EDUCATION FOR ALL CHILDREN

More children with diverse learning needs and disabilities are being educated in general education than ever before (Fuchs & Fuchs, 1994; McLeskey & Pacchiano, 1994). Estimates of the range of instructional levels within general education classrooms are already high, with more than five grade levels represented per classroom in some schools (Jenkins, Jewell, Leceister, Jenkins, & Troutner, as cited in Fuchs & Fuchs, 1994). How are teachers currently accommodating this range of instructional variation? Typically, teachers and classrooms in general education are *not* prepared to address the learning and curricular needs that diverse learners bring to classrooms (Baker & Zigmond, 1990; Moats, 1994). Extensive observa-

TABLE 15.3. Demographics of Individuals with Disabilities

- More than 5.4 million children with disabilities, or 7.7% of the resident population from birth to age 21, received special education services during the 1993–1994 school year.

- The number of children and youth who receive special education has grown every year since a national count was initiated in 1976, with an overall increase of 39% since the 1976–1977 school year.

- Ninety-four percent of all school-age children receiving special education are reported under four disability categories: (1) learning disabilities (52.4%), (2) speech and language impairment (22.2%), (3) mental retardation (10.9%), and (4) emotional disturbance (8.3%).

- The vast majority—approximately 90%—of school-age children receiving special education have "mild disabilities."

- The "typical" child receiving special education in the United States is a 9-year-old boy with learning disabilities who spends part of each school day in the regular classroom and part in a resource room.

tional and self-report data indicate that the type and quantity of instructional adaptations in general education classrooms are insufficient to effect "optimal growth" for many low-performing students in general education (Fuchs, Fuchs, Hamlett, Phillips, & Karns, 1995; Zigmond et al., 1995).

Recently we conducted a 10-week observational study of 20 first-grade classrooms involving 22 teachers and 10 elementary schools in three public school districts (Chard & Kameenui, 1997). We found that 65 first-graders who were not independent word readers, and who were at-risk for reading failure, responded to the teacher, on average, one third as often as did students receiving a combination of general education and Chapter 1 instruction. These students responded one-fourth as often as did students receiving reading instruction only in Chapter 1 classrooms. Not surprisingly, results of stepwise regression analyses revealed that pretest scores on measures of oral reading fluency, phonemic segmentation, nonsense word reading fluency, and the word attack subtest of the Woodcock Reading Mastery Test accounted for the largest amount of variance. The finding that entry-level performance best predicts exit-level performance is simply unacceptable for children who are already far behind when they first walk through the school door. Clearly the majority of students with diverse learning needs in general education classrooms rely on the same teachers and the same technology, educational media, and print materials as their achieving peers. Unfortunately, these aspects of education do not serve them well.

As I understand it, as an adjective, *all* means *the whole amount or number* (e.g., waited *all* day, beyond *all* doubt); as a noun it means *every one of, the greatest possible, entire, complete, each and every,* and *without exception* (e.g., *all* children); as a pronoun it means *all persons concerned,* everything (e.g., *all* are agreed); and as an adverb it means *entirely* (e.g., dressed *all* in white). When we call for educating *all* students, as we do in *Goals 2000* (1994), and in the full sweep of standards called for by the National Council for Teachers of Mathematics (1989), the National Center for History in the Schools (1992), the National Science Education Standards (1993), and the Standards for English Language Arts (see Table 2), what are we saying? Are we issuing a call to educate every single, individual student in public schools today; that is, all 44,034,416 students currently served by the 85,393 elementary and secondary schools in the United States (U.S. Department of Education, 1995)? Is that what we mean by *all*?

Let me share with you one example of *all*. The data reported in Figures 15.1 and 15.2 are fluency data that were obtained in the fall of 1996 and represent *all* students in the sixth grade at one middle school in Oregon (Baker, Simmons, Smith, Thomas, & Kameenui, 1996). Students read two passages, one literature-based and one expository from a social studies textbook commonly used in sixth grade. As indicated in Figures 15.1 and 15.2, the distributions appear very normal. In other words, there is a fairly smooth spread of scores from low to high, with more scores in the middle and fewer scores at the extremes. Students' scores were consistent across the two passages. The correlation between scores on the first and second passage was above .90, which supports the reliability or stability of the scores.

According to my colleague Scott Baker, who is immersed in reading fluency research, most of this research examines students through the fifth grade. Approximately 120 words per minute is his best guess about an adequate fluency rate for sixth-grade students in the fall who are reading in grade-level material. He notes that many reading fluency experts believe the fluency rate for sixth-grade students should be higher, and that even students reading at this level will benefit from an intensive reading intervention. When you examine the graphs in Figures 15.1 and 15.2 and select students in the bottom *five intervals,* you will identify between 100 and 125 students who are reading less than 100 words per minute. In other words, of all the sixth-grade students in this particular middle school, 47%, or nearly *half,* are at reading fluency levels below that expected of them.

Here's the surprise. These data are from one of the highest SES schools in the state of Oregon, and the students are well beyond the "learning to read" stage and well entrenched in the "reading to learn" stage of schooling. Students who read less than 100 words per minute require serious attention, or in Stanovich's words, a "surgical strike." The strike,

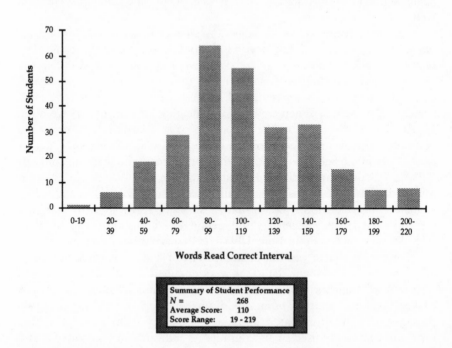

Words Read Correct Interval

Summary of Student Performance	
N =	268
Average Score:	110
Score Range:	19 - 219

FIGURE 15.1. Sixth-grade reading fluency data for passage 1: Literature book.

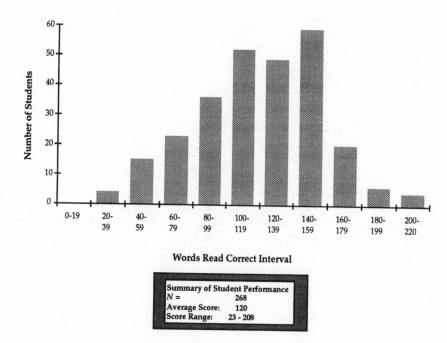

FIGURE 15.2. Sixth-grade reading fluency data for passage 2: Social studies text-book.

as converging evidence suggests, must ensure that all students acquire fundamental reading fluency by grade 3.

What is required then to ensure that all students reach the appropriate reading fluency level, or for that matter, any targeted criterion level of performance? Whose problem is it? Is it the responsibility of all sixth-grade teachers, or just the reading specialists? What school-level system is re-quired to ensure that the selected intervention is effective, reliable, cost-effective, efficient, and has a high probability of correcting the problem for all students? What is required to bring teachers who really don't believe in fluency, assessment, or even reading *instruction* on board? What kind of building-level leadership is required to make a commitment to student performance and to reading-instruction practices that are effective and have a high probability of succeeding with these students? What kind of accountability system is required so that parents are assured their children's instructional needs are being addressed and teachers are rewarded, not punished, for their efforts?

These questions suggest that the problem of reading instruction for *all* is a problem that requires a fundamental reformulation of how educators think about student performance and the roles of teachers and schools. It is not a problem that can be addressed through brief inservice training but, rather, requires a reformulation of school-building goals and a schoolwide commitment to the goals. Grappling with this problem requires vigilant and tenacious leadership at the school-building and district levels, allocation of resources to support the goals, and a results-driven evaluation system that holds everyone at the school-building and district level responsible for satisfactory student achievement.

READING PRACTICE THAT IS VALID, TRUSTWORTHY, AND WARRANTED

The first question that Wingspread Conference participants were asked to address is, "What is the agreed-upon common knowledge base for the teaching and learning of reading and writing?" Whatever the agreement, a professional knowledge base must have as its foundation the warranted evidence—evidence that is coercive, substantial, trustworthy, valid, and publicly defensible (Carnine, 1996; Hanson, 1958; Larrabee, 1964). There is growing consensus that research-based practices are pivotal to improving learning outcomes, not just for diverse students and students with disabilities, but all students.

A recent report by the Education Commission of the States (1995) noted:

> States must decide how to respond to these forces with reforms that work: that is, those that have real and measurable improvements in student performance. However, few of the reforms initiated during the past decade have been subjected to rigorous research. And the existing evidence . . . is often inconclusive and incomplete. (p. 3, emphasis added)

The Education Commission of the States report also identifies how to bring about such improvements:

> Reforms aimed at changing what goes on in the classroom—improving the teaching and learning process, strengthening the interaction between students and teachers, enhancing the curriculum—have strong, positive effects on student performance. Reforms aimed primarily at changing how adults interact with one another—reshaping school governance, for example—have substantially less impact on student performance. (p. 21)

The second question that Wingspread Conference participants were asked to address is, "What are the essential components of reading and writing instruction in American Schools?" My colleagues and I at the National Center to Improve the Tools of Educators (NCITE) at the University of Oregon recently conducted a review of the research from 1985 to 1996 on the design of beginning reading instruction (Simmons & Kameenui, in press). In this review, we extracted foundation concepts or "big ideas" common to the architecture of beginning reading instruction for students with diverse learning needs (see Adams, 1990; Ehri, 1991; Juel, 1991; Stanovich, 1986; Vellutino, 1991; Wagner & Torgesen, 1987). We use big ideas as the first and primary instructional design principle to refer to a set of unifying curricular activities necessary for successful beginning reading instruction. Such curricular activities are instructional anchors that, when established, provide learners with enormous capacity to identify printed words and translate the alphabetic code into meaningful language. The three big ideas we identified are (1) phonological awareness, (2) alphabetic understanding, and (3) automaticity with the code. These big ideas are sequenced from simple to more complex with phonological awareness prerequisite to alphabetic understanding and alphabetic understanding fundamental to automaticity with the code. The big ideas also represent the instructional priorities for diverse learners; they are the essential components of reading instruction. Because they are essential, we must give top instructional priority to each of these big ideas.

Phonological Awareness

One of the most compelling and well-established findings in the research on beginning reading is the important relationship between phonological awareness and reading acquisition (see reviews by Adams, 1990; Ehri, 1991; Felton & Pepper, 1995; Juel, 1991; Wagner & Torgesen, 1987; Snider, 1995; Spector, 1995; Stanovich, 1994). Central to phonological awareness is the "ability to analyze and synthesize the sound structure of words" (Spector, 1995, p. 8). In other words, children must come to know (i.e., become aware) that words are made up of individual sounds (i.e., phonemes). In addition, children must come to know that when the individual sounds are combined in specific ways, they make up words. Moreover, they must recognize that the same sounds are found in many different words (e.g., s in sit has the same sound as the s in miss). The research we reviewed suggests that poor readers have difficulty using the sounds of language in processing written and oral information.

Phonological awareness includes many different features. For example, children lacking phonological awareness do not (1) segment words into sounds (e.g., "What sounds do you hear in the word hot?"); (2) retain sounds in short-term memory and combine them to form a word (e.g., "What word would we have if you put these sounds together: /s/, /a/, /t/?"); (3) detect and manipulate sounds within words (e.g., "Is there a /k/ in bike?"); or (4) isolate beginning, medial, and ending sounds (e.g., "What is the first sound in rose?") (Stanovich, 1994, p. 283).

The overall importance of phonological awareness appears convincingly clear: Students who enter first grade with little phonological awareness experience less success in reading than students who enter school with the ability to analyze and synthesize the sound structure of words. Moreover, because of its powerful causal connection to reading (Adams, 1990;

Ehri, 1991; Juel, 1991; O'Connor, Jenkins, Leicester, & Slocum, 1993), phonological awareness should be an integral part of formal instruction that precedes instruction on reading words.

Alphabetic Understanding

Another big idea in beginning reading is alphabetic understanding, which is a necessary requirement for operating in an alphabetic writing system. The relationship between phonological awareness and alphabetic understanding is closely linked. The primary difference is that in alphabetic understanding, the importance is linking sounds to letters, whereas in phonological awareness, the importance is in hearing and manipulating sounds that make up words. Thus, alphabetic understanding tasks are focused on print stimuli and are concerned with the "mapping of print to speech." Our research review identified three critical points about alphabetic understanding:

1. A primary difference between good and poor readers is the ability to use letter–sound correspondences to identify words (see Juel, 1991).
2. Students who acquire and apply alphabetic understanding early in their reading careers reap long-term benefits (Stanovich, 1986).
3. Teaching students to listen, remember, and process letter–sound correspondences in words is a difficult, demanding, yet achievable goal with long-lasting effects (see Liberman & Liberman, 1990).

Students with diverse learning needs who lack alphabetic understanding are not able (1) to associate an alphabetic character or letter) with its corresponding phoneme or sound (e.g., "What is the sound of this letter?" [point to letter *b*]); (2) to blend letter–sound correspondences to identify decodable words; (3) to segment written words into their constituent sounds (e.g., "The word is *plan*. What sounds do you hear in the word *plan*?"); (4) to identify and manipulate letter–sound correspondences within words (e.g., "What word would *bat* be without the /*b*/?"), and to read pseudowords (e.g., *tup*) with reasonable accuracy and speed.

Automaticity with the Code

A third big idea is automaticity with the phonological/alphabetic code or the ability to translate letters-to-sounds-to-words fluently. Poor readers do not code the sounds of words automatically. Consequently, they have less capacity to allocate toward comprehension (see Juel, 1991; Sawyer, 1992; Stanovich, 1986, 1994). Poor readers do not code the sounds of words as fully or efficiently as good readers, thus impairing their ability to remember and recall needed information (Mann & Brady, 1988; Torgesen, 1985). The strong relationship between reading fluency (i.e., decoding words accurately and quickly) and reading comprehension (i.e., deriving meaning from print) has received strong empirical and theoretical support (Fuchs et al., 1988; Potter & Wamre, 1990; Shinn et al., 1992).

Poor word-reading fluency places heavy demands on a reader's ability to remember and process information. Unless readers become automatic with the alphabetic code, the time and attention required to identify a "word" directly limits the cognitive resources available to process the meaning of the sentence in which the word appeared. Stanovich (1994) explained this relationship by indicating that comprehension fails "not because of overreliance on decoding, but because decoding skill is not developed enough" (p. 283). Apparently, word decoding automatically activates a word's meaning in the learner's lexicon. Thus, the third big idea underscores the importance that readers must move beyond the ability to relate sounds and symbols to the ability to use the alphabetic code automatically and with little or no conscious effort.

These three big ideas—phonological awareness, alphabetic understanding, and automaticity with the code—permeate current beginning reading research. Their importance indicates that they must be instructional priorities when educators design and assess beginning reading instruction. In addition, these three big ideas should align with curricular objectives and state standards and consequently be included in the pedagogical framework of published reading materials. In a recent analysis (Simmons et al., 1995) of the teacher editions of four current kindergarten-level basal reading programs, we found that:

1. Phonological awareness activities are included but in limited quantity and scope.
2. The phonological awareness activities of segmenting and blending, which are most highly correlated with beginning reading acquisition, were not included in any of the basal reading programs.
3. The phonological activities included require students to manipulate primarily single-syllable and multi-syllable words instead of phoneme-level units.

Big ideas, however, are insufficient and do not comprise an instructional system. We have identified a set of features we think represent a minimal set of requirements for designing instruction for students with diverse learning needs (Baker et al., 1994; Kameenui & Carnine, 1998). These include the following:

1. *Conspicuous strategies*: A series of steps that can be purposefully and explicitly employed to achieve a particular outcome. Diverse learners often fail to intuit or pick up the critical information being taught in conventional instruction.

2. *Mediated scaffolding*: External support provided by a teacher, tasks, and materials during the initial phases of learning new and difficult information. Diverse learners have difficulty developing efficient and effective strategies for solving problems and often require high levels of support and guidance.

3. *Strategic integration*: Linking the big ideas across and within curricular activities. Diverse learners often may not see the relations/connections among ideas.

4. *Primed background knowledge*: Accommodating the learner's own reading development, background knowledge, and reading experience. Diverse learners often lack the prerequisite knowledge in their own repertoire and sometimes are not able to activate what they already know in ways that connect with new ideas and experiences.

5. *Judicious review*: Providing opportunities to develop facility and generalization. Diverse learners often fail to retain information over time and may not generalize to related tasks.

The application of this framework of principles of instructional design to beginning reading instruction provides one answer to the question, "What are the essential components of beginning reading instruction in American schools?"

The principles are predicated on the assumption that sufficient instructional time is allocated to teaching the big ideas. Diverse learners

> constantly face the tyranny of time in trying to catch up with their peers, who continue to advance in their literacy development. . . . The pedagogical clock for students who are behind in reading and literacy development continues to tick mercilessly, and the opportunities for these students to advance or catch up diminish over time. (Kameenui, 1993, p. 379)

If we are to close the gap, we must either *teach more in less time* or *teach less more thoroughly.* To do so, we must allocate sufficient time for students to learn the big ideas and protect that time fiercely.

SCHOOLS FOR ALL

The final question posed in the letter of invitation to the Wingspread Conference is perhaps the most difficult; it is the Gordian knot of our profession: "How do we prepare teachers and manage schools so that almost all students achieve acceptable standards of performance in reading and writing?"

To answer this question honestly and not academically, I recommend that we examine the nature and purpose of educational research in the context of public policy issues. Tinkering away with research at the phoneme, word, and text level (or any level for that matter) is very important, but it is entirely inadequate in the long run unless the broader public and noneducational community (stakeholders and tax payers) comes to understand and value research-based tinkering and precision. In the absence of this, conducting research and tinkering with phonemes, for example, have no greater value than the isolated phonemes themselves. That is, the program of research is without context, without political power, and without any genuine linkage to real world actions that make a difference in the lives of children, teachers, parents, policy makers, and administrators. In his 1977 Presidential AERA address, Kerlinger argued that there was little direct connection between research and educational practice; that the purpose of scientific research was theory (Kerlinger, 1977). With enormous deference to Dr. Kerlinger, whose last academic appointment was at the University of Oregon, I am afraid the current political and economic contexts insist on a strong connection between research and practice.

Answering the question, "How do we prepare teachers and manage schools so that almost all students achieve acceptable standards of perform-ance in reading and writing?" requires confronting the most difficult educational policy and reform issues at the most intense level. To answer this question, I defer to the work of my colleague, Doug Carnine, who as Director of NCITE has grappled with this issue. I refer you to his paper entitled, "Ideas for Legislation/Policy to Reform Teacher Education." I must warn you, it is not a paper for the pedagogically squeamish or the educational chauvinist who finds no fault with education.

Similarly, I also defer to the paper "Public School Accountability—The Texas Story" written by Charles Miller, the Chair of the Governor's Business Council Education Committee, and Darvin M. Winick, Organiza-tional Consultant, Center for Houston's Future. According to Carnine, and Miller and Winick, the key to permanently improving education is to institutionalize in legislation and policy a role for research-based practices and accountability.

To address the question, "How do we prepare teachers and manage schools so that almost all students achieve acceptable standards of perform-ance in reading and writing?" requires facing some unpleasant and brutal realities. According to Miller and Winick (1996), these realities include the following:

- Taxpayers expect educators to accept some responsibility for aca-demic achievement, not to point the finger or to find fault.
- The public wants to know how well their schools are doing and how effectively tax revenues are used.
- The public wants high standards for their children and the latitude to organize, program, and manage their schools as they see fit. (In Texas, according to Miller and Winick, "It is now state policy to

give local trustees, administrators and teachers the authority to act to get results and to hold them accountable for what happens. Poorly performing schools are now on notice that they face 'receivership' if results do not improve. Unless test scores rise, hundreds of schools face serious consequences. As a result, academic standards are higher and test scores are up" (p. 2).

- "Educators (and those who train educators) have little experience with results-driven accountability" (p. 2). Results-driven management and results-based accountability systems are not part of the culture of education. "Educators tend to define their responsibilities in terms of process (what they do), not by the results of their efforts" (p. 4).
- We must reject the notion that schools have little influence over student behavior and educators are not responsible for student achievement. Part of the difference in academic success among students depends on the effectiveness of their schools.
- Educators like to adopt nonacademic goals and subjective performance measures to validate current practice.

This characterization of education, educators, and the educational enterprise is not personal and should not be taken as an indictment of the profession. Instead, it should incite us to purposeful and strategic action—action that requires grappling seriously with improving the profession. After all, the profession is about serving *all* children.

CONCLUSION

Is the call for educating *all* children frivolous? Is its use a convenient tidiness of expression or a mere artifact of vision and slogan building? Is its use contemptibly silly with little more than a slender connection to reality? In short, is the education of *all* children attainable? Absolutely!

In *King Lear,* the Earl of Gloucester says to Lear, "Oh let me kiss that hand!" Lear answers, "Let me wipe it first; it smells of mortality." The poet Robert Bly offered an important insight about words: "Every word has thousands of dead bodies hanging on to it. Musicians are lucky because they can go directly to the heart without passing through the history of mankind." The word *smells* is rarely neutral and can connote a negative meaning, that of perceiving an offensive odor. But it also can mean "to perceive, detect, or discover by shrewdness or sagacity." So how does mortality smell? As Shakespeare, Robert Bly, and other great writers have taught us, mortality smells of human dilemmas, wrought with impulses and great twitches. Sometimes it requires a shrewd nose to discover our individual and collective mortality. As Lear quickly learned, we cannot wipe away our mortality.

The challenge of educating *all* is Sisyphean in nature, but it need not be Sisyphean in results. It will require all who take this challenge seriously to be without doubt about who we serve, and to be marked with a sustained and irritable reaching after fact and reason. In short, it requires facing the brutal realities of educating all children and doing it, which is the unmistakable smell of mortality.

ACKNOWLEDGMENTS

I would like to thank Scott Baker, Deborah C. Simmons, and Douglas W. Carnine for their input on the development of this chapter. Preparation of this chapter was supported in part by The National Center to Improve the Tools of Educators (HS96013001) funded by the U.S. Department of Education, Office of Special Education Programs.

REFERENCES

Adams, M. J. (1990). *Beginning to read: Thinking and learning about print.* Cambridge, MA: MIT Press.

Baker, J., & Zigmond, N. (1990). Are regular education classes equipped to accommodate students with learning disabilities? *Exceptional Children, 56,* 515–526.

Baker, S. K., Kameenui, E. J., Simmons, D. C., & Stahl, S. (1994). Beginning reading: Educational tools for diverse learners. *School Psychology Review, 23*(3), 372–391.

Baker, S. K., Simmons, D. C., Smith, S. B., Thomas, C., & Kameenui, E. J. (1996). *Oral reading fluency and corrective reading strategies in middle schools.* Eugene: University of Oregon, National Center to Improve the Tools of Educators.

Bryson (1990). *The mother tongue: English and how it got that way.* New York: Morrow.

Carnine, D. (1996). *Ideas for legislation/policy to reform teacher education.* Eugene: National Center to Improve the Tools of Educators, University of Oregon.

Chard, D. J., & Kameenui, E. J. (1997). *An observational study of low-performing readers' oral responses in first grade reading instruction.* Eugene: National Center to Improve the Tools of Educators, University of Oregon.

Children's Defense Fund. (1992, July). *SV Entertainment,* p. 13.

Education Commission of the States. (1995). *Bridging the gap: School reform and student achievement.* Denver, CO: Education Commission of the States.

Ehri, L. C. (1991). Development of the ability to read words. In R. Barr, M. L. Kamil, P. B. Mosenthal, & P. D. Pearson (Eds.), *Handbook of reading research* (Vol. 2, pp. 383–417). New York: Longman.

Felton, R. H., & Pepper, P. P. (1995). Early identification and intervention of phonological deficits in kindergarten and early elementary children at risk for reading disability. *School Psychology Review, 24*(3), 405–414.

Felton, R. H., & Wood, F. B. (1992). A reading level match study of nonword reading skills in poor readers with varying IQ. *Journal of Learning Disabilities, 25*(5), 318–326.

Fuchs, D., & Fuchs., L. (1994). Classwide curriculum-based measurement: Helping general educators meet the challenge of student diversity. *Exceptional Children, 60,* 518–537.

Fuchs, L. S., Fuchs, D., Hamlett, C. L., Phillips, N. B., & Karns, K. (1995). General educators' specialized adaptation for students with learning disabilities. *Exceptional Children, 61*(5), 440–459.

Fuchs, L. S., Fuchs, D., & Maxwell, L. (1988). The validity of informal reading comprehension measures. *Remedial and Special Education, 9,* 20–28.

Goals 2000: Educate America Act of 1994. (1994). H.R. 1804, 2nd Session.

Hanson, N. R. (1958). *Patterns of discovery.* Cambridge, England: University Press.

Hart, B., & Risley, T. R. (1995). *Meaningful differences in the everyday experience of young American children.* Baltimore, MD: Brookes.

Hodgkinson, H. L. (1991). Reform versus reality. *Phi Delta Kappan, 73,* 9–16.

Hodgkinson, H. L. (1992). *A demographic look at tomorrow* (Report No. ISBN-0-937846-57-0). Washington DC: Institute for Educational Leadership. (ERIC Document Reproduction Service No. ED 359 087)

Hodgkinson, H. L. (1993). American education: The good, the bad, and the task. *Phi Delta Kappan, 74,* 619–623.

Juel, C. (1991). Beginning reading. In R. Barr, M. L. Kamil, P. B. Mosenthal, & P. D. Pearson (Eds.), *Handbook of reading research* (Vol. 2, pp. 759–788). New York: Longman.

Kameenui, E. J. (1993). Diverse learners and the tyranny of time: Don't fix blame; fix the leaky roof. *The Reading Teacher, 46*(5), 376–383.

Kameenui, E. J., & Carnine, D. W. (Eds.). (1998). *Effective teaching strategies that accommodate diverse learners.* Columbus, OH: Merrill Education, Prentice-Hall.

Kerlinger, F. N. (1977). The influence of research on education practice. *Educational Researcher, 6*(8), 5–18.

Larrabee, H. A. (1964). *Reliable knowledge.* Boston: Houghton Mifflin.

Liberman, I. Y., & Liberman, A. M. (1990). Whole language vs. code emphasis: Underlying assumptions and their implications for reading instruction. *Annals of Dyslexia, 40,* 51–76

Mann, V. A., & Brady, S. (1988). Reading disability: The role of language deficiencies. *Journal of Consulting and Clinical Psychology, 56*(6), 811–816.

McLeskey, J., & Pacchiano, D. (1994). Mainstreaming students with learning disabilities: Are we making progress? *Exceptional Children, 60,* 508–517.

Moats, C. L. (1994). The missing foundation in teacher education: Knowledge of the structure of spoken and written language. *Annals of Dyslexia, 44,* 81–102.

Miller, C., & Winick, D. M. (1996). *Public school accountability: The Texas story.* Austin, TX: Governor's Business Council Education Committee.

National Center for History in the Schools. (1992). *Lessons from history: Essential understandings and historical perspectives students should acquire* (S. Crabtree, G. B. Nash, P. Gagnon, & S. Waugh, Eds.). Los Angeles: University of California at Los Angeles.

National Council of Teachers of Mathematics, Commission on Standards for School Mathematics (1989). *Curriculum and evaluation standards for school mathematics*. Reston, VA: The Council.

National Research Council, National Committee on Science Education Standards and Assessment. (1993). *National science education standards: A sampler*. Washington, DC: Author.

O'Connor, R., & Jenkins, J. R. (1995, April). *Predicting children bound for reading acquisition problems*. Paper presented at the annual meeting of the American Educational Research Association, San Francisco.

O'Connor, R. E., Jenkins, J. R., Leicester, N., & Slocum, T. A. (1993). Teaching phonological awareness to young children with learning disabilities. *Exceptional Children, 59*, 532–546.

Porter, A. C. (1993). School delivery standards. *Educational Researcher*, June–July, 24–30.

Potter, M. L., & Wamre, H. M. (1990). Curriculum-based measurement and developmental reading models: Opportunities for cross-validation. *Exceptional Children, 57*, 16–25.

Resnick, L. B. (1987). *Education and learning to think*. Washington, DC: National Academy Press.

Sawyer, D. (1992). Language abilities, reading acquisition, and developmental dyslexia: A discussion of hypothetical and observed relationships. *Journal of Learning Disabilities, 25*, 82–95.

Shinn, M. R., Good, R. H., Knutson, N., Tilly, W. D., & Collins, V. (1992). Curriculum-based reading fluency: A confirmatory analysis of its relation to reading. *School Psychology Review, 21*, 458–478.

Simmons, D. C., & Kameenui, E. J. (in press). *What reading research tells us about children with diverse learning needs: Bases and basics*. Mahwah, NJ: Erlbaum.

Snider, V. E. (1995). A primer on phonemic awareness: What it is, why it's important, and how to teach it. *School Psychology Review, 24*(3), 443–455.

Spector, J. E. (1995). Phonemic awareness training: Application of principles of direct instruction. *Reading and Writing Quarterly, 11*, 37–51.

The Standards Project for English Language Arts. (1996). Newark, DE: International Reading Association; Urbana, IL: National Council of Teachers of English.

Stanovich, K. E. (1986). Matthew effects in reading: Some consequences of individual differences in the acquisition of literacy. *Reading Research Quarterly, 21*(4), 360–407.

Stanovich, K. E. (1994). Romance and reality. *The Reading Teacher, 47*, 280–291.

Torgesen, J. K. (1985). Memory processes in reading disabled children. *Journal of Learning Disabilities, 18*(6), 350–357.

U.S. Department of Education. (1995). *To assure the free appropriate public education of all children with disabilities: Seventeenth annual report to Congress on the implementation of The Individuals with Disabilities Education Act*. Washington, DC: U.S. Government Printing Office.

U.S. Department of Education, National Center for Education Statistics. (1995). *The condition of education*. Washington, DC: U.S. Government Printing Office.

Vellutino, F. R. (1991). Introduction to three studies on reading acquisition: Convergent findings on theoretical foundations of code-oriented versus whole-language approaches to reading instruction. *Journal of Educational Psychology, 83,* 437–443.

Wagner, R., & Torgesen, J. (1987). The nature of phonological processing and its causal role in the acquisition of reading skills. *Psychological Bulletin, 101,* 192–212.

Zigmond, N., Jenkins, J. Fuchs, L. S., Deno, S., Fuchs, D., Baker, J. N., Jenkins, L., & Couthino, M. (1995). Special education in restructured schools: Findings from three multi-year studies. *Phi Delta Kappan, 76,* 531–540.

Appendix:
A Principled Statement
about Beginning Reading

The overarching goal of reading instruction is for children to learn to read well. That means they can read text fluently and understand it. The road to fluency and comprehension includes a great deal of reading. Children should read a wide variety of texts. They also should write for a wide variety of purposes.

The systematic and explicit instruction in decoding and comprehension skills has been neglected in recent years, however. The evidence that skills instruction is necessary is overwhelming. Particularly problematic is that many children do not acquire word recognition skills merely as a by-product of immersion in reading and writing. Moreover, a prominent argument made by whole-language-oriented literacy educators is that semantic and syntactic cues are more important than letter and sound cues for the beginning reader. The evidence against this proposition is simply overwhelming. What is supported by evidence is that systematic and intensive decoding instruction provides an excellent start toward becoming a fluent reader.

Learning about letters and their sounds and how those sounds can be blended to form words is an essential understanding that does not develop naturally, even for many children who have rich language experiences before coming to school. Thus, instruction about letters and phonemic awareness, which is the understanding that words are composed of sounds that correspond to letters, is important in the kindergarten year. Phonemic awareness alone, however, will not lead to the development of the ability to decode words and certainly not to fluent recognition of words. What phonemic awareness *does* is prepare children for explicit decoding instruction in which they learn to analyze the sounds of words and to blend them while reading. Much practice is needed for decoding to become skilled. That practice should include reading of a variety of texts. Important for the development and reinforcement of beginning reading skills are texts written to provide a great deal of practice in the common letter and sound combinations in English. Another excellent source of practice comes as children write and read what they write for others.

Our vision of the development of word recognition skills is that they emerge best in a world—including the classroom—filled with rich and diverse literacy experiences. These experiences include children hearing stories and talking about what they have heard and read, relating information they have encountered in texts to the understandings of the world that they have developed in their homes and culture.

As a general developmental guideline, children need to be phonemically aware by the end of kindergarten. This must be followed by great progress in the development of decoding and word recognition skills during grade 1. Children who do not make good progress during this crucial first year are at great risk for failing to become good readers. And thus, we recommend intensive tutorial intervention for any child who at the end of grade 1 cannot recognize the words most frequently encountered in grade 1 books.

Index

Page numbers in italics refer to tables or figures.

341